DATE DUE

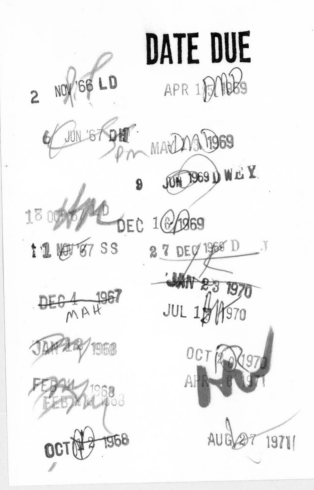

2 NOV '66 LD   APR 1 1969

6 JUN '67 DH   MAY 1969

9 JUN 1969 DWEY

15 OCT D   DEC 16 1969

11 NOV 67 SS   2 7 DEC 1969 D J

DEC 4 1967   JAN 23 1970
MAH

JAN 1968   JUL 1 1970

FEB 1968   OCT 2 1970
FEB 1968   APR 6 1971

OCT 2 1968   AUG 27 1971

MONEY AND FINANCE:

READINGS IN THEORY, POLICY, AND INSTITUTIONS

MONEY AND FINANCE:

READINGS IN THEORY, POLICY, AND INSTITUTIONS

EDITED BY

DEANE CARSON

ASSOCIATE PROFESSOR OF FINANCE
NORTHWESTERN UNIVERSITY

JOHN WILEY & SONS, INC.
NEW YORK · LONDON · SYDNEY

Library of Congress Catalog Card Number: 66–14129
Printed in the United States of America

FOREWORD

In preparing this book, I have examined the syllabi and outside reading lists of more than forty professors of Money and Banking throughout the country. From this examination, and the frequently expressed comments of individual instructors, I have formed a fairly strong opinion on the criteria which should guide the selection of a book of readings in the field.

First, I am impressed by the sophistication that such reading lists impute to the student. In general, assigned or suggested readings are considerably more advanced than the level of the typical Money and Banking textbook. In effect, I believe this means that instructors—or at least my sample, for which I claim no lack of bias—are not entirely satisfied with the level at which textbooks must be pitched if they are to sell at all well. For example, many reading lists that I studied contained substantial references to developments in the theory of money that thus far, with a few exceptions, have not been extensively treated in Money and Banking texts. The quantity theory, as well as the liquidity preference theory of the demand for money, are usually presented in forms that quantity theorists, as well as Keynesians, have long since ceased to consider seriously. I believe, then, that a book of readings should attempt to bridge the gap between theoretical developments and their incorporation in the textbook literature.

Second, it is apparent that many instructors wish to acquaint their students with the controversial issues in the world of money and finance. Since there are many of these, and since the content of the issues changes fairly rapidly, textbooks can be usefully supplemented in this direction. I have usually found interest in the course quickening when students become aware of the fact that the field is dynamic, volatile, and peopled with individuals who often fight rather bitterly over concrete issues in the field. Accordingly, I have not steered clear of controversial issues in preparing this book; if anything, I may be justly accused of seeking them out.

[v]

Third, it is a rare Money and Banking textbook that adequately treats the money market and its institutions. These, to be sure, are handled in other courses and other texts. It seems to me, however, that a knowledge of these areas enhances the student's appreciation of both commercial banking and the aims and techniques of monetary control.

I am indebted to all those professors of Money and Banking who kindly responded to my invitation to submit reading lists and advice. I am particularly grateful for the assistance of Mrs. Helen O'Bannon, who read and commented on many articles from the recent student's point of view and who provided valuable comments at every stage of preparation. Mrs. Yvonne Levy typed the manuscript with the efficient accuracy that I have been grateful for throughout my sojourn in Washington.

Finally, I wish to thank all of the authors and publishers who generously granted permission to use the articles that appear in this book.

DEANE CARSON

Northwestern University
January 1966

CONTENTS

ONE | MONEY AND MONETARY SYSTEMS   1

The Economy's Changing Money Needs   3

Modern Money Mechanics   7

Federal Reserve Open Market Transactions and
the Money Supply   23
Leonall C. Anderson

✓ Eight Questions on Gold   32
Fritz Machlup

On Gold Reserve Requirements   44
William McChesney Martin

Predictability: The Criterion of Monetary
Constitutions   52
James M. Buchanan

TWO | COMMERCIAL BANKING   59

The Goldsmith Banker   61
Anonymous

An Integrated Model for Commercial Banks   69
David A. Alhadeff and Charlotte P. Alhadeff

Multiple Expansion of Bank Deposits   88
James Tobin

Reserve Adjustments of City Banks   91
D. R. Cawthorne

THREE | MONEY MARKET INSTITUTIONS AND
INSTRUMENTS   97

The New York Money Market   99
Carl H. Madden

The Mechanics of Transactions in Federal Funds   111
Parker Willis

Certificates of Deposit   118
Helen B. O'Bannon

Bankers' Acceptances   125
Carl H. Madden

General Features of the Commercial Paper Market   128
Richard T. Selden

Call Loans   136
Anonymous

FOUR | MONETARY THEORY   143

The Supply of Money and the Price Level   145
Milton Friedman

Changes in Prices and Changes in Output   155
Milton Friedman

The Demand for Money   162
Richard T. Selden

The Role of Money in Keynesian Theory   165
Lawrence S. Ritter

The Market for Loanable Funds, Creation of
    Liquid Assets, and Monetary Control   177
John G. Gurley

Postwar Trends in Monetary Theory and Policy   184
Milton Friedman

FIVE | CENTRAL BANKING AND MONETARY
        POLICY   197

The Objectives and Instrumental Role of
    Monetary Policy   199
Harry G. Johnson

The Political Structure of the Federal Reserve
    System   202
Michael D. Reagan

Does Monetary History Repeat Itself?   213
William McChesney Martin, Jr.

What Is the Lesson of 1929?   223
James Tobin

Federal Reserve Independence   227

The Open Market Policy Process   230
Peter M. Keir

Transactions for the System Open Market
    Account   244
Robert Roosa

The Structure of Reserve Requirements on
    Demand Deposits   248

Monetary Restriction through Open-Market
    Operations and Reserve-Requirement Vari-
    ation   253
Joseph Aschheim

The Need for Reserve Requirements and Reserve
    Balances at the Federal Reserve Banks   266
Deane Carson

The Discount Mechanism and Monetary Policy 271

Lender of Last Resort   276

Member Bank Borrowing: Right or Privilege? 281
Karl Brunner and Allan H. Meltzer

Possible Reforms in Discount Policy   284
Warren L. Smith

Open Market Operations in Long-Term Securities 291
Winfield W. Riefler

The Bills Only Doctrine in Retrospect   309
Deane Carson

SIX | INTERNATIONAL MONETARY RELATIONS   327

International Monetary Organization   329
Harry G. Johnson

The International Monetary System   339
Irving S. Friedman

Alternative International Monetary Systems 349
J. M. Culbertson

Exchange Rates—How Flexible Should They Be? 366
Milton Friedman

ONE

MONEY AND
MONETARY SYSTEMS

MONEY is only one among many kinds of financial assets that consumers, business firms, governments, and other economic units hold in their wealth portfolios, but the economist's emphasis on money *per se* is certainly not misplaced. Unlike other financial assets (savings deposits, savings and loan association shares, government securities, and corporate stocks and bonds, to name some of the more important nonmonetary financial assets), money is the essential ingredient in carrying out most economic transactions. Both the supply of money and the demand for it as an asset have persuasive repercussions on economic activity.

It is not an accident that the most highly developed nations have the most completely organized monetary systems, markets, and institutions. Without a stable monetary system, and without well-functioning monetary institutions, trade and industry are not likely to develop and prosper.

In this section, elementary facts about monetary demand and supply are presented, along with materials that supplement the chapters in your textbook on monetary standards. You may wish to return to this section before reading the selections in Parts Four and Six.

THE ECONOMY'S

CHANGING MONEY NEEDS

The American public's holdings of liquid assets—money and financial assets readily convertible into money—have risen fairly steadily in the postwar period. Although the growth in the total has been steady, the "mix" has changed significantly in recent years.

Most noticeable, the vast growth in economic activity since World War II has been accompanied by only modest growth in what is usually referred to as "the money supply"—the public's holdings of currency and demand deposits.

How and why has this happened? Obviously, the money supply has been used with increasing intensity to accommodate the much greater increase in the volume of transactions. Recently, the rate of turnover of the demand deposits component of the money supply has been nearly twice the rate at which deposits were used at the beginning of the postwar period. A major reason for the slow growth in the money supply, and for the rapid growth in money's turnover, has been the attractiveness of substitutes for demand deposits and currency—other liquid assets having the attributes of money.

Individuals, businesses, and other holders of liquid assets have chosen, in recent years, to add more to their holdings of "near monies" than to their holdings of money. Holders of demand deposits have been attracted to time deposits, savings and loan shares, short-term U.S. Government securities, and other liquid assets, by high interest rates. At the same time, many businesses and some individuals have minimized checking account balances carried to cover operating requirements.

Reprinted from Business Conditions, Federal Reserve Bank of Chicago, July 1960, pp. 5–10.

TYPES OF NEAR MONIES

In a sense, any financial asset is an alternative to demand deposits for individuals and businesses with funds not immediately needed for consumption or operations. The closest substitutes for money, however, are those financial assets which are highly liquid—that is, which can be converted into money readily at little or no cost. High on the scale of "moneyness" are nonmarketable financial assets which ordinarily can be redeemed at a fixed value without delay, and marketable securities of high quality which have a broad market in which price fluctuations are relatively small. Classifying some liquid assets as near monies and others as less close substitutes for money is essentially an arbitrary decision.

As a form of liquid reserves, commercial bank time deposits are probably the closest substitutes for demand deposits or currency. Time deposits, like demand deposits, are legal obligations of a bank to creditors. Moreover, on regular savings accounts, the major type of time deposits, banks in practice honor withdrawal requests without exercising their right to require a waiting period between the request and payment. Time certificates and other types of time accounts can be redeemed at maturity or after a notice period of usually thirty days.

Funds placed with savings and loan associations and credit unions represent equities, not creditor claims on the associations. However, such associations ordinarily endeavor to redeem their shares on demand. Consequently, share accounts, along with U.S. savings bonds, are often used as a repository for liquidity. But, like time deposits, share accounts and savings bonds are not money in the narrow sense of the term since they must be changed into currency or demand deposits before being spent.

Also in the category of so-called near monies are Government securities with near-term maturities, usually arbitrarily taken to include those maturing within a year. Such securities are more actively traded than any other assets, and their short maturities limit the price fluctuations.

INDIVIDUALS TURN TO NEAR MONIES

Close to 80 per cent of the total stock of near monies is now held by individuals, as distinct from businesses, state and local governments, and other holders of liquid assets. The shift to near monies by individuals has extended over the past sixty years, though with some interruptions. In the booming 1920's, gains in deposits at mutual savings banks and time deposits at commercial banks were on the whole greater than those in money. However, during the depression, lower interest rates and lessened confidence in financial institutions led to a general decline in savings balances. Reflecting the rise in personal income and the scarcity of goods during World War II, holdings of the near monies rose at an accelerated pace. The newly introduced U.S. savings bonds accounted for a very large portion of the increase.

The much faster growth of near monies than of money during the postwar period is attributable to several factors. In general, individuals have been induced, by high returns and prospects of capital gains to shift away from money to other financial assets, including common stocks as well as the liquid assets considered here. Higher interest rates have been the principal attraction of the near monies. This is reflected partly in the falling off in demand deposits and the surge in time deposits immediately following the announcement by banks of a boost in the rate paid on time funds. The apparent increase in the sensitivity of individuals to rates of return shows up also in the rapid growth in recent years of the higher-paying media—savings and loan associations and credit unions. In addition, savings and loan associations have pursued aggressive promotion policies in the postwar period.

Savings in the near monies have been stimulated also by such special techniques as payroll savings plans and the bank plans covering automatic regular transfers of specified sums from the demand to the savings account of a customer. Then, too, holders of larger savings balances seem more prone to shift among alternative media, and the average size of balances has been rising along with family incomes in the postwar period.

On the other hand, with the increased availability and use of instalment credit, consumers have been under less pressure to accumulate demand deposits or currency, by reducing their near money holdings, or otherwise in anticipation of durable goods purchases. The shorter intervals between pay periods and the greater speed in check clearing, also have worked in the direction of reducing the amount of funds temporarily held in currency and checking accounts.

NEAR MONEY USE BY BUSINESSES

Businesses have stepped up their additions to near monies during recent boom periods. This results largely because short-term Government securities have been the predominant type of near money held, and yields on marketable securities have risen sharply in recent periods of prosperous business. Additions to near monies may mean reductions in demand deposits. Individuals, in contrast, hold only small amounts of Treasury bills, though their use of this near money instrument seems to have been stimulated during [recent years].

Corporations, in their efforts to use demand deposits more efficiently, have also increased their use of time and share accounts. Their holdings of these assets, however, remain small relative to their holdings of short-term Government securities.

The use of time and share accounts by businesses has varied with short-term market rates. The sharp expansion in time deposits during the period of declining business in early 1958 [for example] was in part attributable to the much larger relative gains in corporate as compared to personal time deposits. The switches by investors between time and share accounts on the one hand, and Government securities on the other, reflect their response to changing interest rates on the various kinds of near monies over the course of the business cycle.

MODERN MONEY MECHANICS

Because the stock and flow of the money supply is an important (some experts would say most important) factor involved in determination of aggregate demand for a nation's output of goods and services—and hence the level of employment and prices—it is crucially important to understand how money is created and destroyed in a fractional reserve banking system and how the central bank authorities can influence the process.

PRELIMINARY CONCEPTS

What Is Money? If money is viewed simply as a tool used to facilitate transactions, only those media that are readily accepted in exchange for goods, services and other assets need to be considered. Many things—from stones to cigarettes—have served this monetary function through the ages. Today, in the United States, there are only two kinds of money in use in significant amounts—*currency* (paper money and coins in the pockets and purses of the public) and *demand deposits* (checking accounts in commercial banks).

The amount of currency in use at any time depends solely on the public's preferences. Since currency and demand deposits are freely convertible into each other at the option of the holder, both are money to an equal degree. However, for specific transactions, one form may be more convenient than the other. When a depositor "cashes" a check, he reduces the amount of deposits and increases the amount of currency in circulation. Conversely, when more currency is in circulation than is needed, some is returned to the banks in exchange for

Reprinted from Modern Money Mechanics: A Workbook on Deposits, Currency and Bank Reserves, *Federal Reserve Bank of Chicago.*

deposits. Currency held in bank vaults is not a part of the money supply available for spending by the nonbank public.

While currency is used for a great variety of small transactions, most of the dollar volume of money payments in our economy is made by check. Eighty per cent, or $112 billion, of the $140 billion total money supply at the beginning of 1961 was in the form of demand deposits.

What Makes Money Valuable? Neither paper currency nor deposits have value as a commodity. Intrinsically, a dollar bill is just a piece of paper. Deposits are merely book entries. Coins do have some intrinsic value as metal, but considerably less than their face amount.

What, then, makes these instruments—checks, paper money, and coins—acceptable at face value in payment of all debts and for other monetary uses? Mainly, it is the confidence people have that they will be able to exchange such money for real goods and services whenever they choose to do so. This is partly a matter of law; currency has been designated "legal tender" by the Government. Paper currency is a liability of the Government, and demand deposits are liabilities of the commercial banks which stand ready to convert such deposits into currency or transfer their ownership at the request of depositors. Confidence in these forms of money seems also to be tied in some way to the fact that there are assets on the books of the Government and the banks equal to the amount of money outstanding, even though most of these assets themselves are no more than pieces of paper (such as customers' promissory notes) and it is well understood that money is not redeemable in them.

But the real source of money's value is neither its commodity content nor what people think stands behind it. Commodities or services are more or less valuable because there are more or less of them relative to the amounts people want. Money, like anything else, derives its value from its *scarcity* in relation to its usefulness. Money's usefulness is its unique ability to command other goods and services and to permit a holder to be constantly ready to do so. How much is needed depends on the total volume of transactions in the economy at any given time and the amount of money individuals and businesses want to keep on hand to take care of unexpected or future transactions.

In order to keep the value of money stable, it is essential that the *quantity* be controlled. Money's value can be measured only in terms of what it will buy. Therefore, changes in its value vary inversely with the general level of prices. If the volume of money rises faster (assuming a constant rate of use) than the production of real goods and services grows under the limitations of time and physical facilities, prices will rise because there is more money per unit of goods. Such a development would reduce the value of money even though the monetary unit were backed by and redeemable in the soundest assets imaginable. But if, on the other hand, growth in the supply of money does not keep pace with the economy's current production, either prices will fall or, more likely, some resources and production facilities will be less than fully employed.

Just how large the stock of money needs to be in order to handle the work of the economy without exerting undue influence on the price level depends on how intensively the supply is being used. All demand deposits and currency are a part of somebody's spendable funds at any given time, moving from one owner to another as transactions take place. Some holders spend money quickly after they get it, making these dollars available for other uses. Others, however, hold dollars for longer periods. Obviously, when dollars move into hands where they do little or no work more of them are needed to accomplish any given volume of transactions.

Who Is Responsible for the Creation of Money? Changes in the quantity of money may originate with actions of the Federal Reserve System (the central bank), the commercial banks or the public, but the major control rests with the central bank.

The actual process of money creation takes place in the commercial banks. As noted earlier, the demand liabilities of commercial banks are money. They are book entries which result from the crediting of deposits of currency and checks and the proceeds of loans and investments to customers' accounts. Banks can build up deposits by increasing loans and investments so long as they keep enough currency on hand to redeem whatever amounts the holders of deposits want to convert into currency.

This unique attribute of the banking business was discovered several centuries ago. At one time bankers were merely middle-men. They made a profit by accepting gold and coins brought to them for safekeeping and lending them to borrowers. But they soon found that the receipts they issued to depositors were being used as a means of payment. These receipts were acceptable as money since whoever held them could go to the banker and exchange them for metallic money.

Then, bankers discovered that they could make loans merely by giving borrowers their promises to pay (bank notes). In this way banks began to create money. More notes could be issued than the gold and coin on hand because only a portion of the notes outstanding would be presented for payment at any one time. Enough metallic money had to be kept on hand, of course, to redeem whatever volume of notes was presented for payment.

Deposits are the modern counterpart of bank notes. It was a small step from printing notes to making book entries to the credit of borrowers which could be spent by the use of checks.

What Limits the Amount of Money Banks Can Create? If deposit money can be created so easily, what is to prevent banks from making too much, i.e., more than is needed to handle the volume of transactions resulting from optimum use of the nation's productive resources at stable prices? Like its predecessor, the modern bank must keep a considerable amount of currency (or balances with the central bank) on hand. It must be prepared to convert deposit money into currency for those depositors who request currency. It must make remittance on checks written by depositors and presented for payment by other banks (settle adverse clearings). Finally, a member bank [1] must maintain legal reserves equal to some prescribed percentage of deposits.

How do operating needs and legal requirements affect the amount of deposits that the commercial banking system can create? The public's demand for currency varies greatly, but generally follows a seasonal pattern which is quite predictable. The effects of these swings are usually offset by central bank action and are thus prevented from causing large temporary fluctuations in the quantity of money. Moreover, for all banks taken together, there is no net drain of funds through clearings. A check drawn on one bank will normally be deposited to the credit of another account in the same or another bank. The main factor, therefore, which limits the ability of the banking system to increase demand deposits by expanding loans and investments is the *reserves* that banks must hold against deposits.

Growth of deposits can continue only to the point where existing reserves are just sufficient to satisfy legal requirements. If reserves of 20 per cent are required, for example, total deposits can expand only until they are five times as large as reserves. Ten million dollars of "excess" reserves, i.e., reserves in excess of the 20 per cent requirement, could support up to $50 million of additional deposits. The lower the percentage requirement, the greater the expansion power of each reserve dollar. It is this "fractional-reserve system" that sets the potentials and the limits to money creation.

---

[1] For reasons of simplicity, all commercial banks are assumed to be members of the Federal Reserve System.

What Are Bank Reserves? Currency held in member bank vaults may be counted as legal reserves. The major part of member bank reserves, however, is in the form of deposits (reserve balances) at the Federal Reserve Banks. A bank can always obtain reserve balances by sending currency to the Reserve Bank and can obtain currency by drawing on its reserve balance. Because either can be used to support a much larger volume of ordinary bank deposits, currency and member bank reserve balances together are often referred to as "high-powered money."

For individual banks, reserve balances serve as clearing accounts. Member banks may increase their reserve balances by depositing checks, as well as currency. Banks may draw down these balances by writing checks on them or by authorizing a debit to them in payment for currency or remittance for customers' checks.

Despite the fact that reserve accounts are used as working balances, over every reserve period (one week for city banks and two weeks for country banks) each bank must maintain average reserve balances and vault cash which together are equal to the percentage of its deposit liabilities required by law.

Where Do Bank Reserves Come From? Changes in bank reserves reflect the net effect of a number of factors discussed later in this booklet. But the essential point from the standpoint of money creation is that the reserves of commercial banks are, for the most part, liabilities of the Federal Reserve Banks and that their volume is largely determined by actions of the Federal Reserve System. Thus, the Reserve System, through its ability to vary both the total volume of reserves and the required ratio of reserves to deposit liabilities, influences the amount of bank assets and deposits. One of the major responsibilities of the Federal Reserve System is to provide a sufficient but not excessive amount of reserves to permit deposit expansion at a rate that will serve the needs of a growing economy while maintaining reasonable price stability. Such actions take into consideration, of course, any changes in the pace at which money is being used.

But a given increase in bank reserves does not necessarily cause an expansion in the money supply equal to the theoretical potential as determined by the legal ratio of reserves to demand deposits. What happens to the money supply will vary, depending upon the reaction of the commercial banks and the public. A number of leakages may occur. How many reserves will be drained into the public's currency holdings? To what extent will the increase in the reserve base remain unused as excess reserves? Which banks will gain the reserves? How much will be absorbed by time deposits against which, though they are not money, banks must also hold reserves? The answers to these questions hold the explanation as to why deposit changes may be smaller than expected or may develop only with a considerable time lag.

In the succeeding pages, the way in which various transactions change the quantity of money is described and illustrated. The basic working tool employed is the "T" account, which provides a simple means of tracing, step by step, the effects of these transactions on bank balance sheets. Changes in asset items are entered on the left half of the "T" and changes in liabilities on the right half. For any one transaction, of course, there must be at least two entries in order to maintain the balance between assets and liabilities.

The illustrations are grouped into three sections: (1) how bank deposits can respond to reserve changes originating from Federal Reserve actions or other sources; (2) how the public's demand for currency and other factors, such as gold inflow or outflow, affect bank reserves; and (3) how equal changes in bank reserves may sometimes result in widely different effects on the supply of money.

How the Multiple Expansion Process Works. Let us assume that expansion in the money supply is desired. One way the central bank can initiate such an expansion is through purchases of securities in the open market, thus adding to the reserves of member banks. Such purchases (and sales) are called "open market operations."

How do open market purchases add to bank reserves and deposits? The Federal Reserve System, through its New York office, buys $1,000,000 of Treasury bills from a Government securities dealer in New York. The Federal Reserve Bank pays for the securities with a check issued on itself (and signed by one of its officers). The dealer deposits this check in his account with a commercial bank (Bank A) which sends it for collection and immediate credit to its reserve account at the Federal Reserve Bank of New York. The Federal Reserve System has added $1,000,000 of securities to its assets which it has paid for in effect by *creating* member bank reserves. On the commercial bank's books these reserves are matched by $1,000,000 of additional demand deposits (money) which did not exist before. (See illustration 1.)

If the process ended here, there would be no "multiple" expansion, i.e., deposits and bank reserves have changed by the same amount. However, member banks are required to maintain reserves equal to only a fraction of their deposits. Reserves in excess of this amount may be used to increase earning assets—loans and investments. Under current regulations, banks in large cities are required to have a higher percentage of reserves against demand deposits than are banks in smaller communities, but the average for all member banks is about 15 per cent. Assuming, for simplicity, a uniform 15 per cent reserve ratio and further assuming that all commercial banks attempt to remain fully invested, we can now trace the process of *expansion* in demand deposits which can take place on the basis of the *additional* reserves provided as a result of the Federal Reserve System's purchase of securities.

The expansion process may or may not begin with Bank A, depending on what the dealer does with the money he received from the sale of securities. If he immediately writes checks for $1,000,000 and all of them are deposited in other banks, Bank A loses both deposits and reserves and shows no net change as a result of the System's open market purchase. However, other banks have received them. Most likely, part of the deposits will remain with Bank A and a part will be shifted to a number of other banks as the dealer's checks clear.

It does not really matter where this money is at any given time. The important fact is that *these deposits do not disappear*. They are in some deposit accounts at all times. All banks together have $1,000,000 of deposits and reserves that they did not have before. However, they are not required to keep $1,000,000 of reserves against the $1,000,000 of deposits. All they need to retain, under a 15 per cent reserve requirement, is $150,000. The remainder, $850,000, is "excess reserves." This amount can be loaned or invested. (See illustration 2.)

If business is active, these banks will probably have opportunities to loan the $850,000. Of course, they do not really make loans out of the money they receive as deposits. If they did this, they would be acting just like financial intermediaries and no additional money would be created. What they do when they make loans is to accept promissory notes in exchange for credits they make to the borrowers' deposit accounts. Loans (assets) and deposits (liabilities) both rise by $850,000. Reserves are unchanged by the loan transactions. But the deposit credits constitute new additions to the total deposits of the banking system. (See illustration 3.)

This is the beginning of the deposit expansion process. In the first stage of the process total loans and deposits of the commercial banks rise by an amount equal to the excess reserves existing before any loans were made (85 per cent of the original deposit increase). At the end of Stage 1 deposits have risen by $850,000, in addition to the original $1,000,000 provided by the Federal Reserve's action, and $127,500 (15 per cent of $850,000) of excess reserves have been absorbed by this additional deposit growth. (See illustration 4.)

The lending banks, however, do not expect to retain the deposits they created through their loan operations. Borrowers write checks which will probably be deposited in other banks. As these are cleared the Federal Reserve Banks debit the reserve accounts of the paying banks (Stage 1 banks) and credit those of the receiving banks. (See illustration 5.)

Whether Stage 1 banks actually do lose the deposits to *other* banks or whether any or all of the borrowers' checks are redeposited in these *same* banks makes no difference in the expansion process. Because the lending banks *expect* to lose these deposits and an equal amount of reserves they are not likely to lend more than their excess reserves. Like the original $1,000,000 deposit, the loan-created deposits may be transferred to other banks, but they remain somewhere in the banking system. Whichever banks hold them also have equal amounts of reserves, of which all except 15 per cent will be "excess."

Assuming that the banks holding the $850,000 of deposits created in Stage 1 in turn make loans equal to their excess reserves, then loans and deposits will rise by a further $722,500 in the second stage of expansion. This process can continue until deposits have risen to the point where all the reserves provided by the purchase of Government securities by the Federal Reserve System are just sufficient to satisfy reserve requirements against those deposits. [See pages 11 and 12.]

An individual banker, of course, is not concerned as to the stages of expansion in which he may be participating. In his operations he is constantly experiencing inflows and outflows of deposits. Any deposit he receives is new money to him, regardless of its ultimate source, but if he maintains a policy of making loans and investments equal to whatever reserves he has in excess of his legal requirements, he will be carrying on the expansion process.

DEPOSIT EXPANSION

The amounts in the following illustrations are in thousands of dollars.

(1) When the Federal Reserve Bank purchases Government securities, the reserve deposit of a member bank is credited. This happens because the seller of the securities deposits the check he receives in

payment in his bank (Bank A), and the bank forwards this check to its Reserve Bank for credit to its reserve account.

Federal Reserve Bank		Commercial Bank A	
Assets	Liabilities	Assets	Liabilities
U.S. Government securities +1,000	Member bank reserve deposits: Bank A +1,000	Reserves with F.R. Bank +1,000	Customer deposit +1,000

This "customer" deposit is likely to be transferred in part to other banks and quickly loses its identity amid the huge interbank flow of deposits.

(2) Some banks now have "excess" reserves on the basis of which deposit expansion can take place.

Total reserves gained from new deposits	1,000
Required against new deposits (at 15%)	150
Excess reserves	850

Expansion—Stage 1

(3) Expansion takes place only if the banks which hold these excess reserves increase their loans or investments. Loans are made by crediting the borrower's deposit account, i.e., by creating additional deposit money.

Stage 1 Banks		
Assets		Liabilities
Loans	+850	Borrower deposits +850

How Much Can Deposits Expand in the Banking System? The total amount of expansion that can take place is illustrated on page 12. Carried through to theoretical limits, the initial $1,000,000 of reserves is distributed throughout the banking system, gives rise to an expansion of $5,666,667 of commercial bank credit (loans and investments) and supports a total of $6,666,667 of deposits under a 15 per cent reserve requirement. The expansion factor for a given amount of excess reserves is thus the reciprocal of the required reserve percentage (1/15 per cent = 6⅔).

Although an individual bank can expand its loans only by the amount of its excess reserves, commercial banks as a group can expand credit by a multiple of any addition to their reserves. This is because the banks as a group are like one large bank in which checks drawn against borrowers' deposits result in credits to accounts of other depositors, with no net change in total deposits or reserves.

Expansion Through Bank Investments. Deposit expansion can proceed from investments as well as loans. Suppose that the demand for loans at some Stage 1 banks is slack. These banks would then probably purchase securities. If the sellers of the securities are customers, the banks would make payment by crediting the customers' demand deposits; deposit liabilities would rise just as they did when loans were made. More likely, these banks would purchase the securities through dealers, paying for them with checks on themselves or on their reserve accounts. These checks would be deposited in the sellers' banks. In either case, the net effects on the banking system are identical with those resulting from the loan operations described above.

	All Commercial Banks	
	Assets	Liabilities

As a result of the process so far, total assets and total liabilities of all commercial banks together have risen 1,850.

Assets		Liabilities	
Reserves with F.R.		Deposits	
Banks	+1,000	Initial	+1,000
Loans	+850	Stage 1	+850
Total	+1,850	Total	+1,850

(4) Excess reserves have been reduced by the amount required against the deposits created by the loans made in Stage 1.

Total reserves gained from initial deposits		1,000
Required against initial deposits	150	
Required against Stage 1 deposits	128	278
Excess reserves		722

Why did these banks stop increasing their loans and deposits when they still had excess reserves?

(5) . . . because borrowers write checks, which are deposited in the payees' banks, on their accounts with the lending banks. As these checks are cleared, the deposits created by Stage 1 loans and an equal amount of reserves may be transferred to other banks.

Stage 1 Banks

Assets	Liabilities
Reserves with F.R. Banks −850	Deposits −850

Federal Reserve Bank

Assets	Liabilities
	Member bank reserve deposits:
	Stage 1 banks −850
	Other banks +850

Other Banks

Assets	Liabilities
Reserves with F.R. Banks +850	Deposits +850

Deposit expansion has just begun!

Expansion—Stage 2

(6) Expansion continues as the banks which have the excess reserves increase their loans by that amount, crediting borrowers' deposits—creating still more money—in the process.

Stage 2 Banks

Assets	Liabilities
Loans +722	Borrower deposits +722

All Commercial Banks

Now the banking system's assets and liabilities have risen by a total of 2,572.

Assets		Liabilities	
Reserves with F.R. Bank +1,000		Deposits:	
Loans:		Initial +1,000	
Stage 1 +850		Stage 1 +850	
Stage 2 +722		Stage 2 +722	
Total +2,572		+2,572	

(7) But there are still 614 excess reserves in the banking system.

Total reserves gained from initial deposits		1,000
Required against initial deposits	150	
Required against Stage 1 deposits	128	
Required against Stage 2 deposits	108	386
Excess reserves		614

↓

to Stage 3
banks

(8) As borrowers make payments, these reserves will be further dispersed, and the process can continue through many stages, in progressively smaller increments, until the entire 1,000 reserves have been absorbed by deposit growth. As is apparent from the summary table below, more than four-fifths of the expansion potential is reached after the first ten stages.

It should be understood that the stages of expansion do not occur simultaneously. Because some banks use their reserves incompletely or only after a considerable time lag, the process is in fact continuous. Expansion, moreover, may never reach its theoretical limits. Thus

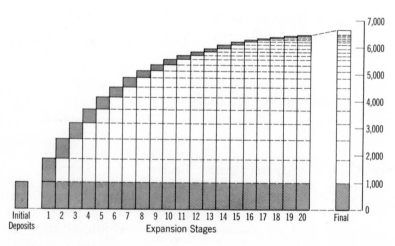

Cumulative expansion in deposits on basis of 1,000 of new reserves and reserve requirements of 15 per cent.

through stage after stage of expansion, "money" can grow to a total of 6⅔ times the new reserves supplied to the commercial banking system as the new deposits created by loans at each stage are added to those created at all earlier stages and those supplied by the initial reserve-creating action.

	Assets				Liabilities
		Reserves		Loans and	
	Total	(Re-quired)	(Ex-cess)	Invest-ments	Demand Deposits
Initial reserves provided	1,000	150	850	...	1,000
Expansion—Stage 1	1,000	278	722	850	1,850
Stage 2	1,000	386	614	1,572	2,572
Stage 3	1,000	478	522	2,186	3,186
Stage 4	1,000	556	444	2,708	3,708
Stage 5	1,000	623	377	3,152	4,152
Stage 6	1,000	680	320	3,529	4,529
Stage 7	1,000	728	272	3,849	4,849
Stage 8	1,000	769	231	4,121	5,121
Stage 9	1,000	803	197	4,352	5,352
Stage 10	1,000	833	167	4,549	5,549
.	.	.	.	.	.
.	.	.	.	.	.
Stage 20	1,000	961	39	5,448	6,448
.	.	.	.	.	.
.	.	.	.	.	.
Final stage	1,000	1,000	0	5,667	6,667

DEPOSIT CONTRACTION

How Open-Market Sales Reduce Bank Reserves and Deposits. Now suppose some reduction in the money supply is desired. Just as purchases of Government securities by the Federal Reserve System can provide the basis for deposit expansion by adding to bank reserves, sales of securities by the Federal Reserve System reduce the money supply by absorbing bank reserves. The process is essentially the reverse of the expansion steps just described.

The Federal Reserve System sells a $1,000,000 Treasury bill to a dealer in Government securities and receives in payment a check drawn on Commercial Bank A. When the check clears, Bank A's reserve account at a Federal Reserve Bank is reduced $1,000,000. As a result, the Federal Reserve System's holdings of securities and the reserve deposits of member banks are both reduced $1,000,000.

The $1,000,000 reduction in Bank A's deposits constitutes a decline in the money supply. (See illustration 1.)

Contraction Is Also a Cumulative Process. While Bank A may have regained deposits from other banks as a result of interbank deposit flows, all commercial banks taken together have $1,000,000 less in both deposits and reserves than they had before the Federal Reserve's sales of securities. The amount of reserves freed by the decline in deposits, however, is only $150,000 (15 per cent of $1,000,000). Unless these banks had excess reserves, they are left with a reserve deficiency of $850,000 (see illustration 2). Although they may borrow from the Federal Reserve Banks to cover this deficiency temporarily, sooner or later the banks will have to obtain the necessary reserves in some other way.

The easiest way for a bank to obtain the reserves it needs is by selling securities (see illustration 3). But as the buyers of the securities pay for them with checks drawn on their deposit accounts (in the same or other banks), the net result is an $850,000 decline in securities and deposits in *the first stage of the contraction process* (see illustration 4). Now deposits have been reduced by a total of $1,850,000, but there is a reserve deficiency of $722,500 at banks whose depositors drew down their accounts to purchase the securities. As these banks, in turn, make up this deficiency by selling securities or reducing loans, further deposit contraction takes place.

It is now clear that the contraction proceeds through reduction in deposits and loans or investments in one stage after another, until total deposits have been reduced to the point where the smaller volume of reserves is adequate to support them. The contraction multiple is the same as that which applied in the case of deposit expansion. Under a 15 per cent reserve requirement, a $1,000,000 reduction in reserves would ultimately entail reductions of $6,666,667 in deposits and $5,666,667 in loans and investments.

As in the case of deposit expansion, contraction of demand deposits may take place as a result of either commercial bank sales of investments or reduction of loans. While some adjustments of both kinds undoubtedly would be made, the initial impact is likely to be reflected in sales of Government securities. In addition, although most types of outstanding loans cannot be called for payment prior to their due dates, the bank may cease to make new loans or renew outstanding ones to replace those currently maturing. Thus, deposits built up for the purpose of loan retirement are extinguished as loans are repaid.

There is, however, one important difference between the expansion and contraction processes. When the Federal Reserve System adds to bank reserves, expansion of credit and deposits *may* take place up to the limits permitted by the minimum reserve ratio that commercial banks are required to maintain. But when the System acts to reduce the amount of bank reserves, contraction of credit and deposits *must* take place (except to the extent that existing excess reserves are utilized) to the point where the required ratio of reserves to deposits is restored.

(1) When the Federal Reserve Bank sells Government securities, the buyer of the securities makes payment with a check drawn on Bank A. When this check is collected, Bank A's reserves decline.

Federal Reserve Bank		Commercial Bank A	
Assets	Liabilities	Assets	Liabilities
U.S. Government securities −1,000	Member bank reserve deposits: Bank A −1,000	Reserves with F.R. Bank −1,000	Deposits −1,000

(2) The reduction in deposits may be spread among a number of banks through interbank deposit flows. But some banks now have reserve deficiencies:

Total reserves lost from deposit withdrawal	1,000
Reserves freed by deposit decline (at 15%)	150
Deficiency in reserves against remaining deposits	850

Contraction—Stage 1

Stage 1 Banks

	Assets	Liabilities
(3) These banks can sell Government securities to acquire reserves, but	U.S. Government securities −850 Reserves with F.R. Bank +850	
(4) this causes a decline in the deposits and reserves of the buyers' banks.	Reserves with F.R. Bank −850	Deposits −850

All Commercial Banks

	Assets	Liabilities
As a result of the process so far, assets and total deposits of all commercial banks are down 1,850. Stage 1 contraction has freed 128 of reserves, but there is still a reserve deficiency of 722 . . .	Reserves with F.R. Bank −1,000 U.S. Government securities −850	Deposits: Initial −1,000 Stage 1 −850
Further contraction must take place!	Total −1,850	Total −1,850

FEDERAL RESERVE OPEN MARKET

TRANSACTIONS AND THE

MONEY SUPPLY

LEONALL C. ANDERSON

The Federal Reserve System has the task of managing the nation's money supply in accord with maintaining the country's economic wellbeing. The author of this article discusses some of the techniques used by the Federal Reserve to control the money supply. He also points to some of the factors outside its direct control which contribute to the discrepancy that exists between the potential rate and the actual rate of growth in the money supply.

The nation's money supply has an important influence on economic activity. Changes in the supply are effected by the Federal Reserve System with a view to promoting a high level of employment, reasonably stable prices, and a viable balance of payments. A major means by which the Federal Reserve affects the quantity of money is changing its holdings of assets. In addition, numerous other factors, which are beyond immediate Federal Reserve control, impinge on money. The Federal Reserve can compensate for these factors, but to give precision to its monetary management it must continually measure and study them.

Changes in the volume of assets—primarily U.S. Government se-

Reprinted from Review, Federal Reserve Bank of St. Louis, April 1965, pp. 10–16.

curities—held by the Federal Reserve System directly change the amount of member bank reserves. Bank reserves, in turn, have an important bearing on the movement in the nation's money supply (demand deposits plus currency).[1] As the chart suggests, however, in many periods there have been large divergences between the rates of change in the System's holdings of Government securities and in the money supply. For example, form December 1963 to December 1964 the Federal Reserve increased its holdings of Governments $3.4 billion, a 10 per cent rise. During the same period the money supply rose $6.4 billion, or 4.1 per cent.

If all of the increase in Federal Reserve holdings of Governments last year had been used to expand the demand deposit component of money at member banks, the money supply would have risen about $22 billion, or 18 per cent.[2] That is, the money supply would have expanded at a rate more than three times as great as it actually did.

MONEY SUPPLY CONCEPTS

The money supply, as usually defined, consists of: (1) demand deposits of all commercial banks other than those due to domestic commercial banks and the U.S. Government, less cash items in the process of collection and Federal Reserve float; (2) foreign demand balances at the Federal Reserve Banks; and (3) currency outside the Treasury, the Federal Reserve System, and the vaults of all commercial banks.

DETERMINANTS OF THE MONEY SUPPLY

The major factors which influence the behavior of the money supply are changes in: (1) System holdings of Government securities; (2) other factors affecting member bank reserves; (3) nonmonetary deposits; (4) excess reserves at member banks; and (5) currency held by the public. These factors reflect decisions of the Federal Reserve, Treasury,

---

[1] Purchases and sales of these assets—called open market operations—is the chief tool used by the System in managing money. In addition, changes in reserve requirements and the discount rate are used.

[2] The $22 billion potential expansion in money is 6.62 (the reserve expansion factor for monetary deposits for December 1963) times the $3.4 billion increase in holdings of Governments.

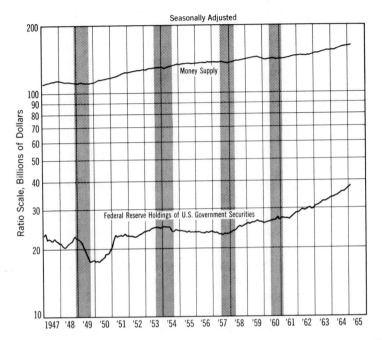

Money supply and Federal Reserve holdings of U.S. Government securities, monthly averages of daily figures. Latest data plotted: March estimated. Shaded areas represent periods of business recession as defined by the National Bureau of Economic Research.

commercial banks, and the public (see Exhibit on page 27). Each of these factors will be discussed in turn.

Federal Reserve Holdings of Government Securities. Federal Reserve purchases of U.S. Government securities are made by adding to member bank reserves, and sales are made by subtracting from reserves.[3] Decisions to buy or sell Government securities are discretionary on the part of the Federal Reserve System. Generally, these decisions are based on a consideration of the level and rate of growth in domestic economic activity along with other ultimate economic goals. In the very short run, such proximate goals as bank reserves, money, bank credit, and interest rates affect open market decisions.

Other Reserve Factors. Reserves are also affected by changes in such other factors as currency in the hands of the nonbank public, the

[3] Total reserves of member banks consist of member bank deposits at Reserve Banks and vault cash.

gold stock, Treasury operations, member bank borrowings from Reserve Banks, and Federal Reserve float. These factors—which are determined, for the most part, by forces beyond the direct and immediate control of monetary authorities—may absorb or reinforce the impact on bank reserves of Federal Reserve open market transactions.

Nonmonetary Deposits. Member banks are required to hold reserves equal to a prescribed proportion of their deposits. Consequently, a rise in nonmonetary deposits reduces the maximum volume of monetary deposits which may be supported by a given reserve base. Reserves required for member bank nonmonetary deposits—consisting of Government demand deposits, interbank deposits, and time and savings deposits—were about 30 per cent of total reserves last year.

Changes in United States Government demand deposits at commercial banks result from variations in tax and borrowing receipts held in accounts at these banks. While additions to these accounts tend to center around tax periods, withdrawals are made as funds are needed by the Government. Government deposits are left in commercial banks until the funds are spent in order to reduce the impact of large Treasury financing operations on the monetary system. While flows of Government receipts and expenditures are the major determinant of these deposits, Treasury balances at commercial banks are further affected by transfers of funds from Government demand deposits at commercial banks to the Treasury's active account at Federal Reserve Banks.

Interbank deposits (demand deposits due to U.S. commercial banks) at member banks arise as the result of correspondent banking relationships among member banks and between member and non-member banks. The amount of these deposits is set by individual banks and is generally related to the volume of banking activity.

Time and savings deposits at member banks account for the major portion of reserves required for nonmonetary deposits. These deposits are a form of "intermediation deposits," arising out of the flow of funds from saving units to units which borrow to purchase investment or consumption goods and services. As in the case of other intermediation-type deposits (e.g., savings and loan shares and deposits in mutual savings banks), the growth in time and savings deposits is related to yields offered, to yields on other short-term investment opportunities, to the amount of personal and business saving, and to the amount of wealth. Time and savings deposits are in the nature of a "tap issue": that is, the public determines the flow into time deposits at the interest rate offered by commercial banks.

Excess Reserves. Not all of member bank reserves are used to support deposits; some reserves are held in excess of reserve require-

EXHIBIT

SUMMARY OF DETERMINANTS OF THE MONEY SUPPLY

Immediate Determinant	Chief Forces Influencing Determinants
Federal Reserve holdings of U.S. Government securities	Discretionary actions of the Federal Reserve

Other reserve factors
  Currency held by the nonbank public
  Gold stock
  Treasury operations
  Member bank borrowing from F.R.
  Miscellaneous factors
	Business activity, balance of payments, Treasury decisions, relationship of market interest rates to the discount rate, and many irregular and seasonal forces

Reserve utilization factors
  Nonmonetary deposits
    Government demand deposits
	Government taxing, spending, and financing, and transfers by the Treasury of balances from commercial banks to Reserve Banks

Interbank deposits	Volume of banking business and bank decisions regarding liquidity
Time and savings deposits	The public, on the basis of interest rates paid on these deposits and similar investment instruments, the volume of saving, and wealth
Excess reserves	Member bank decisions based largely on yields on short-term investment instruments, on the discount rate, and on distribution of member bank reserves
Expansion ratio factors Reserve requirements	Federal Reserve decisions
Location of deposits in member banks with different reserve requirements	The public and the movement of deposits within the country
Other components of money Monetary deposits at nonmember banks	The public, state regulatory agencies, and activities of nonmember banks
Currency held by the nonbank public	Public decisions based primarily on business activity
Foreign deposits at Reserve Banks	Decisions of foreigners

ments. Other things constant, banks change their holdings of excess reserves by taking actions which result in opposite changes in reserves to support monetary deposits. Since excess reserves are a nonearning asset, banks desire to keep their holdings at a minimum consistent with efficient operations. Alternative yields on short-term investments, particularly Treasury bills, and costs of managing a bank's reserve position largely determine the average volume of excess reserves. Within short periods of time there may be considerable variation in excess reserves, depending on the magnitude and timing of flows of funds into and out of individual banks.

Currency. Currency in the hands of the public plays a dual role in money supply determination; it is both a factor tending to reduce total bank reserves (as noted in other factors affecting reserves) and a factor adding directly to the money supply. On balance, a rise in the currency component of money tends to reduce the demand deposit portion by a greater amount than it adds directly to the money stock. This results from the fractional reserve system whereby reserves support a multiple, presently over six times, of demand deposits. The volume of currency in the hands of the public depends on the public's demand for currency which, in turn, is closely related to business activity.

Recapitulation. The following simplified outline may be helpful in explaining changes in the stock of money outstanding.[4] The volume of member bank reserves is affected by System open market transactions and other reserve factors outside direct Federal Reserve control, particularly currency movements. A portion of total reserves is used to support nonmonetary deposits: Government demand deposits determined primarily by the Treasury; the volume of time and savings deposits determined by the public; and interbank deposits. Total reserves less reserves required to support these nonmonetary deposits establishes the amount of reserves available to support monetary deposits. Member bank operations require a certain amount of excess reserves. The remaining portion of reserves are used to support monetary deposits, the major component of money.[5]

In addition, a change in the deposit expansion ratio permits a

---

[4] There probably are interactions between the factors affecting the money supply, but little is known of the relative importance of such interactions at the present time.

[5] Each bank keeps excess reserves at a desired level; additional reserves are quickly used to make loans or to buy securities resulting in an expansion of deposits. Because of the fractional reserve system, the process can be repeated within the banking system until the total deposit expansion is about 6 to 7 times the amount of surplus reserves.

difference in the amount of deposits supported by a given reserve base. Shifts in demand deposits between reserve city banks (16½ per cent reserve requirement) and other member banks (12 per cent requirement) change the reserve expansion ratio.

Money may also increase without direct reference to the member bank reserve base. Growth in nonmember bank monetary deposits does not require reserves at Federal Reserve Banks; hence this component of money is not directly related to the reserve base.[6] Movements in currency and foreign deposits at Reserve Banks affect money directly, as well as via changes in the reserve base.

FACTORS AFFECTING THE MONEY SUPPLY DURING 1964

The Federal Reserve contributed directly to member bank reserves during 1964 by increasing its holdings of U.S. Government securities by $3.4 billion. Changes in other reserve factors absorbed most of the addition to reserves (Table I), and total member bank reserves expanded only $900 million. Chief reserve factors absorbing the expansion in the System's account in 1964 were an increase of $1.8 billion in currency held by the public, a reduction of $200 million in the nation's gold stock, and a drain of $400 million because of Treasury operations.

The net addition to total reserves was used largely by a $600 million increase in reserves required for nonmonetary deposits (Table I), chiefly time deposits. Hence, only $300 million, one-third of the expansion in the reserve base (and less than one-eleventh of that provided by the System), were available for support of member bank monetary deposits.

Reserves required for monetary deposits at member banks increased $400 million during last year, reflecting the increase of $300 million in reserves available for monetary deposits and a $100 million decrease in excess reserves. This rise in reserves required for monetary deposits permitted the member bank demand deposit component of money to increase by $2.6 billion. An increase in the expansion ratio contributed an additional $600 million, so that the member bank component of money actually expanded $3.2 billion. Monetary deposits expanded less rapidly at reserve city banks (2.2 per cent) than at country banks (4.1 per cent). Since reserve requirements are higher (16½ per cent) at reserve city banks than at country banks (12 per cent), the expansion

---

[6] Nonmember banks must keep reserves in an amount and form specified by state law or regulation. The amount of reserves held by nonmember banks is influenced to some extent by the amount of reserves provided to member banks.

TABLE I   SUMMARY OF FACTORS AFFECTING THE MONEY
SUPPLY DURING 1964

(Averages of daily figures, in billions of dollars)

Factors	Dec. 1964	Dec. 1963	Change
U.S. Government securities held by Federal Reserve	37.1	33.7	+3.4
Other reserve factors			
Currency held by the nonbank public	−34.9*	−33.1*	−1.8
Gold stock	15.4	15.6	−0.2
Treasury operations	3.9	4.3	−0.4
Member bank borrowing from Federal Reserve	0.2	0.3	−0.1
Miscellaneous factors	−0.1*	−0.1*	—0—
Net other reserve factors	−15.5*	−13.0*	−2.5
Total reserves	21.6	20.7	+0.9
Reserve utilization factors			
Reserves required for nonmonetary deposits †	−5.7*	−5.1*	−0.6
Excess reserves	−0.4*	−0.5*	+0.1
Total	−6.1*	−5.6*	−0.5
Reserves required for monetary deposits	15.5	15.1	+0.4
Expansion ratio factors	6.66‡	6.62‡	+0.04‡
Member bank monetary deposits	103.2	100.0	+3.2
Other components of money			
Nonmember bank monetary deposits	25.3	23.9	+1.4
Currency held by the nonbank public	34.9	33.1	+1.8
Foreign deposits at Reserve Banks	0.2	0.2	—0—
Money supply	163.6	157.2	+6.4

* These factors have a negative relationship to the money supply; hence, the minus sign.

† Includes adjustment for reserve credit which is allowed, according to Federal Reserve regulations, for deposits due from banks.

‡ Actual figure, not in billions of dollars. The 6.66 in December 1964 resulted from a weighted average reserve requirement on monetary deposits of 15.02 per cent, and the 6.62 in December 1963 resulted from a 15.11 per cent average.

ratio increased from 6.62 to 6.66. The reserve base, therefore, was able to support a larger amount of monetary deposits than otherwise.

Changes in other components of the money stock resulted in a further increase in money last year. Monetary deposits at nonmember banks, which are not directly supported by the reserve base, grew more rapidly (6 per cent) than at member banks. During 1964 currency in the hands of the public increased 5.4 per cent.[7] Foreign deposits at Reserve Banks were unchanged.

In summary, the acquisition of $3.4 billion in Government securities by the Federal Reserve during 1964 was necessary, given the changes that occurred in other factors affecting money, in order that the money supply could continue to expand at about 4 per cent a year. This rate of expansion in money was somewhat less than the rate of expansion of total output.

CONCLUSION

The Federal Reserve System has the major responsibility of managing the nation's money supply so as to assist the economy in achieving a high level of employment and output, a relatively stable price level, and a viable balance of payments. There are many factors beyond direct and immediate control of the monetary authorities which make the task of effective monetary management difficult.

This article has presented a framework for identifying some of the more important elements or "slippages" interposed between Federal Reserve open market transactions and the money supply. Currently, research is under way within the Federal Reserve System to quantify these "slippages" and to develop methods for predicting their movements. The purpose of this research is to make monetary management more a science and less an art.

[7] While currency growth added to the money supply, its growth also reduced member bank reserves. Therefore, currency flows into the hands of the public, as mentioned previously, were a major factor offsetting the impact of Federal Reserve open market transactions on the money supply.

EIGHT QUESTIONS ON GOLD

FRITZ MACHLUP

In a session on "Gold and the Monetary System" at the Annual Meeting of the American Economic Association in December 1940, Charles O. Hardy and Hans Neisser presented two papers which I was asked to discuss. Since I agreed substantially with both speakers, I decided to reshuffle some of the arguments and formulate them in a more provocative manner, to take a few questions about the gold problem which were widely discussed at the time and attempt to answer them bluntly and without scholarly caution.

Perhaps the selection of the questions will be better understood if I recall to the reader's mind that the United States in 1933 had gone off gold and in 1934 had fixed the new gold price at $35 an ounce, or almost 60 per cent above the old price. In seven years, from 1934 to 1940, the United States imported almost $15 billion worth of gold. Frank D. Graham and Charles Raymond Whittlesey were inveighing against this "golden avalanche."

At the end of 1940, when this discussion took place, World War II was in its second year in Europe, but the United States was still a noncombatant and remained so for another year.

Reprinted from International Payments, Debts, and Gold: Collected Essays of Fritz Machlup (New York: Charles Scribner's Sons, 1964), originally printed in The American Economic Review, Volume XXX (February 1941), Proceedings, pp. 30–37.

THE DEVALUATION OF THE DOLLAR IN 1933–1934

QUESTION 1. Was the devaluation of the dollar in 1933–1934, that is, the raising of the price of gold by the United States, on balance a wise or an unwise policy?

A wise policy, to economists, is one which considers not only the short-run effects but also those which are more indirect and less immediate. There were probably several short-run advantages derived from the devaluation; the short-run price increase of some export articles, cotton in particular, may be admitted as such an advantage; psychological effects on business expectations were perhaps of importance at the time. But how about the more lasting consequences?

The devaluation might have been a proper measure in view of a serious gold scarcity. There was no such scarcity, says Hardy. And "the gold scarcity never was a decisive factor during the postwar era," says Neisser.

The devaluation may have prevented an embarrassing outflow of gold from the United States. But the domestic credit situation was not controlled by the gold situation, says Hardy. And he speaks, very much to the point, "of the ancient prejudice against losing gold, even under conditions where no economic purpose was served by restricting its outflow."

The devaluation was supposed to raise quickly the level of domestic commodity prices, something which was considered desirable at the time. This supposed effect was said to rest on a "statistically proven" relationship between gold and the price level. Neisser has shown that this notion is absolutely fallacious, and I believe I may state that most monetary theorists knew this at the time. To these theorists it was, therefore, no surprise that prices of nonstaple commodities failed to rise with the price of gold, but rose only later and to a much smaller extent when demand was increased gradually by other means.

The gold inflow during the first years following the devaluation may be said to have given our banks the reserve increase and thus the investing capacity needed to finance the large government expenditures. Surely, the desired increase in bank reserves could have been brought about just as well by open-market operations of the Federal Reserve banks.

What the boost of the gold price really has brought about was this: First, it shattered all attempts at world cooperation discussed at the 1933 World Economic Conference. Second, as Neisser shows, it

caused a deflationary pressure upon countries then on the gold standard
—a deflationary pressure to which they finally succumbed by abandoning
their gold standard. And, third, it added impetus to an enormous increase in gold production, an increase which is absolutely useless,
wasteful, and embarrassing. (It must be admitted, however, that the
boost in gold production was due much more to British than to American gold price policies. The sterling price of gold—and this is the one
which is relevant for the greatest part of world gold production—rose
before 1933 by more than 45 per cent. The further increase during 1933
and 1934, which can be ascribed to the effects of the American devaluation, amounted to less than 15 per cent of the increased, or 20 per
cent of the original, sterling price.[1]

Hence, with the actual motives recognized as fallacious, with other
purposes achievable by better methods, and with indirect effects undesirable, we seem to be justified in stating that the devaluation was a
mistake.

A POSSIBLE REDUCTION OF THE PRICE OF GOLD

QUESTION 2. Would a reduction of the gold price at this time be a
wise policy?

If it is found that a certain move was a mistake, it is not always
possible to repair it by moving back; moving back may often be just
another mistake.

The effects of a reduction of the gold price in the United States
might depend largely on whether Great Britain and other trading
nations would follow suit. Hardy assumes, justifiably I believe, that
they would do so. He concludes that "the principal effect of the reduction would be to impair the purchasing power of Great Britain in this
country. In the short run, *more* gold might be shipped (to the United
States), but the stocks available for shipment would be exhausted that
much sooner."

Neisser recommends "applying a gold price policy of greater
flexibility in order to secure the repatriation of American securities now
in British possession: the lower our gold price the more England will
be inclined to send over securities first and gold only in the second
place."

I do not believe that it would be in our interest for the British to
finance their purchases in the United States first by selling out their

[1] For this point I am indebted to Dr. Peter Drucker.

security holdings and only afterwards by gold shipments. If they first unload all security holdings, an unwelcome and unnecessary pressure on our securities market may be exerted. If they sell both their gold and their American securities simultaneously and gradually, our gold purchases create new balances for the British and our security purchases transfer existing balances to them. The British, in turn, transfer all these balances to the American producers in payment for airplanes and other matériel. By proceeding with both methods of finance at the same time, the funds newly created through the gold purchases indirectly help our public to absorb the American securities offered by the British.

It is proper at this point to mention the proposal of an import duty on gold, suggested by Professors Graham and Whittlesey. Such an import duty would create a two-price system for gold by lowering the dollar price of gold abroad without changing our official buying price. This indirect gold-price reduction through an import duty would differ from an outright reduction of our price only in optical, political, and bookkeeping respects. The effect upon foreign nations would be the same as that of an outright reduction of our gold price; for an ounce of gold they would get only $35 minus the duty.

What the gold-price reduction, outright or concealed, would mean in effect is that more gold would be needed to pay for an American airplane. With the demand for airplanes practically inelastic, gold imports would probably increase in physical amount and remain unchanged in dollar terms. And since the British gold stocks would be exhausted sooner, the problem of credits to Great Britain would arise sooner.

Hence, a reduction of the dollar price of gold at this time would mean little to us but it would definitely harm the British, whom we seem to have decided to aid. Of course, if we thus find it unwise to reduce the gold price at this time, we must be clear that the situation may change, especially when the war is over.

THE COSTS OF LARGE IMPORTS OF GOLD

QUESTION 3. Do our large imports of gold constitute a sacrifice of wealth or income?

The huge quantities of gold which we have purchased are a rather useless asset. We have neither an industrial use for them nor a monetary use in domestic circulation nor a monetary use in the sense that we may ever intend to have sufficient import surpluses to use substantial portions of the gold for international payments. If this is correct, has it not been utterly foolish to buy all this gold? Not if the gold has cost us little or nothing and if the purchase has had desirable secondary effects.

And this is just the opinion of Hardy, Neisser, and myself. We must, of course, distinguish between the budgetary or financial cost to the buyer, i.e., the U.S. Treasury, and, on the other hand, the real cost to the American public.

There is no budgetary cost to the government, at least if the purchased gold is not sterilized. And we have not permanently sterilized any gold. Neither tax receipts nor borrowed funds were employed in buying the gold, but only new bank funds created *ad hoc* through the issuance of gold certificates; hence at no cost to the government.

And, as Hardy continues, until now or until very recently there has been no real cost to the American public because what we have given in exchange for the gold has been largely commodities produced with equipment and labor which would have been unemployed otherwise. If the goods which we have exported would otherwise have remained unproduced, one cannot say that the exports constitute a sacrifice to the American public. Neisser concurs with this view, qualifying only concerning the "embodied natural resources," meaning the materials which we have taken out of the ground from exhaustible resources and used in the production of exported commodities. Both Hardy and Neisser emphasize, of course, that such costless gold purchases are confined to periods of unemployment and idle capacity.

But not only have we bought the gold at almost no cost to ourselves but we have also enjoyed a beneficial indirect effect, in the form of a contribution to our national income that has resulted indirectly from our gold purchases, even though the gold as such is of no use to us. If foreign nations use the dollars received for the gold to purchase American products, income is created in the United States. If the respending of this income creates demand for more commodities which would otherwise not be produced, further income is created. As Neisser points out, a chain of additional domestic buying is initiated by the foreign buying, which in turn is financed by our gold buying.

I suppose that Professors Graham and Whittlesey would like to object to this point. They would perhaps admit that the foreign purchases of our products have created income in the United States, but they would hold that more relief payments or more public works would have done this equally well or better.

Perhaps, but perhaps not. Would it have been politically wise to raise our government expenditures to still higher levels? Is it not better to have both exports and government spending in more palatable doses than only government spending in much more terrifying doses? We have financed commodity exports through our gold purchases, and deficit spending through our public-debt increase. Granted that the export multiplier and the government-spending multiplier may theoretically be the same, do rising export-business activity and rising government-debt figures have the same effects on business confidence and private investment? Should we neglect the fact that businessmen become paralyzed with fear when they think of the debt, whereas they nurse an old affection for gold and cheer each increase in merchandise exports? On the basis of this reasoning even Graham and Whittlesey may be persuaded to accept the thesis that our gold purchases have financed commodity exports of recent years at almost no opportunity cost to ourselves.

The results of gold purchases which have financed foreign purchases of American securities may be a different matter, because these securities may be resold to us in exchange for American products at a time when we no longer have unemployed labor and unused capacity. Indeed, as soon as some bottlenecks are reached, foreign purchases do involve real costs to us. But why should we fool ourselves with an analysis which neglects all political considerations? Are not the British purchases, even in serious bottleneck situations, of such a nature that we do not mind foregoing new 1942 model automobiles and several other things which may constitute the opportunity cost of our aid to Britain? We are in fact quite glad that the British have still some American securities—at one time acquired with the help of our gold purchases— because we have an easier political problem if we repurchase American securities than if we have to buy British government obligations.

I must guard myself against the charge of inconsistency in my answers to the first question and to this one. How can I consistently state that the raising of the gold price was, on balance, unwise but that the gold imports have had beneficial effects on the American economy? This is not inconsistent. The gold imports of the last four years were not the consequence of our devaluation. Neither the European capital flight nor the European demand for our products were, after 1936, a function of the price of gold.

Summing up, I feel justified in stating that the large gold purchases in recent years have cost us little or nothing and have made sizable contributions to our national income. Continued purchases of gold and exports of war matériel from now on do involve a larger cost, but on account of extraneous circumstances we seem to be willing to shoulder this cost for the time being.

GOLD AS INTERNATIONAL MEANS OF PAYMENT

QUESTION 4. Are the other nations likely to abandon gold as an international means of exchange even if the United States wishes to retain it?

This question can be answered with confidence in the negative. As long as the United States is prepared to take gold at a fixed price, other nations which have access to gold will not be so foolish as to refuse to use gold in international exchange. Both Hardy and Neisser share this opinion.

Popular apprehension on this point, particularly in case of a German victory, is perhaps the result of propaganda which is attempting to create unrest and fear. Mere common sense should make us realize that any country which controls gold stocks and gold mines would be only too glad to maintain the exchange value of these assets. If anyone pictures a victorious Germany not only as possessing the remaining gold stocks of Europe but also as controlling the gold production of one or more of the British dominions, he should extend his imagination to the logical consequence of all this; namely, that the Germans will not do anything to prejudice the international acceptance of so reliable an export product. In the case of a complete German victory the question should run exactly the other way around; that is, whether the United States would be willing to continue accepting gold from a victorious Germany. Neisser does "not doubt" that in such a case we would stop.

In the case of a British victory or in the case of a survival of a sufficient number of free, trading nations, gold is likely to retain its status, in the opinions of both Neisser and Hardy. If one or more nations without access to gold prefer to do foreign trade on a barter basis, this cannot greatly affect the status of gold in the rest of the world. People are apt to confuse two different aspects of the much propagandized barter methods of foreign trade. One is that trade is controlled through government agencies rather than private business firms. The other refers to the settlement of balances. Under the barter system temporary balances remain unpaid, shown in blocked accounts in the country which has imported more, forcing the country with the export surplus either to wait patiently or to buy things which it otherwise would not care to buy or to cut down its exports. These are certainly not advantages which should tempt more countries to adopt the barter system. The authoritarian export monopoly may possibly secure advantages, but the absence of gold can hardly ever benefit a country, least of all a country that is more interested in exports than in imports but would be able to export only if it were willing to accept blocked accounts in exchange for its products. Even if some countries adopt barter agreements in foreign trade, this need not really affect the status of gold among the other nations.

The United States need not be much concerned that other nations after the war may repudiate gold as long as the United States itself does not repudiate it.

THE VALUE OF GOLD

QUESTION 5. Can gold lose its value?

Yes, if the United States decides against gold; no, if the United States continues to support it. If I may borrow a phrase from William Adams Brown, I may say that gold is perfectly safe as long as we redeem it in paper dollars or bank-deposit dollars.

There are at least three meanings in which we may be concerned with the "value of gold." Gold may lose value in terms of dollars, in terms of foreign currencies, or in terms of commodities.

The value of gold in terms of dollars depends on our government policy and nothing else; as long as our Treasury is willing to buy and sell it at $35 an ounce, gold will be worth $35 an ounce. There is nothing under the sun which should make it impossible for our government to uphold that price, although there may be many things which may make it undesirable to do so. When we feel that it is no longer desirable to maintain the price of gold we may of course lower it. Gold can lose value in terms of dollars only through an action of our own, not through actions of foreign nations.

The value of gold in terms of foreign currencies depends on other nations. But what does it mean that gold loses value in terms of foreign currencies? It means—if the dollar price of gold is maintained—that these foreign currencies become more and more valuable in terms of dollars; that is to say, that the foreign-exchange rates of these countries rise steadily with all the awkward deflationary pressures which this would have on their markets. We can be fairly sure that countries would not normally like to embark on such a policy. Hence, unless gold production becomes as exuberant as silver production once did, it is not likely that gold will lose value in terms of foreign currencies while we maintain its dollar value. As long as other nations feel sure that the conversion of gold into bank-deposit dollars remains possible, they will be glad to accept gold, too.

The value of gold in terms of commodities is, as long as the dollar price of gold is fixed, nothing but a matter of commodity prices. With inflationary armament and war expenditures all over the world, commodity prices are likely to rise in the next years, and in this sense the value of gold is likely to decrease. Increased gold production is only one of several and not the most powerful factor tending in this direction. Should new gold mines be discovered or new production methods be developed, the inflation through gold purchases might become very serious. Even at the present rate of gold production we may find, after the war, that the inflationary pressure is more than we like and we may find it desirable to lower the dollar price of gold. But we need not fear anything like a runaway inflation through a gold deluge. The commodity value of gold is much more a function of government spending and credit expansion than a function of the gold supply.

I suspect it is not the rise in commodity prices of which people are afraid when they ask the question whether or not gold can lose its value. What people have in mind is the $35 which an ounce of gold is now worth, or perhaps the value in terms of foreign money. In these respects, however, the United States has the decisive say and we need not worry much about outside forces.

DOMESTIC CIRCULATION OF GOLD COINS

QUESTION 6. Would it be a good idea to readmit gold into domestic circulation?

Such a step would do no harm but it would do no good either. Gold coins in actual circulation could never mean much in our monetary system. Even if people did prefer gold coins to $10 and $20 bills—which is more than doubtful—not much of our $21 billion of gold would be absorbed by circulation, because the circulation of bills in these denominations amounts to no more than $3 billion. In actual fact only a very much smaller sum would be absorbed by active circulation.

Gold hoarding might possibly absorb more. But would gold for purposes of private hoarding be very popular in times when the possibility of a reduction in the dollar price of gold is constantly under discussion? Of course, if Congress decides on new gold coinage, the people may take it as a determination to refrain from further changes in the gold content of the dollar. The present low interest rates on savings deposits and government bonds are factors favorable to the development of new gold-hoarding habits of our people.

But what is the good of such hoarding? One advantage might be that private gold hoarding would reduce the present excess reserves of our banks, something which ought to be done but can be done by other methods. Otherwise there is little that one may claim for the proposal. The prospects of possible fluctuations in the popularity of private gold hoarding would definitely be an important argument against the proposal. And there is absolutely no advantage in committing ourselves to a definitive gold price at this moment when everything is in flux and nobody knows how the world will look in a few months.

GOLD AND THE PUBLIC DEBT

QUESTION 7. Can the United States use some of its gold to reduce the government debt?

This is only a naive layman's question, but it pops up so frequently in discussion that it deserves an answer. When I deal with it from this forum I speak, as it were, for the galleries.

First of all, the gold in the possession of the Treasury is not at its free disposal; gold certificates have been issued against the gold; before the gold is used otherwise, the gold certificates would have to be replaced by something else: by new government debt perhaps? Increase the debt in order to decrease it?

Secondly, the present holders of the government debt—individual savers, corporations, insurance companies, and banks—are not interested in gold and would not for a moment think of holding gold coins instead of interest-bearing bonds. The gold coins paid to the present holders of government securities would be deposited and would be back at the Federal Reserve banks withing twenty-four hours. The member banks' excess reserves would have grown immensely within that day. And all the newly created funds, both those of the bank customers and those of the banks themselves, would then desperately try to seek investment outlets. The savers, insurance companies, etc., could hardly be expected to hold on to their noninterest-earning bank deposits, nor could the banks afford to carry nothing but idle reserve balances in place of interest-bearing government bonds. The inflationary effect of all this would not in the least be different from that of a debt redemption through greenback issues.

Let us follow through the greenback way of paying debts in order to compare it with the "golden" way of paying debts. If the government decided to redeem its bonds with new greenbacks, there is no chance that the paper currency would be kept by the repaid bondholders. Instead it would be deposited in banks, and by the banks with the

Federal Reserve banks. Excess reserves would jump sky-high and the newly created funds, both of bank customers and banks, would struggle for outlets. Knowing that the greenbacks would not stay in circulation but be exchanged for bank deposits, the Treasury could easily short-cut the whole procedure by depositing the newly issued greenbacks directly with the Federal Reserve bank and redeeming its bonds by check. Now it should be clear that it would make little difference whether the statement of the Federal Reserve banks showed new gold coins or new gold certificates or new greenbacks among its assets. In any case, excess reserves would be in dizzy height and the masses of new funds in the possession of former bondholders would start a wild, inflationary chase for earning assets. The banks would be drowned in their liquidity and would probably find themselves unable to pay salaries from their deficient earnings.

Thus the consequences of both methods of repaying government debt—using the gold or using a greenback issue—are the same and, of course, equally dangerous; but one must say that the greenback issue would be much simpler than the roundabout transactions with the gold.[2]

THE VALUE OF LARGE GOLD RESERVES

QUESTION 8. If the world retains gold as an international medium of exchange, will our large gold reserve be of advantage to us?

So large a reserve as the United States has can hardly ever be of any service. It can be of disservice if it is allowed to be a psycho-political temptation with regard to inflationary experiments. Otherwise the buried gold does us no harm and no good.

We shall probably never use the gold in exchange for commodity imports unless we change our attitude concerning large import surpluses. The people of the United States have too long been taught that unfavorable trade balances are something really unfavorable. Only in case the United States has to fight a long war or to indulge in a heavy inflation would large imports find a friendly reception. In an extended war we might be willing to buy sufficiently from South America and from India and use some of our gold to pay for the import surplus. In a serious inflation fast-rising prices might create and permit an import

---

[2] Hardly any of the U.S. Government debt in 1940 was in the hands of foreign holders. The use of gold to reduce foreign debts is therefore not discussed in the text. (Added in 1963.)

surplus, and in payment for this import surplus, as well as in a flight of capital, we might lose a portion of our gold stock. Apart from these (rather improbable) possibilities there is little chance at the time being that we shall use substantial parts of the gold for payments abroad.

Perhaps the possession of the vast gold stock can prove to be a valuable weapon at a future peace conference; however, we must not forget that the weakened nations after the war may have to use any credits they can get to purchase imports rather than to build up new gold reserves.

Given our attitude toward imports we seem to be justified in regarding as very unlikely that the gold which we now have will ever again leave our country. Even if the greater part of the world retains gold as the international medium of exchange and returns to some form of a gold standard, the gold to be produced in the next few years and the gold now held by other nations will probably be sufficient to take care of all international payments in the postwar period.

If this is correct then it would not be incorrect to speak most irreverently of our large monetary gold stock. One might, for example, make the drastic and cruel statement that if some $15 billion of our gold stock suddenly evaporated into thin air the nation would have lost nothing.

POSTSCRIPT AFTER 23 YEARS [3]

The forecasts made in answer to Question 8 proved sound for some eighteen years, but turned sour after 1958. What was held to be "improbable" became a fact: the United States had occasion to "use substantial parts of the gold for payments abroad." This came about after (1) several increases in the price of gold in terms of foreign currencies, leaving some of the "undervalued" relative to the dollar, (2) substantial increases in U.S. commodity prices, tending to make the dollar overvalued relative to some other currencies, and (3) large dollar payments for foreign aid, loans, investments, and military expenditures abroad.

To reexamine old forecasts which have proved to be wrong and to reflect on the reasons for the unexpected outcome is a wholesome practice. It is more customary, though, to let the forecasts be forgotten.

[3] Postscript appended in 1963.

ON GOLD RESERVE REQUIREMENTS

WILLIAM McCHESNEY MARTIN, JR.

Economic growth requires an expansion in the stock of money (unless velocity is rising or the price level is falling appropriately), and this normally entails an increase in both currency and bank deposits.

The Federal Reserve Act has required, until recently, a 25 per cent gold reserve against both the notes issued by the System and the deposits held with Federal Reserve Banks by the member commercial banks. As monetary requirements of the economy here expanded, therefore, more and more of the nation's monetary gold stock has been allocated to meet these requirements. This, together with the outflow of gold to other countries since 1958, brought the level of "free" gold (not required for domestic reserve purposes) perilously close to the legally required minimum.

In this selection, the Chairman of the Federal Reserve Board discusses some of the alternative methods of dealing with the situation. On March 4, 1965 President Johnson signed legislation abolishing the gold reserve requirement against member bank deposits with the Federal Reserve Banks. In reading this selection, the student should consider whether the remaining gold requirement against Federal Reserve notes serves any worthwhile purpose.

You have asked for comment on three bills relating to the requirement of present law that each Federal Reserve Bank maintain a gold

Statement of William McChesney Martin, Jr., Chairman, Board of Governors of the Federal Reserve System, before the Senate Committee on Banking and Currency, February 2, 1965. Reprinted from Federal Reserve Bulletin, February 1965, pp. 226–230.

[44]

certificate reserve of at least 25 per cent against its Federal Reserve notes in actual circulation, plus a further gold certificate reserve of at least 25 per cent against the deposits it holds. S. 743, introduced by Senator Douglas, would repeal both requirements. S. 797, introduced by your Chairman at the request of the President, would drop the requirement against Federal Reserve Bank deposits, but retain that against Federal Reserve notes. S. 814, introduced by Senator Javits, would keep both requirements, reducing that against deposits to 10 per cent and that against notes to 15 per cent.

That conditions now call for some change in these requirements seems clear. By the end of 1964, the ratio of the Federal Reserve Banks' gold certificate holdings to their deposits and notes combined was 27.5 per cent, down 2 points from a year earlier and only 2½ points above the legal minimum now prescribed in Section 16 of the Federal Reserve Act. If developments well within the range of possibilities should be realized, the legal minimum could be penetrated soon, possibly within a year.

Nevertheless the dollar is strong, and so is our economy. We are enjoying vigorous economic growth, and have been reasonably success-ful in maintaining a relatively stable average of prices. American goods and services are doing well in competition in world markets, as indicated by the substantial surplus in our trade balance. Therefore action on this legislation can be taken now, not to deal with a dollar crisis but to maintain the dollar's current strength.

Gold certificate reserves of the Federal Reserve Banks reached their peak of $23.4 billion in September 1954 when the total U.S. gold stock amounted to about 70 per cent of the free world's monetary gold. Over the period from 1949 through 1964, net sales of U.S. Gold to foreign monetary authorities reduced our gold certificate reserve by $8.4 billion. In the same period growth in Federal Reserve deposit liabilities and notes in circulation absorbed into required reserves $3.5 billion. Over these 15 years, therefore, Federal Reserve Bank holdings of gold certificates in excess of the minimum required by statute have on balance declined by $11.9 billion.

In substantial part, United States sales of gold to foreign monetary authorities since 1949 have reflected postwar recovery of the free world from the monetary chaos created by the Second World War, and the desire of the major foreign industrial countries to re-establish con-vertibility of their currencies. These countries sought to accomplish this by accumulating monetary reserves partly in the form of gold and partly in the form of dollar balances. Between the end of 1949 and the end of 1964, the dollar component of monetary reserves of foreign countries rose by $10 billion (from $3 billion to $13 billion) while their monetary gold stocks rose by $16 billion (from $9 billion to $25 billion). Foreign private holdings of dollars also increased by $8 billion, from about $3 billion to nearly $11 billion.

In the half century since the enactment of the Federal Reserve Act, the function of gold in our monetary system has undergone fundamental change. More than three decades ago, coinage of gold, redemption of bank notes and deposits in gold, and private acquisition and holding of monetary gold were discontinued in this country. Domestically, these actions in effect ended the private use of gold as a store of value. Internationally, they enlarged the availability of U.S. gold for official settlements with other governments in response to the needs of our foreign commerce and investment.

Today, throughout the free world, when a citizen of one country does business with a citizen of another—whether or not either of them is an American—the chances are that they will settle their accounts in U.S. dollars. When foreign bankers, merchants, and investors acquire in their transactions more dollars than they wish to hold for working balance or investment purposes, they usually sell them to their central bank. The central bank may keep the dollars as part of its monetary reserves or use them, if it desires, to purchase gold from the U.S. Treasury. On the other hand, if a country's international settlements should use up its dollar balances, its central bank may acquire dollars by selling gold to the U.S. Treasury.

In short, the readiness of the U.S. Treasury to buy and sell gold at the fixed price of $35 an ounce in transactions with foreign monetary authorities has greatly contributed to the willingness of foreign monetary authorities and private foreign residents to hold a growing total of dollar reserves and working balances. Consequently, the U.S. gold stock has come to play the dual role of supporting the international convertibility of the dollar and of facilitating the interconvertibility of other currencies among themselves and into the dollar.

This dual role of the U.S. monetary gold has helped the dollar to attain a unique position in international commerce and finance. And the universal acceptability of dollars has greatly facilitated the record expansion of international trade over the past 15 years, with world trade rising from less than $60 billion to nearly $160 billion. For this reason, the availability of U.S. monetary gold holdings to meet international convertibility needs is a matter of vital importance not only to the United States but to the entire present system of international payments on which the free world relies.

These developments underscore the need for speedy correction of the deficit in our international payments, which for all too many years has been eroding our gold reserves. The President, in his *Economic Report*, has stressed the seriousness of the problem, and has unequivocally stated that "we must and will reduce and eliminate" the deficit.

In consequence of the large and persistent deficit in the U.S. balance of payments after 1957, many foreign countries accumulated dollar balances in excess of their needs for working balances, reserves, and investments. Their monetary authorities used such excess dollar balances to purchase gold from the U.S. Treasury, and the resulting decline in the U.S. gold stock has contributed to the sharp reduction in the System's reserve ratio.

In order to avoid any deflationary impact from this outflow, the Federal Reserve offset the effects of the decline in its gold certificate holdings by expanding its holdings of U.S. Government securities. In addition, the Federal Reserve further increased its Government security holdings in order to sustain an expansion of bank credit consistent with a growing economy and a relatively stable average of prices.

Over the years ahead, the continued growth of U.S. economic activity will require continuing monetary expansion consistent with a stable dollar. Under prospective conditions, it appears all but certain that the gold certificate reserve ratio of Federal Reserve Banks, for domestic monetary reasons alone, will steadily decline, even if gold sales to foreign monetary authorities are small. Of course, any substantial further outflow of gold would accentuate the decline.

Accordingly, the time is ripe for legislative action that will, as President Johnson said in his *Economic Report* last week,

. . . place beyond any doubt the ability of the Federal Reserve to meet its responsibility for providing an adequate but not excessive volume of bank reserves.

and

. . . place beyond any doubt our ability to use our gold to make good our pledge to maintain the gold value of the dollar at $35 an ounce with every resource at our command.

As you know, the President himself expressly requested that Congress "eliminate the arbitrary requirement that the Federal Reserve Banks maintain a gold certificate reserve against their deposit liabilities." The specific provisions to accomplish this are encompassed in S. 797, introduced by your Chairman.

To me, the question before us is a practical one. Removing the reserve requirement against deposits would free approximately $4.8 billion in gold now earmarked for cover purposes and raise the total free gold certificate holdings to about $6.2 billion.

Moreover, by retaining the traditional gold "backing" for Federal Reserve notes, the proposal would be reassuring to those who, in their continuing concern for the stability of the dollar, see in a gold cover requirement an important element of strength. The value of any currency is so much a product of confidence that one should not disregard this advantage.

The removal of the reserve requirement against deposits would seem to me fully adequate to meet our present and foreseeable needs and sufficiently ample to remove any doubt anywhere about our ability to defend the dollar abroad, and to further advance the progress of our domestic economy.

I might note here that, on an earlier occasion, Congress reduced the gold reserve requirements by lowering the percentage of reserves required against Federal Reserve notes as well as deposits in the Federal Reserve Banks. Specifically, in 1945, Congress reduced the gold cover requirements from 40 per cent against notes and 35 per cent against deposits to the present figure of 25 per cent of both. That action was taken after the amount of free gold certificates had dropped from $12.4 billion at the beginning of the war to $3.2 billion by mid-1945. If an across-the-board reduction of the present 25 per cent requirement were to be made now—say to 15 per cent—it would release about $5.5 billion of the earmarked gold, as compared with the $4.8 billion released by S. 797. Or the requirement against deposits could be reduced further, as in S. 814, to 10 per cent, coupled with a reduction in the note cover to 15 per cent; this would release an additional $1 billion in gold.

From a technical viewpoint this approach may be just as sound as that taken by S. 797. What counts, in my judgment, is which approach would be more acceptable to the public. And from that standpoint, I believe it is preferable to preserve the 25 per cent requirement for Federal Reserve notes and thus to keep intact the symbolic tie between our circulating currency and gold.

The Congress could, on the other hand, take a more all-out approach and repeal the gold cover requirements altogether. This would release our entire gold certificate holdings of $15 billion by severing the last statutory link between the volume of our Federal Reserve notes in circulation and gold. The theory here is that, since neither Federal Reserve notes nor deposits in Federal Reserve Banks can be redeemed in gold, there is no need to have any gold "backing" against either of them. Further, it is suggested that outright repeal of both gold reserve requirements would eliminate the possibility that Congress might be called upon to take further action later. Those who would keep the "discipline" of gold, however, answer that this very possibility offers added protection against irresponsible public policies.

While judgments differ as to the value of this kind of statutory protection, we need not attempt at this time to resolve forever the problem of whether or not a gold cover requirement serves a useful end. We need only to adapt our traditional cover requirements so that we can better meet present and foreseeable needs. If we keep the gold cover requirement for our currency, our free gold certificate holdings of more than $6 billion will be enough to accommodate normal growth in circulating Federal Reserve notes for some time to come.

We face the prospect of some additional gold losses this year. But if we persevere in efforts to correct our balance of payments deficit, we can look forward to a cessation of gold outflow and, over the longer run, a gradual growth of our gold stock from world supplies, in consequence of international settlements and at times by sharing in new production.

In considering these proposals, I think we must be careful to keep in mind that, regardless of what is done about legal requirements, there is an inescapable practical requirement that we maintain an adequate gold stock to back up the role of the dollar as a key currency in world trade. Hence the need to conserve our gold stock will continue to exert a disciplinary influence on monetary and other policies, and a statutory gold reserve requirement for notes will serve to emphasize this need.

All of us need to be mindful that sound money is not established by statute alone. In the end, our nation cannot have sound money unless its monetary and fiscal affairs are well managed. The fundamental elements in keeping our financial house in order are thus sound and equitable fiscal and monetary policies.

It may be helpful to your consideration of legislation for me to say at this point a few words about the present provisions of the law respecting the suspension of gold reserve requirements. The Board's authority in this regard is contained in Section 11(c) of the Federal Reserve Act. It provides that we can suspend the gold reserve requirements for a period of 30 days, and renew such suspensions for 15-day periods thereafter.

Upon action to suspend the requirements, the Board would have to establish a tax on the Reserve Banks graduated upward with the size of their reserve deficiencies. The tax could be very small so long as the reserve deficiencies were confined to the reserves against deposits and the first 5 percentage points of any deficiencies against Federal Reserve notes. But if the reserve deficiencies should penetrate below 20 per cent of the Federal Reserve notes outstanding, the tax would undergo a fairly steep graduation in accordance with statutory specification.

The Federal Reserve Act further specifies that, should the reserve deficiencies fall below the 25 per cent requirement against notes, the amount of the tax must be added to Reserve Bank discount rates. But if the deficiencies were confined to reserves against Reserve Bank deposits, the required penalty tax could be nominal and no addition to Reserve Bank discount rates would be necessary.

From a technical point of view, it might be possible under existing law for the Board to suspend gold reserve requirements indefinitely, since there is no limit on the number of times the Board might renew suspen-

CONSOLIDATED RESERVE POSITION OF THE FEDERAL RESERVE BANKS

(In millions of dollars, unless otherwise noted)

Item	Sept. 21, 1949	Dec. 31, 1963	Dec. 31, 1964
F.R. Bank deposits	17,523	18,392	19,454
F.R. notes	23,248	32,878	35,342
Liabilities requiring reserves	40,771	51,270	54,796
Required reserves			
Against deposits	4,381	4,598	4,864*
Against notes	5,812	8,220	8,835
Total required reserves	10,193	12,818	13,699
Free gold certificate holdings	13,247	2,419	1,376*
Gold certificate reserves	23,440	15,237	15,075
Ratio of gold certificate reserves to deposit and note liabilities (per cent)	57.5†	29.7	27.5

* Elimination of required reserves against deposits, as recommended in the President's *Economic Report*, would raise free gold certificate holdings to $6,240 million. "Free gold" includes some additional gold held by the Treasury (amounting to $240 million on Dec. 31, 1964) that is not pledged as cover for gold certificates or U.S. notes.
† Postwar peak.

sions for periods of 15 days each. Yet it seems clear that the purpose of the provision for suspension was to facilitate adjustments by those Reserve Banks whose reserves fall temporarily below required levels, and not to provide a solution to a national problem of more than temporary import.

In a world in which the role of the dollar as an international means of payment and a reserve asset has been under criticism, it is important for the Congress to assure the world of the availability of U.S. monetary gold for legitimate monetary uses in international commerce, to re-affirm the relationship between the dollar and gold, and to reassert the intention of the United States to maintain an adequate gold reserve for the dollar. Enactment of S. 797 would accomplish this triple purpose.

In conclusion, I would re-emphasize that we do not need now to resolve this question of gold cover for all time, for monetary arrangements and institutions are constantly evolving in accordance with domestic and international needs, and these changes call for adaptation from time to time in monetary legislation. The all-important need for legislation at this juncture is to assure the world that U.S. monetary gold is always available to maintain the convertibility of the dollar and that the United States will honor its debts and liabilities in the form of foreign dollar holdings—as I have said many times before—down through the last bar of gold, if that be necessary.

PREDICTABILITY: THE CRITERION

OF MONETARY CONSTITUTIONS

JAMES M. BUCHANAN

> The decline and fall of the gold coin standard in the
> United States and elsewhere after World War I was not
> universally hailed as a blessing. Opponents of "managed
> money"—the system under which the quantity of money is
> controlled by governmental authority without fixed rules—
> have in recent times called for a return to the domestic
> gold-coin standard. Your textbook contains the pros and
> cons of this proposal; in general very few economists would
> advocate such a step.
>   On the other hand, some economists are convinced
> that, while gold should not serve as the commodity stand-
> ard money, some commodity (or group of commodities)
> should be adopted as standard money to avoid the alleged
> abuses of the managed paper standard. In this selection the
> author discusses the possibility of adopting a brick standard.

There exists no "ideal" commodity for purposes of achieving monetary predictability under an automatic system. There is no single real
commodity or service that serves at all adequately to represent composite
production over the whole economy, or that could appropriately be used
as an image of the economy. Having recognized this, however, we
should not dismiss all automatic or commodity money systems as un-

Reprinted from essay of same title in L. B. Yeager (ed.), In Search of a Monetary Con-
stitution (Cambridge: Harvard University Press, 1962), pp. 171–179.

workable and impracticable. There are still better and worse commodity standards, "better" and "worse" being measured in terms of the degree to which specific real commodities possess the characteristics required of the "ideal" commodity discussed above.

It is in this sense that the use of common brick as the standard commodity should be considered. Among existent real commodities, a good argument can be made out for common building brick as the best practicable commodity that could be employed as the basis for an automatic monetary system. The ingenious proposal that the value of money be based on common building brick was first advanced by Dr. C. O. Hardy, one of the seminal minds in monetary theory during the interwar and early postwar years. So far as I can discover, Dr. Hardy never published the proposal in a formal paper.[1] It has, however come to be recognized as one of his many important contributions to monetary theory, and its substance has been passed along in an oral tradition by several scholars, among them Professor Lloyd Mints and a few of his former students, who have been impressed by the logical completeness and, confessedly, by the shock value of the common-brick proposal.

It will be useful to consider the advantages and disadvantages of common brick as the basis for an automatic monetary system. First let us specify briefly but carefully the structure of the system as it is expected to operate. The government sets a schedule of money prices for common building brick of specified quality. For simplicity in exposition, let us assume that this schedule of prices can be represented by a single price that is to be held constant over time. Again I should emphasize, however, that neither a single price nor constancy over time is significant to the proposal. At the same time that this price is announced, a public authority, which we shall call the Mint, announces its willingness to buy and sell units of common brick at the specified price in unlimited amounts. Money is issued from the Mint only in exchange for common brick, and money proceeds from the sale of common brick by the Mint are impounded in the Mint. Every individual has the assurance that he can, at any time, take a common brick, or any quantity of common brick (or a certificate of ownership of brick) to the Mint and receive in exchange a monetary unit, say, a paper dollar. He also knows that he can, at any time and in any desired amount, go to the Mint and purchase, for paper dollars, common brick of the specified quality. No additional monetary or fiscal policy need take place. Having no

[1] In my search for some published version of the original proposal, I am indebted to Mrs. Myra M. Hardy of Washington, D.C., and to Dr. William H. Moore of the staff of the Joint Economic Committee.

powers to create or to destroy money other than those implicit in the rules governing the operations of the Mint, the government has to finance expenditures through taxation or through real borrowing. Commercial banks may be assumed to operate on the basis of 100 per cent reserves behind deposits, although this assumption is not essential to the analysis of the brick standard itself.[2]

This sort of monetary system could be predicted to work in a manner analogous to any other monetary system based upon a commodity standard. When the general level of prices rises above some presumed initial or "equilibrium" level, it becomes profitable for traders in common brick to *purchase* physical units of the standard commodity from the Mint. They can do so readily by exchanging paper money for brick or certificates of ownership of brick. As these traders turn in units of paper money to the Mint, the money supply outside the Mint is reduced, since the Mint is obligated to destroy or neutralize paper so received. As the supply of money in the system is reduced, the upward pressure on general prices is changed into downward pressure, and the price level begins to fall toward a predicted value. At the same time, of course, the brick-production industry becomes depressed in relation to other industries. The rate of brick production is reduced and resources tend to shift to other industries. This induced increase in the supply of nonstandard commodities and services does, of course, exert an effect that is substantially less significant than the demand effect resulting from the monetary contraction generated by the expansion of brick purchases from the Mint. Both the demand and the supply processes continue until they, along with supporting speculation in nonstandard commodities, are successful in bringing the absolute price level back into some accepted relation with a generally expected or predicted value. This result is accomplished, however, without any agency, authority, business firm, or single individual paying explicit attention to the absolute price level as such. Traders and potential traders in the standard commodity, brick, are guided by profit-maximization criteria, not by any private or public concern for monetary stability.

The system is fully symmetrical in the case of a fall in the absolute price level below some predicted value. This fall generates offsetting equilibrating behavior. Firms find it profitable to sell brick to the Mint. As this takes place, additional money finds its way into the pay-

---

[2] I should point out that the brick-standard proposal as outlined here, and the analysis of its operation that follows, represent my own version of the original proposal. I should like to give Dr. Hardy the full credit due him for originating the proposal without attributing to him any of the possible errors that might be present in this version.

ments stream of the economy. This primary effect tends to increase aggregate demand for all nonstandard goods and services. It is supplemented by a supply-side effect generated by the shift of resources away from the production of nonstandard commodities, reducing the excess supplies forthcoming and into the production of brick, the standard commodity. Again, the process continues until the absolute price level returns to some expected or predicted value, or to state the same thing in terms of the criteria directing private actions, until the relative profitability of production and sale of brick to the monetary authority disappears.

To this point, the same analysis might be applied to any physical commodity designated as the standard for an automatically operating monetary system. Indeed one of the points in discussing this analysis in terms of an everyday commodity like common building brick is the demonstration that a commodity standard need not be conceived in terms of precious metals. But we may go much further than this. There are many positive advantages of the brick-standard system in comparison with other possible commodity systems. In reviewing some of these advantages, it is useful to compare and contrast common brick with gold as the basis for an automatic monetary system.

First of all, common brick can be produced advantageously in almost every local area in the United States. The required adjustments in the industry producing the standard commodity would not, therefore, be localized in particular regions or areas. When general inflationary or deflationary pressures in the economy imposed depression or boom on this brick-producing industry, the dispersion of production over space would tend to prevent differential regional impact. Contrast this situation with one involving a standard commodity, such as gold or anthracite coal, which is produced only in highly localized areas. In periods of incipient depression or recession, the employment effects of the brick-standard system would be noteworthy. Opportunities for employment in local brickyards would tend to mitigate the necessity for the accelerated labor mobility that would be required in the shifting of resources into a regionally localized industry. This advantage is symmetrical with respect to the unemployment effects during periods of inflation.

A second major advantage lies in the fact that production processes for common brick do not seem to be overly complex, although I plead technical ignorance here. Efficient producing plants probably need not be of extremely large size, and entry into and egress from the industry should not be difficult. For these and other reasons, reactions to relative price and cost changes should take place rapidly and without serious dislocation of resources. A closely related third advantage is that production seems to require relatively few highly specialized resources. These three features combine to ensure that the elasticity of supply would be reasonably high.

A final advantage that should not be overlooked is that common building brick would probably not be suitable for adjusting international balances of payments. The system would, in this way, facilitate rather than hinder the separation of the domestic monetary system from the international payments mechanism, a separation whose impossibility would seriously restrict the use of gold as the standard commodity. The brick-standard system would be a suitable companion to a system of floating exchange rates.

On each of the four counts noted, a monetary standard of common building brick would seem superior to one of gold or any other precious metal.

There would, of course, be some offsetting disadvantages to the brick-standard system. Any commodity standard must involve some storage costs not present under managed systems: some proportion of the resources of the economy must of necessity be devoted to maintaining a stock of the commodity designated as the monetary standard, a stock over and above that which would be normal for nonmonetary uses. With brick, there would be little deterioration or depreciation involved in storage over time, but the sheer bulk of the commodity could make storage costs substantial. Economic resources would be tied up in maintaining unused a sizable stock of common brick. This stock need not go entirely unused, however. A substantial proportion could be devoted to the construction of government buildings. If in fact it could be predicted that the system would operate effectively on some fractional-reserve withdrawal, that is, if it could be predicted that the required responses to general upward or downward pressures would involve no more than, say, one-fourth of the existing stock of "money brick," then three-fourths of this stock, against which the Mint would at some time have issued dollars, could be employed in the construction of government buildings. In this way, the general taxpayer would secure some indirect benefit. As a recognized ultimate reserve or backing for the outstanding money issues, the brick used in such construction projects would have to be carefully distinguished from those government bricks acquired through ordinary market channels, and a potential withdrawal of this "money brick" would have to be acknowledged. Should a general wave of dishoarding on the part of the public generate serious inflationary pressure, thus making it highly profitable for private buildings to be constructed with brick purchased from the Mint, then offsetting destruction of some government buildings might have to take place. It is difficult to imagine that such major swings around a predicted norm would take place, however, once a monetary system of this nature came to be in full operation. For this reason there would seem to be little grounds for concern about the periodic possible destruction of private or public buildings.

One of the major disadvantages of any commodity standard, especially when viewed in the light of the predictability norm, lies in its vulnerability to unpredictable changes in the relative costs of producing standard and nonstandard commodities. A major technological improvement in production processes in the brick industry could, for example, be the source of serious inflation in the economy. We know that one of the disadvantages of the historical gold standard was its subjection of general economic conditions to the sometimes fortuitous discoveries of new gold fields. While brick would on this count clearly be superior to gold, the possible inflation that could result from a differential technological breakthrough should not be neglected in any thorough comparative evaluation. There would seem to be little chance of such a depletion of suitable raw materials as to make deflation from this source a serious possibility.

A second disadvantage of any commodity standard lies in its potential vulnerability to unpredictable shifts in the nonmonetary demand for the standard commodity. For example, an upsurge in the fashionableness of brick houses would, under the operation of a brick standard, impose deflationary pressure on the economy generally. To some extent, however, these unpredictable shifts in the private demand for the monetary commodity could be offset by variations in the government demand. Insofar as such demand shifts occur and are not effectively offset, the commodity standard will not be able to produce monetary predictability. But broadly considered, such shifts are different in degree only from shifts in the desire to hold money, that is, hoarding and dishoarding, which seem to reduce the predictability of any monetary system.

TWO

COMMERCIAL BANKING

MOST textbooks on money and banking contain a thorough treatment of the role of commercial banking in the monetary system, with considerable emphasis on these institutions as creators of a large part of the nation's supply of money. (This will already be evident to you from a reading of "Modern Money Mechanics" in the preceding section.)

The key selections in Part Two are "An Integrated Model for Commercial Banks" and "Multiple Expansion of Demand Deposits." The former presents the commercial banking industry in a significantly different framework from that which is found in the typical textbook. As such, it supplements the elementary presentation of banking with some important and subtle refinements. The latter selection is also a sophisticated supplement to the mechanical discussion of money-creation activity of the commercial banking system.

THE GOLDSMITH BANKER

ANONYMOUS

This essay traces the early development of modern banking practices in 17th Century England.

In 1924 Glyn, Mills & Co. purchased the business of Child's Bank and thus acquired what is probably the oldest existing bank in the country. Its origins as a goldsmith business date back to 1559, to the days of Queen Elizabeth I, when it was owned by John Wheeler who lived in Cheapside. About 1620 the business was transferred to the present premises at the "Marygold," No. 1 Fleet Street, and in the middle of the seventeenth century passed by marriage into the hands of Robert Blanchard and Francis Child.

Although there had been a crude form of money-lending and money-changing in Elizabethan times, the goldsmiths seem to have been moving towards some form of banking. "The crucial innovations in English banking history seem to have been mainly the work of the goldsmith bankers in the middle decades of the seventeenth century," as a recent writer has pointed out.[1]

Before the Civil War it was the custom for London merchants to use the Mint (then in the Tower) as a repository for their surplus cash. But when, in 1640, Charles I requisitioned some £200,000 which had been thus deposited, they naturally began to seek elsewhere for a place

---

[1] D. M. Joslin, in *Economic History Review*, December 1954.

Reprinted from The Three Banks Review, No. 27, September 1955, pp. 42–52.

safe from such royal interference. The goldsmiths, with the facilities which they had for the safe storage of their own valuables, were a logical choice, and their acceptance of money deposits in trust, returnable on demand, was really the first stage in the evolution of goldsmith into banker. From "working" goldsmiths—jewellers and makers and sellers of gold and silver ware—providing safe custody facilities, they developed into bankers in the modern sense, and by 1694, when the Bank of England was founded, banking as we now know it was recognisably in being.

The earliest surviving ledger of Child's Bank covers the period 1662–1670, and the numbering of subsequent ledgers indicates that it was number 3 of a series. It seems reasonable, therefore, to assume that No. 1—the first methodical record of their banking transactions—must have started in the mid 1650's, almost exactly 300 years ago.

An analysis of these ledgers shows quite clearly the change from goldsmithing to banking. In 1663, 60 new accounts were opened, of which 41 were goldsmith accounts, 9 banking and 10 mixed accounts—containing entries of both types of business. The following year the figures were 48, 25 and 16 respectively, indicating that the business was expanding in an encouraging manner. But disaster was at hand. December of 1664 saw the beginning of the Great Plague of London, and its effect was such that the number of new accounts opened in 1665 dropped to only 9. True, the numbers grew slowly each succeeding year, but it was not until 1679 that the figures rivalled those of the years before the Plague. And by that time the growth of new business had shown a definite change of pattern. Whereas in 1663–1664 the majority of the accounts were devoted entirely to goldsmith business, by 1667 purely banking accounts exceeded the purely goldsmith accounts, and in 1679 the figures for new accounts opened were—banking 206, goldsmith 27 and mixed accounts 20. Despite this change of emphasis, however, the older traditional side of the business remained an important factor until the end of the century.

In the initial stages the goldsmith merely accepted money for safe custody and gave in exchange a receipt which took the form of a promise to pay on demand. But the practice soon developed of these receipts being presented from time to time for part payment; the face value of the receipt being reduced on each occasion. Thus it was that the goldsmith bankers became known as "keepers of running cashes."

The following is an example of this simple type of early "running cash" account; the forerunner of the modern current account.

Mr. Martyn

Cr.			Dr.		
1663			*1663*		
July 30	Recd. being left		Oct. 4	Payd Mr. Martyn	£16
	here	£56	*1664*		
			Jan. 9	p. himselfe	10
			23	pd. more	10
			May 16	pd. in full	20
					£56

The growth of this practice of keeping "running cashes" led to the goldsmith receipts becoming assignable and passing from one party to another with their eventual development into the modern bank note, the wording of which has changed surprisingly little since those early days.

Novr 28: 1684
I promise to pay unto ye Rig^t Honble ye L^d
North & Grey or bearer Ninty pounds at
demand————

for Mr. ffran Child & my Self
JN^o ROGERS

£90———

Another point of interest is that in the modern bank note the letters "I" and "P" of the words "I Promise to pay" are linked together in a rather peculiar form. In fact many people do not realise that the letter "I" is there at all. This method of writing it dates back to the earliest days and a scrap of paper in Francis Child's own handwriting, bearing the date "Mar. 25th 1685," shows his attempts at design. The first printed bank notes were issued in 1729, but even on these the amount and payee's name were still written by hand.

A further method by which a customer could withdraw money was by writing a "note" requesting a sum of money to be paid to a third party, or to bearer, adding "and place it to my accompt," or "the receipt shall bee yr. sufficyent discharge." These "drawn notes" were the forerunners of the modern cheque but, though there is an isolated reference in the ledger for 1680 to such a "checque," the expression does not appear to have become current usage until very much later.

The purely goldsmith accounts operated as one would expect, customers being debited for plate or jewels supplied—often with a charge for making or engraving—and credited either with cash which they paid in or allowances for old plate returned. The account of Francis Wyndham, for example, was debited 31st July 1663

	£	s	d
for the silver of 6 forged forkes wt. 12.9 at 5s. 2d.	£3	4	3
for makeing them		15	0

On the same date his account was credited with

	£	s	d
Old spoones & forkes wt. 54. 14. at 5s. 2d.	£13	2	7

A fascinating variety of items may be noted from the various accounts, such as

			£	s	d
1673	(Countess of Devonshire)				
	A warming pan wt. 79 oz. 7 dwt. at 6s.		£22	6	0
	For handle and graveing			7	6
1686	(H.R.H. Prince George of Denmark)				
	24 Trencher Plates wt. 505 oz. at 5s. 8d. p. oz.		143	1	8
	A stewing pan wt. 112 oz. 5 dwt. at 6s. 4d. p. oz.		35	10	11
1686	(Duke of Beaufort)				
	For a chamberpott & cover 38 oz. 7 dwt.		11	10	0
1687	(Earl of Kingston)				
	For a gold plate wt. 31 oz. 00 dwt. 12 gr. at 4l 5s. p. oz.		131	17	0

When the plate was out of fashion and they wanted a change, or some ready cash was needed, customers would sell it back or, alternatively, make use of another facility provided by the goldsmith banker, and pawn the plate, receiving a loan against its deposit. These "pawnes" were a common feature of the business and the records show that the facility was availed of by many customers, including the famous "Nell" Gwyn, for whom there are several entries, including—"Nov. 26. (1685) Lent on plate £4,600," [2] for which she paid interest at 6 per cent.

---

[2] The security for this loan appears to have been over-valued, for when she died two years later, in debt to the bank, they purchased the plate in part settlement for the sum of £3,791 5s. 9d. only.

Eventually all loans, of whatever description, were entered in a separate "P" or "Pawns" ledger, a practice which continued until well into the present century.

There are isolated instances of mortgages on property in the early days, but they all occur in Francis Child's "Own Posting Book," and appear to have been undertaken by him as a private venture rather than as part of the normal business. This book also contains details of exchange accounts showing dealings in foreign bills, as well as references to his "Adventures" in the East India trade.

Acting as goldsmith and banker to many national figures of the period, the firm's ledgers contain a large number of interesting accounts, amongst them being that of King William and his Queen, Mary. The first entries on the debit side of this account, dated 17th May 1689, are

> For Loan of Jewells for ye Coronation to ye Queen £222
> For a pre. of Diamd. Earrings to ye Queen 300

In his own personal account book, Francis Child records £10, 18s. 6d. "Paid for a Place att ye Coronation," while a later entry, dated 30th April 1691, records the receipt of £50 "Recd. of ye Queen to be given away."

The ledgers, then called posting books, varied considerably in size and shape, being referred to as "ye greate poaste Booke," "little Posting booke," "long new Po. Booke," etc. The earliest surviving ledger for 1662–1670 contains 235 accounts and occupies 514 pages. Most of these are simple accounts consisting of only a few entries each. The second ledger, running concurrently with the first—from 1663 to 1679—is a larger volume of 656 pages but contains only 18 accounts. Of these, three alone occupy two-thirds of the ledger; Christopher Cratford has 205 pages, Roger Jenyns [3] 100 pages and Lord Herbert (subsequently Marquess of Worcester) 106 pages. This division of the accounts into active and nonactive seems to have been the regular practice, for the ledgers show a similar pattern throughout the whole of the seventeenth century. Taking one year with another, 11 per cent of all the accounts were those of ladies.

By the 1680's the practice had developed of sending the customer a copy of his account on a sheet of paper, similar to the modern statement of account. The ledger would be balanced and a note made that the account had been sent. The Earl of Danby's account, for example, was balanced on 9th November 1686 and the entry made—"By an acct

[3] Cousin of the celebrated Sarah, Duchess of Marlborough.

then delld his honr there rested due to his honr £2362.—. 9¼." An entry in another account, dated 22nd March 1686/7, records the sending of the account "with all his Vouchers since Aprill the 2d." The issue of passbooks was a logical development of this practice and the earliest mention of these is found in the records in 1715.

Balance night, for so long a headache each half-year to banking staffs, was a very different affair in the seventeenth century. Then known as "Casting up ye Shop," it was done at very irregular intervals, varying from eighteen months to as long as eight years. Individual accounts were not necessarily balanced on these occasions, this usually being done only when an account was asked for, or the customer called to agree and sign the ledger. Records of these periodic assessments of the state of business survive from 1686 onwards and, in most cases, sufficient information is available to draw up fairly accurate balance sheets. It is interesting to note that the dates chosen for this irregular "Casting up ye Shop" usually bore some relationship to national events. For example, William of Orange landed at Torbay on 5th November 1688 and James II abdicated on 11th December; the books were balanced on 8th December. Similar action was taken six days prior to the final incorporation of the Bank of England on 27th July 1694.

The balance sheets reveal that the ratio of cash to deposits was normally about 35 per cent. On two occasions, however, in September 1697 and again in October 1712, it rose to over 50 per cent. Today the corresponding figure is under 10 per cent, but the higher figure then is understandable. The comparative newness of the system, together with the fact that the times were uncertain, made it difficult to assess just what demands would be made by customers withdrawing their cash, and the banker of the day had to keep a large stock of actual cash in his strong-room ready to meet any eventualities.

Apart from the actual cash, the assets included the stock of jewels, gold and plate held in the shop, and the figures show very clearly the decline in this side of the business as the partners concentrated more and more on banking. From 1686 until 1696 the ratio of these assets to deposits averaged just over 17 per cent. In 1697 and 1704 they were 7 per cent and in 1712 only 1 per cent. On two occasions the assets included an item "Sweep" of £40 and £220, obviously referring to the sweepings from the goldsmith's workship.

The total of deposits varied fairly considerably, being £109,000 in 1694 and again in 1712, while the figure rose to £160,000 in 1690 and to £177,000 in 1704.

In 1686 the balance sheet shows liabilities exceeding assets by £39 0s. 11d., but thereafter a credit balance was maintained varying up to £8,500. Only once—in 1697—do the balance sheets mention any division of profits. On that occasion the amount divided was £2,250 and at the same time £1,878 8s. 5d. was allocated as "Provision for Bad Debts." Some idea of the profits, however, can be obtained by reference to the partners' own accounts. Francis Child joined Robert Blanchard as a partner in the goldsmith business at about the time he married Blanchard's step-daughter, Elizabeth Wheeler, in 1671, and we find him credited with £50 on 22nd October 1674, "p. Pfitt to Mich. 74," with a further £50 a year later. No further entry can be found until 1697, by which time Blanchard had died and Sir Francis Child (he was knighted in 1689) was the senior partner. In September of that year, as has already been stated £2,250 was divided, of which Sir Francis received £1,000. There is then a further gap until 1701 from which year the figures are more regular—and astonishing considering the size of the business. In August 1701 he was credited with £3,000; October 1702 with £4,000; February 1704 with £8,000 together with a further £4,000 in the July of the same year. From that time until his death in 1713, Sir Francis took a smaller share in the profits amounting only to £1,200 a year: a further £1,000 being divided between the other partners. It is of interest to note that throughout this latter period the entries always record the same detail—"Recd. on acct. of profits of ye Shop since Mich. 1704," confirming the fact that there was no "Casting up ye Shop" during the intervening years.

Sir Francis Child kept accounts in his books for a number of his fellow goldsmith bankers, entries which show that they were in the habit of paying each other's notes and leaving amounts with each other to meet such liabilities. Examination of these accounts raises an interesting question as to their business arrangements. It would appear that while not actual partners in their business as bankers, they did, in fact, combine for the purpose of their goldsmith business in some form of co-partnership. The ledger for 1669–1679, for example, contains a lengthy and detailed account, headed by the clerk—"Inventory of Dyamonds and Jewells betweene Mr. E(ast) and my M(aste)r." And for the better identification of these partnership assets there are appended several pages of drawings of individual items with a note of their value and eventual disposal.

In the same ledger is the account of this John East—who carried on his business in the Strand, only a few doors away from Child's—and this is debited and credited with "½ pte" of sales and purchases of jewels. As an instance of the way this worked, Robert Flatman's account with Child's is debited 30th September 1670 with £23 10s.—for a diamond ring; John East's account being credited the following 22nd

February with £11 15s.—"½ pte of a ring sold Mr. Flatman." Similarly, debit entries in John East's account, such as "Pd. by ½ pte of a Ring he sold of ours," shows that the partnership operated both ways.

Contemporary with these accounts, but in the ledger for 1677–1682, there is a further account of "Dyamonds bought betweene Mr. Mawbert, Mr. Churchey, Mr. East and ourselves," and Mr. Churchey's separate account in the same ledger is debited and credited with items "in pte of" various transactions.

As has already been said, the prominence of the goldsmith side of the business diminished considerably towards the end of the seventeenth century, but cheques continued to be addressed to "Sir Francis Child & Compy., Goldsmiths" until well into the next century, and it is not until 1729, the year they first issued printed bank notes, that we find a cheque addressed to the firm as "Bankers."

The personal banking, started so many years ago, is still carried on at Child's Branch on the very same site where it started, and among the bank's customers are many who can find the accounts of their ancestors in the early ledgers. These contain not only much material of considerable banking interest, but they also have a lighter side. What could be more human, for instance, than the little note penned by the young son of the 1st Duke of Beaufort in 1686—when he would have been about eighteen—addressed to his father's banker?

> Pray do mee the favour to pay this bird-man four
> guineas for a paire of parckeets that I had of him.
> Pray dont let any body either my Ld. or Lady know
> that you did it and I will be sure my selfe to pay
> you honestly againe.
>   ARTHUR SOMERSET
> Chelsey
> the 23d. of September 86

AN INTEGRATED MODEL

FOR COMMERCIAL BANKS

DAVID A. ALHADEFF AND CHARLOTTE P. ALHADEfF

In this selection we gain unusually keen insight into the mysterious business of commercial banking. The authors clearly demonstrate the fact that individual banks are both buyers and sellers of money, and that costs and revenues of various asset portfolios and deposit-mixes determine bank profitability.

INTRODUCTION

Banking problems are conventionally discussed either under the heading of internal bank management or as an adjunct of monetary theory and policy. The former is concerned with the allocation of bank funds and with bank costs and earnings; the latter stresses particularly the effects on the money supply of bank lending and investing operations. Both approaches are treated elsewhere and need not be repeated here. What does not exist is a model to integrate systematically the results of these two approaches.

These two approaches to banking reflect the different interests of those who, on the one hand, are primarily interested in banking as a business, and those who, on the other hand, are primarily interested in banking, because bank operations affect the money supply, which, in turn, influences the kind and level of total economic activity. The results of individual bank operations are summarized in the profit and

Reprinted from The Journal of Finance, March 1957, pp. 24–42.

loss statement for the bank; the effects of bank operations on the money supply are summarized in the balance sheet of the bank, particularly the relation between liquidity reserves and deposits. It is the purpose of this paper to present a model which systematically integrates both the income statement and balance sheet aspects of commercial bank operations. The model presented in this paper is thus a very useful device for examining the probable effects of alternative bank policies, like lending versus investing, making different kinds of loans, increasing or decreasing rates on time deposits, accepting or rejecting marginal business which does not cover its full cost, the desirability of holding excess reserves, etc. In addition, the model can serve to examine the impact on the individual bank of numerous external factors, like a change in reserve requirements, internal and external drains and return flows, open market operations by the central bank, actual or prospective changes in interest-rate levels, etc.

A DIAGRAMMATIC MODEL FOR COMMERCIAL BANKS

Although it is not our purpose to review portfolio policy in this paper, a few brief comments may help to clarify the ensuing discussion. In determining portfolio composition, bankers generally avoid rate competition. At any moment of time, therefore, bankers accept the going rates for different kinds of credit and adjust their portfolios to existing rate schedules. Moreover, cost accounting is not sufficiently developed in most banks to permit precise cost allocation for different kinds of credit. As a result, fixed costs are not generally divided among the different products of a bank. Similarly, bankers appear to believe that, within the normal range of probable output variation, variable costs for different kinds of output are probably constant. Although the variable costs for different kinds of output are not likely to be known with precision, bankers do know in a rough way the ordinal ranking of the variable costs for different kinds of output.

If portfolio composition were motivated exclusively by profit-maximization in the simplest sense, and assuming perfect homogeneity within each credit category, bankers would produce each product as far as they could, giving priority to the product with highest markup over variable costs, and then proceeding to successively lower markup items.[1] Bankers produce different kinds of output partly because product

[1] In practice, this might be modified by business strategy and other considerations, just as the simple descriptions of profit-maximization for single firm monopoly are, in practice, far more complex than is usually mentioned in the abstract, theoretical description.

specialization is limited by the extent of the market for any given kind of loan. The allocation of bank funds is partly determined by three other dominant considerations: liquidity, solvency, and legal considerations. Briefly, liquidity considerations affect portfolio composition by restricting the total volume of earning assets, and by forcing banks to hold part of their earning assets in comparatively low-yielding assets. Solvency considerations based on the risk of default losses affect profit-making in two direct ways: higher profits may be precluded by the arbitrary limitation on acceptable loan and investment risks, regardless of the risk premium; and higher profits may be precluded by diversification, which limits product specialization in high-profit assets within the selected risk categories.[2] In general, legal considerations affect bank profits by limiting the total volume of earning assets in a bank, by limiting risks, by limiting specialization, by excluding certain categories of assets entirely, etc.

The Modified Profit Graph. With the preceding comments in mind, we can proceed to develop a model to combine the income statements and balance sheet aspects of commercial bank operations. The analysis of commercial bank operations could be cast exclusively in terms of the variables of the economic theory of the firm, but the model derived in this way would be nonoperational. In striving for an operational model, we have translated the concepts of the theory of the firm into variables which bankers deal with in their daily operations. The variables in our model include all the major items in the income statement and balance sheets of commercial banks.

A preliminary difficulty in integrating the income and expense items with balance sheet items concerns the different time periods for the two sets of variables. The income statement summarizes the experience of a business *over a definite period of time*, whereas the balance sheet depicts a cross section of the values of the business *at a particular moment of time*. In other words, the income statement items are flow concepts, whereas the balance sheet items are stock concepts. The complications presented by the different periods can be overcome as follows. At any moment of time, a bank has certain balance sheet items. Most of the asset items and some liabilities generate expenses at a certain rate per period. Thus, at any moment of time, depending on the relation between earning rates and expenditure rates, the bank generates net profits (or losses) at some particular rate per period. By depicting income statement items as rates per period at any moment of time, we can legitimately combine income statement items with balance sheet

---

[2] Diversification may also raise bank costs by sacrificing possible economies of specialization.

items which are also given at any moment of time. By modifying the diagram, we can show a change in any of the variables of our problem. Thus, the diagrammatic model is accurate at any moment of time, and a series of adjusted diagrams accurately portray the bank's situation over time. Moreover, if the time period of the diagram is the conventional accounting period of a year, and if the variables remain unchanged during this period, the income and expense rates shown in the diagram would coincide exactly with the absolute values for the income and expense items during the period.

With these introductory observations, we can turn directly to the analysis of our model which attempts to integrate the balance sheet and income statement items. The major variables in this problem are listed in Table 1.

TABLE 1   MAJOR BALANCE SHEET AND INCOME STATEMENT ITEMS

Major Assets

    Cash and due from banks
    Loans and discounts
    Investments

Major Liabilities

    Capital (including surplus, undivided profits, and reserve for losses)
    Time deposits
    Demand deposits

Sources of Earnings

    Interest and dividends on securities
    Interest and discount on loans
    Other charges on loans
    Service charges on deposits
    Other charges, fees, etc.
    Trust department earnings
    Miscellaneous earnings

Expenses

    Officers' salaries
    Non-executive wages and salaries
    Directors' fees
    Interest on time deposits
    Interest on borrowed money
    Taxes other than income taxes
    Recurring depreciation
    Miscellaneous expenses

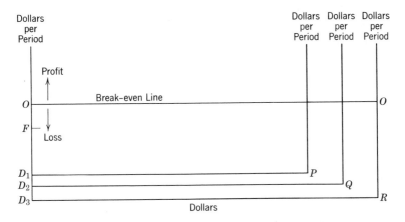

Figure 1. Source and cost of bank funds.

Balance sheet and income statement variables can be integrated in a modified profit graph (Figure 1). The x-axis of the modified profit graph is measured in dollars, and the y-axis is measured in dollars per period. The x-axis measures the different sources and use of bank funds. The y-axis measures the income or expense associated with different volumes of funds (for both sources and uses) along the x-axis. The zero point along the y-axis indicates the break-even position of the bank, and is the base from which profits or losses are measured along the vertical axis. A positive y-coordinate shows the amount of profits per period, and a negative y-coordinate shows the amount of losses per period from bank operations.[3]

Sources of Bank Funds. Every bank has a certain amount of basic fixed costs at zero levels of output. Of the expenses listed in Table 1, basic fixed costs include part of the officers' salaries, at least part of the nonexecutive wages and salaries (other than those associated with deposits), directors' fees, taxes other than income taxes, recurring depreciation (other than on machinery and equipment to handle deposit ac-

[3] Strictly speaking, the diagram shows the amount of net current earnings before income taxes. For brevity, these are called "profits." Profits before income taxes (which we call "adjusted profits") are the difference between net current earnings before income taxes and the net balance of the net amount of recoveries, transfers to and from reserves, profits, losses, and charge-offs on loans, securities, and other assets. We call net profits after income taxes "final profits." The items between profits and final profits are handled verbally rather than in the diagrammatic model. These different profit concepts are based on the Federal Reserve tables of member bank earnings. Cf., for example, *Federal Reserve Bulletin* (May 1955), p. 564.

counts and process checks), and at least part of the miscellaneous expenses (e.g., heat, light, insurance, etc.). The sum of these basic fixed costs is measured by a negative y-intercept. In Figure 1, basic fixed costs are OF.

The major sources of a bank's funds [4] are capital (including surplus, undivided profits and reserves for losses) and (time and demand) deposits.[5] In the short run,[6] we consider capital to be costless, because dividends are a residual disbursement from profits. A bank's failure to pay dividends in any one year is not likely to force liquidation of the bank for the purpose of permanently withdrawing capital funds. In the long run, however, bank capital definitely has a cost, and, if bank capital does not earn what is considered a "normal" return, stockholders will permanently withdraw funds from the banking industry and seek alternative employment for those funds. Alternatively, bank capital can be considered to have a cost even in the short run, if practical considerations dictate paying a dividend each year. In that case, the amount of the dividend is the short-run cost of capital, and would be shown diagrammatically as a fixed cost.

Deposits are a more important source of funds than capital; neither time nor demand deposits are costless. Time deposit costs include depreciation on bank machinery for time accounts, labor for these accounts, and interest paid on time deposits. Time deposits earn no *directly* compensating income. Demand deposit costs include labor costs for handling these deposits, and depreciation on machinery and equipment for processing checks. Demand deposits earn a directly compensating income in the form of service charges. Since it is generally conceded that service charges fail to cover the direct cost of demand accounts, we may presume that most banks incur net costs on demand accounts. The sum of the time deposit costs and the net demand deposit costs is called the deposit cost.

The nature of deposit costs is ambiguous, because deposit costs exhibit characteristics of both fixed and variable costs. A variable cost varies with short-run variations in output. For given reserve requirements and a given deposit mix, deposit costs appear to satisfy the requirements of a variable cost, because the bank generally cannot increase

---

[4] Funds borrowed either from the Federal Reserve Banks or from other banks are considered at a later point.

[5] The deposits are the bank's stable deposits, and not deposits which appear transitorily after a loan transaction, but which are fairly promptly lost to the bank through adverse clearing balances.

[6] The analysis of this paper is short run in the usual sense of holding certain factors fixed. The discussion of fixed and variable factors follows shortly.

output without a prior increase in deposits.[7] On the other hand, a variable factor is variable at the discretion of the management. At any moment of time, however, a bank has no real option about making quick changes in its stable deposits. Indeed, it may carry some of these deposits unused (in the form of excess reserves) for years, even though they cost the bank money and the bank is not employing the funds in earning assets. From this viewpoint, deposit costs are like fixed costs. For graphical convenience in this paper, deposit costs are treated primarily like fixed costs, with a negative y-intercept. Changes in deposit costs are assumed to be associated with changes in deposit volume, and the different deposit costs are shown by different y-intercepts.[8] On a profit graph, the volume of capital (minus the amount of capital invested in fixed factors) and deposits is measured along the x-axis. The actual volume of capital and deposits is D_1P in Figure 1. The net deposit cost is measured along the y-axis. The actual net deposit cost is FD_1.

Two factors are unambiguously fixed in the short run; the basic fixed factors and the bank's capital. Each imposes a quasi-independent restriction on the bank's basic capacity in the short run. At any moment of time, a given bank has a certain size building, a certain amount of machines and equipment, a permanent managerial staff, etc. These basic fixed factors limit the amount of deposits and output which the bank can handle. In Figure 1, this restriction is D_2Q, and FD_2 is the net deposit cost for this capacity.[9] On the other hand, the absolute amount of capital (for a given portfolio mix) limits the amount of deposit liabilities a bank can safely carry.[10] This limit is D_3R, and FD_3 is the net deposit cost for this capacity.

For any given bank, the *actual capacity line* (D_1P) varies with

[7] There are, of course, certain circumstances under which earning assets can be increased without an increase in deposits. See Lauchlin Currie, "Treatment of Credit in Contemporary Monetary Theory," *Journal of Political Economy* (February, 1933), p. 62. Some of these are discussed at a later point.

[8] Deposit costs do not always vary with changes in deposit volume. In practice, most banks have enough slack to handle small increases in deposit volume with no additional cost. Moreover, larger deposit volumes need incur no greater deposit costs, if, for example, the size of checks drawn on the accounts increases with no other change in the activity or number of accounts. Indeed, such changes could even reduce total deposit costs despite an increasing volume of deposits. In this paper we ignore the possibility of decreasing or constant *total* deposit costs with increasing deposit volume.

[9] We assume a given deposit mix and a given activity, number, and size distribution of deposit and loan accounts.

[10] Expansion limits with given capital are not absolute, except in some states which specify the maximum capital-deposit ratio by law; in others, custom is strong.

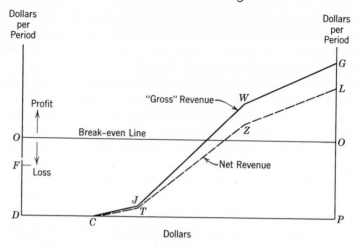

Figure 2. Use of bank funds.

changes in the volume of deposits, except that the limit to this variation is the earliest restriction. In our example, this limit is the capacity line for basic fixed factors (D_2Q). The first restriction encountered, whichever it happens to be, is the *effective capacity* limit for the given bank. Banker decisions about basic capacity variations are important, but they are long-run decisions and are ignored in the (essentially) short-run analysis of this paper.

Uses of Bank Funds. The uses of a bank's funds are shown by its assets. The bank's primary reserves [11] earn no income. These include legal reserves, vault cash, and due from banks. Legal reserves are determined by the volume of time and demand deposits, and by the fractional reserves required for each; vault cash is determined by the day-to-day cash requirements of the bank; and due from banks depends mostly on business connections with other banks. Diagrammatically, primary reserves are DC (Figure 2).

The bank's secondary reserves [12] are held for seasonal liquidity needs above the normal daily liquidity requirements. The requisite volume of secondary reserves is rather closely determined for any bank by the character and volume of its deposits, the number of depositors,

---

[11] Primary reserves *explicitly exclude excess reserves,* which are treated later.
[12] Secondary reserves are composed primarily of Treasury bills and secondarily of prime bankers' acceptances, open market commercial paper, and call and time loans on stock exchange collateral. Longer-term securities may also be part of secondary reserves when the remaining maturity of the securities is short.

size distribution of accounts, and location of the bank. Given these factors, and with a certain amount of experience, a banker can generally forecast seasonal liquidity requirements, and hence, the necessary volume of secondary reserves. The volume of secondary reserves is measured along the x-axis, and starts at the terminal point of the primary reserves line segment. The "gross" [13] revenue curve for secondary reserves is CJ (Figure 2). To show the net earnings of secondary reserves, we subtract the direct wage and salary costs of securing and holding these assets from their relatively small gross earnings. In Figure 2, this is CT.

After a banker has allocated funds to primary and secondary reserves, he stands ready to meet the loan demands of customers. The loan portfolio of a bank is not homogeneous; it consists of business loans, real estate loans, consumer loans, etc. Each kind of loan can be shown separately on the diagram, with line segments of different slopes for different net rates of return. Indeed, each individual loan could be shown separately, for both gross and net loan rates often differ for different loans within a single loan category, especially business loans. For simplicity in this paper, we treat all loans together. The volume of loans is measured along the x-axis, and starts at the terminal point of the secondary reserves line segment. The "gross" revenue curve for all loans is JW (Figure 2). To show the net earnings on loans, we subtract all direct loan costs from the "gross" earnings (both interest rate and other loan charges) on loans. The net earnings curve for loans and discounts is the line segment TZ (Figure 2).

Investment for income in open-market securities is largely a residual use of bank funds after primary reserves, secondary reserves, and loans to customers. A net earnings curve on securities is derived in a similar manner to the net earnings curve on loans. Hence, the slope of the investment line is less than the slope of the loan line. The "gross" investment revenue curve is WG, and the net investment curve is ZL (Figure 2). Profits are measured directly along the right-hand vertical axis and are OL in Figure 2.

Excess Reserves and Borrowed Funds. Under ordinary circumstances, the banking system can create money, but the individual bank generally cannot. Thus, a bank can lend or invest only the funds it already has. The bank's funds are allocated to different uses in accordance with the principles of portfolio management. The profit or loss per period from the bank's operations is shown directly by the net earnings curve.

---

[13] By its construction, the diagram automatically subtracts basic fixed costs and deposits costs from the gross revenue curves.

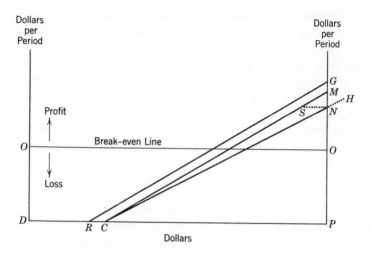

Figure 3. Excess reserves and borrowed funds.

We have thus far ignored excess reserves as a use of funds and borrowed funds as a source of funds. These remaining items can readily be included in our model. Consider how the model accommodates borrowed funds. In Figure 3, the total volume (source) of funds from capital and deposits is DP, and total fixed costs (basic fixed costs and net deposit costs) are OD. The use of funds is for primary reserves of DC and earning assets of CP. The net revenue curve for secondary reserves, loans, and investments is CM,[14] and profits are OM. The primary reserves of DC are just adequate to the amount of deposits. Now let the bank increase its earning assets by RC. Total earning assets are now RP, and the net revenue line is RG. Assuming a complete loss of derivative deposits, the source of funds from *stable* deposits (plus capital) is unchanged at DP, and the use of funds for necessary primary reserves is still DC. Since primary reserves are only DR, the reserve deficiency is RC. By borrowing RC at the Federal Reserve, the bank can correct the reserve deficiency. After the funds have been borrowed, the curve RG shifts to the right until R coincides with C. The volume of earning assets is still equal to the amount RP as shown in Figure 3, but the net revenue curve after borrowing from the Federal Reserve is CH. Borrowed funds are a temporary increment to the bank's loanable funds, and increase the

---

[14] For simplicity, we use a single net revenue line rather than individual line segments for different earning assets.

bank's variable costs. Accordingly, the slope of CM is reduced by the cost of the borrowed funds, and the slope of CH is less than the slope of CM. For discounts or advances from the Federal Reserve, the cost of borrowed funds is determined by the appropriate discount rate.[15]

Now consider how bank profits are affected by excess reserves as a use of funds. Let DP (Figure 3) be the total source of funds from capital and deposits, and let OD be the total fixed costs. DC are the necessary primary reserves. The net revenue curve for secondary reserves, loans, and investments is CS. The bank is left with unused funds or excess reserves equal to SN, and the bank's profits are ON (measured directly along the right-hand vertical axis).

Excess reserves may develop when a bank has surplus funds, i.e., "funds not needed or demanded by local business activity, or by the customer bank-loan market." [16] The absence of a satisfactory loan demand would normally lead a banker to the open market for investment of the surplus funds. That might not happen, however, when interest rates are expected to rise. To be sure, those expectations per se would mean simply that bankers should invest in short terms rather than in long terms. Bankers might not invest in short terms, however, if the demand for short terms drove the rate to an unprofitable level, i.e., the net increment to adjusted profits from the marginal investment is negative. Capital losses from rate fluctuations on short-term investments are negligible. Hence, it is substantially correct to say that excess reserves develop when the net profit from the marginal investment is negative, i.e., when the interest return on the marginal credit is less than its direct variable cost (excluding deposit costs which are considered fixed in the short run). Alternatively, excess reserves might develop when high-grade short terms are not available in sufficient quantities to absorb the surplus funds of banks. Excess reserves for either reason are consistent with individual equilibrium. It should be mentioned that the existence of excess reserves reduces the importance of liquidity and risk considerations in the composition of a bank's portfolio.

Excess reserves are one kind of excess capacity in banking; we call this "excess actual capacity." Excess actual capacity is perfectly compatible with individual equilibrium. Another kind of bank excess capacity in the short run is "excess effective capacity," the difference between actual capacity and effective capacity. Excess effective capacity is also

---

[15] The slope of the entire line is reduced and not just the slope of the marginal segment, because we are using an average net revenue line.
[16] Benjamin H. Beckhart, *The New York Money Market* (New York, 1932), III, 5. We ignore "frictional" excess reserves.

compatible with short-run individual equilibrium assuming the bank is otherwise in an equilibrium position. This is because the bank cannot in the short run significantly vary its stable deposits by its own action. In the long run, stable deposits can be varied by an advertising campaign, by changing the interest rate on time deposits, by altering the service charge policy on demand deposits, etc. Outside influences, largely beyond the bank's control, can bring about short-run variations in stable deposits, and a bank would have to adjust to these changes to achieve an equilibrium position. At any moment of time, however, the volume of stable deposits is given for the individual bank, and its short-run equilibrium is achieved in terms of these deposits. Excess effective capacity can affect the banker's decisions, but mostly in the long run.

With this inclusion of excess reserves and borrowed funds, our diagrammatic model has succeeded in integrating into one conceptual framework all important sources and uses of bank funds, as well as all important sources of income and expenses.

IMPACT OF EXTERNAL FACTORS ON THE BANKING SYSTEM

In this section, we examine the group equilibrium adjustment. Specifically, we propose to show how our model can be employed to examine different possible effects on bank earnings from different factors which can affect the aggregative level of deposits, even when the aggregative level is assumed to be the same in all cases. Only one of these disequilibrating factors will be examined in detail to show how the model works; the effects of some of the other forces can then be summarized briefly. Since the individual banks differ in important respects, it is convenient to proceed initially under the assumption that all banks have identical costs, demand, portfolio composition, etc. Under this symmetry assumption, a representative bank can serve to show the effects on all banks. Later, this symmetry assumption will be dropped.

Let us consider the effects on bank profits when a disequilibrium develops between the reserves and deposits of the banking system as a result (say) of a decrease of money in circulation and/or a gold inflow which increase the reserves of the banking system.[17] Let us posit a banking system with one hundred banks. Total primary reserves [18] are

---

[17] To simplify the analysis, we use a single (average) net rate of return curve for all the earning assets together.

[18] The reader is reminded that primary reserves include vault cash, and legal reserves, but specifically exclude excess reserves.

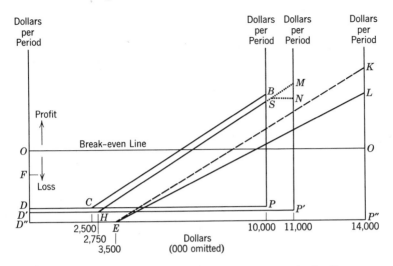

Figure 4. Group equilibrium adjustment (representative bank).

$250,000,000, loans and investments are $750,000,000, and deposits are $1,000,000,000. Primary reserves are assumed to be 25 per cent of deposits. Since there are one hundred banks in the system, the representative bank is 1 per cent of the size of the banking system. The representative bank has primary reserves of $2,500,000, loans and investments of $7,500,000, and deposits of $10,000,000. In Figure 4, basic fixed costs are OF and deposit costs are FD; actual capacity is DP, and DCB is the use of funds or net revenue curve.

Now suppose the decrease of money in circulation and the gold inflow together amount to $100,000,000, or 10 per cent of the system's deposits. Let the representative bank receive a proportionate share of this sum. In Figure 4, the representative bank's use of funds (net revenue) curve shifts from DCB to D'HSN. The bank's new profits of ON ·(measured along the vertical axis) are less than the former profits of OB, because liabilities (and expenses) have increased without a corresponding increase in earning assets.[19] By lending or investing the bank's excess reserves (=SN), the management can increase profits. Assuming a complete loss of derivative deposits, the use of funds curve shifts from D'HSN to D'HM. This is not the end of the story, however, since the action in the representative bank is repeated in the ninety-nine

[19] As we explained earlier, we are ignoring in this paper the possibility of decreasing or constant total deposit costs with increasing deposit volume. However, the analysis could readily accommodate either of these excluded possibilities.

other banks as well. Thus, although the representative bank loses its derivative deposits, it gains incremental primary reserves in successive rounds. After each round, the management of the representative bank finds that it can increase profits (or decrease losses) by lending or investing the newly acquired excess reserves. When the expansion process has worked itself out, the representative bank has no excess reserves, and the bank's net revenue curve has shifted from $D'HM$ to $D''EL$.

Interest rates fall in the process of expansion by all banks together. If the representative bank's assets had been expanded at the former rate [20] assuming constant variable costs, the bank's profits would have been OK in Figure 4. Instead, they are OL. The profits of OL can be greater than, less than, or equal to the original profits of OB, depending on demand and cost patterns and the particular portfolio composition at the original and at the final output levels. The group equilibrium is stable when no bank is operating with undue final profits or undue final losses, given the imperfections of entry and of exit.

This discussion of the group equilibrium adjustment has ignored the possible desirability of holding excess reserves. As we have already shown in the previous section, the individual bank will hold excess reserves when there are surplus funds in the loan market and the net adjusted profits from investing all or part of the surplus funds in the open market are negative, or, alternatively, when the surplus funds of the banking system exceed the acceptable demand for those funds on the open market. The group equilibrium with excess reserves is only stable, however, when the individual banks are operating with neither undue final profits nor losses. To the extent that excess reserves develop, the total expansion of the representative bank will, of course, be less than the amount shown in Figure 4.

Diversity among Banks. DIVERSITY OF BANKING MARKETS. We can now drop the symmetry assumptions and recognize the considerable diversity among banks. The demand, costs, portfolios, and "products" of different banks are not identical. The importance of elements of monopolistic competition varies widely in different banks. As a result, some bankers exercise a much greater degree of control over their loan markets than do others. In the prime borrower markets, the elements of monopolistic competition are very weak, and the market control by bankers operating primarily in this market is also very weak. In other words, the prime borrower markets are reasonably competitive, and exhibit rate flexibility in response to changing credit conditions.

[20] Under the symmetry assumptions, we ignore rate rigidities, which are discussed later.

In the prime borrower markets, loan expansion is associated with a reduction in loan rates. The initial reduction in loan rates is not identified with a fall in the *schedule* of rates, because "Declines in the prime rate generally come when competition for loans has widened eligibility for the rate. . . . " [21] In other words, the initial loan expansion is not associated with a reduction in the schedule of rates, but rather is associated with reduced rates for particular borrowers who are reclassified within the existing schedule of rates. Some borrowers who just missed being prime borrowers, and paid more than the prime rate, are reclassified as prime borrowers—that is what widened eligibility means—and pay the (lower) prime rates. The result is to lower the bank's net rate of return curve.

In due course, the eased credit situation affects the rate schedule, too, for the original prime borrowers can force reductions in the prime rates.[22] The prime rate reduction is usually accomplished under a kind of barometric leadership in which the *de facto* rate reductions are acknowledged by an official reduction in prime rates. Although prime borrower banks are numerically small, their officers cannot collude either directly or implicitly to maintain loan rates, because prime borrowers have access to the open-money market for commercial paper. Since the open market is supplied by thousands of banks, open-market rates could not be held rigid by outright collusion or by an oligopoly rationale.

At the other extreme, the elements of monopolistic competition are very strong in small borrower markets and permit bankers in these markets to exercise semimonopolistic control. A bank serving primarily small borrowers (with very weak bargaining power and possibly no alternative sources of supply) is not under the same pressure as a prime borrower bank to reduce lending rates to expand loans.[23] A banker operating in a semimonopolistic market is comparatively insulated against the price action of other banks. Loan rates in these markets are administered and comparatively inflexible. In these markets, funds are allocated less by the price (rate) mechanism and more by banker rationing under an administered price system. This system often permits

---

[21] *Monthly Letter on Business and Economic Conditions,* First National City Bank, October 1955, p. 111.

[22] The change in the prime rate sparks the change in the schedule of rates.

[23] However, a fall in the prime rate tends eventually, to greater or less degree, to filter through the banking system so that the effects of the fall in the prime rate tend to be fairly widely felt. The greater the fall in the prime rate and the longer its duration at the new low levels, the greater is the likelihood of widespread dissemination—in some cases affecting even the relatively monopolistic banking markets.

the banker to increase loan output without reducing rates. Given an increase in lending capacity, bankers in such markets would increase loans as long as it was profitable to do so.

Although bankers in semimonopoly markets are not under strong pressure to reduce rates to increase loans, their profits may not reach the level OK (Figure 4). This is because the limitation of acceptable borrowers in local markets may force the banker to turn to the open market to dispose of his surplus funds. In the open-money markets for long-term and short-term funds, the local monopolist has no monopoly influence, and open-market investments earn the reduced rates consistent with the eased reserve position of the banking system. The lower interest rate on open-market investments reduces the average rate of return earned on the bank's total portfolio. Diagrammatically, therefore, the slope of the average rate of return curve falls.

Owing to this diversity of banking markets, the profitability of different banks at the equilibrium position can vary widely. The elements of product differentiation and monopolistic competition which surround different producers in different degrees protect the higher profits in some banks from encroachment by other (existing) banks. Similarly, they protect these "extra" profits against encroachment by new entrants, by making entry imperfect.[24]

OTHER DIVERSITIES AMONG BANKS. Under the symmetry assumptions, we assumed homogeneity in the composition and average maturity of the portfolio of different banks. In fact, of course, bank portfolios vary widely. Moreover, that part of the equilibrium process described under diversity of banking markets holds strictly only for business loans. For consumer loans, for example, the terms of the credit are often more important than the rate charged. For real estate loans, both loan terms and loan rates are important factors in demand. Moreover, bank costs differ for different kinds of output. Accordingly, an eased reserve position can result in different equilibrium profits for banks with different portfolio composition.

Bank profits are also affected by the different average maturities of loan portfolios in different banks. Reduced loan rates associated with increased output directly affect (with some exceptions) either new loans or loans which are being renewed. In banks with short average loan maturities, the renewable portion encompasses a larger percentage of the loan portfolio than in banks with longer average loan maturities. Accordingly, a larger percentage of the loan portfolio is subject to the

[24] Additionally, entry into banking is imperfect because of legal barriers to free entry.

reduced rates in the former rather than in the latter banks. Other things being equal, bank profits would also differ for this reason.

The diversity among banks extends to their risks and losses, too. Bankers' attitudes toward risk-bearing on individual loans are at least partly subjective and differ for this reason. Since portfolio risks on individual loans differ among banks, portfolio losses also may differ. Moreover, the collective risk [25] also varies among banks. For example, the collective risk is likely to be greater for a small bank with limited diversification opportunities in local loan markets than for a large metropolitan bank. When different individual and collective risks result in different bank losses, the equilibrium adjusted profits may differ for different banks.

Banks also differ in their liquidity buffers. The calculation of liquidity needs is based on expectations about future liquidity drains. The allowance for possible error in these forecasts varies in different banks partly because banker conservatism varies. Moreover, bankers differ in their willingness to rely upon the Federal Reserve for liquidity in an emergency. Or, again, the amount of excess reserves—and excess reserves are also a liquidity buffer—varies in different banks. For example, excess reserves are generally smaller in money market banks than in country banks. For these and similar reasons, liquidity buffers are not the same in different banks. Other things being equal, different liquidity buffers are responsible for different profits in equilibrium.

Finally, legal factors exert a strong influence on the composition and size of bank portfolios. This influence is not uniform, however, because different regulations are issued by many of the forty-nine chartering jurisdictions and the various other bank regulatory agencies in the United States. An obvious example is the different legal reserve requirements for member and nonmember banks of the Federal Reserve System. Because of this diversity of legal regulations, the profits of different banks can be different in equilibrium.

Other Disequilibrating Factors. We can now consider briefly how bank profits might be affected by some of the other factors which alter bank reserves. In all such cases, the group equilibrium analysis follows

---

[25] The individual risk depends upon the circumstances of each loan and is evaluated by conventional credit analysis. Uncertainty remains about the individual risk, because unusual or unpredictable circumstances can affect the borrower's ability to meet his commitments. The possibility of uncertainty losses increases for a bank with an increase in the volume of similar loans. We call this risk from a large volume of similar loans in a bank's portfolio the collective risk.

that outlined above. However, the final equilibrium position may not be the same after different disequilibrating factors even when total deposits are the same.[26]

Consider the following cases, for which we resume the symmetry assumptions. Suppose the central bank engages in open-market operations and purchases securities from the public. Let the reserves of the individual bank and of the banking system increase to the same extent as they would after a corresponding decrease of money in circulation. *Ceteris paribus,* the equilibrium profits for the representative bank after open-market operations would be the same as after a reversal of the internal drain. On the other hand, suppose the bank's equilibrium is disturbed by a reduction in legal reserve requirements. The bank's earning assets would be smaller after the open-market operations than after the reduction in reserve requirements, although we posit the same volume of final deposits in both cases. Under the symmetry assumptions, the comparative profits depend on the revenues and costs for the total portfolios after the two cases. Because of these factors, we cannot state a priori whether profits after the change in legal reserve requirements would be greater than, less than, or equal to the profits after open-market operations despite the different volume of earning assets.

Although an individual bank cannot be permanently indebted to the Federal Reserve, a bank can achieve a temporary equilibrium with such borrowed funds. The temporary equilibrium achieved with these borrowed funds differs from the final equilibrium after reducing reserve requirements and after open-market operations, even when the amount of the expanded deposits is the same for the three cases. Assuming no excess reserves, the earning assets after Federal Reserve borrowing would be greater than after open-market operations and would be the same as the earning assets after the reduction in reserve requirements. When these situations are plotted in terms of our earlier diagrammatics, it is apparent that profits (losses) would be greater (smaller) after reducing reserve requirements than after borrowing from the Federal Reserve (during the period of outstanding indebtedness to the Federal Reserve). This is because the volume of earning assets is identical and the composition of earning assets is assumed to be identical. Hence, the slopes of the gross earnings curves are identical for both cases. The slopes of the net earnings curves would differ only by the cost of borrowing. Moreover, when profits after open-market operations are the same or greater than after reducing reserve requirements, the profits would also

[26] In these examples, the intensity of the change is measured in terms of final deposits, assuming a full expansion of the banking system in all cases.

be greater than after Federal Reserve borrowing. When profits after open-market operations are less than profits after reducing reserve requirements, the comparative profitability after open-market operations and Federal Reserve borrowing would depend upon the discount rate in addition to the factors that determined the relative profitability after open-market operations and reduced reserve requirements.

In the foregoing discussion, we assumed that the disequilibrating force increased the reserves of the banking system. The same analysis would hold, *mutatis mutandis*, for a decrease in reserves. However, two considerations deserve special mention in discussing the contraction process. First the existence of excess reserves can, to that extent, prevent the liquidation of earning assets. Second, the liquidation of earning assets can be partly forestalled by temporary borrowing from the Federal Reserve.

— really says absolutely nothing about a bank's *desired* equilibrium.

MULTIPLE EXPANSION

OF BANK DEPOSITS

JAMES TOBIN

The usual textbook approach to the multiple expansion
of bank credit and deposits is not entirely realistic, since
assumptions concerning the utilization of available bank
resources do not always hold in the "real world." Professor
Tobin brings us a step closer to a general explanation of the
expansion process and its constraints.

Without reserve requirements, expansion of credit and deposits
by the commercial banking system would be limited by the availability
of assets at yields sufficient to compensate banks for the costs of attracting and holding the corresponding deposits. In a regime of reserve
requirements, the limit which they impose normally cuts the expansion
short of this competitive equilibrium. When reserve requirements and
deposit interest rate ceilings are effective, the marginal yield of bank
loans and investments exceeds the marginal cost of deposits to the
banking system. In these circumstances additional reserves make it
possible and profitable for banks to acquire additional earning assets.
The expansion process lowers interest rates generally—enough to induce
the public to hold additional deposits but ordinarily not enough to
wipe out the banks' margin between the value and cost of additional
deposits.

Reprinted from "Commercial Banks as Creators of 'Money,'" Banking and Monetary
Studies, Deane Carson, ed. (Homewood: Richard D. Irwin, 1963), pp. 416–418.

It is the existence of this margin—not the monetary nature of bank liabilities—which makes it possible for the economics teacher to say that additional loans permitted by new reserves will generate their own deposits. The same proposition would be true of any other system of financial institutions subject to similar reserve constraints and similar interest rate ceilings. In this sense it is more accurate to attribute the special place of banks among intermediaries to the legal restrictions to which banks alone are subjected than to attribute these restrictions to the special character of bank liabilities.

But the textbook description of multiple expansion of credit and deposits on a given reserve base is misleading even for a regime of reserve requirements. There is more to the determination of the volume of bank deposits than the arithmetic of reserve supplies and reserve ratios. The redundant reserves of the thirties are a dramatic reminder that economic opportunities sometimes prevail over reserve calculations. But the significance of that experience is not correctly appreciated if it is regarded simply as an aberration from a normal state of affairs in which banks are fully "loaned up" and total deposits are tightly linked to the volume of reserves. The thirties exemplify in extreme form a phenomenon which is always in some degree present: the use to which commercial banks put the reserves made available to the system is an economic variable depending on lending opportunities and interest rates.

An individual bank is not constrained by any fixed quantum of reserves. It can obtain additional reserves to meet requirements by borrowing from the Federal Reserve, by buying "Federal Funds" from other banks, by selling or "running off" short-term securities. In short, reserves are available at the discount window and in the money market, at a price. This cost the bank must compare with available yields on loans and investments. If those yields are low relative to the cost of reserves, the bank will seek to avoid borrowing reserves and perhaps hold excess reserves instead. If those yields are high relative to the cost of borrowing reserves, the bank will shun excess reserves and borrow reserves occasionally or even regularly. For the banking system as a whole the Federal Reserve's quantitative controls determine the supply of unborrowed reserves. But the extent to which this supply is left unused, or supplemented by borrowing at the discount window, depends on the economic circumstances confronting the banks—on available lending opportunities and on the whole structure of interest rates from the Fed's discount rate through the rates on mortgages and long-term securities.

The range of variation in net free reserves in recent years has been from −5 per cent to +5 per cent of required reserves. This indi-

cates a much looser linkage between reserves and deposits than is suggested by the textbook exposition of multiple expansion for a system which
is always precisely and fully "loaned up." (It does not mean, however,
that actual monetary authorities have any less control than textbook
monetary authorities. Indeed the net free reserve position is one of their
more useful instruments and barometers. Anyway, they are after bigger
game than the quantity of "money"!)

Two consequences of this analysis deserve special notice because
of their relation to the issues raised earlier in this paper. First, an increase—of, say, a billion dollars—in the supply of unborrowed reserves
will, in general, result in less than a billion-dollar increase in required
reserves. Net free reserves will rise (algebraically) by some fraction of
the billion dollars—a very large fraction in periods like the thirties, a
much smaller one in tight money periods like those of the fifties. Loans
and deposits will expand by less than their textbook multiples. The
reason is simple. The open-market operations which bring about the
increased supply of reserves tend to lower interest rates. So do the
operations of the commercial banks in trying to invest their new reserves.
The result is to diminish the incentives of banks to keep fully loaned up
or to borrow reserves, and to make banks content to hold on the average
higher excess reserves.

Second, depositor preferences do matter, even in a régime of
fractional reserve banking. Suppose, for example, that the public decides
to switch new or old savings from other assets and institutions into
commercial banks. This switch makes earning assets available to banks
at attractive yields—assets that otherwise would have been lodged either
directly with the public or with the competing financial institutions
previously favored with the public's savings. These improved opportunities for profitable lending and investing will make the banks content
to hold smaller net free reserves. Both their deposits and their assets
will rise as a result of this shift in public preferences, even though the
base of unborrowed reserves remains unchanged. Something of this
kind has occurred in recent years when commercial banks have been
permitted to raise the interest rates they offer for time and savings
deposits.

RESERVE ADJUSTMENTS

OF CITY BANKS

D. R. CAWTHORNE

*Large banks typically attempt to minimize excess re-
serves over the reserve accounting period. How this is
accomplished is the subject of this selection.*

The distribution of bank resources among loans to customers, primary and secondary reserves, and the bond account is one of the major decisions relating to bank asset management. Such decisions often are based on an estimate of the need for liquidity to meet deposit losses or to satisfy loan requests, as well as on expectations about future movements of interest rates. The degree of confidence placed in the reliability of such estimates also is important. Allowance must be made for the fact that deposits fluctuate—sometimes predictably but often without warning—which at times raises the investable reserves of the bank and at other times reduces them.

In this respect, the unique characteristic of large banks compared with smaller institutions is that while the day-to-day fluctuations of reserves are relatively small in percentage terms, the amount is large enough to justify special action to gain earnings on these transitory balances. Larger banks in the Tenth Federal Reserve District encounter widely varying conditions with respect to the short-run volatility of their deposits. In banks where the accounts of oil companies represent a

Reprinted from Essays on Commercial Banking, Federal Reserve Bank of Kansas City, 1962, pp. 31–40.

substantial part of the total, intramonth fluctuations are quite wide but have a fairly regular timing and magnitude. Some of the banks in which interbank deposits are important also experience distinct seasonal deposit flows. In still others, state funds produce both predictable and unforeseen changes in deposits. All of these movements, together with the ebb and flow of other depositors' accounts, may either yield short-run gains of reserves or result in short-run losses.

It is common knowledge that, despite this somewhat random movement of deposits and reserves, larger banks are able to hold their excess reserves to low levels, measured in terms of absolute values or percentages. Not so well known is the fact that rather wide disparities exist between the comparative performance of larger banks in minimizing their excess reserves. District reserve city banks, for example, maintain relatively.high excess reserves in comparison with the national average for all reserve city banks. This fact is often attributed to time differences between New York and District municipalities which make adjustment through the federal funds market more difficult. Another argument is that banks in District cities having no Federal Reserve office are handicapped in adjusting reserves through the use of discounting. It appears, however, that the widely varying holdings of excess reserves by larger District banks cannot be explained by these factors.

It is the purpose of the ensuing discussion to examine the nature of the reserve adjustment problem, the process by which excess reserves are minimized, the instruments employed in making the adjustment, and the comparative behavior of large District banks in their holdings of excess reserves.

THE OPERATION OF THE ADJUSTMENT PROCESS

The task of adjusting the reserve position of a large bank is assigned to a money desk which may be operated by the cashier, the investment vice president, or, less frequently, by another officer of the bank. The principal bank policies which affect the nature of the operation are management's attitude toward borrowing, whether from the Reserve bank or from the federal funds market, and restrictions on the method employed to dispose of excess funds.

One of the requisites of the management of the reserve position is the establishment of a system throughout the bank whereby the money desk is informed of all major actions that affect the money position. Such actions include large transfers into or out of customers' accounts, purchases or sales of securities for customers or the bank's own portfolio, withdrawals from or additions to the U.S. Treasury Tax and Loan accounts, and sizable extensions or retirements. These known changes, together with any events whose effects can be foreseen—such as redemptions of securities, loan commitments, and so forth—constitute the principal data used to gauge the forces affecting the current reserve position of the bank.

Federal Reserve regulations governing the determination of legal required reserves form another part of the framework within which the adjustment is made. Reserve requirements are applied to average deposits in a week that begins with the opening of business on Thursday morning and closes the following Wednesday morning. The balances which fulfill these requirements are the deposits of the bank at the Reserve bank in the week which begins with the close of business on Thursday and ends with the close of business on the following Wednesday.[1] Thus, on any Wednesday morning, the bank knows its requirement for the preceding seven days and its reserve balance for the preceding six days. Therefore, if it becomes evident during the day that a deficiency will occur, steps can be taken to raise the balance by a sufficient amount to meet the minimum requirement. On the other hand, expected surpluses can be placed in assets that will yield earnings for the bank.

Subject to approval in the individual case, current regulations allow a member bank to carry a reserve deficiency of not more than 2 per cent into the succeeding reserve period, provided a deficiency did not occur in the preceding period and provided the reserve balance in the next period is sufficient to counterbalance the deficiency. Banks occasionally employ this privilege, not perhaps as a conscious policy, but rather a result of minor errors in forecasts. Penalties are assessed against larger reserve deficiencies at a rate 2 per cent above the discount rate, so banks have an incentive to hold somewhat more than the minimum to avoid this charge.

The process of reserve adjustment may be illustrated from the records of two District banks of approximately equal size. One trims its reserve position very closely and the other runs larger-than-average excesses, as shown by the data. Bank A had a cumulative excess reserve of $663,000 in the reserve period which on a daily basis was $94,714. Bank B had a cumulative excess of $13,124,000, an average daily excess of almost $1,875,000. Bank A curtailed its reserves on the last day of the reserve period by sales of federal funds, but the cumulative excess of Bank B expired, as the surpluses of one reserve period cannot be used to

---

[1] Since November 24, 1960, all vault cash held by member banks also has counted as reserves in meeting legal requirements.

	Bank A	Bank B
	Excess (+) or deficiency (−) of reserves	
Thursday	$−1,144,000	$+1,650,000
Friday	+996,000	+986,000
2-day total	−148,000	+2,636,000
Saturday	+273,000	+392,000
3-day total	+125,000	+3,028,000
Sunday	+273,000	+392,000
4-day total	+398,000	+3,420,000
Monday	+579,000	+1,594,000
5-day total	+977,000	+5,014,000
Tuesday	+1,160,000	+5,642,000
6-day total	+2,137,000	+10,656,000
Wednesday	−1,474,000	+2,468,000
7-day total	$ +663,000	$+13,124,000

meet the requirements of the following period. Assuming an interest rate of 3 per cent, a sale of $13 million for one day would have produced earnings of $1,083; at a rate of 3½ per cent, the transaction would have yielded $1,264.

METHODS OF RESERVE ADJUSTMENT

The principal methods employed by the larger District banks in adjusting reserve positions include variations of indebtedness to the Reserve bank, purchases or sales of funds in the federal funds market, and purchases or sales of short-term Treasury issues. These three methods may be compared first as ways of covering a deficiency of reserves and then as methods for disposing of excess funds.

The use of the Reserve bank discount privilege has the advantage that the exact sum needed to cover the deficit of reserves can be borrowed. Also important to some banks is the fact that no borrowing limit is imposed apart from the necessity of having acceptable collateral or rediscountable paper. Banks which experience rather wide fluctuations of deposits may rely heavily on this source of reserves since their ability to borrow from other sources is limited by law. Other advantages of discounting are the ease with which the transaction is consummated and the ready availability of funds. A bank can wait until very late in the business day before covering its deficiency, and while this also may be possible in the securities and federal funds markets, the earlier closing of eastern markets would make these avenues of adjustment less reliable for District banks.

Funds also may be borrowed—usually for one day—from other banks, security dealers, or other organizations, in what is known as the federal funds market. Most of these transactions flow through the wire transfer system of the Federal Reserve banks, moving reserve balances from banks having deficiencies. Under normal circumstances, the minimum transaction is $1 million. This restriction prevents banks from borrowing from the federal funds market when they require less than $1 million, or from using that market to dispose of excess reserves of less than $1 million. Another important restriction on use of this market is the prohibition against national banks borrowing a greater amount than their capital stock.[2] Since banks often experience short-term outflows of reserves that exceed their capital, these exigencies cannot be met through the federal funds market.

There are two principal advantages of this market as a source of funds. At times, the rate of interest is less than the discount rate, permitting reserve deficiencies to be covered at reduced cost. A substantial part of the purchases of funds by District banks over the past year has coincided with declines in the federal funds rate. Use of the market also permits a bank to curtail its borrowing from the Reserve bank. Since continuous borrowing is not in accord with the provisions of Federal Reserve Regulation A, a number of banks employ the market for ordinary adjustments and conserve the privilege of borrowing from the Reserve bank for more extreme emergencies.

The chief problem in using the Treasury bill market as a source of funds arises from rate fluctuations and the costs of the transaction. If rates should rise and prices fall after bills are purchased, losses may occur when the security is sold. Moreover, the spread between bid and asked quotations, which is the dealer's margin, may absorb interest earned over a short period. These disadvantages often are surmounted by the use of repurchase agreements in which bills or other securities are sold for immediate delivery and purchased for regular delivery a day later. The rate on the transaction for the one day is usually the same as the rate on federal funds and thus the purchase and sale prices are fixed in advance. Recent rulings have declared these contracts to be loans, rather than purchases and sales of securities, and to be subject to the

---

[2] Editor's note: Since this was written, the Comptroller of the Currency has ruled that Funds transactions are purchases and sales, and therefore do not come under the lending limitation for National Banks.

restrictions placed by law upon loans.[3] In fact, this type of transaction bears a closer resemblance to a reserve adjustment via the federal funds market than to an adjustment through the bill market as such.

Each of these instruments is used as a method of disposing of excess reserves. Banks with indebtedness to the Reserve bank can pay down their discounts. Those without debts either sell funds or acquire Treasury bills. If the excess is large compared with the loan limit of the bank, several separate transactions in federal funds may be required to reduce the reserve balance to an acceptable level. If the amount is small, the minimum size of a transaction may prevent the use of the funds market. Several banks follow the practice of purchasing the maturing Treasury bill late in the reserve period to be presented for redemption on Thursday—the first day of the new reserve period. This operation carries the excess forward into the next period and a return is earned for the period of investment. Demand for the maturing bill for this purpose frequently makes it difficult to obtain and drives the interest rate below the rate obtainable on federal funds.

[3] Editor's note: The Comptroller of the Currency has since ruled that these agreements are to be considered outright sales and purchases and therefore not subject to the lending limit of National banks.

THREE

MONEY MARKET
INSTITUTIONS
AND INSTRUMENTS

M ONEY is the ultimate financial asset, as far as liquidity is concerned. Other financial assets have near-money characteristics in varying degree, with varying degrees of liquidity, depending upon how quickly they can be converted to money without significant loss in value.

At any moment in time, there will be some holders of money whose balances are considered excessive, and who therefore wish to exchange money for other assets. At the same moment, it is likely that some asset-holders require money for one reason or other, and who therefore would like to sell nonmonetary assets.

The money market consists of a number of closely connected institutions which serve to bring together, quickly and efficiently, those who have more money than they require and those who have less. Although the money market is centered in New York, it is closely connected by rapid communication to the regional markets which exist in other large cities. The money market has developed a series of instruments to effect transactions. Both the institutions and the instruments are considered in the following sections.

THE NEW YORK MONEY MARKET

CARL H. MADDEN

*Carl Madden has an intimate acquaintance with the
geography and functions of "Wall Street," having worked
there for many years. The money market instruments discussed in the following selections have their central locus
in the area he describes.*

THE PLACE

Wall Street is a surprisingly small place. Only seven blocks long, it
runs from Broadway's old Trinity Church less than half a mile gently
downward to the East River. But the name also refers to a small district
lying a few hundred yards to its north and south. In this area, less than
half a mile square, bounded by Maiden Lane (called Cortlandt Street
west of Broadway) on the north and by Whitehall Street on the south,
and lying eastward of Trinity Place, are found most of the purely
financial institutions of the City. Here, in a gloomy forest of concrete
and steel where the sun shines on some streets only hours during the
entire year, are the head offices of most of the nation's largest banks,
the great stock and commodity exchanges, Government security dealers,
investment bankers, corporate and municipal bond houses, foreign exchange dealers, and a host of subsidiary financial specialties.

The northern boundary of the financial district proper is marked
by the neo-Florentine *palazzo* of the Federal Reserve Bank of New
York on Liberty Street. Almost hidden by the gleaming 60-story shaft

Reprinted from The Money Side of "The Street," (New York: Federal Reserve Bank
of New York, 1959), pp. 7–17.

of a new bank skyscraper, the "Fed" of New York, largest of the nation's twelve regional Reserve Banks, represents the nation's central banking system, apex of Wall Street's and the nation's financial structure. At the southern boundary near the Battery the Produce Exchange, for 75 years housed in Victorian red, has a new 30-story glass and steel sky-scraper home. The Exchange links the paper world of Wall Street with the tangible goods and the human skills whose production, storage, marketing, or employment the Street finances.

The inner sanctum of pure finance stretches upward within its narrow confines sometimes 40, 50, and 60 stories—as much as a fifth of a mile—above crowded streets with names like Cedar, Pine, Nassau, Broad, William, New, Beaver, and Market. These streets were once the pleasant lanes of little Nieuw Amsterdam and later the fashionable, gilded-age thoroughfares of the growing city. Now they crisscross a com-pact area of probably the most intensive land use in the world. So many bricks and so much mortar are packed on top of each square foot of Manhattan bedrock here that engineers once fretted whether the island might sink from their weight. So many people work here that they can-not all, it is said, get onto the crowded streets at once.

Within or nearby this area the expansion and rebuilding of the last few years is to add 6,525,000 square feet of office space—nearly 800,000 more than all the rentable area in the fifteen buildings of Rockefeller Center. This construction, with a total cost of almost a quarter billion dollars, includes a new Coffee and Sugar Exchange Building, Produce Exchange Building, a giant new bank, three insurance company build-ings, and at least three large new general office buildings. Also, plans have been completed for redevelopment of some of the older downtown areas surrounding Wall Street's financial district. The building boom is only one sign of the renewed vigor and activity of the financial district that, since World War II, has stimulated renewed inter-est in its functioning.

Spreading out from its center in Wall Street a larger financial and insurance center runs south to Bowling Green, north to City Hall Park, and east and west almost from the East to the Hudson River. Also scattered out from Wall Street are a dozen or so specialized quarters still recognizable in the jumbled conglomerate of downtown New York, though becoming less distinctly specialized with time. Some are com-modity markets in the traditional sense. Examples are the dilapidated, old Washington wholesale market for fruits and vegetables along the West Street waterfront (the retail market is now closed), or the famous Fulton Fish Market on the East River opposite; the Mercantile Ex-change on Hudson and Harrison Streets (market for butter and eggs);

the coffee (fourth largest import for the city) market around Depeyster Street and the wholesale leather market near Franklin Square. Others serve the Wall Street population of commuters, more than half a million people with jobs located below Canal Street. These are the discount houses of Cortlandt Street (retail specialty stores that first flouted "suggested" manufacturers' prices), the downtown branches of Madison Avenue men's shops, sprawling department stores and the crannied lingerie shops for the working girls.

The New York Stock Exchange at Wall Street and the American Stock Exchange at Trinity Place are perhaps Wall Street's best known market centers. Other basic centers near the area are the shipping district of lower Broadway, the Produce Exchange at Bowling Green and Whitehall, the Cotton and Wool Exchange at Hanover Square, the Coffee and Sugar Exchange on Pine Street, and the Maritime and Commodity Exchanges on Broad Street. In these markets hundreds of million dollars' worth of wheat, cotton, coffee, copper, tin, lead, zinc, and other basic materials are bought and sold each year. To be sure, none of these things is made in the Wall Street area. What is more important to understand, only a small proportion ever comes within miles of its boundaries. As surely and swiftly as the shares traded on the stock exchanges switch ownership of plants in Poughkeepsie, Pittsburgh, or Podunk, the deals on these exchanges pass from hand to hand ownership of materials that may be stored thousands of miles away.

So we must carefully remember, when we speak of the markets for all these goods being located in the Wall Street area, that we use the word "market" in a much wider sense than its old dictionary meaning of "an open space or covered building in which cattle, provisions, etc., are exposed for sale" (*Oxford Universal Dictionary*). A market in the modern sense is any arrangement that helps buyer and seller to come together and allows them to swap opinions about the value of things traded quickly and cheaply, where demand and supply of a traded commodity can be expressed. Whether there is a hall for the purpose is a matter of convenience. The money market has no single meeting place, but as we shall see operates largely in Wall Street through dealers and bankers talking over the telephones.

In fact, within the Wall Street area an alert visitor can observe the evolution of the market from its ancient to its modern form in a morning stroll. A little before nine o'clock he'd first glimpse the crates of lettuce, carrots, celery, and greens, iced and glistening in stacks on West Street sidewalks, and surrounded by haggling merchants and tired handlers. Or, on the East River side, he'd see the six-block bedlam of the Fulton Fish Market. There, rubber-booted men weigh, clean, bone, pack, and re-pack tons of fish, moved each morning from stubby trawlers and draggers dockside, or trucked to market from other fish piers, to be sold and loaded on waiting refrigerated trucks from Connecticut or New Jersey.

In the exchanges, open later in the morning, he'd find swarms of busy brokers congregated at trading posts and rings or moving briskly about a great floor littered with paper slips from completed transactions. They move in answer to signals given by clerks who flash the brokers' numbers, like license plates, onto a giant scoreboard called an annunciator, whenever they receive an order to purchase or sell some shares. The brokers take the orders to the proper posts to carry them out.

After eleven the short-term open market in money, officially open at ten o'clock, begins to hum. To see a part of it, our visitor might go to the trading room of a Government securities dealer. Here is the workplace of shirt-sleeved traders at desks cluttered, perhaps, with paper containers left from a hasty mid-morning snack. Most desks have little "turrets"—direct-wire switchboxes connecting with other dealers, banks, and the Federal Reserve Bank (sometimes marked by a special light, different in color from the others). Dealers make decisions to buy or sell bonds and their traders haggle for the best price. Listening to the cryptic negotiations of the quiet-voiced traders and watching dealers glance at small quotation boards or read messages from the broad-tape news ticker, he might be reminded of an Army communications center. He might also experience mild disappointment to observe the modest size of the establishment and small number of people, considering the size of the operations—that in this part of the market some $180 billion of securities are available to be traded.

From gleaming vegetables and smelly fish to little slips of paper, and from slips of paper to the airy vibrations of telephone diaphragms, Wall Street—and other national money and securities centers—squeeze out of ancient trading devices the bare essentials of bringing buyer and seller together to express demand and supply pressures by sending and receiving market judgments, the indispensable ingredients of decisions to buy or sell.

THE NEED

Why are the basic commodity markets, the center of banking, insurance, and stock trading all located in so small an area? Part of the answer lies in the history of Wall Street—it just grew. Also, information is vital to trading, and word of mouth passes quickly in "The Street." But most of all, despite this electronic age, the physical facilities must be close together to do business in the volume done by Wall Street. Billions of dollars move from lender to borrower, from buyer to seller, from depositor to banker or back again each day. This money must physically pass from hand to hand along with the papers showing owner-ship rights or indebtedness for which it is swapped. To be sure, the money (as we shall see) nearly always takes the form of checks, some in very large denominations. But it must be handed over, and the matter of "delivery" thus makes proximity important.

Equally important, the merchants, brokers, dealers, and others who operate in these great markets do not normally possess the ready money to pay for the purchases they make. Normally they have to borrow it, and this is where the money market comes in. By virtue of the monetary resources it commands, the money market is able and willing to lend the large amounts which security and commodity markets may require.

Indeed, every day money must be found somewhere in very large quantities though often for short periods to keep goods moving on the conveyor belt that takes them from raw material to finished products. It takes money in large quantities to make payment to a construction contractor for a new manufacturing plant on the agreed completion date, to buy a shipload of coffee arriving from Brazil, to finance a tanker of oil from the Middle East. It is the money market's job to find these dollars. It takes money in large quantities to bridge the gap—a day or two perhaps—between the time when an underwriting syndicate of bond dealers buys directly from the issuing corporation a $50 million block of securities and the time when it has sold all the bits and pieces to the customers it may already have spent weeks lining up. It is the money market's job to find these dollars. It takes a lot of money to pay on a single day for $3 billion of Government IOU's being offered in the market by the U.S. Treasury, say, to cover a deficit in its budget. The money market must help find these dollars, too.

The services of a financial center such as Wall Street's money mar-ket, by quickly bringing together lender and borrower and dependably arranging for them to borrow and lend large amounts of funds, are thus essential to the smooth, day-to-day workings of banking and financial institutions, businesses, the Government, and the economy as a whole. The money market enables commercial banks to supply extra funds to one another or make up much of their unexpected needs for funds quickly and cheaply. Banks have the job of receiving their de-positors' cash and paying it on demand, but they earn income by lend-ing to customers, setting aside only a portion of their cash as "reserves." Because banks can invest temporarily idle funds in the money market and be sure of getting them back again quickly and with little risk of loss, they can as a result of using the money market operate on a narrower margin of nonearning cash. This is particularly important for large banks, which may experience with only a few hours' notice (or none at all) withdrawal demands for considerable sums, as large depositors make payments of all kinds.

The money market serves businesses by providing a swift and safe mechanism for paying money. Huge sums move by check or wire. The market also furnishes money to "finance" the production and marketing of raw materials into finished products. That is to say, the market finds money to pay for these services before businessmen who organize these activities might otherwise be able to do it. It also allows businesses to economize their use of cash by investing extra sums for short periods with assurance that investments can be quickly "liquidated" or turned back into cash. And finally, the market forms a highly efficient mechanism through which the Federal Reserve monetary authorities pump new credit into the economy at times and siphon it off at others to carry out their Congressional mandate. Responsible for using their powers to foster orderly economic growth and stability in the value of the dollar, the authorities use the money market to spread the effects of their actions taken in New York City throughout the banking system and the economy.

The money market in Wall Street is thus an integral part of the economy. Countries lacking well-developed capital and credit institutions, taken for granted in the United States, find great difficulty in getting together sums of money large enough to finance private voluntary enterprise, and must rely on Government taxing and borrowing powers. What Wall Street does affects the economy. On the other hand, the economy affects Wall Street's money markets. In 1956–1957, a time of high employment and near-capacity output, too many people wanted to borrow and spend; too many businessmen wanted to borrow at the same time to expand or replace equipment. The economy, already operating at near capacity, was unable to turn out products as fast as businessmen wanted to use them in order to expand their plants. In a word, savings could not keep pace with the boom level of investment, and we had "tight money" and rising interest rates.

WHY WALL STREET?

Why is the nation's central money market located in New York rather than in some other city? Fundamentally, the reason is largely historical. In any integrated financial system with markets, there tends to arise a single central market through which transactions in secondary markets can be brought together. During the nineteenth century there developed, along with the rivalry for transportation routes connecting with the West, a spirited competition among the eastern seaboard cities for the financial custom of the burgeoning centers of the trans-Appalachian hinterland. New York emerged victorious from this struggle early in the century. Its superior harbor attracted trade; trade generated finance; both promoted economic growth. Favorable banking legislation went hand in hand with the Erie Canal to attract business from the West and to build institutions that could finance it. As a result of its success in trade, finance, and production, New York City soon outstripped its rivals in size, adding economies of size such as increased specialization to those inherited from nature.

Today, though Wall Street covers a small parcel of land it is big by almost any other standard of size, and its size continues to give The Street advantages of convenience and economy. Take a look at a few figures. In 1958 stock turnover on the New York and American Stock Exchanges totaled 1.2 billion shares valued very roughly at $36 billion.[1] While turnover figures are not published in over-the-counter markets, new offerings of corporate securities in 1958 totaled more than $11.5 billion. The Government securities market traded in issues adding up to more than $177 billion outstanding. Loans of Wall Street's 17 money market banks expanded at the end of 1958 to a level of $16.2 billion.

The New York money market serves the largest local market area in the country. It's hard to realize just how big a market New York City and its environs make up. For example, almost one out of ten people in the United States lives within a 40-mile radius of New York City. More than four million people have jobs located in the City's five boroughs—more people than live in most other United States cities.

The central business district—Manhattan below 60th Street— forms a concentrate of all kinds of economic activity, employing six out of ten people working inside the City limits—roughly 2,300,000. Draw a circle with a three-mile radius around a point in the East River near Houston Street (thus taking in downtown Brooklyn as well), and you encompass the place of employment of more than 2,600,000 workers. More than one-fourth of the nation's clothing workers, one-fifth of its light-manufacturing workers, one-sixth of printing, publishing, finance, insurance, and real estate workers are employed in Manhattan's central business district. Moreover, 90 of the country's 100 largest corporations have main or branch offices here. It is the nation's center of

[1] By 1964 these figures had increased to 1.8 billion shares and $66.6 billion. (Ed.)

manufacturing and wholesale trade, origin and terminus of transport and communication, and concentration point for specialized business services. It is the nation's and world's greatest port, with a total export and import trade of better than 40 per cent of the nation's total. More than $9 billion worth of merchandise came into or left the port in 12,000 ships from 100 different lines during 1957. The central business district could hardly avoid being a national financial center as well.

Wall Street, by centering highly specialized activities, reduces the effort and cost of carrying on the business of the money market. At the market's core, the specialists who lend and borrow millions each day for their institutions are brought ear-to-ear in a flick of a direct wire telephone key. A short walk to one of the downtown lunch clubs brings them face to face to hear word of latest developments and their meaning. In a world where "keeping up" is vital to success, they save unmeasured hours of time and energy by talking "the language of The Street," full of shorthand jargon stemming from a common background. Such constant, easy checking and rechecking, such a flow of information reduces the tremendous risks inherent in large-scale transactions with money.

What's more, The Street has vital ancillary services to offer to the market. It houses the country's largest concentration of specialized lawyers highly selected and skilled in finance; management services like engineering and economic consulting, public relations, and a host of other such specialties immediately available and ready to perform; and, quite important to a world where paper is the tangible product, custom printers who take overnight deadlines in stride and specialize in accuracy. Through experience with increasing volume of paper-swapping, The Street has developed easier and cheaper ways to effect physical delivery, like the New York Clearing Corporation, the clearing arrangement for delivery of Treasury securities at one of the money market banks.

Of course, as the nation has grown in population, other cities have become capable of supporting more and more specialized activity once unique to New York. Today some of the nation's largest banks are located outside Wall Street and several other money centers have stock exchanges and other important financial markets. With the postwar movement of people to the West, Southwest, and Southeast coastal areas, and with U.S. industry building more plants in and near smaller cities around the country, New York has lost some of its financial pre-eminence. Also, its money market banks have felt the effects of the move beyond their reach of middle income receivers and of plants to surrounding suburbs, where banking laws have prevented City banks from operating. Still, the New York metropolitan area remains roughly double the size of any other metropolitan area in the country, and with its continuing and perhaps increasingly vital role in international finance, the City's money center in Wall Street remains far and away the nation's most extensive complex of credit facilities.

ITS SPECIAL JOBS

Besides its role as the nation's largest local financial center, Wall Street is the focal point of the nation's credit system. Some jobs, peculiarly its own, flow from its very size and high degree of organization. Internally, Wall Street's money market is arranged in three levels that are interwoven and interconnected in many ways.

First comes the *local market* itself, with direct loans to the giant corporations and many businesses and individuals of the City by the large banks, commercial insurance companies, and others. Take apparel, for example. Banks extend credit for a year or less to cutters, converters, and mill operators to help them prepare for their "season"—whether it's summer for bathing suits or winter for ski togs. And in an industry that depends heavily on style and weather, where the last 25 years have seen startling shifts in taste towards informality and new fabrics, the banker must know his customers intimately.

At the same time this customers' market is interconnected with wholesale markets. For example, the New York commercial banks may be lending to "factors." These concerns compete with banks in part by combining lending to apparel firms with collecting their bills. The banks also extend short-term credit to finance companies. Wholesale borrowing and retail lending is their business. They use wholesale borrowings to extend instalment credit to families that borrow to buy cars, television sets, other "big ticket" items, and also clothes. But finance companies may at times (when they can get better terms) prefer to borrow long term, placing their notes directly with insurance companies or floating debentures in the long-term markets, rather than borrowing from commercial banks.

Next, New York also is the nation's *central market* for long- and short-term borrowing. We find there the so-called *capital* markets, that is, the markets for corporate, state, and municipal bonds, for long-term U.S. Government securities, and for new and secondary issues of equity shares. Through nationwide contacts by direct wire and long distance or direct telephone, brokers and dealers can seek out, bring together, and match off demands and supplies of long-term funds that cannot be satisfied locally in other cities. For example, after World War II the nation's people moved to the suburbs and built millions of new homes. Atomic energy, aluminum, steel, and many other industries grew and developed. As a result the demand for electrical power grows steadily. Long-term borrowings in that basic industry total billions yearly and require getting money from all over America.

Large New York commercial banks extend short-term business credit not only to large corporations with head offices in the City, but lend to businesses with head offices outside the City which cannot get funds in sufficient amounts or on satisfactory terms elsewhere. In October 1955 almost half of the $8 billion of business loans on the books of the downtown New York City banks went to businesses with head offices located outside metropolitan New York City or New York State. The biggest part of this outside credit went to borrowers in the Federal Reserve Districts of Chicago, Dallas, San Francisco, and Richmond, growing areas short of funds compared with more stable "capital surplus" areas like New England. For example, in the Southwest, aluminum, airplanes, chemicals, vegetable oils, and ladies' dresses have come to the area recently. Since 1944 personal income has doubled; new plants have increased 80 per cent. This kind of growth couldn't have happened if industry had not been able to get money from investors all over the country. When needs for bank credit are big or specialized, local banks share the lending with large New York City "correspondent" banks.

Finally, the third level of the New York money market is the short-term, impersonal "open" market—the money market proper—where the nation's temporary funds find useful employment at a price without much risk of loss. Because New York is the nation's largest center for short- and long-term business credit needs, it is also the center towards which idle money is drawn to find employment and earn a small return until it may be needed. Large businesses and some financial institutions, because of seasonal changes in demand for their products or services, or because of accumulations for dividend or tax payments, have funds temporarily in excess of needs; others as a matter of policy hold excess liquid funds as a buffer against the unexpected. Wall Street's money market facilities gather up, bring together and set off demands and supplies for such money that is to be used for brief periods, sometimes only a day or two.

And, equally important, such money is immediately available when needed, either at a stated time or within a few hours or a day's notice. Because such surplus funds can be both invested and liquidated quickly, the money market serves the nation's credit system much as your bank balance serves you. The ability of the money market to furnish cash to any part of the country at almost a moment's notice is vital to the smooth working of the economy.

The open market is impersonal in that neither borrower nor lender feels any obligation to a particular counterpart, and price considerations among participants who are known to one another usually prevail over established relationships. Because the short-term, impersonal market uses funds from all over the country, it also mirrors changing needs for funds throughout the nation. It is the market where the final adjustments between the supply and demand for funds are made for the nation as a whole and where the money market in the broader sense is cleared from day to day. This is why it is the place where the Federal Reserve Bank of New York, acting for the nation's central banking system, injects cash into the nation's money stream or drains it off through what are known as "open market operations," in the System's continuing attempt to influence our money supply to promote economic growth and stability.

Funds in this "open" money market, aside from Federal Reserve Funds, are supplied primarily by commercial banks, business corporations, insurance companies, and foreign central banks. Such funds are in turn used by other commercial banks, the Federal Government, finance companies, business firms, and others, or at times partly withdrawn by the Federal Reserve. Its two most important institutions—aside from the Federal Reserve itself—are the big money market banks and the Government securities dealers. The most important assets in which the money market deals are "Federal Funds" and short-term Government securities. Trading on a nationwide basis in these assets through New York now forms the heart of the short-term money market. Other less important markets include bankers' acceptances, commercial and finance paper, and short-term Government agency obligations.

New York is linked to the nationwide market in three ways: First, commercial banks located throughout the United States are themselves linked with larger commercial banks in money centers and through them to New York by a network of correspondent relationships. A "correspondent" bank—one in Wall Street had $1.6 billion of deposits from other banks at the end of 1958—performs many services in exchange for deposits of funds by smaller banks and for other benefits stemming from holding these deposits. Second, the Federal Reserve System and the correspondent banking system together form a nationwide mechanism for moving funds swiftly throughout the country. Third, the various securities dealers have branch offices in the major cities and banking and business connections across the country, and can use these to seek out available funds. By these means money lying temporarily idle nearly anywhere in the country can be speedily moved to New York and other centers for investment in assets that can in turn be readily sold. In this way the short-term money market makes the day-to-day adjustments of cash balances easier and also marshals funds for all kinds of large payments that keep the economy operating smoothly.

THE MECHANICS OF TRANSACTIONS

IN FEDERAL FUNDS

PARKER WILLIS

On any given day, some commercial banks will have excess reserve balances at their respective Federal Reserve Banks, while others will find that their reserve balances are below the required level. The goal of a profit-maximizing money manager in a commercial bank is to maintain a zero average daily excess reserve position over the reserve accounting period.

The money manager is aided in this goal by the existence of several markets for short-term money. In the past, the call loan market (see the selection on p. 136) was a major outlet for excess reserves; more recently, the Treasury Bill and the Federal Funds markets have been the major vehicles for adjusting reserve positions to desired levels.

In this selection, Parker Willis explains the methods employed in making purchases and sales of reserve balances in the Federal Funds market.

FEDERAL FUNDS

This term is shorthand for "immediately available Federal Reserve Funds" and means, essentially, title to reserve balances (of member banks) at Federal Reserve banks. For example, a check drawn on a member bank's reserve account at the Federal Reserve bank is collectible

Reprinted from The Federal Funds Market (Boston: The Federal Reserve Bank of Boston, 1964), pp. 71–76.

there, upon presentation, in Funds immediately available at the Reserve bank. In contrast, a check drawn on a clearing house bank is collectible in funds available at the Reserve bank the next day, when clearing balances are settled on the books of the Reserve bank.

In addition to checks on member bank balances, title to Federal Funds may be acquired through checks issued by the U.S. Treasury, certain clearing nonmember banks, foreign official banks when drawn against their balances at the Reserve banks, and by Reserve System disbursing officers.

Using the Federal Reserve wire transfer facilities, banks may wire Federal Funds to other banks in different localities for their own use or that of their customers. Funds for wire transmission come from the sending bank's reserve account, and the proceeds at the other end flow into the receiving bank's reserve account.

No interest is paid by the Reserve banks on balances held with them. Considerations of profit dictate that member banks continuously employ any surplus reserves in interest-earning outlets. Thus, a bank with temporary excess reserves may employ excess reserves in several ways in the short-term money market, and among these are Federal Funds sales. A conventional Funds sale of $1 million for one day (overnight lending) would return the seller $83.33 if Funds are trading at 3 per cent. The Funds rate is determined by the day's trading and is figured on a 360-day basis. If sold on Friday—over the weekend—the return would be $249.99 since the next clearing is three days away.

UNITS OF TRADING AND TYPES OF TRANSACTIONS

The common unit of trading is $1 million, although at times transactions are accomplished in blocks of $250 thousand or larger multiples under $1 million. Trades are infrequently made in amounts less than $250 thousand; but some liberalization of trading units has developed at times during the monetary ease of the last three years as a result of competition by the accommodating banks. Trades in some accommodating arrangements have been reported in units of $50,000.

Until the recent ruling of the Comptroller, Funds sales were considered unsecured loans made by one bank to another. They came under the single-borrower limitation for unsecured loans in the National Bank Act, and individual transactions were limited to 10 per cent of capital and surplus. There are similar limitations in many state statutes. The provision imposed on national banks and many state banks, stipulating that aggregate borrowings cannot exceed capital stock and a percentage of surplus, also limited purchases. Thus, direct trades of Funds in size were generally confined to the larger banks. During the 1950's however, the practice of using repurchase agreements, buy backs, or general U.S. Government short-term security collateral transactions was developed by the smaller banks in order to enter the Funds market on the selling side. The common unit for accomplishing these transactions is also $1 million.

Until 1957, these secured transactions were carried in the bank's investment account and were considered investment transactions to avoid the loan limits. Rulings of the Comptroller in 1957 and 1958 required such transactions to be classified as loans by national banks and permitted certain exceptions from the limits when secured by U.S. Government securities. State member banks met similar conditions. The recent ruling of the Comptroller in June, 1963, however, frees all Funds transactions of national banks from lending and borrowing limits. Market practice generally continues to observe the old regulations in amount of transactions, but there has been some reduction in number of collateral transactions.

REPURCHASE AGREEMENTS, OR BUY BACKS, WITH DEALERS

These terms are practically synonymous, and in their more technical usage are applied to transactions by which a bank makes a firm purchase of government securities for delivery and payment in Federal Funds the same day. Concurrently, the bank makes a firm sale with the same dealer of the same amount of the same issue of government securities for delivery and payment in Federal Funds on the following business day at an agreed price. The transaction prices (usually at, or below, the bid side of the market) include interest. Written confirmations of the sale and purchase are delivered, and the payments in Federal Funds are made on the respective settlement dates. Less frequently, banks may borrow Funds from banks or dealers in an analogous transaction known as a "reverse repurchase." The volume of these transactions, however, is small.

The transaction frequently arises as follows. A corporation may have some surplus money and wish to invest in a repurchase agreement. Even though the dealer may have no need for Funds, he sometimes will execute the repurchase to satisfy the customer. The dealer then finds a bank needing Funds and makes a reverse repurchase obtaining the securities from the bank and supplying the bank with Funds. The two transactions ordinarily have the same maturity and are equal in amount, thus cancelling out. Less frequently, the corporation may need cash and not wish to disturb its portfolio of investment securities. In this case the dealer will buy the securities and provide the corporation with Funds. When the cash shortage has passed, the corporation returns the securities and pays the dealer in Funds.

Repurchase agreements are generally made for overnight, but they may be "open," particularly when they arise between a dealer and a bank and run for two or three days, the exact period being indeterminate when initiated. Some provide automatic renewal until terminated. The parties to the transaction usually agreed to ignore the coupon rate on the securities and the yield to maturity. The specified rate is related to the going rate on Federal Funds, the dealer loan rate in New York and, to a lesser extent, the Treasury bill rate. If the transaction is "open," the rate is set from day to day. Repurchases may provide automatic adjustment of the rate to the market; and some agreements may permit substitution of collateral. The use of the transactions between banks and between banks and dealers varies; overnight transactions between dealers and banks outside New York City have been widespread, and they may also occur between dealer banks in New York and out-of-town banks. New York banks do not make repurchase agreements with dealers because these agreements carry a lower rate than can be obtained from dealer loans. More generally, secured direct transactions between banks do not involve the precise pricing of securities as is characteristic of repurchases with dealers.

If the transactions originate between a bank and a dealer's office outside New York, the tickets are billed to the local office, but settlement is made in New York for their accounts. Virtually all of these transactions outside New York are accomplished by wire transfer, with debits and credits of Federal Funds to correspondent account balances maintained in New York City. The instructions to pay the Funds to the borrower against delivery of the securities flow over the "bank wire." The securities involved in the transaction are held in safekeeping accounts in New York.

ACCOMMODATING BANKS

Some 30–40 large banks, principally in New York and other reserve cities, will operate on both sides of the market during the same day. They buy and sell Funds to meet their own reserve needs, but in addition, provide or absorb Funds as a service to correspondent banks and others. About seven of the banks aggressively promote their Funds service. Depending on conditions in the market, some of the banks limit the service at particular times. Usually there are three methods by which transactions are handled, but regardless of the method the accommodator deals as principal directly with the customer bank.[1]

(1) The accommodator generally will, to the extent possible, match on its own books buy and sell orders which are received from a correspondent or customer bank.

(2) When the accommodator's own reserve position is on the other side from that of the correspondent, it will generally care for the correspondent's needs out of its own position.

(3) When it is not possible to accomplish transactions by either means (1) or (2), the accommodator will extend its best efforts to cover a correspondent's needs in the national Funds market. At times it may borrow from the Federal Reserve bank.

There may be a very small profit or loss in their purchases from and sales to customers, which arises from rate fluctuations during the day. In some banks the Funds are traded even—a good 3 per cent market would mean a bid in size at 3 per cent and an offering in size at 3 per cent. Profits in this instance may come from differences in rates during the reserve period, selling at 3 per cent early in the period in hope of buying them at a lower rate at the end of the period.

In contrast to the accommodating banks, the other regular participants usually come into the market on only one side, either borrowing or selling on a particular day unless their money position undergoes a marked swing during the day. Over a period of time they tend to be net buyers or net sellers.

MARKET RULES

Selling banks may impose their own limits on borrowing banks and may restrict their transactions to banks on an approved list. Some banks which view the market on an impersonal basis may develop their lists without reference to correspondent relationships, but will honor direct requests from correspondents for purchases if Funds are available in their position. The list of banks with which another bank may deal may be more closely observed in tight markets than when they are easier.

[1] The correspondent banks may execute a collateral loan agreement.

MECHANICS OF ACCOMPLISHING TRANSACTIONS

Intracity. Among banks within a city, direct transactions in buying or selling Funds are made by telephone between borrowing and lending banks and may be initiated by either one. The lending bank then telephones the Federal Reserve bank, to charge its account and credit the borrowing bank. The call to the Reserve bank is followed by a letter of instruction to the Reserve bank and an exchange of letter confirmations by the lending and borrowing banks. The entries are reversed the next day by the borrowing bank. Interest is handled separately by treasurer's or cashier's check.

In a few cities, local transactions are still accomplished by the selling bank's check on the Federal Reserve bank, and the transaction is discharged by the borrower's clearing house check plus one day's interest at an agreed rate. Until three years ago this was also the practice in New York. Currently, under an agreement by the clearing house banks, the issuance of the clearing house check by the buyer is enough acknowledgment and the seller no longer issues a check, but merely instructs the Reserve bank by telephone to charge its account and credit the buyer. Generally, the New York City banks do not arrange transactions directly with one another, but use the brokers as an intermediary.

Intradistrict. Transactions arranged between banks in different cities within a district are usually accomplished by telephone or telegraph instructions to the Reserve bank, both in opening and closing. The transaction may be arranged by a broker or through direct communication from one bank to another by telephone or the commercial bank wire. Letters of instruction follow the telephone calls or telegrams to the Reserve bank, and the borrowers and lenders exchange written confirmations. Interest is settled by cashier's or treasurer's check.

Interdistrict. The lending bank instructs the Federal Reserve bank by telegram, telephone, or telautograph to wire Funds to the borrowing bank in another district for immediate payment, and the borrower repays the loan with a return wire of Funds on the following business day. Telegrams or letters are exchanged (sometimes both) confirming the transactions. Interest is settled by credit to correspondent accounts, or flows back by draft or check if no correspondent relationship is involved. This practice is usually followed because the Federal Reserve levies a charge on wires involving odd sums.

FUNDS BROKERS

Two member firms of the New York Stock Exchange, Garvin Bantel & Co. and Mabon & Co.; and the Irving Trust Company, a New York commercial bank, maintain desks in regular daily contact with both buyers and sellers of Funds. None of these organizations deals as principals. They match purchases and sales orders received from banks desiring to use their services.

For their services Garvin Bantel & Co. is compensated by stock exchange business which it may receive. The firm also offers the banks a brokers' loan facility when it suits the banks' loan needs. At the request of a bank, a commission of $\frac{1}{16}$ of one per cent may be charged.

Mabon & Co. in return for their services may charge the banks a $\frac{1}{16}$ of 1 per cent commission. As an alternative the firm may receive stock exchange business.

The Funds brokerage service offered by Irving Trust Company is separate and independent of any other transactions which the bank may conduct in Funds. The service is supplied at no charge, but the bank may, through the offer of this service, receive other business from the customer banks.

CERTIFICATES OF DEPOSIT

HELEN B. O'BANNON

There has been recently much unfavorable publicity surrounding certificates of deposit because of the importance banking authorities and congressional investigators have attached to their role in several isolated bank failures. In addition, extraordinary growth in the past four years of this money market instrument has made it second only to short-term U.S. Government securities held by the public, and made it assume significant importance in the financial world.

BACKGROUND

Certificates of deposit, that is, pieces of paper stating that so much money has been deposited (usually by the holder) with the issuing bank for a fixed period of time and at a fixed rate of interest, have existed for many years. Prior to 1961, these certificates were generally nonnegotiable because of written or tacit agreement between the issuing bank and the customer and could not be legally transferred. They were also nonmarketable because of a lack of an established secondary market for such paper. The funds behind these certificates were relatively stable, placed with the issuing bank for the depositor's convenience.

Many other commercial banks had been unwilling, however, to even hold time deposits for commercial customers, much less issue certificates of deposits (CD's) which guaranteed the deposits would remain in the bank for a specified length of time. These banks felt that if they offered certificates of deposit their customers would merely shift some of

Reprinted from original manuscript commissioned by the editor.

the idle cash they held in demand deposits (on which no interest was paid) to these short-term, interest-yielding securities, raising the banks' costs of keeping such deposits without significantly increasing the lending ability (although some reserves would be freed for investments and loans by shifting to time deposits requiring less reserves).

In the late 1950's, however, the giant banks in the New York money market began to feel the pressure of improved cash management by corporate treasurers. Increased demands on working capital to accelerate corporate growth, increased cash flows arising in part from the application of rapid depreciation schedules, and rising interest rates encouraged scientific money management. Corporations turned first to the Treasury bill market with their surplus short-term funds, and then became even more sophisticated by branching their investments into municipals, commercial paper, and sales finance company paper, so that by 1961 nonfinancial corporations held more than $25 billion in short-term, interest-yielding assets. At the same time there was a trend for corporations to decentralize their operations with accompanying shifts in deposits from New York banks to regional banks. Thus these New York banks had to seek ways to encourage corporations to return some of these interest-rate-sensitive, invested funds to their banks so that they, in turn, could increase their own lending ability.

In February, 1961, The First National City Bank of New York announced it would offer its corporate and noncorporate customers negotiable certificates of deposit. At the same time the Discount Corporation, a Government securities dealer, indicated it would maintain a trading market for these new securities. Similar announcements by other New York banks followed immediately and other Government securities dealers began to participate in the secondary market. Quickly, banks around the country were offering negotiable certificates of deposit.

NEW CERTIFICATES

Certificates of deposit are issued to increase the bank's deposits and lending ability by attracting new funds. Banks are not encouraging customers to shift deposits from demand accounts into time certificates. To discourage such shifting, most issuing banks tend to establish high minimum limits on the size of individual certificates. These denominations are generally $500,000 to $1 million in order to attract funds that are already invested or are seeking profitable use in short-term securities markets. A recent study by the American Bankers Association indicates that 80 per cent of the dollar volume of CD's are in denominations of $500,000 or more.[1]

Smaller banks tend to issue certificates in denominations of $100,000 or less for two reasons. First, the smaller bank may have difficulty securing customers for such large denominations, as these deposits are insured only to $10,000 by the Federal Deposit Insurance Corporation; second, by issuing small denominations the bank would not be faced with a severe liquidity problem if the maturing certificate of deposit could not be rolled over into a new certificate.

Banks have also used CD's to try to attract funds to their time deposit account in order to stabilize their deposits. By acquiring funds guaranteed to be on deposit for a certain length of time, banks feel they have greater freedom in investment commitments. This stability exists, however, only as long as maturing certificates can be reissued, since the majority of these negotiable certificates are held by interest-sensitive purchasers.

For customers—corporations, savings and loan associations, credit unions, labor unions, pension funds, and other—negotiable certificates of deposit enable them to put money to work for a fixed short period of time at a relatively higher rate of interest than prevails in the Treasury bill market. The establishment of a secondary market makes the certificates of deposit even more attractive, guaranteeing, in most cases, the holder a market for the certificate if it is necessary or desirable to liquidate it.

New certificates are classified as "prime" and "nonprime." These two classifications and the many grades within each are appraisals of the relative marketability of the certificates if the holder chooses to liquidate them before maturity. "Prime" certificates are usually issued in large denominations and purchased by large corporations from large, nationally known banks. These instruments can be quickly sold and resold in the secondary market. "Nonprime" certificates of generally smaller denominations are often issued by less well-known banks and, consequently, are more difficult to trade. They must be issued, therefore, at a higher rate of interest initially and are resold at higher rates of interest in the secondary market.

[1] *Business Week*, April 3, 1965.

COST OF CERTIFICATES OF DEPOSIT

The maximum rate of interest which may be paid on negotiable and nonnegotiable certificates of deposit is fixed by the Federal Reserve Board through Regulation Q. At the present time (effective November 24, 1964) the ceiling on instruments 90 days and over is 4.5 per cent, and under 90 days, 4 per cent. The actual rates offered by New York banks (prime certificates) in March, 1965, were 4 per cent on 30–89 day certificates, 4.30 per cent on 90—179 day certificates and 4⅜ per cent on certificates of more than 180 days.

Interest rates on prime certificates of deposit tend to be ¼ of 1 per cent higher than Treasury certificates of comparable maturity, and about ⅛ of 1 per cent higher than sales finance company paper.

The negotiability and marketability of certificates of deposit have enabled banks to tap new sources of funds, although the exact proportion of new funds which has been invested with banks is undeterminable. These new funds have permitted banks to expand their loans and investments. At the same time, however, the funds are relatively high cost. The attention given to CD's arose because several of the banks that have recently failed used certificates of deposit unwisely or illegally. Banks attempting to make their CD's more attractive to potential buyers may offer them at a discount price (giving a yield in excess of the 4.5 per cent ceiling imposed by Regulation Q), and violate the regulation. These are banks that can only offer "nonprime" CD's and would probably be small or newly chartered banks. Buyers are concerned only with the interest rate advantage and give little or no regard to the "nonprime" classification and the probably nonmarketable status of such CD's.

Other banks aggressively seeking deposits have resorted to money brokers to contact potential buyers of the bank's certificates. The use of a money broker by a bank is not illegal, but may be unwise, since the brokerage charges add to the already high cost of CD money. Recent disclosures show that these broker charges have run from ½ of 1 per cent to 3 per cent, the latter bringing the cost of certificates of deposit to over 7 per cent. At this rate, the bank finds it increasingly difficult to secure profitable, safe investment and lending opportunities that would yield a return higher than 7 per cent.

SECONDARY MARKET

The establishment of a secondary market for certificates of deposit greatly aided their initial acceptance by purchasers and partly accounts for their phenomenal growth. It is estimated that between 80 and 90 per cent of the purchasers of new certificates of deposit hold them until maturity, but the existence of a secondary market has assured even these holders of a considerable degree of liquidity if necessary. The market's primary operative function, though, has been to provide certificates of less than six months' maturity to organizations wishing to hold very short-term securities. It has also assisted purchasers who buy new issues to take advantage of the demand for them as they approach maturity by the aforementioned buyers. Data on the extent of the secondary market in terms of volume and dealer inventories are too fragmentary to be included here,[2] but the market must be of adequate size since the market seems to serve the function for which it was established—that is, providing a considerable degree of liquidity.

CONCLUSIONS

The rapid growth of certificates of deposit in the past four years has significantly altered the banking system. A Federal Reserve Board study of 410 banks indicated that as of December 31, 1961, $3,223 million of CD's had been issued. By the end of 1963, this amount was nearly $9,800 million. As of March 31, 1965, 350 weekly reporting member banks had CD's outstanding amounting to $13,962 million.

This growth has been uneven. The declines in the rate of new issues have come at quarterly tax payment times and at traditional dividend payment times. Since two-thirds of the holders of certificates of deposit are corporations, this behavior indicates that much of the buying is a result of improved corporate money management. Additional lulls were noted in 1964 when the short-term U.S. Treasury bill rate approached the ceiling rate of interest set in Regulation Q. In November, 1964, the rates payable on negotiable time certificates of deposit were raised to the present levels of 4 per cent on certificates of 30–89 days and 4.5 per cent on certificates of 90 days or more. This behavior

---

[2] "Certificates of Deposit," *Monthly Review*, Federal Reserve Bank of New York, June 1963, pp. 83–84.

seems to substantiate the claim that much of the money in CD's is volatile, i.e., interest-rate sensitive.

Such volatility could make it difficult for banks at times to turn over maturing certificates of deposit. The American Bankers Association study estimates that 70 per cent of maturing CD's are reissued. However, there is evidence that the length of maturity on new issues has declined as a result of pressure from rising interest rates on other securities. The ABA study estimates that 40 per cent of the new issues are for six to nine month maturities and the average maturity of CD's is six months. When the market dictates the length of maturity on an issue, the bank cannot fully control its portfolio of certificates and arrange the maturities of outstanding certificates in an optimally desirable fashion. This difficulty may force banks to reconsider the value of CD's in relation to their asset and liquidity position.

As a money market instrument, negotiable certificates of deposit have aided Treasury balance of payments efforts by encouraging funds to remain here rather than seek short-term investment abroad. As interest rates on CD's have risen, so have interest rates on other securities reducing some of the incentives for foreign investment. CD's have also contributed to the significant expansion of bank credit since 1961 that has enabled the nation to continue its economic growth with a minimum expansion of bank reserves.

Certificates of deposit are weighed by the Federal Reserve Board as an important factor responding to its general monetary operations. The Fed has raised Regulation Q three times since 1961 in response to other money market trends and has thus forestalled any liquidity crisis and credit contraction for the banking system. Nonetheless, if it desired, the Fed could use the interest sensitivity of the funds invested in CD's if it wished to contract credit with a minimum of overt action such as raising reserve requirements. By maintaining the levels in Regulation Q, the Fed could allow other interest rates to rise and compete for some of the funds now invested in CD's. As the certificates matured, the money might be withdrawn from CD's and invested in other securities, forcing the banks to liquidate some of their assets in order to pay off the maturing CD's. Or the holder might choose just to shift the money into demand deposits with the same bank which would also squeeze a member bank since it would force it to increase its reserve holdings with its Federal Reserve Bank. If the holder chose to shift CD funds at maturity to another bank, the issuing bank would have to liquidate some assets to pay off the CD. In either case, the banking system as a whole would have to contract credit.

Individual banks would face the credit squeeze in different ways.

Well-managed banks that held readily liquid, safe assets in the proper proportion against their outstanding certificates would be able to pay them off as they matured. If these banks had carefully balanced the maturities of their CD's as they were issued, they could handle the drain on liquidity over the months as the certificates fell due and could not be turned over. Other banks, however, would suffer a severe liquidity contraction, especially if they paid additional fees to secure CD money and, in turn, had to invest it in risky, long-term illiquid investments.

It can be seen that this new money market instrument has enabled many banks to expand credit. Undoubtedly, most banks have managed their portfolios of CD's in a sound and sophisticated manner and will be able to meet any pressure that the market may exert on them. A few banks (usually smaller or newly chartered) will find that they do not have the special skills or experience to use the certificate of deposit money wisely without regulation and close supervision from banking authorities. Already, a few banks that have failed have shown that they were unequal to dealing with this new instrument. They were unwise and, on occasion, illegal, in their pursuit of this money and its utilization.

BANKERS' ACCEPTANCES

CARL H. MADDEN

FROM DEBT TO CREDIT

A banker's acceptance is an ingenious financial device by which a bank, without having to put up a dollar of its own, turns the debt of a merchant into what is in effect a cashier's check payable at a future date by agreeing to pay it at maturity. Here's how it works. Caffeine, a New York City coffee importer, goes to the First of Wall Street Bank to ask for a letter of credit in favor of a Brazilian exporter, Greenbean, to cover a shipment. The credit letter states the details of the shipment and the credit terms—say 90 days—and tells Greenbean that he may draw drafts on the First of Wall up to, say, $10,000, the value of the shipment. Caffeine agrees to put the First of Wall in funds to cover the accepted draft at its maturity.

The First of Wall cables its branch or correspondent in Rio to tell Greenbean about the letter. Greenbean then ships the coffee. But to make sure the deal doesn't go awry, he keeps the bill of lading and other documents that will be needed in New York to get the coffee from the shipping company. He draws a draft on the First of Wall, ordering the bank to pay $10,000, say 90 days after "sight," and presents it, together with the necessary documents, to the bank in Rio which pays him a lesser, or discounted, amount. Greenbean is then ordinarily out of the transaction. The Rio bank, which now owns the draft, sends it and all the papers to its New York office or correspondent for presentation to the First of Wall.

When the Rio bank presents the draft and documents, the First

Reprinted from The Money Side of "The Street," Federal Reserve Bank of New York, 1959, pp. 63ff.

of Wall stamps "Accepted" on the draft, if everything is in order. Now the Rio bank has the First of Wall's commitment to pay the draft at maturity, 90 days hence, and can sell what is now a banker's acceptance in the acceptance market at a discount to a dealer and have the proceeds credited to the Rio bank. The acceptance buyer has the First of Wall's obligation to pay $10,000 in 90 days from the date it has stamped on the bill. Now the First of Wall gives Caffeine the shipping documents, in exchange for a trust receipt; he takes his coffee, roasts it, packs it, sells it, and uses the proceeds to pay the First of Wall before the maturity date of the acceptance.

Acceptances may cover a wide variety of particular transactions, usually the movement or storage of commodities, in both foreign and domestic trade. At years-end 1958 there were $1,194 million of acceptances outstanding, a decrease of $113 million from the December 31, 1957 level of $1,307 million but more than double the 1951 total of $490 million. Of this total about 72 per cent financed foreign trade (about 29 per cent exports, 21 per cent imports, and 22 per cent foreign storage or shipment); 19 per cent financed domestic storage; 2 per cent domestic shipments and about 7 per cent were "dollar exchange" bills.

The bank's act of accepting a bill of exchange, by removing the need for costly and often difficult credit investigation, makes it as salable as any other top-grade short-term IOU in the money market, at rates which depend upon the maturity of the acceptance and the state of market conditions. On February 2, 1959, bankers' acceptances were quoted in the New York market to buyers at 2¾ per cent for 30–90 days, 2⅞ per cent for 91–120 days, and 3 per cent for 121–180 days. Still, acceptances are more complicated and less flexible than renewable short-term bank notes and thus have not been so popular in financing domestic shipments.

COST OF FINANCING

As we have seen, the cost to the borrower is made up of two parts: the bank's charge, usually 1½ per cent a year, plus a discount set from time to time in the market by dealers. This discount, quoted as the bid-offer rates of acceptance dealers and printed in the newspapers, pays almost entirely the cost for simply using the money, since scarcely any credit risk is left after acceptance by the bank. On February 2, 1959, the bank rate on short-term loans to substantial depositors with highest credit ratings was 4 per cent, compared with the cost of borrowing through acceptances totaling 4⅜ percent; of course, not all acceptance borrowers would qualify, either, for the prime loan rate.

The return to the investor, we saw, is the offered rate of the acceptance dealer. His 2¾ per cent return on February 2, 1959 compared with a rate on 91-day Treasury bills of 2¾ per cent. He could earn only 3 per cent on 90–179 day, directly placed finance paper, and though the rate on 4- to 6-month paper was 3⅜ per cent, this meant a slightly longer period of tying up his money. In both these instances, too, there is the security, not of a bank's obligation, but a commercial firm's.

THE MARKET: NEW YORK

New York City holds a dominant place in the acceptance market, in recent years accounting for approximately 70 per cent of the total outstanding. In a 1954 survey, nearly two-thirds of the year-end total was accounted for by 10 banks and 25 banks were responsible for seven-eighths of the remainder. Because acceptance financing is specialized and closely tied to foreign trade, it is not surprising that New York is its center. San Francisco, Dallas, Boston, and Chicago follow in importance.

Fewer than half a dozen firms in New York City, most engaged primarily in dealings in United States Government and other securities, act as dealers in bankers' acceptances, and trading in acceptances is a fairly small part of their activity. Most dealers hold only a small inventory overnight and avoid the practice of holding bills to earn interest.

Acceptances are traditionally attractive investments for foreign dollar balances, and so foreign central and commercial banks are important buyers. Also, acceptances have a tax advantage over Treasury bills for some foreign holders. Income from them is not subject to Federal income taxes for foreigners and so they have a tax advantage over taxable investments except where tax treaties in effect between the United States and the countries in which some buyers are resident make all investments for such buyers tax exempt. Finally, acceptances are a more familiar financing device in many foreign countries and their use is better understood.

GENERAL FEATURES OF THE

COMMERCIAL PAPER MARKET

RICHARD T. SELDEN

HISTORICAL BACKGROUND: THE MID-NINETEENTH CENTURY AND 1920

The term "commercial paper" is sometimes used broadly to include virtually all short-term business debt, and sometimes narrowly to include only short-term promissory notes issued by businesses and offered on the more or less impersonal open market. In the latter sense, the United States has had a commercial paper market for perhaps 150 years. Up to the closing decades of the nineteenth century, this paper consisted largely of trade notes received by manufacturers, wholesalers, or jobbers, in payment for goods shipped to other firms. The recipients endorsed them over to banks, to their own creditors, or to note brokers who in turn sold them to banks. Note brokers were operating in most of the larger cities by the 1850's.[1]

Thus, at the time of the National Currency Act, commercial paper was almost exclusively two-name paper, the maker being a buyer of goods and the payee being the seller; the denominations were in odd

[1] For the early history of the commercial paper market see Margaret G. Myers, *The New York Money Market*, Vol. I (New York: Columbia University Press, 1932); and Albert O. Greef, *The Commercial Paper House in the United States*, Cambridge: Harvard University Press, 1938).

Reprinted from "Commercial Paper, Finance Companies, and the Banks," Deane Carson, ed., Banking and Monetary Studies (Homewood: Richard D. Irwin, 1963), pp. 334–340.

amounts, reflecting the value of particular shipments. At maturity most of it probably was held by banks. Little is known about the position of open-market notes (i.e., paper obtained from dealers) in bank earning assets a century ago, but it is reasonable to suppose that holdings of such paper were significant.

By 1920 a number of important changes had taken place. First, nearly all open-market commercial paper had become single-name promissory notes issued in round denominations and unrelated to shipments of goods, in contrast to the "trade" paper that had predominated earlier. A sizable share was secured paper ("collateral trust notes"). Second, the note brokers of the 1850's and before had been replaced by dealers, about 30 in all, who purchased paper outright for resale. Several of these firms maintained extensive branch systems across the country, and most of them were heavily engaged in securities underwriting or other financial activities.

Third, banks remained the major holders of commercial paper, but there is reason to believe that open-market notes occupied a decidedly less important place in bank earning assets than in 1860 (see Table 1). Call loans, customer loans, and government security holdings of banks had grown much more between 1860 and 1920 than open-market paper. In addition, the volume of bankers' acceptances expanded after passage of the Federal Reserve Act. It is fair to say that by 1920

TABLE 1   COMMERCIAL PAPER AND OTHER FORMS
OF DEBT, 1919

Type of Debt	Amount (Billions)	Ratio to Commercial Paper
1. Commercial paper	$ 1.2	1.0
2. Corporate short-term debt	22.3	18.6
3. Corporate long-term debt	31.0	25.8
4. Total corporate debt	53.3	44.4
5. Federal government debt	25.6	21.3
6. Bankers' acceptances	1.0	0.8
7. Total loans of commercial banks	25.7	21.4
8. Non-real estate loans of commercial banks	22.8	19.0

Source: Richard T. Selden, *Trends and Cycles in the Commercial Paper Market*, Occasional Paper No. 86, NBER, 1963, Table 1.

commercial paper had been relegated to the position of a secondary reserve asset, along with acceptances and call loans, useful as a means of diversifying risks and, because of the absence of a customer relationship, as a supplemental source of liquidity.

THE RISE OF FINANCE COMPANIES

Since 1920 the commercial paper market has experienced sweeping changes. The number of borrowers shrank from 4,395 in 1920 to 327 in 1960, and the number of dealers declined from about 30 to 10. On the other hand, outstanding paper quadrupled between 1920 and 1960, although it, too, declined during the 1920's and early 1930's. These conflicting trends were accompanied by major shifts in the identity of borrowers and lenders, in the role of the dealers, and in the character of the paper itself. In one way or another most of these changes were related to the growth of consumer credit since 1920 and the associated growth of sales finance and personal loan companies.

Finance companies of both types were already well established by 1920. And even in those early days finance companies were highly leveraged, with debt to equity ratios of four or five to one for the largest sales finance companies, and one or two to one for the smaller firms. Nearly all of these borrowings were short-term and came from banks in one form or another. However, it is doubtful that any significant portion was obtained through the sale of commercial paper on the open market, for only 9 of the 2,259 paper borrowers in 1922—the earliest figures available—were finance companies.

During the 1920's the growth of finance companies was phenomenal, and these firms relied more and more on the commercial paper market. They already accounted for perhaps 15 per cent of total paper borrowings by 1925, and by 1934, at the latest, for 50 per cent. In terms of the number of borrowers, finance company growth was equally impressive: between 1922 and 1926 the number rose from 9 to 86; and though the number declined for several years thereafter, the decline in nonfinance borrowers was even greater.

The period following World War II has witnessed continued growth of consumer credit and finance companies, and finance companies have extended their dominance of the commercial paper market. By 1962, 132 of these firms (including business finance companies) sold paper, and they made up 35.6 per cent of all borrowers; they probably accounted for about 90 per cent of the amount outstanding.

DIRECT PLACEMENT

Closely associated with the rising importance of finance companies has been the development of directly placed paper to its currently dominant position in the commercial paper market. Direct placement (i.e., sale of notes without a dealer's assistance) was initiated in 1920 by a sales finance company, General Motors Acceptance Corporation. Two other sales finance companies, Commercial Credit Company and CIT Financial Corporation, entered the direct placement market in 1934, and these three have been joined by at least 10 others in the postwar period.[2] All of these firms are large; collectively they held at least 90 per cent of sales finance company receivables in 1962. Seven of them are subsidiaries of manufacturers or retailers.

In contrast to the traditional dealer paper, direct paper grew persistently in the 1920's and 1930's, except during recessions, and by 1935 the two divisions of the market were about the same size. Direct paper was 83 per cent of total paper outstanding at the August, 1957, cycle peak, but it receded to 65 per cent of the total at the end of 1962.

CHARACTER OF THE PAPER AND DEALER PRACTICES

Along with these shifts in borrowers and in methods of placing notes, there have been other significant changes in commercial paper in recent decades. These include a pronounced shift in lenders (which I shall discuss later), changes in the character of the paper itself, and changes in dealer practices.

One change in the character of commercial paper has been a definite improvement in quality beginning in the mid-1930's. Between 1920 and 1934 a total of 170 defaults occurred, and there were losses of several million dollars. In contrast, between 1935 and 1962 there were only eight defaults, five of which occurred before World War II, and the only loss sustained was $47,250 in 1936. Another change was the grad-

[2] Associates Investment Company (1953), Ford Motor Credit Company (1961), General Electric Credit Corporation (1952), General Finance Corporation (1955), International Harvester Credit Corporation (1957), Montgomery Ward Credit Corporation (1960), Pacific Finance Corporation (1958), Sears Roebuck Acceptance Corporation (1957), James Talcott, Inc. (1962), and Westinghouse Credit Corporation (1961). Several other firms are expected to begin direct scales of paper in the near future.

ual disappearance of secured paper, a process that was completed by 1956.

A much more fundamental change relates to maturities. Four decades ago most paper was sold with maturities of four, five, or six months; today's maturity span is from five days (in the case of direct paper) to more than a year.[3] Moreover, finance company paper is now sold to mature on any date requested, a feature that has made it much more attractive to lenders.

Finally, the rise of direct placement has added significantly to the liquidity of commercial paper. There has never been an active secondary market in dealer paper, and its qualifications as a liquid asset are based on short maturities, together with the lack of any customer relationship that might compel lenders to renew loans at maturity.[4] Of course, direct paper has no secondary market either, but direct sellers will repurchase their notes if the lender is faced with an unforeseen need for cash. While direct sellers certainly do not encourage such repurchases, their willingness to make them does increase the liquidity of direct paper substantially. There are indications that the dealers may be moving in this direction as well.

Under the heading of dealer practices two changes are worth mentioning. First, since the maturity of most finance company paper is not established until it is placed with the lender, the dealer does not buy it from the borrower until the resale is arranged. In the lingo of Wall Street, finance company paper is "bought as sold." This means, in effect, that the "dealers" are now functioning very largely as brokers rather than as true dealers. Another change relates to commissions: in the 1920's they were usually a flat ¼ of 1 per cent, regardless of a note's maturity; now they are usually ⅛ of 1 per cent *per annum*.

In summary, the commercial paper market of the early 1960's is in a far better state of health than the market of the 1920's, despite the reduced number of borrowers and dealers. Most obviously, the volume of paper outstanding is now much larger. But more significantly, today's paper is less risky, more flexible, and more liquid.

---

[3] At least one direct seller borrows funds over weekends.
[4] Mention should be made of the fact that since October 1, 1937, finance company paper within 90 days of maturity has been eligible for rediscount at Federal Reserve Banks. However, the practical import of this change has been minor.

REASONS FOR RECENT TRENDS

As was already suggested, to a great extent recent trends in the commercial paper market are attributable to the rise of sales finance companies (and in lesser degree, of personal loan companies) as important financial intermediaries. These firms operate largely with borrowed funds—not merely during busy seasons but at all times. Moreover, they have always relied fairly heavily on *short-term* funds, because of the cyclical volatility of their assets; hence, their interest in commercial paper.

The fact that finance companies are continuous paper borrowers, in contrast to the mainly seasonal "industrial" borrowers, goes far toward explaining the innovations in the commercial paper market in the last four decades. Only continuous borrowers are willing to borrow over a wide maturity range and for periods determined by lenders; industrial borrowers, it should be noted, still sell paper on the old 4- to 6-month basis for the most part. In addition, it is evident that flat percentage commissions, irrespective of maturities, were quite acceptable when maturities were kept within a fairly narrow range, but that adoption of a really wide range of maturities would require some method of scaling the commission to the maturity of the note, as is currently done.

Furthermore, only heavy and continuous borrowers would find it profitable to make the sizable initial investment in trained personnel necessary for direct placement of paper. As noted, all direct sellers are large sales finance companies. Their mean amount outstanding was well over $200 million at the end of 1961, in comparison with the $156.4 million average of dealer-handled paper per dealer. Even the smallest direct seller ordinarily has outstandings of $50 million or more.

These facts also help explain the shrinking number of borrowers and dealers in recent decades. On one hand, the growth of direct placement undoubtedly has been partly at the expense of dealer paper growth. Measured in constant dollars, the $798 million of dealer paper outstanding at the end of 1924 was not equaled again until the summer of 1961. With less paper outstanding one would expect fewer dealers, and fewer borrowers as well. But even the smaller finance companies that borrow via dealers are relatively large firms, and they are heavy borrowers per dollar of net worth. Consequently, the dealers have gradually found it to their advantage to work with a few sizable and continuous finance company borrowers rather than with a large number of small and sporadic industrial borrowers. One result of this shift is that the dealers have been able to watch their clients more closely, thereby assuring the maintenance of high quality paper.

It would be wrong to leave the impression that the rise of finance companies has been the only important source of change in the commercial paper market. This would ignore important developments on the supply side of the market. The banks, which in 1920 were virtually the only paper holders, now hold no more than 20 or 25 per cent of outstanding paper, their place having been usurped by nonfinancial corporations, with about half of the total, and a wide variety of other lenders. Not only have the banks become relatively unimportant among commercial paper lenders, but commercial paper is now distinctly unimportant among bank earning assets (see Table 2).

Again there is probably no single explanation of the disengagement of the banks from the commercial paper market. In part this change seems to be related to the abandonment of interest payments on demand deposits, brought about by the Banking Act of 1933. Corporate treasurers, being denied any yield on their cash balances, began to discover commercial paper as an alternative liquid asset. The existence

TABLE 2   COMMERCIAL PAPER AND OTHER FORMS OF DEBT, 1961

Type of Debt	Amount (Billions)	Ratio to Commercial Paper
1. Total commercial paper	$ 4.7	1.0
2. Paper placed through dealers	1.7	.4
3. Directly placed paper	3.0	.6
4. Corporate debt other than bonds and mortgages	38.2	8.1
5. Total corporate debt (except trade debt)	155.6	33.1
6. U.S. Treasury bills	43.4	9.2
7. U.S. marketable debt maturing within one year	84.4	18.0
8. Bankers' acceptances	2.7	.6
9. Total loans of commercial banks	124.9	26.6
10. Commercial loans of commercial banks	45.2	9.6

Source: Richard T. Selden, *Trends and Cycles in the Commercial Paper Market*, Occasional Paper No. 86, NBER, 1963, Table 3.

of large corporate tax accruals since the 1930's probably also created a demand for an investment medium such as paper. At the same time, finance companies and other borrowers responded by making paper much more enticing to corporate lenders. Furthermore, the existence of Treasury bills as an attractive substitute source of liquidity since 1929 has caused the banks to lose interest in paper.

The serious implication of these developments from the standpoint of the banks is not that they have lost commercial paper as a relatively high-yield earning asset, but rather that they have increasingly lost customer loans to finance companies and others who have been turning to the open market for their short-term funds. Before elaborating this theme, however, I shall describe more fully the role of commercial paper in finance company operations.

CALL LOANS

ANONYMOUS

*Once a major money market instrument, the call loan
no longer holds a prominent place in Wall Street banking
and finance. Still its present and past importance warrants
a brief examination.*

The call loan is one of the oldest money market instruments; it was
first introduced in the United States in the mid-1800's. Although the
call loan is not currently one of the more important money market
instruments, it was at one time not only the most important instrument,
but was the chief source of secondary reserves for commercial banks.

The call loan represents short-term funds loaned by banks to securities brokers and dealers for the purpose of financing their customers'
purchases of common stock. The securities purchased with the proceeds
of the loan, in turn, become the principal collateral. The call provision
allows termination of the loan by either lender or borrower on one-day
notice. While customer borrowings from brokers are also on a call basis,
they are excluded from the usual definition of the call loan.[1]

[1] Although call loans represent only a portion of total security credit, the two terms
are often, and incorrectly, used interchangeably. Other sources of security credit are
customer net free credit balances (funds left on deposit with brokers) and bank loans
made to others than brokers and dealers for the purpose of carrying or purchasing
securities. While bank loans to "others" are extensive, the call loan rate refers specifically to collateralized broker borrowings. Occasionally, security collateral loans are
made on a time basis, but because of the dominance of the call provision, all brokers'

Reprinted from Money Market Instruments, Federal Reserve Bank of Cleveland, pp.
55–61.

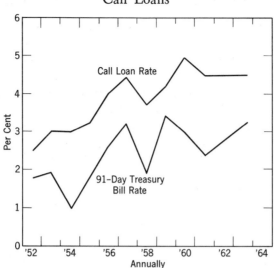

Figure 1. Call loan rates and yields on 91-day Treasury bills, 1952–1963. Note: Call loan rate refers to loans secured by customers' stock exchange collateral at New York City banks. Yields on 91-day Treasury bills refer to new issues. *Source:* Board of Governors of the Federal Reserve System.

The bulk of call loan activity occurs in New York City because securities trading is concentrated there. For example, at the end of 1963 about one-half of the $5.4 billion in commercial bank loans to brokers and dealers was carried by New York City banks.[2] The relative de-emphasis of call loans in bank portfolios is reflected in the change in the percentage of total earning assets accounted for by call loans between 1929 and 1963. At the end of 1929 call loans represented 45 per cent of earning assets ($8.1 billion) of New York City banks; at the end of 1963 the comparable figures were 8 per cent of $34.8 billion.

Although the call rate displays a secular relationship with other money market rates, it is not a particularly sensitive indicator of money market conditions. The behavior of the call loan rate during 1952–1963 is plotted in Figure 1, where it is compared with the market yield on 91-day Treasury bills, which is the pivotal money market rate. As the

loans are generally designated as the call money market. In addition, security credit often is extended to facilitate underwriting and distribution of new issues, overall operations of security dealers, and for a variety of reasons not necessarily related to the money market.

[2] These and other data included in this article, unless otherwise indicated, are from various issues of the Federal Reserve Bulletin.

chart shows, the bill rate fluctuates much more widely in response to changes in both economic and money market conditions. Moreover, the call loan rate usually exceeds the bill rate by approximately one percentage point.

A clear indication of the relative insensitivity of the call loan rate has been demonstrated during the current economic recovery that began in 1961. The chart shows that the call rate has remained unchanged despite variation in other money market rates. This is shown quite clearly in Figure 2, where the range of yields on various interest rates during 1961–1964 is presented.

The experience of the 1920's, however, would indicate that the demand for call loans is not closely related to the cost of this form of credit. As shown in Figure 3, despite the fact that the call loan rate rose dramatically between January 1927 and September 1929, there was an increase in the absolute amount of security loans outstanding as well as an increase in the ratio of security loans to total commercial bank loans. This experience indicates that restraint in the use of call loans

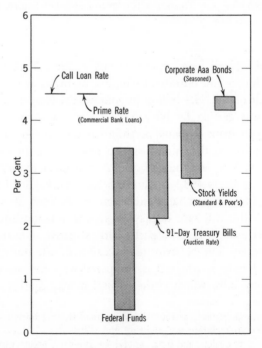

Figure 2. Range of selected interest rates, 1961–1964. Note: 1964 rates as of July 10, 1964. *Source:* Board of Governors of the Federal Reserve System.

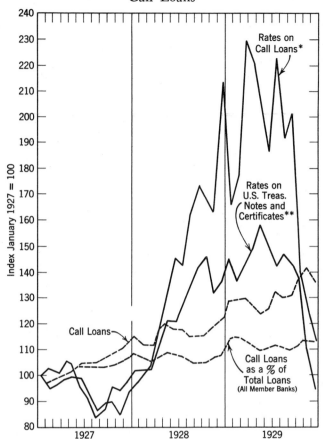

Figure 3. Indexes of selected rates and call loans, 1927–1929. * Daily average rate.
** Daily average rate; 6–9 month maturities used in some cases, 3–6 month maturities in most cases. *Source:* Board of Governors of the Federal Reserve System.

would have to be achieved through a curtailment of demand for this
form of credit rather than through an increase in cost.

HISTORICAL BACKGROUND

The call loan market developed in New York City around 1830.
Call loans served as secondary reserves of large city banks partly because
the United States did not have the developed Treasury bill or commercial bill markets such as existed in London.

After the termination of the Second Bank of the United States in 1836, country banks began to use banks in New York City and Chicago as reserve depositories. In turn the large city banks began to compete for the reserve balance of country banks by offering competitive interest rates. Because such deposits were subject to immediate withdrawal, city banks employed them primarily in the call loan market. Call loans were regarded as highly liquid because the collateral behind such loans could be sold quickly to obtain funds. By the end of the nineteenth century, approximately 50 per cent of New York City bank loan portfolios were represented by call loans.

The relative liquidity of call loans was subjected to wide fluctuations primarily because of seasonal swings in rural economic activity. For example, farmers needing funds to facilitate harvesting or planting usually withdrew deposits and requested loans at country banks. These institutions, in turn, frequently found it necessary to draw on their correspondent balances in New York City and Chicago banks to meet the deposit drain and demands for credit. Since call loans constituted the secondary reserves of large banks, the call privilege was widely exercised in order to meet the withdrawals of banks. However, brokers and dealers were frequently unable to meet the calls on their loans and were forced to request that their customers, for whom the funds had been borrowed, repay the amount due on the securities purchased on margin. Because many customers were unable to meet the payments, the securities were sold to meet the call. Since calls were concentrated in short periods of time mass liquidations of securities and sharp declines in securities prices usually occurred. As a result, the financial system underwent severe pressures as the demands for credit far outstripped the amount of credit available, and the value of securities declined sharply under repeated forced liquidations. In addition, the lack of liquidity and decline in security prices frequently resulted in bank failures, which further aggravated financial conditions. At times these pressures were so intense that financial panics resulted, e.g., in 1884, 1893, 1903 and 1907.

The Federal Reserve Act in 1913 provided facilities to member banks for alternative sources of liquidity to meet temporary deposit drains. This was done through the rediscounting of short-term business loans. However, call loans were not rediscounted by the Federal Reserve System, and the denial of rediscounting facilities for call loans resulted in a temporary demise of call loans as secondary reserves of banks. A surge in equity financing after World War I brought about a widespread return to using call loans. Portfolios of commercial banks thus began to include larger amounts of call loans during the 1920's. For example, between 1922 and 1929, brokers' loans held by commercial banks rose from $1.5 billion to $8.5 billion. By September 1929 brokers' loans accounted for 44 per cent of all member bank loans and 50 per cent of New York City bank loans.

When stock values collapsed in late 1929, however, call loans were once again relegated to limbo. In many instances, call loans could not be repaid and the collapse of the market reduced the demand for such credit. In less than three years after October 1929, the volume of call loans dropped from $8.5 billion to only $335 million.

FOUR

MONETARY THEORY

MONETARY theory, in the broadest sense, involves the question of whether the supply of and demand for money exert independent influences on the level of prices and employment, or whether the latter are principally affected by *real* factors such as saving and investment. The question "Does money matter?" has been the focal point of a great deal of controversy among economists for many years.

Although clear-cut labels disguise significant nuances in view and approach, the controversy has principally involved "The Chicago School"—money matters—and Keynesians and neo-Keynesians—money is relatively passive.

In this section, both schools of thought are represented. Professors Friedman and Selden present the "Chicago" view, while Professor Ritter outlines a neo-Keynesian position. The remaining selection, by Professor Gurley, is a somewhat separate treatment of monetary and financial theory.

If students are perplexed that experts cannot agree on the role of money, it should be noted that only recently have empirical data been brought to bear on the question. Many models are being developed and tested; perhaps not too far in the future we will have a closer consensus on the importance of money.

THE SUPPLY OF MONEY

AND THE PRICE LEVEL

MILTON FRIEDMAN

How does the stock of money affect the level of prices and output over time? In this and the following selection, the leader of the "Chicago School" of monetary thought presents a widely held view of the processes involved. Note should be taken of the distinction the author makes between short (cyclical) and long (secular) run effects of changes in the supply of money relative to other influences on prices and output.

As a result of his empirical work in monetary history, Professor Friedman concludes that a steady increase in the stock of money (say, 3–4 per cent per year) would lead to better results than variation through discretionary central bank policy.

RELATION OF STOCK OF MONEY TO PRICES OVER LONGER PERIODS

There is perhaps no empirical regularity among economic phenomena that is based on so much evidence for so wide a range of circumstances as the connection between substantial changes in the stock

Reprinted from "The Supply of Money and Changes in Prices and Output," The Relationship of Prices to Economic Stability and Growth, compendium of papers submitted to the Joint Economic Committee (Washington: Government Printing Office, 1958), pp. 242–251.

of money and in the level of prices.[1] To the best of my knowledge there is no instance in which a substantial change in the stock of money per unit of output has occurred without a substantial change in the level of prices in the same direction. Conversely, I know of no instance in which there has been a substantial change in the level of prices without a substantial change in the stock of money per unit of output in the same direction. And instances in which prices and the stock of money have moved together are recorded for many centuries of history, for countries in every part of the globe, and for a wide diversity of monetary arrangements.

There can be little doubt about this statistical connection. The statistical connection itself, however, tells nothing about direction of influence, and it is on this question that there has been the most controversy. It could be that a rise or fall in prices, occurring for whatever reasons, produces a corresponding rise or fall in the stock of money, so that the monetary changes are a passive consequence. Alternatively, it could be that changes in the stock of money produce changes in prices in the same direction, so that control of the stock of money would imply control of prices. The variety of monetary arrangements for which a connection between monetary and price movements has been observed supports strongly the second interpretation, namely, that substantial changes in the stock of money are both a necessary and a sufficient condition for substantial changes in the general level of prices. But of course this does not exclude a reflex influence of changes in prices on the stock of money. This reflex influence is often important, almost always complex, and depending on the monetary arrangements, may be in either direction.[2]

This general evidence is reinforced by much historical evidence of

---

[1] "The stock of money" is not of course an unambiguous concept. There is a wide range of assets possessing to a greater or lesser degree the quality of general acceptability and fixity in nominal value that are the main characteristics of "money." It is somewhat arbitrary just where the line is drawn which separates "money" from "near-money" or "securities" or "other financial claims." For most of what follows, the precise line drawn will not affect the analysis. For the United States at present, I shall treat as "money in the hands of the public" the sum of "currency outside banks," "demand deposits adjusted," and "adjusted time deposits in commercial banks," as these terms are defined in Federal Reserve monetary statistics. I shall note explicitly any point at which the precise definition adopted affects the statements made.

[2] For example, under a gold standard, a rising level of prices discourages gold production and so, after a lag, tends to produce a decline in the stock of money. On the other hand, under a fractional reserve banking system, if rising prices lead banks to reduce the ratio of cash to liabilities, rising prices may tend to produce a rise in the stock of money.

a more specific character demonstrating that changes in the stock of money, at least when they are fairly large, can exert an independent influence on prices. One dramatic example is from the experience of the Confederacy during the Civil War. In 1864, "after 3 years of war, after widespread destruction and military reverses, in the face of impending defeat, a monetary reform that succeeded in reducing the stock of money halted and reversed for some months a rise in prices that had been going on at the rate of 10 per cent a month most of the war. It would be hard to construct a better controlled experiment to demonstrate the critical importance of the supply of money."[3] The discoveries of precious metals in the New World in the sixteenth century and of gold in California and Australia in the 1840's, the development of the cyanide process for extracting ore, plus gold discoveries in South Africa in the 1890's, the printing of money in various hyperinflations, including our own Revolutionary War experience and the experience of many countries after World War I and World War II, are striking examples of the effect of increases in the stock of money producing increases in prices. The long price decline in the second half of the nineteenth century in many parts of the world is a less dramatic example of a decline in the stock of money per unit of output producing a decline in prices.[4]

The relationship between changes in the stock of money and changes in prices, while close, is not of course precise or mechanically rigid. Two major factors produce discrepancies: changes in output, and changes in the amount of money that the public desires to hold relative to its income.

For the moment, we shall treat output as if it were determined independently of monetary and price changes. This is clearly a simplification that is to some extent contrary to fact, but certainly for the longer periods and larger changes that are discussed in this section, the simplification neither does serious violence to the facts nor leads to any significant errors in conclusions.

Suppose the stock of money were to remain unchanged for a period of years but total output over the same period were to double. Clearly,

[3] Milton Friedman, "The Quantity Theory of Money—a Restatement," *Studies in the Quantity Theory of Money*, p. 17. The quotation summarizes one item from a study by Eugene M. Lerner, summarized in his article, "Inflation in the Confederacy, 1861–65," in the same volume, pp. 163–175.

[4] The decline in the stock of money per unit of output occurred as a result of (1) exhaustion of then-known gold mines; (2) the shift of many countries from a silver to a gold standard; (3) the rapid increase in output.

one would expect prices to fall—other things the same—to something like half their initial level. The total amount of "work" for the money stock to do, as it were, is doubled, and the same nominal quantity of money could perform the "work" only at lower levels of prices. Roughly speaking, this is what happened in the United States in the period from the end of the Civil War in 1865 to the resumption of specie payments in 1879: the stock of money was roughly the same in 1879 as in 1865—if anything, some 10 per cent higher; output grew very rapidly over the period, probably more than doubling; and wholesale prices were half their initial level. Thus, for price movements, the relevant variable is the stock of money per unit of output, not simply the global stock of money.

The second major factor that can introduce a discrepancy between movements in money and in prices is a change in the ratio that the public desires to maintain between its cash balances and its income [5]— the public including individuals, business enterprises other than banks, nonprofit institutions, and the like. The number of dollars an individual wants to keep in cash depends of course on the price level—at twice the price level he will want to hold something like twice the number of dollars—and on his income—the higher his income, presumably the larger cash balances he will want to hold. But the price level is what we are trying to explain, and we have already taken account of the effect of changes in output. This is why we express this factor in terms of the ratio that the public desires to maintain between its cash balances and its income, rather than in terms of the number of dollars it desires to hold.

Broadly speaking, the public as a whole cannot by itself affect the total number of dollars available to be held—this is determined primarily by the monetary institutions. To each individual separately, it appears that he can do so; in fact an individual can reduce or increase his cash balance in general only through another individual's increasing or reducing his. If individuals as a whole, for example, try to reduce the number of dollars they hold, they cannot as an aggregate do so. In trying to do so, however, they will raise the flow of expenditures and hence of money income and in this way will reduce the ratio of their cash balances to their income; since prices will tend to rise in the process, they will thereby reduce the real value of their cash balances, that is, the quantity of goods and services that the cash balances will com-

---

[5] The reciprocal of this ratio is termed "the income velocity of circulation."

mand; and this process will continue until this ratio or this real value is in accord with their desires.

A wide range of empirical evidence suggests that the ratio which people desire to maintain between their cash balances and their income is relatively stable over fairly long periods of time aside from the effect of two major factors: (1) The level of real income per capita or perhaps of real wealth per capita; (2) the cost of holding money.

(1) Apparently, the holding of cash balances is regarded as a "luxury," like education and recreation. The amount of money the public desires to hold not only goes up as its real income rises but goes up more than in proportion. Judged by evidence for the last 75 years in the United States, a 1 per cent rise in real income per capita tends to be accompanied by nearly a 2 per cent increase in the real amount of money held and thus by nearly a 1 per cent increase in the ratio of cash balances to income. This tendency is highly regular over the long sweep of time from 1875 to World War II; it has not been operative since the end of World War II but it is yet too soon to judge whether this is a fundamental change or simply a reaction to the abnormally high ratio of cash balances that was reached during the war.

(2) The cost of holding cash balances depends mainly on the rate of interest that can be earned on alternative assets—thus if a bond yields 4 per cent while cash yields no return, this means that an individual gives up $4 a year if he holds $100 of cash instead of a bond—and on the rate of change of prices—if prices rise at 5 per cent per year, for example, $100 in cash will buy at the end of the year only as much as $95 at the beginning so that it has cost the individual $5 to hold $100 of cash instead of goods. The empirical evidence suggests that while the first factor—the interest rate—has a systematic effect on the amount of money held, the effect is rather small. The second factor, the rate of change of price, has no discernible effect in ordinary times when price changes are small—of the order of a few per cent a year. On the other hand, it has a clearly discernible and major effect when price change is rapid and long continued, as during extreme inflations or deflations. A rapid inflation produces a sizable decline in the desired ratio of cash balances to income; a rapid deflation, a sizable rise.

Of course even after allowance is made for changes in real income per capita and in the cost of holding money, the ratio of cash balances to income is not perfectly steady. But the remaining fluctuations in it are minor, certainly far smaller than those that occur in the stock of money itself.

RELATION OF STOCK OF MONEY TO PRICES OVER
SHORTER PERIODS

Over the longer periods considered in the preceding section,
changes in the stock of money per unit of output tend to dominate
price changes, allowance being made for the effect of the growth of
real income per head. This is less so over the shorter periods involved
in the fluctuations we term business cycles, though the general and
average relationship is very similar. The reason for the looser connection in such periods presumably is that movements in both the stock
of money and in prices are smaller. Over longer periods, these movements cumulate and tend to swamp any disturbance in the relation
between desired cash balances, real income, and the cost of holding
money; in the ordinary business cycle, the disturbances, though perhaps
no more important in an absolute sense, are much more important
relative to the movements in money and prices.

On the average, prices rise during an expansion phase of a business
cycle, fall during the contraction phase. In the usual fairly mild cycle of
peacetime since 1879, wholesale prices have on the average risen about
10 per cent from trough to peak, and have fallen by somewhat less
than half that amount from peak to trough. The general pattern has
not changed much except for the relation of the rise to the fall. During
the period of generally declining prices from the 1880's to the mid-1890's,
prices tended to fall more during the contraction than they rose during
expansion; during the subsequent period of generally rising prices, the
reverse was the case and in some instances prices continued to rise during part of the contraction; in the 1920's the rise and fall were roughly
the same; in the two postwar cycles the rise was decidedly larger than
the fall, as in the pre-1914 period.

Taken as a whole, these mild cycles would have imparted a generally upward drift to prices. The failure of such a drift to develop during
peacetime was a consequence of the more severe depressions that occurred from time to time. In the five business cycles for which the contractions were most serious and can be designated deep depressions
(1891–1894, 1904–1908, 1919–1921, 1927–1933), wholesale prices on the
average rose about 10 per cent during expansions, about the same as
in the mild cycles, but then fell during the contractions over twice
as much, ending up on the average some 12 per cent below their level
at the start of the cycle. It was the price declines during these deep depressions that, as a matter of experience, offset the upward tendency

during mild cycles—"creeping inflation" in this sense is by no means a unique post-World War II phenomenon.

The stock of money shows the same relation to these cyclical price movements as that depicted for long periods. During the mild cycles, the stock of money almost invariably rose during both expansion and contraction, but at a faster rate during expansions than during contractions. On the other hand, during the deep depression cycles listed above, the stock of money invariably fell during the course of the contraction, and there is only one other cycle during which there was an appreciable absolute decline during any part of the contraction (1894–1897). This resemblance between the cyclical movement in the stock of money and in prices holds not only on the average but also from cycle to cycle, though of course with more variability for the individual cycles.[6]

There can be little doubt on the basis of this evidence that there is a close link between monetary changes and price changes over the shorter periods within which business cycles run their course as well as over longer periods and during major wartime episodes. But three important considerations must be borne in mind if this fact is not to be a misleading guide to policy.

The first is that the direction of influence between the money stock and income and prices is less clear-cut and more complex for the business cycles than for the longer movements. The character of our monetary and banking system means that an expansion of income contributes to expansion in the money stock, partly through inducing banks to trim more closely their cash reserve position, partly through a tendency for currency in public hands to decline relative to deposits; similarly, a contraction of income contributes to a reduction or a slower rate of rise in the money stock by having the opposite effects on bank reserve ratios and the public's currency ratio. Thus changes in the money stock are a consequence as well as an independent cause of changes in income and prices, though once they occur they will in their turn produce still further effects on income and prices. This consideration blurs the relation between money and prices but does not reverse it. For there is much evidence—one important piece on timing will be presented in the next paragraph—that even during business cycles the money stock plays a largely independent role. This evidence is particularly direct and clear for the deep depression periods. There can be little doubt, for example, that Federal Reserve action in sharply raising discount rates

[6] One difference between the comparison made here and in the preceding section is that the money series used is the stock of money, not the stock of money per unit of output.

in January 1920 and again in June 1920 (five months after the onset of the contraction in January 1920) played an important role in the subsequent decline in the money supply and unprecedentedly rapid fall in prices or that Federal Reserve policy in the early 1930's played an important role in producing a decline of a third in the stock of money from 1929 to 1933—by far the largest decline in the whole period covered by our data.[7]

The second, and perhaps more important consideration, has to do with the timing of the changes in the money supply and in income and prices. The generally upward trend in the money supply which accounts for its continuing to rise, though at a slower rate, during most contractions in economic activity as well as during expansions makes it difficult to judge timing relations from ups and downs in the supply itself. For this and other reasons, we have found it most useful to examine instead the ups and downs in the rate at which the money supply is changing. The rate of change of the money supply shows well-marked cycles that match closely those in economic activity in general and precede the latter by a long interval. On the average, the rate of change of the money supply has reached its peak nearly 16 months before the peak in general business and has reached its trough over the 12 months before the trough in general business.[8]

This is strong though not conclusive evidence for the independent influence of monetary change. But it also has a very different significance. It means that it must take a long time for the influence of monetary changes to make themselves felt—apparently what happens now to the rate of change of the money supply may not be reflected in prices or economic activity for 12 to 16 months, on the average. Moreover, the timing varies considerably from cycle to cycle—since 1907, the shortest time span by which the money peak preceded the business cycle peak was 13 months, the longest, 24 months; the corresponding range at

[7] The other deep depression episodes are a bit more complex. The decline in the stock of money from 1893 to 1894 seems connected with the uncertainty about silver; in 1907, quite clearly from the banking panic which was of course, in part, a consequence of a prior decline in economic activity but not through the particular channels described above and which once begun very likely served as an important factor in making the contraction as deep as it was; in 1937–1938, with the doubling of reserve requirements by the Federal Reserve System in two steps in 1936 and in 1937—the first step coincides with a sharp reduction in the rate of growth of the money stock, the second with the beginning of decline.

[8] The average at peaks is based on 18 observations; that at troughs, on 19. Of course, instead of interpreting the cycles in the rate of change as conforming positively with a lead they could be interpreted as conforming inversely with a lag. A number of pieces of statistical evidence, however, argue strongly for the former interpretation.

troughs is 5 months to 21 months. From the point of view of scientific analysis directed at establishing economic regularities on the basis of the historical record—the purpose for which the measures were computed—this is highly consistent behavior; it justifies considerable confidence in the reliability of the averages cited and means that they cannot easily be attributed simply to the accident of change variation. But from the point of view of policy directed at controlling a particular movement such as the current recession, the timing differences are disturbingly large—they mean that monetary action taken today may, on the basis of past experience, affect economic activity within six months or again perhaps not for over a year and six months; and of course past experience is not exhaustive; the particular episode may establish a new limit in either direction.

The long time lag has another important effect. It leads to misinterpretation and misconception about the effects of monetary policy, as well as to consequent mistakes in monetary policy. Because the effects of monetary change do not occur instantaneously, monetary policy is regarded as ineffective. [A] . . . recent example is the tight money policy of 1956 and 1957 which coexisted with rising prices but whose delayed effects are with us in the current recession. A similar and even more dramatic example is the tight money policy from early 1928 on and the associated lack of growth in the money supply which coexisted with economic expansion but contributed to both the occurrence and the severity of the 1930 downturn. The fact that these policies had a delayed effect in turn misled the monetary authorities; on those occasions, and even more clearly in 1930, they were induced to believe that still stronger measures were required and tended to overdo a repressive policy. On other occasions, notably in 1932 as well as earlier in that major catastrophe, the failure of tentative movements toward easy money to have an immediate effect led them to regard their actions as ineffective and to permit and contribute to the sharp decline in the stock of money which occurred and which played so crucial a role in that episode.

The third consideration is in some ways a different aspect of the one just discussed. The variation in timing means that there is considerable leeway in the precise relation between changes in the stock of money and in prices over short periods of time—there are other factors at work that lead to these variations and mean that even if the stock of money were to change in a highly regular and consistent fashion, economic activity and prices would nonetheless fluctuate. When the money changes are large, they tend to dominate these other factors—or perhaps one might better say, they will force these factors to work in a particular direction. Thus there seems little doubt that a large change in the money supply within a relatively short period will force a change in the same direction in income and prices and, conversely, that a large change in income and prices in short periods—a substantial short-period inflation or deflation—is most unlikely to occur without a large change in money supply. This is certainly the conclusion suggested by the evidence for the deep depression cycles and for sizable inflation. But when the money changes are moderate, the other factors come into their own. If we knew enough about them and about the detailed effects of monetary changes, we might be able to counter these other effects by monetary measures. But this is utopian given our present level of knowledge. There are thus definite limits to the possibility of any fine control of the general level of prices by a fine adjustment of monetary change.

CHANGES IN PRICES

AND CHANGES IN OUTPUT

MILTON FRIEDMAN

CHANGES IN PRICES AND CHANGES IN OUTPUT
OVER LONGER PERIODS

Over the cycle, prices and output tend to move together—both tend to rise during expansions and to fall during contractions. Both are part of the cyclical process and anything, including a monetary change, that promotes a vigorous expansion is likely to promote a vigorous rise in both and conversely. The preceding [selection] implicitly assumes this connection.

Over the longer period, the relation between price changes and output changes is much less clear and in the first section we took the behavior of output for granted. Now this seems clearly valid, not only as an expository device but also as a first approximation to reality. What happens to a nation's output over long periods of time depends in the first instance on such basic factors as resources available, the industrial organization of the society, the growth of knowledge and technical skills, the growth of population, the accumulation of capital, and so on. This is the stage on which money and price changes play their parts as the supporting cast.

One proposition about the effect of changes in the stock of money and in prices that is widely accepted and hardly controversial is that large and unexpected changes in prices are adverse to the growth of output—whether these changes are up or down. At one extreme, the

Source cited in preceding selection, pp. 251–256.

kind of price rise that occurs during hyperinflation seriously distorts the effective use of resources.[1] At the other extreme, sharp price declines such as occurred from 1920 to 1921 and again from 1929 to 1933 certainly produce a widespread and tragic waste of resources.

So much is agreed. The more controversial issue is the effect of moderate change in prices. One view that is widely held is that slowly rising prices stimulate economic output and produce a more rapid rate of growth than would otherwise occur. A number of reasons have been offered in support of this view. (1) Prices, and particularly wages, are, it is said, sticky. In a market economy, the reallocation of resources necessitated by economic growth and development requires changes in relative prices and relative wages. It is much easier, it is argued, for these to come about without friction and resistance if they can occur through rises in some prices and wages without declines in others. If prices were stable, some changes in relative wages could still come about in this way, since economic growth means that wages tend to rise relative to prices, but with no changes in relative prices, there would not be as much scope even for relative wage changes. (2) Costs, and in particular, wages, are, it is argued, stickier than selling prices. Hence generally rising prices will tend to raise profit margins, giving enterprises both a bigger incentive to raise output and to add to capital and the means to finance the capital needed. (3) The most recently popular variant of the preceding point is that costs are not only sticky against declines but in addition have a tendency to be pushed up with little reference to the state of demand as a result of strong trade unions. If the money stock is kept from rising, the result, it is claimed, will be unemployment as profit margins are cut, and also a higher level of prices, though not necessarily a rising level of prices. Gently rising prices, it is argued, will tend to offset this upward pressure by permitting money wages to rise without real wages doing so. (4) Interest rates are particularly slow to adapt to price rises. If prices are rising at, say, 3 per cent a year, a 6 per cent interest rate on a money loan is equivalent to a 3 per cent rate when prices are stable. If lenders adjusted fully to the price rise, this would simply mean that interest rates would be 3 per-

---

[1] However, even open hyperinflations are less damaging to output than suppressed inflations in which a wide range of prices are held well below the levels that would clear the market. The German hyperinflation after World War I never caused anything like the reduction of production that was produced in Germany from 1945 to the monetary reform of 1948 by the suppression of inflation. And the inflationary pressure suppressed in the second case was a small fraction of that manifested in the first.

centage points higher in the first case than in the second. But in fact this does not happen, so that productive enterprises find the cost of borrowing to be relatively low, and again have a greater incentive than otherwise to invest, and the associated transfer from creditors to debtors gives them greater means to do so.

In opposition to this view, it has been argued that generally rising prices reduce the pressure on enterprises to be efficient, stimulate speculation relative to industrial activity, reduce the incentives for individuals to save, and make it more difficult to maintain the appropriate structure of relative prices, since individual prices have to change in order to stay the same relative to others. Furthermore, it is argued that once it becomes widely recognized that prices are rising, the advantages cited in the preceding paragraph will disappear: escalator clauses or their economic equivalent will eliminate the stickiness of prices and wages and the greater stickiness of wages than of prices; strong unions will increase still further their wage demands to allow for price increases; and interest rates will rise to allow for the price rise. If the advantages are to be obtained, the rate of price rise will have to be accelerated and there is no stopping place short of runaway inflation. From this point of view, there may clearly be a major difference between the effects of a superficially similar price rise, according as it is an undesigned and largely unforeseen effect of such impersonal events as the discovery of gold, or a designed result of deliberative policy action by a public body.

Some who believe that slowly rising prices are adverse to economic growth regard stable product prices with slowly rising wage rates as most favorable, combining the advantages of stable price expectations with some easing of frictions involved in relative wage adjustments. Others view gently falling prices and stable wages as most favorable, arguing that additional problems in wage adjustments would be balanced by the stimulus to thrift and accumulation.

Historical evidence on the relation between price changes and output changes is mixed and gives no clear support to any one of these positions. (1) In the United States, the period from 1865 to 1879 was a period of exceedingly rapid progress; and during the same period, prices were cut in half. True, neither price changes nor output changes proceeded regularly within the period. Output apparently grew most rapidly during the cyclical expansions in the period when prices rose mildly or were roughly stable; most of the price declines occurred during cyclical contractions. Yet the problem at issue is less the cyclical relation than the longer period relation and there can be no doubt that during the period as a whole prices fell sharply and output rose sharply. (2) The period from 1880 to 1897 was a period of generally declining prices, from 1897 to 1913, of generally rising prices; taken as a whole, the second period has generally been regarded as displaying more rapid growth than the first. But it is not clear that this is a satisfactory interpretation. The period of great monetary uncertainty in the early 1890's was associated with generally depressed conditions and was followed by a rapid rebound. If both are excluded, the remaining periods show about the same rates of growth in real output per head, although prices were generally falling during the 1880's and rising after the turn of the century. Moreover, the period from 1908-1914 was one of relatively slow growth despite rising prices. (3) The decade of the 1920's, after the recovery from the deep depression of 1920-1921, was a decade of rapid growth and prices were relatively stable. (4) In Great Britain, output per head apparently grew at a definitely higher rate during the period of generally falling prices before the mid-1890's than during the subsequent period of rising prices up to World War I. (5) On the other hand, the attempt to achieve mildly falling prices in Britain in the 1920's was associated with considerable economic difficulties and something close to stagnation.

All in all, perhaps the only conclusion that is justified is that either rising prices or falling prices are consistent with rapid economic growth, provided that the price changes are fairly steady, moderate in size, and reasonably predictable. The mainsprings of growth are presumably to be sought elsewhere. But unpredictable and erratic changes of direction in prices are apparently as disturbing to economic growth as to economic stability.

POLICY IMPLICATIONS

The preceding account of the relation of money to prices over long and short periods and of price changes to output changes has some fairly direct and immediate implications for public policy with respect both to growth and stability.

(1) In order for the price level to be reasonably stable over the decades ahead, the total stock of money will have to grow to accommodate itself to the growth in output and in population. In addition, if past patterns continue, it will have to grow to satisfy the desire of the public to increase the ratio of cash balances to income as their real income rises. Past experience suggests that something like a 3- to 5-per cent

per year increase in the stock of money is required for long-term price stability.[2]

(2) An essential requirement for the avoidance of either substantial inflation or substantial deflation over the coming decades is the avoidance of a substantially more rapid or a substantially less rapid increase in the stock of money than the 3- to 5-per cent per year required for price stability. A substantially more rapid rate of growth in the money supply will inevitably mean inflation; conversely, continued inflation of substantial magnitude cannot occur without such a large rate of growth in the money supply. A substantially slower rate of growth in the money supply, let alone an absolute decline, will inevitably mean deflation; conversely, continued deflation of substantial magnitude cannot occur without such a small or negative rate of growth in the money supply.

(3) A highly fluctuating price level is as disturbing to economic growth as to economic stability. Given that this is avoided, it is not clear what pattern of long-term price behavior is optimum for economic stability—whether a roughly stable price level, a gently rising price level, or a gently falling price level. It does seem clear that any of these is consistent with rapid economic growth. If it is necessary to state objectives in terms of a price level goal, then a stable price level has the very great advantages of (a) ease of public understanding, (b) definiteness, which renders successive alterations in the precise goal less likely, and (c) probably the closest approach to equitable treatment of the various members of the community. However, the difficulty of assuring the close attainment of any price level goal suggests that it might be better to express the immediate policy goal in terms of some variable other than the price level, for example, as being the attainment of a steady 4 per cent per year rise in the stock of money, and then to let the price level be whatever would be consistent with this money goal. The resulting price level behavior could hardly depart much from relative stability and would certainly not be violently unstable.

(4) For cyclical movements, a major problem is to prevent monetary changes from being a source of disturbance. If the stock of money

---

[2] This range is for the stock of money defined as currency outside banks plus adjusted deposits, demand and time, of commercial banks. In a narrower definition, for currency outside banks plus adjusted demand deposits, the required rate of growth is less; for a broader definition, the preceding plus all time deposits, in mutual savings banks and the postal savings system as well as commercial banks, the required rate of growth is greater. The reason is that time deposits have been growing relative to demand deposits and currency, and, until 1957, mutual savings deposits were relative to other time deposits.

can be kept growing at a relatively steady rate, without erratic fluctuations in short periods, it is highly unlikely if not impossible that we would experience either a sharp price rise—like that during World Wars I and II and after World War I—or a substantial price or output decline—like those experienced from 1920–1921, 1929–1933, 1937–1938.

(5) A steady rate of growth in the money supply will not mean perfect stability even though it would prevent the kind of wide fluctuations that we have experienced from time to time in the past. It is tempting to try to go farther and to use monetary changes to offset other factors making for expansion and contraction. Though the available evidence demonstrates a close connection between monetary change and price and income change in the course of business cycles as over larger periods, it also casts grave doubts on the possibility of producing any fine adjustments in economic activity by fine adjustments in monetary policy—at least in the present state of knowledge. The evidence suggests that monetary changes take a fairly long time to exert their influence and that the time taken varies considerably. In terms of past experience, for example, action taken now to offset the current recession may affect economic activity in some six months or not again for over a year and six months. The tight-money policy of late 1956 and most of 1957, which was taken to offset the then existing inflationary pressure, almost surely had little effect on that situation and is only now exerting its influence and contributing to the current recessionary tendencies; the inflationary pressures in 1956 may well have been in part a delayed consequence of the expansionary monetary policy taken to offset the 1953–1954 recession. There are thus serious limitations to the possibility of a discretionary monetary policy and much danger that such a policy may make matters worse rather than better. Federal Reserve policy since 1951 has been distinctly superior to that followed during any earlier period since the establishment of the System, mainly because it has avoided wide fluctuations in the rate of growth of the money supply. At the same time, I am inclined to believe that in our present state of knowledge and with our present institutions, even this policy has been decidedly inferior to the much simpler policy of keeping the money supply growing at a predesignated rate month in and month out with allowance only for seasonal influences and with no attempt to adjust the rate of growth to monetary conditions.[3]

---

[3] This is not intended to be a full statement of the optimum monetary structure. I would prefer automatic arrangements that would reduce the area of discretion. One particular set of such arrangements is suggested in my "A Monetary Fiscal Framework

(6) To avoid misunderstanding, it should be emphasized that the problems just discussed are in no way peculiar to monetary policy. Fiscal action also involves lags. Indeed the lag between the recognition of need for action and the taking of action is undoubtedly longer for discretionary fiscal than for discretionary monetary action: The monetary authorities can act promptly; fiscal action inevitably involves serious delays for congressional consideration. It has been argued that this defect of fiscal action is counterbalanced by a shorter lag between the action and its effects. This may well be, though there is little concrete empirical evidence that I know of; the belief is based on general considerations of plausibility, which can be a misleading guide. And there are certainly no reasons for believing and no empirical evidence to show that the lag, whatever its average length, is any less variable for fiscal than for monetary action. Hence the basic difficulties and limitations of monetary policy apply with equal force to fiscal policy.

(7) Political pressures to "do something" in the face of either relatively mild price rises or relatively mild price and employment declines are clearly very strong indeed in the existing state of public attitudes. The main moral to be drawn from the two preceding points is that yielding to these pressures may frequently do more harm than good. There is a saying that the best is often the enemy of the good, which seems highly relevant. The goal of an extremely high degree of economic stability is certainly a splendid one: our ability to attain it, however, is limited; we can surely avoid extreme fluctuations; we do not know enough to avoid minor fluctuations; the attempt to do more than we can will itself be a disturbance that may increase rather than reduce instability. But like all such injunctions, this one too must be taken in moderation. It is a plea for a sense of perspective and balance, not for irresponsibility in the face of major problems or for failure to correct past mistakes.

---

for Economic Stability," reprinted in my *Essays in Positive Economics* (Chicago: University of Chicago Press, 1953), pp. 133–156.

The extensive empirical work that I have done since that article was written has given me no reason to doubt that the arrangements there suggested would produce a higher degree of stability: it has, however, led me to believe that much simpler arrangements would do so also: that something like the simple policy suggested above would produce a very tolerable amount of stability. This evidence has persuaded me that the major problem is to prevent monetary changes from contributing to instability rather than to use monetary changes to offset other forces.

On the issues in question, see also my "The Effects of a Full Employment Policy on Economic Stability: A Formal Analysis," reprinted in the same book, pp. 117–132.

THE DEMAND FOR MONEY

It should be perfectly clear that the stock of money at any given moment must be held in the aggregate by persons and institutions of various kinds. Why do persons and institutions desire to hold money? What are the causes of changes in the desire to hold money over time? The theory of the demand for money is, in essence, the answer to such questions as these.

In this selection Professor Selden treats real money balances per unit of output as a commodity for which there exists a demand on the part of persons and institutions. Holding money idle has both utility and disutility, and the outcome of their respective magnitudes determines the nature of this demand.

The key to velocity analysis lies in the application of orthodox demand theory to money. The reciprocal of velocity, real balances per unit of output (M/Py), may be regarded as a commodity whose services are in demand. A decrease (increase) in quantity demanded, of course, means a rise (fall) in velocity. Quantity demanded, in this as in all other cases, can by analyzed in terms of the usual categories: the commodity's price, prices of related commodities, incomes, tastes, and expectations.

The "price" of M/Py consists of the opportunity costs sustained by moneyholders. The cost of holding money may be measured in various ways but for our purposes it is the difference between yields on illiquid assets and on money. Since the yield on money is negligible and does not change quickly, corporate bond yields serve as a rough measure of the cost of holding money. Higher bond yields will lead to an increase in velocity.[1]

Money substitutes can be handled in the same fashion. Their attractiveness as sources of liquidity depends on their yields. A rise in the yields of money substitutes will reduce the demand for M/Py, since households and firms will tend to satisfy their liquidity needs by holding near-money rather than money.

The income elasticity of demand for M/Py appears to be well above zero in the long run; that is, a permanent rise in real income per capita leads to greater quantity demanded and thus to a lower velocity. Exactly the opposite relationship exists during cyclical income rises, probably because households adjust their holdings of cash primarily with reference to permanent rather than current income.[2] As current income falls during recessions, the demand for nominal balances (M) does not fall correspondingly, since permanent income falls more slowly. The result is a reduction in velocity, as computed with current income. During business upswings the reverse effect probably occurs.

Tastes may change in the aggregate either as a result of income redistribution or because of alterations in individual desires. One of the more significant redistributional effects occurs when government's share of GNP fluctuates. Obviously, changes in tastes may be either velocity-increasing or velocity-decreasing, although cash-economizing innovations may gradually reduce the basic desire for liquidity.

The final category, expectations, is important for short-run changes in velocity. Most obvious, perhaps, are expectations about the future

[1] Strictly speaking, this argument should be stated in terms of equilibrium interest rates. This is because lending is not the only alternative to holding cash. Real investment is an important additional alternative; hence the expected return on investment also measures the cost of holding money. It is the essence of cyclical disturbances that the relation between returns on loans and returns on investment is out of equilibrium —a fact that complicates the cyclical relation between interest rates and velocity. Under such conditions a rise in the real rate will lead to higher velocity even though the loan rate is constant. This may be visualized as a shift to the right of the investment demand curve, accompanied by a simultaneous and causally related leftward shift in the demand curve for M/Py. The latter shift implies an increase in velocity. This is probably a major reason why studies of earlier periods have found a relatively weak relation between velocity and interest rates.

[2] See Milton Friedman's research report in *National Bureau of Economic Research, Thirty-eighth Annual Report* (May 1958), pp. 39–41. [The term "permanent income" refers to the discounted value of the stream of income one expects over a lifetime; current income is this period's contribution to that stream. Ed.]

value of money. If the public expects the rate of inflation to increase (perhaps because of rapid monetary expansion), the demand for M/Py will fall and velocity will rise. Probably more significant for the general run of cyclical inflations are businessmen's expectations about the productivity of capital and its relation to interest rates. A rise in the expected marginal efficiency of capital will stabilize interest rates, reduce the quantity of M/Py demanded, and velocity will rise.

THE ROLE OF MONEY

IN KEYNESIAN THEORY

LAWRENCE S. RITTER

In this essay, Professor Ritter challenges the simple Keynesian model which the quantity theorists have properly attacked as unrealistic. Showing that money does matter is the Keynesian system (as interpreted by Keynes), he argues that the real challenge intellectually to the Quantity of Money School is not this version (Model B) but a stream-lined Model C, which emphasizes the role of the whole spectrum of liquid assets, not just money, in determining economic activity.

In recent years it has frequently been asserted, primarily by Quantity theorists, that the main characteristic of Keynesian theory is that "money does not matter." The view that "money matters" is held to be the exclusive province of the Quantity theory, and extensive statistical tests are thereupon conducted to demonstrate that the supply of money has had an important influence on the level of economic activity. On this basis, Keynesian theory is, *ipso facto*, declared fallacious.

The purpose of this essay is to examine carefully the role of money in Keynesian theory, in order to evaluate the thesis that in the Keynesian system "money does not matter." It turns out that the validity of this point of view depends in large part on which version of the latter one has in mind.

Reprinted from essay in Banking and Monetary Studies, Deane Carson, ed. (Homewood: Richard D. Irwin, 1963), pp. 134–150.

KEYNES WITHOUT MONEY

The most familiar version of Keynesian economics, which we will call Model A, is the elementary simplification of Keynes in which the only determinants of the level of national income are the consumption function and a given volume of investment (including government) spending. Consumption spending is seen as depending mainly upon income, and investment spending is assumed to be given, determined autonomously. Occasionally, in order to include an accelerator effect, investment spending may also be made to depend partly upon income. Within this context, the equilibrium level of national income is found where realized income, resulting from consumption plus investment expenditures, equals anticipated income, on the basis of which spending decisions are made. Alternatively, equilibrium income is that level of income at which planned investment equals planned saving.

It is this simplified model which has been popularized by the widely known "Keynesian cross" diagram, in which either consumption and investment or saving and investment are plotted on the vertical axis, and anticipated income is plotted on the horizontal axis. Equilibrium income is determined where aggregate demand equals anticipated income or, alternatively, where planned investment equals planned saving. This particular analytical system has also been the basis for the bulk of orthodox Keynesian multiplier theory: a sustained increase in autonomous spending is assumed to raise equilibrium income by a multiple of the initial increment in spending. The specific value of the multiplier is determined solely by the size of the marginal propensity to consume. Such an uncomplicated formula for the value of the multiplier can only be derived from an equally uncomplicated frame of reference, such as that outlined above. For if the value of the multiplier depends solely on the size of the marginal propensity to consume, it must be assumed, implicitly or explicitly, that spending is insensitive to such increases in interest rates and tightening of credit availability as would normally accompany an expansion in income.

On the basis of this model, countless public policy recommendations, dealing almost exclusively with the implications of alternative fiscal policies, have been advanced over the years in the name of Keynesian economics. In this scheme of things, the Quantity theory's characterization of the Keynesian system as one in which "money does not matter" is quite accurate: national income is determined without any reference whatsoever to either the supply of or the demand for money, and public policy prescriptions are confined to the area of fiscal policy. Monetary policy is completely extraneous. That this model evidently commands considerable allegiance, even today, is attested to by the great amount of attention paid in 1962 and 1963 to alternative forms of tax reduction, and to the size of the resulting budget deficit, as compared with the relative lack of interest in how such a deficit should be financed, i.e., whether by monetary creation or otherwise.

KEYNES WITH MONEY

Although Model A is probably the most popular version of Keynesian economics, it is not the same economics to be found in Keynes' *The General Theory of Employment, Interest, and Money.* As far as Keynes himself was concerned, and as the title of his major work indicates, money plays a significant role in the determination of income and employment. Let us call the orthodox Keynesian system, as advanced in *The General Theory* and much subsequent literature, Model B.

Most important, Keynes did not assume that investment spending is exogenous, a given datum, but rather that it depends on relationships *within* the system, namely on comparisons between the expected rate of profit and the rate of interest. The rate of interest, in turn, depends on the supply of and demand for money. The demand for money, or liquidity preference, is viewed as consisting of two parts, the demand for idle money balances (with the amount demanded increasing as the rate of interest falls) and the demand for active or transaction balances (with the amount demanded increasing as the level of income rises).

In contrast to the partial Keynesian system, represented by Model A, the complete Keynesian system, Model B, requires that *two* conditions be fulfilled before income can be said to be in equilibrium. Not only must planned investment equal planned saving, as before, but in addition at any moment in time the amount of money people want to hold must equal the supply of money, the amount that is available for them to hold. If the second condition is not satisfied, the rate of interest will rise or fall, thereby altering the volume of investment and consequently changing the equilibrium level of income.[1]

[1] The diagrammatics of the complete Keynesian system thus are not contained in the "Keynesian cross," but rather in Hicks' *IS* and *LM* curves. See J. R. Hicks, "Mr. Keynes and the Classics: A Suggested Interpretation," *Econometrica*, Vol. V (1937), pp. 147–59, reprinted in *Readings in the Theory of Income Distribution* (Philadel-

If, at a given interest rate and income, planned investment equals planned saving but the amount of money desired exceeds (falls short of) the supply, the interest rate will rise (fall), thereby reducing (increasing) investment spending and lowering (raising) the level of income. As the interest rate rises, the desired amount of idle balances contracts, and as income falls the desired amount of active balances contracts, until the amount of money demanded is reduced to the point where it is equal to the given supply. Thus, the equilibrium level of income eventually is reached, with both planned investment equal to planned saving and the demand for money equal to the supply, but the interest rate is now higher and income now lower than initially postulated.

Here there is room for monetary policy to operate: if the monetary authorities want to prevent upward pressure on the interest rate, and the consequent drop in income, they can increase the supply of money enough to satisfy the demand at the initial interest rate and income level. On the other hand, if they want to permit money income to fall, they can sit back and let nature take its course. Both of these are rather passive policies. More aggressive actions would call for increasing the money supply even more than enough to satisfy the initial demand, in order to stimulate an increase in income rather than merely prevent a decrease; or actually reducing the money supply, even though it is already less than the demand, to provide added impetus to the decline in income.

It is obvious that a policy of doing nothing is but one alternative among a spectrum of possibilities. The Federal Reserve at times seems to suggest that those changes in interest rates which occur when the central bank is passive are none of its doing. It is implied that changes in interest rates which take place when the central bank is holding the money supply constant are solely the result of "free market forces," and are in some sense preferable to changes which result from more active monetary policies. But as long as interest rates could be different if the central bank did something rather than nothing, it follows that interest rates are what they are in part because the central bank prefers them that way.

All this does not mean that the monetary authorities are omnipotent. In the orthodox Keynesian system, monetary policy is important

---

phia: The Blakiston Co., 1946), pp. 461–76. Also see Alvin H. Hansen, *Monetary Theory and Fiscal Policy* (New York: McGraw-Hill, 1949), chapter 5, and his *A Guide to Keynes* (New York: McGraw-Hill, 1953), chapter 7. For a concise exposition see Joseph P. McKenna, *Aggregate Economic Analysis* (New York: Holt, Rinehart & Winston, 1955), chapter 8.

but not always in the same degree. As a general principle, monetary policy is likely to be less effective the more interest-elastic the demand for idle balances (for then a change in the money supply will not succeed in altering the interest rate) and the less interest-elastic the investment and consumption schedules (for then a change in the interest rate will not induce a change in spending). This has typically been construed by most Keynesians to mean that monetary policy is likely to be less effective in combating depression than in stopping inflation. In a severe depression, the public may prefer to hold additional amounts of money at low interest rates rather than lend it out or buy securities, so that the rate of interest may reach a floor below which it will not fall; investment prospects may appear so bleak that reductions in interest rates become of negligible importance; and job prospects may appear so dismal that consumer spending on durable goods is severely inhibited, despite such additions to the public's wealth as are brought about by expanding the stock of money.

In formal Keynesian terms, during severe depressions the interest-elasticity of liquidity preference may become so great as to prevent increases in the supply of money from reducing the interest rate, as they normally would. And investment and consumer spending may become so unresponsive to changes in interest rates and in wealth as to preclude what would be expected to be their normal reactions. In terms of the equation of exchange, $MV = PT$, increases in the money supply would be offset by proportionate reductions in the velocity of money. Under such circumstances, money again "does not matter" in the Keynesian system, in the sense that increases in the money supply beyond a certain point will not affect the volume of spending, and for all practical purposes we are back in the world of Model A above.

It is important to realize, however, that severe depression is only a special case in the general Keynesian system. And even then, *decreases* in the money supply would not be looked upon as trivial. In other instances, the supply of money may be of crucial importance. From the beginning, for example, it has been a basic tenet of Keynesian doctrine that inflation cannot proceed very far without an increase in the supply of money. Rising incomes are seen as leading to larger demands for transactions balances, which in the absence of increases in the money supply must be drawn from formerly idle balances, inducing a rise in interest rates. This process can continue until idle balances are depleted, or perhaps somewhat further if there is some interest-elasticity in the demand for active balances at high interest rates. But, unless the money supply is increased, the expansion in spending is viewed as having to grind to a halt before too long, because rising interest rates and tightening monetary conditions in general will sooner or later choke off investment spending.[2] Indeed, so strongly has this position been held by some orthodox Keynesians that they have at times objected to the use of monetary policy to stop inflation because of the fear that it is likely to be too effective. In brief, in the orthodox Keynesian system sometimes the supply of money is not very important, sometimes it is critically important, and most of the time it is somewhere in between, depending in each instance on the circumstances at hand.

It is rather ironic that Keynes should be the target of a blanket charge by Quantity theorists that he is responsible for propagating the view that "money does not matter." For in Keynes' own mind he was enlarging the scope of monetary theory, not narrowing it. Before Keynes, prevailing monetary theory in the form of the Quantity theory of money, had been concerned almost exclusively with the determination of the general level of prices, to the neglect of the influence of money on real output and employment. As expressed by Jean Bodin in 1569, through John Locke, David Hume, David Ricardo, John Stuart Mill, and Irving Fisher, the Quantity theory had always stressed that the supply of money determined primarily the absolute price level. The velocity of money was held to be an institutional datum and aggregate real output was assumed at the full employment level by virtue of Say's Law. In terms of the equation of exchange, $MV = PT$, V and T were assumed to be given so that changes in the money supply would result in proportionate changes in prices.[3]

The policy implications of the pre-Keynesian Quantity theory were simple and paralyzing. Increases in the supply of money, even in periods of substantial unemployment, could never achieve any permanent benefit. They could only be harmful, by raising prices proportionately—a view that is deeply imbedded in popular folklore to this day. It is this

---

[2] "A rise in prices and incomes leads to an increase in requirements for money balances in active circulation. This tends to reduce the amount available for inactive balances and so causes the rate of interest to rise, which checks investment. The rope which holds the value of money is a limitation on its supply. If the monetary authorities are compelled to increase the supply of money, the rope frays and snaps in their hands." Joan Robinson, *Essays in the Theory of Employment* (London: Macmillan, 1937), pp. 17–21 (spliced quotation). Also see J. R. Hicks, *op. cit.*, p. 470.

[3] As expressed by Irving Fisher, in the most widely accepted pre-Keynesian statement of the Quantity theory: "Since a doubling in the quantity of money will not appreciably affect either the velocity of circulation or the volume of trade, it follows necessarily and mathematically that the level of prices must double. There is no possible escape from the conclusion that a change in the quantity of money must normally cause a proportional change in the price level." Irving Fisher, *The Purchasing Power of Money* (Macmillan, 1911), pp. 156–57 (spliced quotation).

framework, rather than the Keynesian, which in a fundamental sense views money as unimportant. Here money is seen as "neutral," a veil behind which "real" forces work themselves out just about as they would in the absence of money. In the Keynesian approach, on the other hand, money also plays a role in the determination of real output. For the first time money becomes more than merely a veil, and a monetary economy is seen as behaving very differently from a barter economy.

NEW DEPARTURES

Model C is a lineal descendant of Model B, but comes to rather different conclusions. Although Model C uses most of the orthodox Keynesian apparatus, it is so unorthodox in its handling of selected parts of that apparatus as to make it debatable whether it should be classified as a version of Keynesian theory. Perhaps it should be given a category of its own and called Radcliffism, since it has been most closely associated with the work of the Radcliffe Committee and Professors Gurley and Shaw.[4] In any case, in this model changes in the money supply are seen as no more likely to be effective against inflation than they were against depression in Model B!

The analysis of Model C differs from both previous models in that it does not ignore the liquidity preference function, as A does, nor does it stress the significance of its interest-elasticity, as B does. Rather than being ignored, the liquidity preference function is an integral part of Model C, *but the demand for liquidity is no longer viewed as identical with the demand for money.* And rather than stressing the importance of the interest-elasticity of the demand schedule for money, attention is directed instead to the likelihood of *shifts* in that schedule. While the orthodox Keynesian literature has a great deal to say about shifts in the investment demand function, through the influence of changes in expectations, it tends to ignore the possibility of shifts in the demand for money, and instead concentrates almost exclusively on its interest-elasticity.

In the orthodox Keynesian system, Model B, the demand for

[4] Report of the Committee on the Working of the Monetary System (London, 1959), and J. G. Gurley and E. S. Shaw, *Money in a Theory of Finance* (Washington: The Brookings Institution, 1960). See also J. G. Gurley, *Liquidity and Financial Institutions in the Postwar Economy,* Study Paper 14, Joint Economic Committee, U.S. Congress (1960); R. S. Sayers, "Monetary Thought and Monetary Policy in England," *Economic Journal,* Vol. LXX, No. 280 (December, 1960), pp. 710–24; and A. B. Cramp, "Two Views on Money," *Lloyds Bank Review,* No. 65 (July, 1962), pp. 1–15.

liquidity is synonymous with the demand for money. The ready availability of interest-yielding money substitutes, however, destroys that equation. Such near monies as time deposits, savings and loan shares, and Treasury bills are virtually as liquid as cash and in addition yield an interest return. Thus, the demand for money (demand deposits plus currency) may contract even though the demand for liquidity broadly conceived remains stable. Liquidity preference, in other words, may be satisfied partially by holdings of money substitutes in place of money itself.

These are two reasons for the demand for money in the orthodox Keynesian system. In the first place, active money balances are needed for transactions purposes. The demand for active balances is assumed to bear a more or less constant ratio to income, so that an expansion in income will lead to a proportionate increase in the amount of active balances desired. In the second place, idle cash is demanded because of uncertainties regarding the future course of interest rates. Idle cash is held primarily because of the fear that interest rates might rise (bond prices fall), imposing capital losses on bondholders. This is the main reason why Keynes believed that the amount of idle cash desired would increase as the rate of interest falls.[5] The lower the rate of interest, the more it is likely to drop below what are considered "safe" or "normal" levels, leading to the expectation that its future course is likely to be upward, with consequent losses in capital values. Under such circumstances, it is prudent to get out of bonds and into a more liquid asset. In *The General Theory* the only liquid asset available is cash.

The existence of short-term money substitutes, however, provides an alternative to holding money for both of these purposes. With respect to *active* balances, there is no reason to assume that these need to be held solely in the form of money. For immediate transactions purposes, there is little alternative to possessing the medium of exchange itself. But for payments scheduled for several months in the future, there are many assets available which can serve as a substitute for holding cash without diminishing liquidity, and which at the same time provide an interest income. Firms with scheduled payments to make at particular dates in the future can hold Treasury bills, sales finance company paper, or repurchase agreements with government securities dealers, for example —all of which can easily be arranged to come due when the cash is needed. The very purpose of tax anticipation bills is to fill just such a need. Similarly, households can hold time deposits, paying interest from

[5] See *General Theory*, pp. 201–2. Also see Day and Beza, *Money and Income* (New York: Oxford University Press, 1960), pp. 17–20.

date of deposit to date of withdrawal, pending anticipated payments. For possible emergencies, lines of credit can be arranged on a standby basis in place of holding idle cash.

Many other methods exist through which both households and business firms can economize on their average holdings of transactions cash without impairing their liquidity positions. Indeed, there is ample evidence that high short-term interest rates in the postwar period have stimulated the expenditure of considerable ingenuity in the economical management of cash balances, with consequent reductions in the required ratio of active money balances to income. To the extent that this is accomplished, an expansion in income will not lead to a proportionate increase in the amount of transactions cash desired.

With respect to *idle* balances, the existence of short-term money substitutes also provides an alternative to holding cash when it is feared that long-term interest rates might rise (bond prices fall). If it is thought that long-term rates are too low (bond prices too high) for safety, investors need not increase their holdings of idle cash to get liquidity, but instead can purchase Treasury bills or other interest-bearing liquid assets. With highly liquid money substitutes, the concept of a "safe" yield level is almost meaningless and the chance of suffering a capital loss close to nil; indeed, the very definition of a liquid asset is one which can be turned into cash on short notice with little or no loss in dollar value.

The concept of a "safe" yield level is crucial in decisions as to whether or not to buy *long-term* securities, because the existence of uncertainty regarding future long rates gives rise to the fear of taking substantial capital losses (or the hope of making capital gains). The rationale behind buying *short-term* liquid assets is that if yields rise no loss need be suffered. The securities will mature shortly anyway, and thereby turn into cash at their face value. And, in any event, even if one has no choice but to dispose of them before maturity, the resulting capital losses (or gains) are likely to be small. Unlike long-terms, a rather large change in yields on short-term instruments involves but a small change in their price.[6]

---

[6] A rise in yields from 4 per cent on a $1,000 face value 30-year bond bearing a 4 per cent coupon involves a fall in price from $1,000 to $845. A similar rise in yield on a 3-month security of similar coupon involves a fall in price from $1,000 to only $997.

The point can be made even more dramatically. Assume, not too unrealistically, that at the extreme, long-term yields on government securities might be expected to vary between 2 per cent and 6 per cent in the foreseeable future, and short-term yields between 1 per cent and 7 per cent. The holder of a $1,000 30-year bond bearing a 4 per cent coupon might then anticipate, at the extreme, that its price might possibly

In brief, the amount of money desired may not increase when the rate of interest falls, even though the amount of liquidity desired does increase. At least part of the accumulation of liquidity is likely to take the form of interest-bearing near monies instead of nonearning cash. In comparison with Model B, the demand for idle cash balances will have contracted throughout the range of interest rates, even though the liquidity preference function may have remained stable. Under these circumstances, with both segments of the demand for money susceptible to leftward shifts, monetary policies confined to regulating the supply of money are not likely to be as successful in stemming inflation as orthodox Keynesian theory believes. Since the significant variable is not the supply of money, per se, but rather the supply relative to the demand, the flexibility of demand makes control of the supply, alone, an unreliable instrument through which to affect the level of economic activity. These results do not depend, as in orthodox Keynesian theory, on the short-run interest-elasticity of the demand for money, but rather on shifts in that demand.

In Model B, for example, if the economy is initially in equilibrium, with planned investment equal to planned saving and the demand for money equal to the supply, and exogenous increase in spending will raise money income and increase the amount of transactions cash desired proportionately. Limitation of the money supply—holding it constant—will then automatically result in an excess demand for money, which will raise interest rates, check investment, and thereby bring the expansion in income to a halt. There will probably be some slippage, as the rise in interest rates attracts some funds out of idle cash holdings into transactions balances, with the degree of slippage depending on the interest-elasticity of the demand for idle balances and the specific ratio between active cash and income. But that same rise in interest rates, and the related tightening of monetary conditions in general, will tend to discourage some expenditures. In any event, sooner or later idle balances will be depleted. If the monetary authorities want to accelerate the process, they can provide added impetus by actually reducing the money supply rather than merely holding it stable.

In the world envisaged by Model C, on the other hand, these results are not as likely to be realized. If the required ratio of transactions cash to income contracts as income rises, the expansion in income

---

vary between the limits of $723 and $1,450. For a 3-month security of similar coupon, however, the possible range of price variation would be only from $992 to $1,008. In one case, possible range of price variation is $727 on a $1,000 security, and in the other case it is only $16. Safety of principal is tenuous in the former, and practically assured in the latter.

will not lead to a proportionate increase in the amount of active cash desired. It may not even lead to an absolute increase. Limitation of the money supply then may not produce very much of an excess demand for money, so that upward pressure on interest rates will be negligible, investment will not be checked, and the rise in spending will proceed unhindered. If, at the same time, the demand for idle balances has also shifted to the left, then—regardless of its interest-elasticity—formerly idle balances will become available for transactions use, again with minimal increases in interest rates. Instead of an excess demand for money, there might conceivably be an excess supply, with consequent *downward* pressure on interest rates. Even if the monetary authorities were to actually reduce the supply of money, they might be hard put to keep pace with the contraction in demand. And although idle balances must sooner or later be depleted, this will pose no obstacle to the continued rise in spending if the desired active cash to income ratio continues to contract.

Of course, the process need not be this straightforward. Models B and C need not be mutually exclusive, but may be combined over several cycles. Interest rates may indeed rise during periods of cyclical expansion, especially if the expansion is vigorous, as spending increases more rapidly than can be accommodated by contractions in the demand schedules for money. However, rising interest rates are likely to stimulate new financial techniques for economizing on cash balances.[7] These techniques of cash management, introduced during periods of tight money, are not likely to be abandoned when rates recede in the subsequent recession. As a result, the contraction in the demand for money may not be clearly evident until the *next* upturn in business conditions. When that upturn comes, the supply of money may be more than ample to finance it, even though, by past standards, it would appear to be less than adequate. In effect, liquidity is accumulated during the recession, in the form of money substitutes instead of money, and is then released when needed to finance expenditures when economic activity revives.

Presumably, the central bank could always reduce the money supply drastically enough to counteract the decline in the demand for money, and thereby produce the results it wants. But with business

---

[7] See Hyman P. Minsky, "Central Banking and Money Changes," *Quarterly Journal of Economics,* Vol. LXXI, No. 2 (May 1957), pp. 171–87; and L. S. Ritter, "The Structure of Financial Markets, Income Velocity, and the Effectiveness of Monetary Policy," *Schweizerische Zeitschrift für Volkswirtschaft und Statistik,* Vol. XCVIII, No. 3 (September 1962), pp. 276–89.

prospects cloudy, as they generally are, and with past guidelines un-reliable indicators of the current adequacy of the money supply, the monetary authorities are usually not sure enough of where they stand to take decisive action in *any* direction. This inaction is then rationalized by the invocation of moral principles, as ethical values are attributed to the determination of interest rates by "free market forces" and to "minimum intervention" in general.

It is for these reasons that Model C shifts attention away from the money supply narrowly defined to the significance of liquidity broadly conceived. Traditional monetary policy, which is confined to the control of the money supply, is seen as having to give way to a more broadly based liquidity policy if it is to successfully influence economic activity within the context of the present-day financial environment.[8] It is thus Radcliffe monetary theory, rather than orthodox Keynesian theory, which poses the most fundamental challenge to the modern Quantity theory of money.

[8] In the words of the Radcliffe Report (paragraph 981, p. 337): "The factor which monetary policy should seek to influence or control is something that reaches far beyond what is known as 'the supply of money.' It is nothing less than the state of liquidity of the whole economy."

THE MARKET FOR LOANABLE FUNDS,

CREATION OF LIQUID ASSETS,

AND MONETARY CONTROL

JOHN G. GURLEY

During any year, nonfinancial economic units sell new issues of debts and equities in the market for loanable funds. These securities are purchased by other nonfinancial economic units, by the monetary system, and by nonmonetary intermediaries. The following pages develop the broad outlines of this market.

THE DEMAND FOR LOANABLE FUNDS

The net demand for loanable funds, during any year, is the planned net issues of primary securities by nonfinancial economic units—by consumers, business firms, and Government units. Primary securities are the obligations of these economic units, and they include Government securities, corporate bonds and stocks, mortgages, and a variety of short- and intermediate-term debt. The sellers of these new issues are ultimate borrowers.

The following chart illustrates that ultimate borrowers may sell

Reprinted from Liquidity and Financial Institutions In the Postwar Period, Study Paper 14, Joint Economic Committee (Washington: Government Printing Office, 1960), pp. 20–25.

primary securities through any of three channels: (1) Directly to ultimate lenders; (2) indirectly to them through the monetary system; or
(3) indirectly to them through nonmonetary financial intermediaries.

(1) When primary securities are sold directly to ultimate lenders,
the latter acquire these securities rather than claims on financial institutions. These financial transactions may conveniently be called direct
finance.

(2) When primary securities are sold to the monetary system, the
ultimate lenders acquire money balances and time deposits instead of
primary securities. This is called indirect finance through the monetary
system. The monetary system comprises the monetary accounts of the
U.S. Treasury, Federal Reserve banks, and commercial banks.

(3) When primary securities are sold to nonmonetary financial intermediaries, ultimate lenders acquire claims on these intermediaries—
nonmonetary indirect assets—rather than primary securities. This is
called indirect finance through nonmonetary intermediaries. These intermediaries include mutual savings banks, savings and loan associations,
life insurance companies, credit unions, and similar institutions. Nonmonetary indirect assets are mutual savings deposits, savings and loan
shares, policy reserves, and so on. For some purposes the time deposit
departments of commercial banks should be included in the group of
nonmonetary intermediaries.

THE SUPPLY OF LOANABLE FUNDS

The net supply of loanable funds, during any year, is the demand
for primary securities by ultimate lenders, the monetary system, and
nonmonetary intermediaries.[1] When ultimate lenders supply loanable

---

[1] This is what the orthodox definition amounts to. In that definition the supply of
loanable funds is:

Planned saving by economic units

+

Increase in stock of money

−

Increase in economy's demand for money (hoarding)

Assuming that saving and investment are done by different groups and that
savers do not repay debts, planned saving is equal to economic units' increase in
demand for primary securities, money, and nonmonetary indirect assets. The increase
in the economy's demand for money minus that of economic units is the increase in

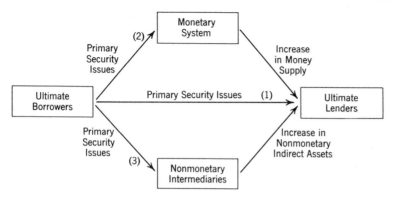

Figure 1. The market for loanable funds.

funds, they acquire primary securities. When the monetary system supplies loanable funds, it acquires primary securities and ultimate lenders accumulate money and time deposits. When nonmonetary intermediaries supply loanable funds, they acquire primary securities and ultimate lenders receive nonmonetary indirect assets. These relationships are shown in Figure 1.

MARKET EQUILIBRIUM

The market for loanable funds is in equilibrium when the demand for loanable funds is equal to the supply of loanable funds. It is in equilibrium, in other words, when issues of primary securities by ultimate borrowers are equal to the incremental demand for primary securities

---

demand for money by nonmonetary intermediaries. With these definitions, the supply of loanable funds becomes:

Economic units' increase in demand for primary securities

+

Economic units' increase in demand for nonmonetary indirect assets

+

Increase in stock of money

−

Nonmonetary intermediaries' increase in demand for money

The second item above is equal to nonmonetary intermediaries' increase in demand for primary securities and money; the third item above is equal to the monetary system's increase in demand for primary securities, neglecting gold. This yields my definition.

by ultimate lenders, the monetary system, and nonmonetary intermediaries.[2] When there is an excess demand for loanable funds, interest rates on primary securities rise and other terms of lending tighten. When there is an excess supply of loanable funds, interest rates on primary securities fall and other terms of lending are eased.

INTERNAL AND EXTERNAL FINANCE

Nonfinancial economic units finance their expenditures for current output either internally or externally. Expenditures are financed internally when they are financed out of current income or from existing holdings of financial or real assets. Expenditures are financed externally when economic units issue primary securities to obtain funds for spending. External finance may take the form of direct finance, when primary security issues are sold directly to other nonfinancial economic units, or of indirect finance, when primary issues are sold to financial intermediaries.

CREATION OF FINANCIAL AND LIQUID ASSETS

All financial assets are created by someone. Primary securities are created by nonfinancial economic units when they sell new issues for money. (The money may then be used to purchase current output, primary securities, or other assets.) Indirect securities are created by financial intermediaries. Money, as one type of indirect security, is created by the monetary system when it purchases primary securities. Nonmonetary indirect securities are created by other financial intermediaries when they sell claims on themselves for money. (The money may then be used to purchase primary securities.)

Liquid assets, as previously noted, comprise those financial assets that nonfinancial economic units consider to be fixed in price and redeemable into money on demand. The money supply itself has the highest degree of liquidity. Some nonmonetary indirect assets, such as time deposits, savings and loan shares, mutual savings deposits, and credit union shares, also qualify as liquid assets. Finally, a small portion of primary securities is highly liquid, the most notable example being savings bonds of the U.S. Government. Thus liquid assets are created

[2] This assumes an initial state of equilibrium—that the stock of primary securities is initially equal to the demand for this stock.

by the monetary system when it purchases primary securities and creates money and time deposits. They are also created by nonmonetary intermediaries when they purchase money and create liquid claims on themselves, and then "sell" money for primary securities. Economic units then end up with more liquid assets, comprising the same amount of money and additional liquid claims on nonmonetary intermediaries. Finally, liquid assets are created, in small part, by those nonfinancial economic units who issue highly liquid primary securities, such as savings bonds.

THE SCOPE OF MONETARY CONTROLS

The monetary authorities have no direct controls over the amount of internal financing done by nonfinancial economic units. Moreover, they have only limited direct control over the amount of external financing done.

With respect to external financing, the monetary authorities ordinarily do not control directly the demand for loanable funds (issues of primary securities). Further, they have no direct control over the supply of loanable funds coming from ultimate lenders and from nonmonetary intermediaries (except that emanating from time deposit departments of commercial banks, when they are included in nonmonetary intermediaries). Instead, monetary controls usually impinge on only one portion of the total supply of loanable funds—that coming from the monetary system.

The monetary authorities seek to regulate the total supply of loanable funds in relation to the total demand for these funds. They try to restrict the supply of loanable funds in relation to the demand when they want credit tightness. They endeavor to increase the supply relative to the demand when they want credit ease. The purpose of credit tightness is to reduce spending for current output and to lower commodity prices. Credit ease is meant to increase spending for current output, which may raise commodity prices. Consequently, by controlling one portion of the total supply of loanable funds, without directly controlling the demand for these funds, and without directly controlling internal financing, the monetary authorities attempt to influence aggregate spending in the economy.

THE EFFICACY OF MONETARY CONTROLS IN
THE POSTWAR PERIOD

Monetary controls were not eminently successful during the postwar period in halting increases in commodity prices, despite the fact that the growth of the money supply was held in check. Many observers feel that the impact of monetary policy on prices and output has been weakened over the past few decades by fundamental changes in the economic environment, and that these changes account for the comparatively poor postwar record of the monetary authorities.

One of the fundamental changes, it is believed, has been the fast growth of nonmonetary financial intermediaries, which lie outside of the monetary authorities' direct control. These intermediaries, by purchasing large amounts of primary securities, have greatly increased the supply of loanable funds and have created a substantial volume of highly liquid assets.

One writer has pointed out the implication of this in the following way:

Since the end of World War II the spectacular growth of the assets of financial institutions other than commercial banks reflect . . . the efficiency of financial markets in assembling "idle" funds and putting them to work in commerce and industry. This process not only can continue in the face of restrictions on the growth of commercial bank assets, but it is even likely for a time to be accelerated by a restrictive credit policy. A rise of interest rates increases the cost of holding demand deposits, on which commercial banks have been forbidden to pay interest since 1935. Hence, rising interest rates, especially if the movement is of considerable magnitude and duration, tend to stimulate both consumers and business firms to convert their cash balances into earning assets. This can often be done without any significant loss of liquidity. For example, when an individual draws on his checking account to buy a life insurance policy or to acquire savings and loan shares or to deposit funds in a mutual savings bank, he obtains against a financial institution a claim which can be readily converted into cash. The institution, in turn, having acquired ownership over a part of his demand deposit, now has additional money to lend to others who are likely to be active spenders. In these and other ways the loans of financial intermediaries can for a time grow quite rapidly even when the reserves of commercial banks are severely restricted by Federal Reserve actions.[3]

[3] Arthur F. Burns, "Prosperity Without Inflation," pp. 50–51.

There is little doubt that ultimate borrowers obtained much of their postwar external financing through the sale of primary security issues to nonmonetary financial intermediaries, that the intermediaries obtained loanable funds by selling claims—often highly liquid ones—on themselves for money balances, and that such financing took place beyond the reach of the monetary authorities. This process of indirect finance not only increased the supply of loanable funds but at the same time it expanded the volume of liquid assets in the economy.

POSTWAR TRENDS IN

MONETARY THEORY AND POLICY

MILTON FRIEDMAN

The postwar period has seen a dramatic change in the views of academic students of economics about monetary theory and of government officials about monetary policy. At the end of the war most professional economists and most governmental officials concerned with economic policy took it for granted that money did not matter, that it was a subject of minor importance. Since then there has been something of a counterrevolution in both theory and policy.

In theory, the direction of change has been toward the earlier attitudes associated with the quantity theory of money, but with a different emphasis, derived from the Keynesian analysis, on the role of money as an asset rather than as a medium of exchange. In the field of policy, the direction of change has been away from what we might call "credit policy," i.e., policy which emphasizes rates of interest and availability of credit, and toward monetary policy, i.e., policy which is concerned with the quantity of money. The emphasis has been away from qualitative controls and toward quantitative controls. And, finally, in the field of policy there has been renewed attention to the problem of relating internal stability to external stability. In examining these changes I shall outline briefly what the situation was at the end of the war; I shall then discuss in more detail the changes in theory that I have just sketched, and finally analyze the changes in policy.

Reprinted from The National Banking Review, *September 1964, pp. 1–10. Originally published by* The Center of Economic Research, Athens, Greece.

THE POSTWAR SITUATION

Economic thought at the end of the war was greatly affected by the Keynesian revolution which occurred in the 1930's. Keynes himself was much less extreme in rejecting the importance of money than were some of his later disciples. Keynes stressed the particular problem of under-employment equilibrium. He argued that under such circumstances one might run into something he called absolute liquidity preference. His analysis concentrated on the relation between money, on the one hand, and bonds or other fixed interest securities, on the other. He argued that bonds were the closest substitute for money, and that in the first instance one could regard people as choosing between holding their wealth in the form of money or holding it in the form of bonds. The cost of holding wealth in the form of money was the interest that could otherwise be received on bonds. The higher the rate of interest, the less money people would want to hold and vice versa. But, Keynes said, there exists some rate of interest so low that if the rate were forced still lower nobody would hold any bonds.

At that interest rate, liquidity preference is absolute. At that rate of interest, if more money were introduced into the economy people would try to get rid of the money by buying bonds. This, however, would tend to lower the rate of interest. But even the slightest decline in the rate of interest would lead people to hold money instead. So, said Keynes, under such circumstances, with the interest rate so low that people were indifferent whether they held money or bonds, no matter what quantity of the one they held or what quantity of the other, changes in the stock of money would have no effect on anything. If the quantity of money were increased by buying bonds, for example, the only effect would be that people would substitute money for bonds. If the quantity of money were decreased by selling bonds, then the opposite effect would occur.

Keynes did not of course deny the validity of the famous quantity equation, $MV = PT$. That is an identity which is a question of arithmetic not of theory. What he said, in effect, was that in conditions of under-employment, V (velocity) is a very unstable, passive magnitude. If M (quantity of money) increases, V will go down and the product will not change. If M decreases, V will go up and the product will not change. I emphasize this point in order to make clear that the question at issue is an empirical question and not a theoretical question.

There was never any dispute on a purely theoretical level in this respect between Keynes and the quantity theorists.

Keynes himself felt that such a position of unstable velocity would occur only under conditions of under-employment equilibrium. He said that under conditions of inflation the quantity theory comes into its own. But some of his disciples went much farther. They argued that even under conditions less extreme than those of absolute liquidity preference, changes in the stock of money would not have any significant effect. It is true, they said, that under such circumstances changes in the stock of money would lead to changes in interest rates. But, changes in interest rates, they argued, would have little effect on real flows of spending: the amounts of money people want to invest in projects is determined by considerations other than the rate of the interest they have to pay; in technical language, the demand for investment is highly inelastic with respect to the interest rate. And consequently, they argued that, even under conditions of full employment or of inflation, changes in the quantity of money are of minor importance. An increase in M would tend to lower the interest rate a little, but this in turn would have very slight effect in expanding investment. And hence, they argued, one would find again that V of the MV equation fluctuated widely, tending to offset changes in M.

The general presumption among most economists at the end of the war was that the postwar problem was going to be depression and unemployment. The problem was going to be to stimulate sufficient investment and sufficient consumption to prevent substantial unemployment. The appropriate monetary policy in their view was very simple. The monetary authorities should keep money plentiful so as to keep interest rates low. Of course, interest rates according to this view did not make much difference, but insofar as they had any effect it would be in the direction of expanding investment slightly and hence contributing to the investment that would be urgently needed to offset deficiencies of demand. Nearly two decades have elapsed since then, and it is hard now to remember how widespread these views were and how strongly they were held by people in responsible positions, as well as by economists in general. For example, in 1945, E. A. Goldenweiser who at this time was the Director of Research of the Federal Reserve Board's Division of Research and Statistics wrote:

This country will have to adjust itself to a 2½ per cent interest rate as the return on safe, long-time money, because the time has come when returns on pioneering capital can no longer be unlimited as they were in the past.[1]

[1] "Postwar Problems and Policies," *Federal Reserve Bulletin*, February 1945, p. 117.

This whole approach was shattered by the brute evidence of experience. In the first place, and most important, the problem of the postwar world turned out to be inflation and not deflation. Country after country which adopted an easy money policy because of the views I have just described discovered that it was faced with rising prices. Equally important, no country succeeded in stopping inflation without taking measures which had the effect of controlling the quantity of money. Italy stopped inflation in 1947. How? By measures designed to hold down the quantity of money. The experience was repeated in Germany after the monetary reform in 1948; in the United States after the Federal Reserve-Treasury Accord in 1951; in Britain, when it restored orthodox monetary policy in 1951 to keep prices down; in Greece; and in France, a recent (1960) addition to the list. Those countries which continued to follow low interest rate policies or continued to increase the quantity of money rapidly, continued to suffer inflation, whatever other measures they took.

Though this experience was in many ways the most important single factor that produced a radical change in attitudes toward money, it was reinforced by several other factors. One was the developments which were proceeding in the world of economic theory in the analysis and re-examination of the body of doctrine which had emerged out of the Keynesian revolution. The most important element here was the emphasis on the role of real cash balances in affecting flows of expenditures, first pointed out by Haberler and then by Pigou in several articles which received more attention. An essential element of the Keynesian approach has been the view that only substitution between money and bonds is important, that real goods or real expenditures are not an important substitute for cash balances, and that when cash balances are larger than people desire to hold, they alter solely their desired holdings of other securities. The intellectual importance of the forces brought to the fore by Haberler and Pigou was the emphasis they placed on the possibility of substitution between cash on the one hand and real flows of expenditures on the other. This contributed to a re-emphasis on the role of money.

Another development that had the same effect, in a negative way, was the disillusionment with fiscal policy. The counterpart of the Keynesian disregard for money was the emphasis placed on fiscal policy as the key element in controlling the level of aggregate demand. In the United States in particular, governmental expenditures have proved to be the most unstable element in the economy in the postwar years, and they have been unstable in a way that has tended to increase fluctuations rather than to decrease them. It has proved to be extremely hard to change expenditures and receipts in advance in such a way as to offset other forces making for fluctuations. This led to re-emphasis on monetary policy as a more flexible instrument which could be used in a sensitive way.

DEVELOPMENTS IN MONETARY THEORY

Let me turn now to the developments in monetary theory that have followed this postwar experience and the re-emphasis on money as an important economic magnitude. One development has been that many economists who continue to use the Keynesian apparatus have revised their empirical presumptions. These economists now say that liquidity preference is seldom absolute, that there is some elasticity in the demand for cash balances, and that if there are changes in the stock of money there will be changes in interest rates. They say also that investment is not completely insensitive to interest rates, that when borrowing becomes more expensive, the amount spent on investment is reduced, and conversely. This view goes along with the attitude that, while money is more important than these economists used to think it was, monetary policy still can influence income only directly. A change in the stock of money may affect the interest rate, the interest rate may affect investment, the change in investment may affect income, but it is only by this indirect route, the argument runs, that monetary changes have an effect on economic change.

This is purely a semantic question of how one wants to describe the channels of influence. The crucial issue is the empirical one of whether in fact the links between money and income are more stable and more regular than the links between investment and income. And it is on this empirical issue that the postwar evidence spoke very strongly and led to a re-examination of the role of money.

A more fundamental and more basic development in monetary theory has been the reformulation of the quantity theory of money in a way much influenced by the Keynesian liquidity preference analysis. That analysis emphasizes money as an asset that can be compared with other assets; its emphasis is on what is called "portfolio analysis," analysis of the structure of peoples' balance sheets, of the kinds of assets they want to hold. This emphasis looks at monetary theory as part of capital theory, or the theory of wealth. This is a rather different emphasis than that derived from earlier approaches, particularly that of Irving Fisher, which put major emphasis on transactions and on money as a mechanical medium of exchange somehow connected with the transaction process.

The emphasis on money as an asset has gone in two different directions. On the one hand, it has led to emphasis on *near moneys*, as an alternative source of liquidity. One example is the work of Gurley and Shaw and their analysis of financial intermediaries as providing money substitutes. Another example, in its most extreme form, is in the Radcliffe Committee report which attempts to widen the concept of money to make it synonymous with the concept of liquidity, itself an undefined term which covers the universe. My own view is that this particular trail toward widening the range of reference of the concept of money is a false trail. It will peter out and will not in fact be followed. The reaction which the Radcliffe Committee analysis has received among academic economists and others seems to suggest that my opinion is widely shared.

The other direction in which the emphasis on money as an asset has led is toward the development of a theory of the demand for money along the same lines as the theory of the demand for other assets and for commodities and services. In such a theory, one asks what determines the amount of cash balances that people want to hold. Here it is essential to distinguish between cash balances in two senses: nominal cash balances, the nominal quantity of money as defined in terms of monetary units such as drachmas, dollars, and so forth; and real cash balances, the real stock of money as defined in terms of command over goods and services.

The essential feature of the quantity theory of money in both its older versions and its more recent and modern version is the assertion that what really matters to people is not the number of things called drachmas or dollars they hold but the real stock of money they have, the command which those pieces of paper give them over goods and services. In talking about the demand for money, one must ask what determines the command over goods and services that people want to keep in the form of money. For example, take a very simple definition of money as consisting only of currency, of the pieces of paper we carry in our pockets. We must then ask what determines whether the amount that people hold is on the average equal to a little over six weeks' income, as it is in Greece, or a little over four weeks' income, as it is in the United States, or five weeks' income, as it is in Turkey. Thus, when we talk about the demand for money, we must be talking about the demand for real balances in the sense of command over goods and services, and not about nominal balances.

In the theory of demand as it has been developed, the key variables include *first*, wealth or some counterpart of wealth, for example, income or, preferably, something like permanent income which is a better index of wealth than measured income. Because the problem is one of a balance sheet, the first restriction is that there is a certain total amount of wealth which must be held in the form of money, bonds, or other securities, houses, automobiles, or other physical goods, or in the form of human earning capacity. Hence, income or wealth acts as a restraint in determining the demand for money in exactly the same way that the total income people have operates to determine their demand for shoes, hats, or coats by setting a limit to aggregate expenditures. The *second* set of variables that is important is the rates of return on substitute forms of holding money. Here, the most important thing that has happened has been a tendency to move away from the division of assets into money and bonds that Keynes emphasized, into a more pluralistic division of wealth, not only into bonds but also into equities and real assets. The relevant variables therefore are the expected rate of return on bonds, the expected rate of return on equities, and the expected rate of return on real property, and each of these may of course be multiplied by considering different specific assets of each type. A major component of the expected rate of return on real property is the rate of change in prices. It is of primary importance when there is extensive inflation or deflation.

I should like to stress the significance of the emphasis on money as one among many assets, not only for the kinds of variables that people consider as affecting the demand for money, but also for the process of adjustment. According to the earlier view of money as primarily a medium of exchange, as something which is used to facilitate transactions between people, it was fairly natural to think of a short link between changes in the stock of money and changes in the expenditure and to think of the effects of changes in the stock of money as occurring very promptly. On the other hand, according to the more recent emphasis, money is something more basic than a medium of transactions; it is something which enables people to separate the act of purchase from the act of sale. From this point of view, the role of money is to serve as a temporary abode of purchasing power. It is this view that is fostered by considering money as an asset or as part of wealth.

Looked at in this way, it is plausible that there will be a more indirect and complicated process of adjustment to a change in the stock of money than looked at the other way. Moreover, it seems plausible that it will take a much longer time for the adjustment to be completed. Suppose there is a change in the stock of money. This is a change in the balance sheet. It takes time for people to readjust their balance sheets. The first thing people will do is to try to purchase other assets. As they make these purchases, they change the price of those assets. As they change the prices of those assets, there is a tendency for the effect to spread further. The ripples spread out as they do on a lake. But as prices of assets change, on the one hand, and flow, on the other, the *relative* price of assets also changes. And now people may adjust their portfolios not only by exchanging assets but by using current income to add to, or current expenditures to subtract from, certain of their assets and liabilities. In consequence, I think that this reformulation of monetary theory with its emphasis on monetary theory as a branch of the theory of wealth has very important implications for the process of adjustment and for the problem of time lags.

DEVELOPMENTS IN MONETARY POLICY

Policy does not always have a close relation to theory. The world of the academic halls and the world of policy makers often seems to move on two wholly different levels with little contact between them. The developments in postwar monetary policy have not been the same throughout the world. However, the makers of monetary policy in different countries have been in closer and more systematic touch with one another than the monetary theorists. As a result, I think one can speak to some extent of general trends in policy without necessarily referring to the country.

As I indicated earlier, I think two features dominate and characterize the trends in postwar monetary policy. The first is the shift of emphasis away from credit policy and toward monetary policy. I think this is a distinction of first-rate importance, and yet one which is much neglected. Therefore let me say a word about the meaning of this distinction. When I refer to credit policy, I mean the effect of the actions of monetary authorities on rates of interest, terms of lending, the ease with which people can borrow, and conditions in the credit markets. When I refer to monetary policy, I mean the effect of the actions of monetary authorities on the stock of money—on the number of pieces of paper in people's pockets, or the quantity of deposits on the books of banks.

Policy makers, and central bankers in particular, have for centuries concentrated on credit policy and paid little attention to monetary policy. The Keynesian analysis, emphasizing interest rates as opposed to the stock of money, is only the latest rationalization of that concentration. The most important earlier rationalization was the so-called real bills doctrine. The belief is still common among central bankers today that, if credit were somehow issued in relation to productive business activities, then the quantity of money could be left to itself. This notion of the real bills doctrine goes back hundreds of years; it is endemic with central bankers today. It understandably derives from their close connection with commercial banking, but it is basically fallacious.

The emphasis on credit policy was closely linked with the emphasis at the end of the war on qualitative controls. If what matters is who borrows and at what rate, then it is quite natural to be concerned with controlling the specific use of credit and the specific application of it. In the United States, for example, emphasis on credit policy was linked with emphasis on margin controls on the stock market, and with controls over real estate credit and instalment credit. In Britain, it was linked with controls over hire purchase credit. In each of these cases, there was a qualitative policy concerned with credit conditions. The failure of the easy money policy and of these techniques of qualitative control promoted a shift both toward less emphasis on controlling specific rates of return and toward more emphasis on controlling the total quantity of money.

The distinction that I am making between credit and monetary policy may seem like a purely academic one of no great practical importance. Nothing could be farther from the truth. Let me cite the most striking example that I know; namely, the experience of the United States in the great depression from 1929 to 1933. Throughout that period the Federal Reserve System was never concerned with the quantity of money. It did not in fact publish monthly figures of the quantity of money until the 1940's. Indeed, the first mention in Federal Reserve literature of the quantity of money as a criterion of policy was in the 1950's. Prior to that time there was much emphasis upon easy or tight money, by which was meant low or high interest rates. There was much emphasis on the availability of loans, but there was no emphasis and no concern with the quantity of money.

If there had been concern with the quantity of money *as such*, we could not have had the great depression of 1929–1933 in the form in which we had it. If the Federal Reserve System had been concerned with monetary policy in the sense in which I have just defined it, it literally would have been impossible for the System to have allowed the quantity of money in the United States to decline from 1929 to 1933 by a third, the largest decline in the history of the United States in that length of time. In reading many of the internal papers of the Federal Reserve Board during that period, the communications between the various governors of the Federal Reserve Banks and the Board of Governors, and so forth, I have been struck with the lack of any quantitative criterion of policy. There are vague expressions about letting the market forces operate. There are comments about "easy" money or "tight" money but no indication of precisely how a determination is to be made whether money is "easy" or "tight." This distinction between emphasis on credit policy and emphasis on monetary policy is a distinction of great importance in the monetary history of the United States, and I think also in the monetary history of other countries.

The failure of the easy money policy was reinforced by another factor which promoted a shift in policy away from qualitative measures involving control of particular forms of credit, and toward quantitative measures involving concern with changes in the stock of money. This other factor was a reduction of exchange controls and quantitative restrictions on international trade, as in the postwar period one country after another began to improve its international position. There was a move toward convertibility in international payments. This shift toward convertibility led to a reduction of emphasis on qualitative direct controls and toward increased emphasis on general measures that would affect the course of events through altering the conditions under which people engaged in trade. In turn, this led to a final development in monetary policy—the renewed concern about the relation between internal monetary policy and external policy, the problem of the balance of payments. In this area we have had, most surprisingly of all I think, a return to an earlier era of something approximating a gold standard.

In the immediate postwar period, concern with the balance of payments tended to be centered in the countries of Western Europe that were having a so-called dollar shortage. Those countries were at that time facing the problem of recurrent drains of their international reserves. They were in the position of having somehow to restrain their residents from converting their local currencies into foreign currencies. Those were also the countries that emerged from the war with fairly extensive exchange controls and direct restrictions on trade. And thus in the first years after the war the solution to this problem took the form of direct control rather than of monetary policy.

At that time the United States was in a very different position. It was gaining gold and it was able to take the position that it could conduct its monetary policy entirely in terms of internal conditions and need pay no attention to the effects that its policies had abroad. Of course, that was not what happened. There is little doubt that during the immediate postwar period the ease in the U.S. gold position contributed toward a greater readiness to accept inflation than would otherwise have prevailed, so that the ease in the international balance produced a relatively easier monetary policy than we otherwise would have had. But once the United States started selling gold on net instead of buying gold on net, to use a more accurate term than the term "losing gold," the situation changed drastically and the United States itself became much more concerned with the effect of monetary policy and much more striven toward a pre-World War I gold standard approach.

In recent years, the concern with the international balance of payments has given rise to greater cooperation among central banks. They have tried to develop techniques which will assure that any temporary drains on the reserves of one country will be matched by offsetting movements by central banks in the other countries. Despite the immense amount of good will and of human ingenuity that has gone into this effort to avoid payments difficulties through central bank cooperation, I must confess that I regard the tendency as an exceedingly dangerous one. The danger is that the arrangements developed will provide an effective system for smoothing minor difficulties but only at the cost of permitting them to develop into major ones.

I am struck by the analogy between what is now happening in this respect and what happened in the United States between 1919 and 1939. The United States in that earlier period developed a monetary system which turned out to be an effective device for smoothing minor difficulties. The system was highly successful in helping to make the years from 1922 to 1929 relatively stable. But this stability was purchased at the cost of major difficulties from 1920 to 1921, from 1929 to 1933, and again from 1937 to 1938. I very much fear that the same results may emerge from present trends toward international cooperation among central banks, because these measures do not go to the root of the problem of international adjustment.

In international financial arrangements, as in personal finances, the problem of having enough liquid assets to meet temporary drains must be sharply distinguished from the adjustment to changed circumstances. The central bank arrangements look only to providing liquidity for temporary drains. More fundamental adjustment to changed circumstances can come only through either: (1) domestic monetary and fiscal policy directed toward holding down or reducing domestic prices relative to foreign prices when the country is experiencing a surplus, or toward permitting domestic prices to rise relative to foreign prices when the country is experiencing a surplus; (2) changes in exchange rates to achieve a similar alteration in the relative level of domestic and foreign prices when expressed in the same currency; or (3) direct measures designed to alter the flows of receipts or expenditures, such as changes in tariffs, subsidies, and quotas, direct or indirect control of capital movements, restrictions on foreign aid or other governmental expenditures, extending ultimately to that full panoply of foreign exchange controls that strangled Western Europe after the war and remains today one of our most unfortunate gifts to many underdeveloped countries.

The great danger is that central bank cooperation and other means to enlarge liquidity, by providing palliatives that can at best smooth over temporary imbalances, will encourage countries to postpone undertaking such fundamental adjustments to changed circumstances. The consequences will be to allow minor imbalances to accumulate into major ones; to convert situations that could have been corrected by gradual and minor monetary tightness or ease, or by small movements in exchange rates, into situations that would require major changes in monetary policy or exchange rates. The consequence is likely to be not only international financial crises, but also the encouragement of the use of the third method of adjustment, direct controls. Paradoxically, most economists and most policy makers would agree that it is the worst of the three; yet it is the one that has most regularly been resorted to in the postwar period.

These developments in monetary policy are much more difficult to pin down precisely than the developments in monetary theory, as may be expected from the fact that monetary policy is and must be much more a matter of opportunism, of day-to-day adjustment, of meeting the particular problems of the time. The theorist can sit in his ivory tower and make sure that his structure is coherent and consistent. This is, I must say, an advantage of the theorist and a great disadvantage of the policy maker, and not the other way around. But I think it is clear that we are likely to see in the future still further developments in monetary policy.

There is almost invariably a long cultural lag before developments in theory manifest themselves in policy. If you were to look at what is being proposed today in domestic policy in the United States, you would say that my analysis of changes in the field of monetary theory must be a figment of my imagination. The policy proposals that are being made in the United States today are all reflections of the ideas of the late 1930's, or at the latest of the early 1940's. That is natural and widespread. The people who make policy, who are involved in policy formation, are inevitably people who got their training and their education and their attitudes some 20 or more years earlier. This is a special case of a much more general phenomenon. I am sure all are aware of that famous book by A. V. Dicey on *Law and Public Opinion in the*

19th Century, the main thesis of which is precisely that trends in ideas take about 20 years before they are effective in the world of action. What is happening in the United States today is a dramatic illustration of his thesis. And so I expect that monetary policy will in the course of the next 20 years show some radical changes as a result of the changes I have described in monetary theory.

FIVE

CENTRAL BANKING
AND MONETARY POLICY

M OST money and banking textbooks have strong and lucid chapters on the history and structure of the Federal Reserve System, and quite adequate discussions of central bank controls and policies.

In order to add flavor to these topics, the selections in this section are designed to point up a number of controversial aspects of Federal Reserve structure and policy.

In the past decade or so, there has developed an increasing concern, chiefly among monetary economists, over the role and effectiveness of the monetary authorities. To some extent this criticism has been intramural—some economists believe the Federal Reserve is ineffective, others believe that it is perversely so, and still others that it is *too* effective. Perhaps all have been right at one time or another, since the stabilizing record of the System has been spotted with major errors, usually seen in retrospect, but indicating that further discussion of the central bank's role in our economy is not out of order.

THE OBJECTIVES

AND INSTRUMENTAL ROLE

OF MONETARY POLICY

HARRY G. JOHNSON

In pre-Keynesian days, monetary policy was the single established instrument of aggregative economic policy, and price stability was its established objective. The Keynesian revolution introduced an alternative instrument, fiscal policy, and a second objective, maintenance of full employment, which might conflict with the objective of price stability. Since the war, debt management has been added almost universally to the list of instruments; and since the middle 1950's many economists have added a third item—adequately rapid economic growth —to the list of objectives. In recent years the balance-of-payments problem has been forcing the admission of a fourth objective—international balance—and may eventually establish a fourth instrument—foreign economic policy.

Recognition of several objectives of economic policy introduces the possibility of a conflict of objectives requiring resolution by a compromise. This possibility and its implications have been more clearly recognized elsewhere than in the United States, where there has been a tendency to evade the issue by denying the possibility of conflict [1] or

[1] This can always be done by giving priority to one objective and defining the others in terms that implicitly impose consistency with the favored objective; an example is the concept of "sustainable economic growth" promulgated by the Federal Reserve System.

Reprinted from "Monetary Theory and Policy," The American Economic Review, June 1962, pp. 335–384.

[199]

by insisting that conflicts be eliminated by some other means than sacrifice of the achievement of any of the objectives.

The availability of alternative policy instruments introduces the question of their absolute and comparative effectiveness; research on this range of problems has been undertaken by a number of economists, but has not progressed far towards an accepted body of knowledge. As already mentioned, monetary policy since 1951 has resumed a large part of the responsibility for short-run economic stabilization—a consequence of both the inadaptability of the budgetary process to the requirements of a flexible fiscal policy and the domination of the budget by other objectives of national policy than stabilization. Reliance on monetary policy for this purpose has raised the question of how effectively the task is likely to be performed. The argument for using monetary policy is usually expressed in terms of the "flexibility" of monetary policy, by which is often meant no more than that monetary policy can be changed quickly. But the real issues are whether the monetary authorities are likely to take appropriate action at the right time, and whether the effects of monetary action on the economy occur soon enough and reliably enough to have a significant stabilizing effect.

As to the first question, there is general agreement that the Federal Reserve has committed errors in the timing, extent and duration of policy changes. Most economists seem inclined to trust the System to improve its performance with experience and the benefit of their criticism. Some, however, are so distrustful of discretionary authority in principle, or so skeptical of the feasibility of effective stabilization by monetary means, as to advocate that the Federal Reserve should not attempt short-run stabilization, but should confine itself (or be confined) to expanding the money supply at a steady rate appropriate to the growth of the economy. The proposal to substitute a monetary rule for the discretion of the monetary authority is not of course new—Henry Simons' classic statement of the case for it appeared in the 1930's—but the definition of the rule in terms of the rate of monetary expansion rather than stability of a price index reflects both the modern concern with growth and a more sophisticated understanding of the stabilization problem.

The question of the extent of the stabilizing effect that monetary action may be expected to achieve was first raised, at the formal theoretical level, by Friedman, who argued that policies intended to stabilize the economy might well have destabilizing effects because of the lags involved in their operation. Subsequent work and discussion on this aspect of monetary policy has concentrated on the length and variability of the lag in the effect of monetary policy, and has become enmeshed in intricate arguments about the proper way of measuring the lag. Two alternative approaches to the measurement of the lag have been employed, direct estimate and statistical inference. The outstanding example of the first is Thomas Mayer's study of the inflexibility of monetary policy.[2] Mayer estimates the lag in the reaction of investment expenditure and consumer credit outstanding to monetary policy changes, sector by sector, and, taking into account lags in monetary-policy changes and the multiplier process, concludes that monetary policy operates on the economy much too slowly for its effects to be quickly reversed; from a computation of the effect that an optimally-timed monetary policy would have had on the stability of industrial production over six business cycles, he concludes that monetary policy is too inflexible to reduce the fluctuation of industrial production by more than about 5 to 10 per cent on the average.

Statistical inference is also employed in the study of lags in fiscal and monetary policy conducted for the Commission on Money and Credit by Brown, Solow, Ando, and Kareken.[3] These authors claim that Friedman's comparison of turning points in the rate of change of the money stock with turning points in the level of activity involves a methodological *non sequitur*, and find from a comparison of turning points in the rates of change of money with the rate of change of aggregate output that the money stock and aggregate output move roughly simultaneously over the cycle. Their own work attempts to estimate the lag between the indication of a need for a change in monetary policy and the effect of the resulting change in policy on output, and finds that a substantial stabilizing effect is achieved within six to nine months. They also find that fiscal policy operating on disposable income is a more powerful stabilizer, achieving as much as half of its effect within six months.

---

[2] "The Inflexibility of Monetary Policy," *Review of Economics and Statistics*, November 1958, pp. 358–374.

[3] "Lags in Fiscal and Monetary Policy" in *Stabilization Policies*, Research Studies prepared for The Commission on Money and Credit (Englewood Cliffs: Prentice-Hall, 1963), pp. 1–164.

THE POLITICAL STRUCTURE

OF THE FEDERAL RESERVE SYSTEM

MICHAEL D. REAGAN

The author of this article contends that the structure of the Federal Reserve System was created to meet needs that are no longer compelling; at the same time, it fails to meet present-day requirements of monetary policy formulation in a democratic society.

The student whose interest is piqued by the following selection may wish to consult the three-volume Hearings, The Federal Reserve System after Fifty Years, Subcommittee on Domestic Finance, Committee on Banking and Currency, H. R., Washington: Government Printing Office, 1964.

STRUCTURE AND FUNCTIONAL DEVELOPMENT

The Pyramid. The Federal Reserve System can be described as a pyramid having a private base, a mixed middle level and a public apex. At the apex stands the Board of Governors (frequently referred to as the Federal Reserve Board or FRB). Its seven members are appointed by the President, with the consent of the Senate, for fourteen-year, overlapping terms, one term expiring at the end of January in each even-numbered year. Members are removable for cause, but the removal power has not been exercised. In making appointments, the President

Adapted from *Joint Economic Committee, Hearings, Review of the Annual Report of the Federal Reserve System, 1960,* Washington: *Government Printing Office, 1961,* pp. *134–146.*

must give due regard to "fair representation of financial, agricultural, industrial, and commercial interests, and geographical divisions of the country," and not more than one member can be appointed from a single Federal Reserve District. The Chairman is selected by the President for a renewable four-year term. The Board is independent of the appropriations process, for its operating funds come from semi-annual assessments upon the twelve Reserve Banks.

At a level of equivalent authority to the Board itself, but in the "middle" of the public-private pyramid, stands the statutory Federal Open Market Committee. It is composed of all FRB members plus five of the twelve Reserve Bank Presidents, with the President of the New York Reserve Bank always one of the five and the others serving in rotation. The Chairman of the Board of Governors is, by custom, the Chairman of the Committee.

The Reserve Banks are quasi-public institutions: their capital stock is subscribed by the member banks—all national banks and about one-third of the state-chartered banks, at the statutory rate of 6 per cent (one-half paid in) of their capital and surplus—but their role is public as a part of the central banking system. While a 6 per cent cumulative dividend is paid to the member-bank stockholders, and a surplus equal to twice the paid-in capital has been accumulated, the remainder of the Reserve Banks' now sizable earnings is surrendered to the national Treasury.

The Reserve Bank Presidents are not government appointees; they are elected by the boards of directors of their respective Banks, subject to FRB veto; and their compensation—far above civil service levels—is fixed in the same way. Thus their selection is initially private, but with public supervision. The Board of Directors of each Reserve Bank consists of nine persons, six of whom are elected by the member commercial banks of that District (these banks, the "owners" of the Reserve Banks, constituting the private base of the pyramid), while three (including the Chairman and Deputy Chairman) are appointed by the FRB in Washington.

Off to the side stands the final element of statutory organization, the Federal Advisory Council (FAC). This group of twelve men is composed of one commercial-banker representative from each District annually elected by the respective regional Boards. The FAC meets quarterly with the FRB to discuss general business conditions and may make recommendations to the Board on matters of policy. The twelve Reserve Bank Presidents constitute a nonstatutory Conference of Presidents that meets three times a year; a Conference of Reserve Bank Chairmen meets annually with the FRB.

The Location of Policy Powers. The three major tools of monetary policy are the rediscount rate charged by Reserve Banks to member bank borrowers on their loans from the System; the setting of reserve requirement levels for the member banks; and—most important today —open market operations in securities of the federal government. Decisions regarding each of these instruments is formally located in a different organ of the System, although (as will be developed below) channels for advice and influence cause a mingling of the decisional powers in fact. The levels of reserve requirements are set by the FRB; open market policy is a function of the Open Market Committee (OMC), thus providing the regional and quasi-private elements of the System with formal access to the heart of monetary policy formation; and the Reserve Bank Boards of Directors share with the FRB formal authority over the discount rate. The rate is "established" every fourteen days by each regional Bank, but "subject to the review and determination" of the Board of Governors. In addition the FRB shares with the Comptroller of the Currency, the FDIC and state authorities, a very considerable list of regulatory and supervisory powers over member banks and their officers.

Functional Change Since 1913. When established, the Federal Reserve System was thought of as exercising only the technical function of quasi-automatic adjustment of an elastic currency supply to the fluctuating needs of commerce and industry. The System was pictured as a "cooperative enterprise" among bankers for the purpose of increasing the security of banks and providing them with a reservoir of emergency resources. To this day the Federal Reserve Act mandate reflects this view: it instructs that the discount rate and open market policy shall be operated with "a view of accommodating commerce and business," and that reserve requirements shall be handled so as to prevent "excessive use of credit for the purchase or carrying of securities." Nothing in the Act relates the monetary authority to the function of national economic stabilization; yet this is its prime task today.

In 1913, it was not foreseen that the techniques of monetary policy would become instruments of economic stabilization with their consequences for employment, growth and price stability overtaking their specific banking objectives in importance. Yet this is what has happened, beginning in the Twenties but more strongly and with more explicit recognition in the policy process since the Great Crash. With this shift, the operation of the Federal Reserve System necessarily moved into the political mainstream, for the goal of stabilization requires making choices among alternatives that have important and visible consequences for substantial interests and community values. Once macro-economic policy had become the primary *raison d'être* of the System, the breadth of interests involved became coterminous with the nation, not just with the bankers; and monetary policy, as well as depositors' safety, became a public concern rather than a private convenience.

A corollary of the rise of stabilization to stage center is that the scope of FRB action has become essentially national, belying the assumption of relative regional independence that underlay the original legislation. Divergent policies for each region become undesirable—even impossible—if national stabilization is to be achieved in an increasingly interdependent national economy.

ROLES AND INTERESTS OF THE COMPONENTS

We turn now to a comparison of formal roles and interest composition with the informal roles and interest-impact of each level of the System's structure.

The Commercial Bank Base. The formal role of the member banks is that of an electoral constituency in the selection of six of the nine directors for each Reserve Bank. While the member banks have no direct policy voice, this electoral role originally gave them an indirect one, on the assumption that the regional boards would be policy-making bodies through their authority over the discount rate. That authority is negligible today. Furthermore, the "ownership" of the Reserve Banks by the commercial banks is symbolic; they do not exercise the proprietary control associated with the concept of ownership nor share, beyond the statutory dividend, in Reserve Bank "profits." As in the large, publicly held corporation, ownership and control have been divorced. No doubt the FRB, for example in the adjustment of reserve requirements, has been solicitous for the maintenance and improvement of commercial bank earnings. But if the record of the other "independent" regulatory commissions is any guide, this would have been true regardless of their stockholdings in the Reserve Banks.

Bank ownership and election at the base are therefore devoid of substantive significance, despite the superficial appearance of private bank control that the formal arrangement creates.

Reserve Bank Boards of Directors. The Reserve Bank Boards' authority to set rediscount rates, subject to "review and determination" by the FRB, is considerably diminished by the ultimate formal authority of the latter, for "determination" includes final decision and even initiation of rate changes. It is further reduced by informal practice: to avoid the embarrassments of public disputes, discount rate policy is discussed at OMC meetings and the determination settled upon therein is usually followed through uniformly at the next meetings of the respective regional Boards of Directors. The special formalities are "of little significance; rediscount policy is made in much the same way and on essentially the same considerations as in reserve and open-market policy." [1] The nationalization of function has thus removed the basis for the assumption of regional autonomy that underlay the original grant of authority to the Reserve Banks. The major tasks of the Directors are now to provide information on regional conditions for OMC and the FRB to take into account, and to serve as a communications and public relations link between the System and local communities—both the general community and the specific "communities" of commercial banking, industry, merchants and other financial institutions. They do not exercise important substantive authority.

This may be fortunate in view of the structure of interests that prevails at this level. For the range of interests, reflecting the banker-business orientation of 1913, is narrow by legal specification and narrower still in fact. By statute, each regional Board has three classes of membership: Class A consists of three commercial bankers; Class B of three men active in commerce, agriculture or "some other industrial pursuit"; and Class C, without occupational restriction. Class C members are appointed by the FRB; the others are elected by the member banks of each region.

Class A directors are elected by a method that groups the member-bank stockholders into size categories for voting purposes and assures the selection of one director from a large bank, one from a middle-sized bank and one from a small bank within the District. Informally, Classes B and C tend to be quite similar. Both are dominated by executives of manufacturing firms, utilities, oil and chemical firms, and large distributors—although Class C also includes an occasional academic economist or publisher. Very large firms predominate; very small firms, "family farmers," and labor are not represented. The list of Directors reads like a *Who's Who* of American industry.

The propriety of excluding other segments of the economy from these Boards is not a substantively important question at present because of the decline in the Board's authority, though the appearances could themselves become a political issue. But it is worth asking what functional value this elaborate structure possesses and whether the Boards

[1] G. L. Bach, *Federal Reserve Policy-Making* (New York: 1950), pp. 81–82.

would be missed if they were simply abandoned. The informational role of the Directors could be as well—perhaps better—performed by the Reserve Bank Presidents, who are full-time officials in close daily contact with their districts.

The Reserve Bank Presidents. The Presidents, by virtue of the membership of five of their number on the OMC (and the participation of all twelve in OMC discussions) are more significantly related to the policy process than are their nominal superiors, the regional Boards.

Selection of the President is by the respective Boards, but subject to FRB veto: initially private but finally public. Increasingly, they are men with substantial Reserve System experience. Two-thirds of the incumbents have had such experience; one-third have come to their posts from careers in commercial banking. Their daily contacts are with private bankers and one observer suggests that they have been "inclined to favor more cautious, mild policies that would be less disturbing to the normal courses of banking and the money markets" than has the FRB.[2]

As a statutory minority on the OMC, the views of the Presidents cannot be controlling in themselves. In the apparently unlikely event of a split within the FRB segment of the Committee, however, a solid front by the five President-members would enable them to determine public policy. Since they are not appointed by the President, nor removable for policy differences with either the President or the FRB within their five-year terms, the present structure allows the possibility that policy with a highly-charged political potential may be made by men who lack even indirect accountability to the national public affected. Former FRB Chairman Marriner Eccles has pointed out the uniqueness of the arrangement in these words: "there is no other major governmental power entrusted to a Federal agency composed in part of representatives of the organizations which are the subject of regulation by that agency." [3]

The situation of the Reserve Presidents reverses that of the regional Boards: while the latter's structurally important place has been downgraded by loss of function, the former's structurally inferior position has been upgraded by increased authority.

The Board of Governors and the Board Chairman. The gap between formal and informal roles in the Federal Reserve is readily appar-

---

[2] Bach, pp. 57–58.
[3] Joint (Douglas) Committee on the Economic Report, *Hearings, Monetary, Credit and Fiscal Policies,* 81st Congress, first session, 1949, p. 221.

ent at the FRB level. By statute, it controls by itself only one of the major monetary instruments, the setting of reserve requirements. In fact, it is in a position to, and does, exercise authority in varying degree over all three instruments of policy—and is popularly recognized as *the* monetary policy authority. Further, the effective voice within the Board is that of the Chairman, despite the formal equality of all seven Members—and this too is popularly recognized.

The Board has final authority over discount rates through its power to "review and determine" the decisions of the Reserve Directors. The Members of the FRB constitute a seven-to-five majority in the OMC and thus—barring defections—control the most important of monetary tools. In fact, decisions on all three instruments of policy are taken on the basis of discussion within OMC. Since 1955 the Committee has been used as a "forum, a clearinghouse for all of the aspects of policy determination in the System." [4] Thus the formal distribution of authority is belied in practice by unified consideration. Unified control seems inevitable, since the types of decisions are logically related and it would be unthinkable to have them operating in contradictory directions. Because of the political importance of monetary policy, however, and the desirability of fiscal-monetary coordination, it is questionable whether a twelve-man, quasi-private body provides an adequate or appropriate locus for policy determination; of this, more presently.

The size, length of term, and interest composition of the FRB have been the subject of considerable Congressional attention and have undergone some change over the years. The Board began with five appointed members with staggered ten-year terms and two *ex officio*— Secretary of the Treasury and the Comptroller of the Currency. Both the latter were removed in the 1935 revision of the Banking Act, at the insistence of Senator Carter Glass, then chairman of the Banking and Currency Committee. Now there are seven Presidential appointees, and the term is fourteen years. The Chairman is selected by the President for a four-year renewable term.

Although replacement of the Board by a single executive has been suggested only rarely, many observers, including Chairman Martin, are on record as favoring a smaller group than seven, on the ground that more capable men might then be attracted to the Board. Clearly a seven-man board cannot collectively negotiate effectively with the President, the Secretary of the Treasury, the Chairman of the Council of

---

[4] Chairman Martin in Senate Committee on Finance, *Hearings, Investigation of the Financial Condition of the United States*, 85th Congress, first session, 1957, p. 1260. Cited hereafter as Senate Finance Committee *Hearings*.

Economic Advisers, or the lending agencies whose programs impinge on economic stability; yet coherent policy requires negotiation, consultation and program coordination constantly. Nor would a five-man board be notably better in this respect.

As it is now, the Chairman *is* the Federal Reserve Board for purposes of negotiation. In recent years he has lunched with the Secretary of the Treasury weekly, and has sat in with the President's informal council on economic policy. Congressional committees rely upon the Chairman to speak for the Board and rarely bother to interrogate other Board members. These arrangements apparently work because none of the other members is strong enough, personally or politically, to challenge the Chairman; and also, it seems reasonable to suggest, because there is no alternative save chaos. It is supported too by the tradition of secrecy that attends the actions of central banks, and that is defended as necessary to prevent the exploitation of leaks to private advantage: the fewer the negotiators, the less the likelihood of leaks. The gap between formal structure and the necessities of action reflected in the informal but decisive accretion of power to the Chairman (not only to the incumbent, but to McCabe and Eccles before him) is too great to be bridged by a minor adjustment in the size of the group.

Because of the importance of the Chairmanship, and the necessity for cordial relations between the head of the FRB and the President, Martin and McCabe have both suggested that the four-year term of the Chairman should end on March 31 of the year in which a President begins his term of office. Simpler still is the suggestion that the Chairman's term should be at the President's pleasure, as with most other national regulatory commissions. Whichever way the matter is handled, the need is for a relationship of mutual trust between President and Chairman, both for the sake of consistent economic policy and for democratic accountability through the President as chief elected representative of the public. The present system of a fixed four-year term that (accidentally) does not coincide with Presidential inaugurations is unfortunate on both counts. Moreover, since the staggered 14-year terms of members expire in January of even-numbered years, a new President—even if the Chairman stepped aside—would be confined to the membership he inherits, in choosing a new Chairman, unless some member resigned to create a vacancy.

The policy suitability of geographic and interest qualifications for membership on the Board is a question that would become moot if the Board were replaced by a single head. If not, the answer must be that such qualifications are unsuitable because they are irrelevant and, in their present form, inequitable as well. They are irrelevant because the function of the Board is no longer simply to accommodate business, but to stabilize the national economy. The Board is not engaged in mediating group conflicts where the direct representation of parties-in-interest may be an irresistible political demand, but in a task of economic analysis and political judgment affecting the interests and values of *all* groups and individuals. Given the agency's function, independence of mind and familiarity with government finance and money markets, and with macroeconomic analysis, are far more desirable qualifications than group representation. Sensitivity to basic political currents—a quite different kind of "expertise"—is also pertinent, but not sensitivity only to the needs of a few special segments of the economy. The geographic qualification is equally irrelevant because of the nationalization of economic forces; five of the twelve districts must go unrepresented at any given time, as it is. And some geographic spread would be secured in any event, although without the severely restrictive effects of the current requirement upon the availability of capable men, simply because Presidential politics would work in this direction in the FRB as it does in cabinet and Supreme Court appointments.

The Open Market Committee and Policy Unification. In origin and development, the OMC represents the leading structural response of the Federal Reserve System to its change in function. But the response has not been entirely adequate and further modifications in the structure and scope of authority of the Committee have been advanced from a number of quarters.

When the System began operations, the discount rate and the levels of reserves were thought to be the major tools of policy. As the public debt grew, and as the macroeconomic function of stabilization developed, open market operations by the Reserve Banks increased in importance. The initial structural response came in 1922 when an Open Market Committee was established informally, more under the leadership of President Benjamin Strong of the New York Reserve Bank than of the FRB. The Banking Act of 1933 gave the OMC statutory recognition as a 12-man group, selected by the Reserve Banks, to carry on open market operations under rules laid down by the FRB, thus substantially increasing the power of the national, public component. The Banking Act of 1935, largely written by then-Chairman Eccles as an effort to enhance the centralized, public character of the monetary authority, reorganized the Committee into its present form: the seven FRB members and five Reserve Presidents. (The House version—not enacted —of the 1935 Act would have gone further with the centralizing process by transferring authority for open market operations to the Board alone, with a requirement of consultation with an advisory committee of the regional Banks.) In short, change in economic circumstance, i.e., the growth of a large federal debt as an inescapable component of the nation's financial structure, and the development of a new function led to an institutional addition to the System. Informally, the change has gone one step further: as mentioned earlier, the OMC is used as a forum for discussion of the entire range of monetary actions, not just for decisions regarding the tool that lies formally within its jurisdiction.

The rationale underlying the all-powers-to-the-Board approach can be summarized in the principle that public functions should be lodged in public bodies, and the assertion that open market operations are in no sense regional in character. Eccles has pointed out that the Reserve Presidents are not appointed by or accountable to either the President or Congress, and for this reason argues that their participation in national, public policy formation is inappropriate. Bach has emphasized the national character of open market policy,[5] and he is joined in this view by Jacob Viner, who has said that:

The regional emphasis in central banking is an obsolete relic of the past. No country, not even Canada, which is much more a collection of distinct economic regions than is the United States, has thought it expedient to follow our initial example of introducing regionalism into central banking. Regionalism in the Federal Reserve—or at least its modern defense—perhaps owes more to an unexamined bias in favor of "federalism" as a matter of political ideology than to an empirical examination of the national economic structure.[6]

Macrostabilization as the major function of the System clearly forecloses regional devolution in the making of policy, yet regional circumstances should be considered. The valid claims of regionalism, however, require only a consultative voice, not a decisional one. And public policy, I would agree with Eccles, should not be made by a body containing men who are not accountable to the national public whose welfare is affected by the decisions made.

In *operations*, as distinct from policy determination, regionalism may well possess continued utility; and centralization of policy is entirely compatible with a considerable degree of regional diversification in operations. The point of greatest overlap between national policy

---

[5] Bach, p. 234.
[6] Subcommittee on General Credit Control and Debt Management, Joint Committee on the Economic Report, *Hearings, Monetary Policy and the Management of the Public Debt*, 82nd Congress, second session (1952), p. 756, cited hereafter as General Credit Control Subcommittee *Hearings*, 1952.

and Reserve Bank operations appears to be in the handling of the "discount window," that is, the ease or difficulty with which a member bank may avail itself of the rediscount privilege. A uniform national policy could, for example, suggest "easier" loan conditions in any District whose area rate of unemployment was "x" percentage points above the national average, and thus provide for regional differentiation while maintaining central policy control.

DOES MONETARY HISTORY

REPEAT ITSELF?

WILLIAM McCHESNEY MARTIN, JR.

When economic prospects are at their brightest, the dangers of complacency and recklessness are greatest. As our prosperity proceeds on its record-breaking path, it behooves every one of us to scan the horizon of our national and international economy for danger signals so as to be ready for any storm.

Some eminent observers have recently compared the present with the period preceding the breakdown of the interwar economy, and have warned us of the threats of another Great Depression. We should take these warnings seriously enough to inquire into their merits and to try to profit in the future from the lessons of the past.

And indeed, we find disquieting similarities between our present prosperity and the fabulous twenties.

Then, as now, there had been virtually uninterrupted progress for seven years. And if we disregard some relatively short though severe fluctuations, expansion had been underway for more than a generation —the two longest stretches of that kind since the advent of the industrial age; and each period had been distorted in its passage by an inflationary war and postwar boom.

Then, as now, prosperity had been concentrated in the fully developed countries, and within most of these countries, in the industrialized sectors of the economy.

Then, as now, there was a large increase in private domestic debt;

Address of William McChesney Martin, Jr. to the Alumni Federation of Columbia University, New York, June 1, 1965.

[213]

in fact, the expansion in consumer debt arising out of both residential mortgages and instalment purchases has recently been much faster than in the twenties.

Then, as now, the supply of money and bank credit and the turnover of demand deposits had been continuously growing; and while in the late twenties this growth had occurred with little overall change in gold reserves, this time monetary expansion has been superimposed upon a dwindling gold reserve.

Then, as now, the Federal Reserve had been accused of lack of flexibility in its monetary policy: of insufficient ease in times of economic weakness and of insufficient firmness in times of economic strength.

Then, as now, the world had recovered from the wartime disruption of international trade and finance, and convertibility of the major world currencies at fixed par values had been restored for a number of years.

Then, as now, international indebtedness had risen as fast as domestic debt; recently, in fact, American bank credits to foreigners and foreign holdings of short-term dollar assets have increased faster than in the closing years of the earlier period.

Then, as now, the payments position of the main reserve center—Britain then and the United States now—was uneasy, to say the least; but again, our recent cumulative payments deficits have far exceeded Britain's deficits of the late twenties.

Then, as now, some countries had large and persistent payments surpluses and used their net receipts to increase their short-term reserves rather than to invest in foreign countries.

Then, as now, the most important surplus country, France, had just decided to convert its official holdings of foreign exchange into gold, regardless of the effects of its actions on international liquidity.

Then, as now, there were serious doubts about the appropriate levels of some existing exchange rate relationships, leading periodically to speculative movements of volatile short-term funds.

And most importantly, then as now, many government officials, scholars, and businessmen were convinced that a new economic era had opened, an era in which business fluctuations had become a thing of the past, in which poverty was about to be abolished, and in which perennial economic progress and expansion were assured.

If some of these likenesses seem menacing, we may take comfort in important differences between the present and the interwar situation.

The distribution of our national income now shows less disparity than in the earlier period; in particular, personal incomes, and especially wages and salaries, have kept pace with corporate profits, and this has reduced the danger of investment expanding in excess of consumption needs.

Perhaps related to that better balance, the increase in stock market credit now has been much smaller.

Instead of a gradual decline in wholesale prices and stability in consumer prices, there has now been stability in wholesale prices though consumer prices have been creeping up.

The worst defects in the structure of commercial and investment banking and of business seem to have been corrected—although we are time and again reminded of our failure to eliminate all abuses.

The potentialities of monetary and fiscal policies are, we hope, better understood—although the rise in government expenditures even in times of advancing prosperity threatens to make it difficult to be still more expansionary should a serious decline in private business activity require it.

In spite of the rise in the international flow of public and private credit and investment, business abroad appears in general to be less dependent upon American funds. The recent restraint on the outflow of U.S. capital has had little effect on business activity abroad, in contrast to the paralyzing effect of the cessation of U.S. capital outflows in the late twenties.

While the cold war makes for sources of friction absent in the twenties, we are no longer suffering from the cancer of reparations and war debts.

We have learned the lessons taught by the failure of trade and exchange restrictions, and of beggar-my-neighbor policies in general, although the temptation to backslide is ever present.

We have become aware of our responsibility for helping those less developed countries that seem willing and able to develop their economies—although the poor countries still are not becoming rich as fast as the rich countries are becoming richer.

The International Monetary Fund has proved to be a valuable aid to a better working of the international payments system.

A network of international, regional, and bilateral institutions and arrangements has reduced the danger of lack of international financial communication.

And finally, the experience of the twenties has strengthened the resolution of all responsible leaders, businessmen and statesmen alike, never again to permit a repetition of the disasters of the Great Depression.

But while the spirit is willing, the flesh, in the form of concrete policies, has remained weak. With the best intentions, some experts seem resolved to ignore the lessons of the past.

Economic and political scientists still argue about the factors that converted a stock-exchange crash into the worst depression in our history. But on one point they are agreed: the disastrous impact of the destruction of the international payments system that followed the British decision to devalue sterling in September 1931. At that time, sterling was the kingpin of the world payments system, exactly as the dollar is today. While changes in the par values of other peripheral currencies affected mainly or solely the devaluing countries themselves, the fate of sterling shook the entire world.

This is not wisdom of hindsight. Only a few weeks before the fateful decision was taken, the most eminent economist of the day stated that "for a country in the special circumstances of Great Britain the disadvantages (of devaluation) would greatly outweigh the advantages" and he concurred with his colleagues in rejecting the idea. His name was John Maynard Keynes.

And soon afterwards, another great British economist, Lionel Robbins, declared that "no really impartial observer of world events can do other than regard the abandonment of the Gold Standard by Great Britain as a catastrophe of the first order of magnitude." This was long before the final consequences of that step had become apparent —the political weakening of the West which followed its economic breakdown and which contributed to the success of the Nazi revolution in Germany, and thus eventually to the outbreak of the Second World War and to the emergence of Communism as an imminent threat to world order.

As if neither Keynes, the founder of the anti-classical school of economics, nor Robbins, the leader of the neoclassical school, ever had spoken, some Keynesian and neoclassicist economists—fortunately with little support at home but with encouragement from a few foreign observers—are urging us to follow the British example of 1931 and to act once more in a way that would destroy a payments system based on the fixed gold value of the world's leading currency. In doing so, they not only show that they have not learned from monetary history; they also impute to our generation even less wisdom than was shown in the interwar period.

The British Government in 1931, and the U.S. Administration in 1933, can rightly be accused of underestimating the adverse international effects of the devaluation of the pound and the dollar. But at least they had some plausible domestic grounds for their actions. They were confronted with a degree of unemployment that has hardly ever been experienced either before or after. They were confronted with disastrously falling prices, which made all fixed-interest obligations an intolerable burden on domestic and international commerce. They were confronted with a decline in international liquidity, which seemed to make recovery impossible.

Neither Keynes nor Robbins have denied that, from a purely domestic point of view, there was some sense in devaluation. In the United States of 1933, one worker out of four was unemployed; industrial production was little more than half of normal; farm prices had fallen to less than half of their 1929 level; exports and imports stood at one-third of their 1929 value; capital issues had practically ceased. In such a situation, any remedy, however questionable, seemed better than inaction.

In the Britain of 1931, things were not quite as bleak as in the United States of 1933; but fundamentally, the economic problems were similar. Ever since 1925, the British economy had failed to grow, and by 1931, one out of five workers had become unemployed, exports—far more important for the British economy than for our own—had declined by nearly one-half, and most observers believed that overvaluation of the British pound was largely responsible for all these ills. Can anybody in good faith find any similarity between our position of today and our position of 1933, or even the British position of 1931?

In 1931 and 1933, an increase in the price of gold was recommended in order to raise commodity prices. Today, a gold price increase is recommended as a means to provide the monetary support for world price stability. In 1931 and 1933, an increase in the price of gold was recommended in order to combat deflation; today it is recommended in effect as a means to combat inflation. In 1931 and 1933, an increase in the price of gold was recommended as a desperate cure for national ills regardless of its disintegrating effect on world commerce; today it is recommended as a means to improve integration of international trade and finance. Can there be worse confusion?

True, most advocates of an increase in the price of gold today would prefer action by some international agency or conference to unilateral action of individual countries. But no international agency or conference could prevent gold hoarders from getting windfall profits; could prevent those who hold a devalued currency from suffering corresponding losses; could prevent central banks from feeling defrauded if they had trusted in the repeated declarations of the President of the United States and of the spokesmen of U.S. monetary authorities and kept their reserves in dollars rather than in gold. To this day, the French, Belgian, and Netherlands central banks have not forgotten that the 1931 devaluation of sterling wiped out their capital; and much of the antagonism of those countries against the use of the dollar as an international reserve asset should be traced to the experience of 1931 rather than to anti-American feelings or mere adherence to outdated monetary theories.

But most importantly, no international agency or conference could prevent a sudden large increase in the gold price from having inflationary consequences for those countries that hoarded gold, and deflationary consequences for those that did not. And the gold holding countries are precisely those whose economies are least in need of an inflationary stimulus since they are most prosperous—not prosperous because they are holding gold, but holding gold because they are prosperous; in contrast, those that do not hold gold are most in need of further expansion. Hence the inflationary and deflationary effects of an increase in the price of gold would be most inequitably and most uneconomically distributed among nations.

If we were to accept another sort of advice given by some experts, we might repeat not the mistakes of 1931–1933 but those of earlier years. We are told that a repetition of the disaster of the Great Depression could be averted only, or at least best, by returning to the principles of the so-called classical gold standard. Not only should all settlements in international transactions between central banks be made in gold; but also the domestic monetary policy of central banks should be oriented exclusively to the payments balance, which means to changes in gold reserves. Whenever gold flows out, monetary policy should be tightened; whenever it flows in, it should be eased.

This is not the place to discuss whether this pure form of gold standard theory has ever been translated into practice. I doubt that any central bank has ever completely neglected domestic considerations in its monetary policy. And conversely, we do not need to adhere to an idealized version of the gold standard in order to agree that considerations of international payments balance need to play a large role in monetary policy decisions. But even strict adherence to gold standard principles would not guarantee international payments equilibrium. As a great American economist, John H. Williams, put it in 1937:

For capital movements, the gold standard is not a reliable corrective mechanism. . . . With capital the most volatile item in the balance of payments, it is apt to dominate and to nullify any corrective effects which might otherwise result from the gold standard process of adjustment. . . . It is surely not a coincidence that most booms and depressions, in the nineteenth century as well as in the twentieth, had international capital movements as one of their most prominent features.

Even countries that advocate a return to gold standard practices do not practice what they preach. Gold reserves of some Continental European countries have been rising strongly and continuously for many years, and according to the rules, these countries should follow a clearly expansionary policy. But in order to offset inflationary pressures, they have done exactly the opposite—and who is there to blame a country that wishes to assure domestic financial stability even at the expense of endangering equilibrium in international payments?

But obviously, if we permit one country to violate the rules of the gold standard in order to avert domestic inflation, we must also permit another country to violate those rules in order to avert domestic deflation and unemployment. In other words, we must agree that a country may be justified in avoiding or at least modifying a tightening of monetary policy even though its gold reserves are declining, if otherwise it were to risk precipitating or magnifying a business recession.

True, this deviation from gold-standard rules could be carried too far. Domestic developments might be taken as a pretext to avoid an unpopular monetary move, although the payments situation would seem to demand it and although the action would be unlikely to be damaging to the domestic economy. But the possibility of abuse and error is inherent in all human decision, and just as no sane observer would ascribe infallibility to the decisions of central bankers, neither should he ascribe infallibility to a set of rules. Few experts today would want to argue that it was right for the German Reichsbank in 1931, in the middle of the greatest depression that ever hit Germany, to follow the gold standard rules by raising its discount rate to 7 per cent merely in order to stem an outflow of gold; or that it was right for our own Federal Reserve to take similar restrictive action, for the same reason, in the fall of 1931.

And just as the success of monetary policy cannot be guaranteed by an abdication of discretion in favor of preconceived gold-standard rules, it cannot be guaranteed by following the advice of those who would shift the focus of policy from national agencies to an international institution. Surely, international cooperation should be encouraged and improved whenever possible. And the functions of the International Monetary Fund might well be enlarged so as to reinforce its ability to act as an international lender of last resort and as an arbiter of international good behavior.

But no institutional change can exclude the possibility of conflicts between national and international interests in specific circumstances. Moreover, there is no reason to believe that such conflicts would necessarily be resolved more wisely, more speedily, and with less rancor and dissent if they were fought out in the governing body of some supra-national bank of issue rather than by discussion and negotiation among national authorities.

It is true that such discussion and negotiation may prove fruitless and that inconsistent decisions may be taken on the national level. But similarly, lack of consensus within a supra-national agency may result in a paralysis of its functions, and the effects of such paralysis could well be worse than those of inconsistent national actions.

If then we doubt the wisdom of the three most fashionable recent proposals—to increase the dollar price of gold, to return to pure gold-standard principles, or to delegate monetary policy to an international agency—what should be our position? And what is the outlook for solving present and future difficulties in international monetary relations, and thus for avoiding a repetition of the disasters of 1929–1933?

In my judgment, it is less fruitful to look for institutional changes or for a semi-automatic mechanism that would guarantee perennial prosperity than to draw from interwar experience some simple lessons that could save us from repeating our worst mistakes.

First, most observers agree that to a large extent the disaster of 1929–1933 was a consequence of maladjustments born of the boom of the twenties. Hence, we must continuously be on the alert to prevent a recurrence of maladjustments—even at the risk of being falsely accused of failing to realize the benefits of unbounded expansion. Actually, those of us who warn against speculative and inflationary dangers should return the charge: our common goals of maximum production, employment, and purchasing power can be realized only if we are willing and able to prevent orderly expansion from turning into disorderly boom.

Second, most observers agree that the severity of the Great Depression was largely due to the absence of prompt anti-recession measures. In part, the necessary tools for this were not then available nor were their potentialities fully understood. Today it is easy to understand where observers went wrong 35 years ago. But it is less easy to avoid a repetition of the same mistake; we always prefer to believe what we want to be true rather than what we should know to be true. Here again, we need most of all eternal vigilance. But we must also be ready to admit errors in past judgments and forecasts, and have the courage to express dissenting even though unpopular views, and to advocate necessary remedies.

Third, and most importantly, most observers agree that the severity of the Great Depression was due largely to the lack of understanding of the international implications of national events and policies. Even today, we are more apt to judge and condemn the worldwide implications of nationalistic actions taken by others than to apply the same criteria to our own decisions.

Recognition of the close ties among the individual economies of the free world leads to recognition of the need to maintain freedom of international commerce. This means not only that we must avoid the direct controls of trade and exchange that were characteristic of the time of the Great Depression. It means also that we must avoid any impairment of the value and status of the dollar, which today acts—just as sterling did until its devaluation in 1931—as a universal means of international payment between central banks as well as among individual merchants, bankers, and investors.

If the dollar is to continue to play its role in international commerce, world confidence in its stability must be fully maintained; the world must be convinced that we are resolved to eliminate the long-persistent deficit in our balance of international payments. The measures taken in accordance with the President's program of February 10, 1965, have so far been highly successful. But some of these measures are of a temporary character, and these include the efforts of the financial community to restrain voluntarily the expansion of credit to foreigners. We should not permit the initial success of these efforts to blind us against the need of permanent cure.

Some observers believe that our responsibility for maintaining the international function of the dollar puts an intolerably heavy burden on our monetary policy; that this responsibility prevents us from taking monetary measures which might be considered appropriate for solving domestic problems. I happen to disagree with that view. I believe that the interests of our national economy are in harmony with those of the international community. A stable dollar is indeed the keystone of international trade and finance; but it is also, in my judgment, the keystone of economic growth and prosperity at home.

Yet even if I were wrong in this judgment, and if indeed an occasion arose when we could preserve the international role of the dollar only at the expense of modifying our favored domestic policies— even then we would need to pay attention to the international repercussions of our actions. We must consider these international effects not because of devotion to the ideal of human brotherhood, not because we value the well-being of our neighbors more than our own. We must do so because any harm that would come to international commerce and hence to the rest of the world as a result of the displacement of the dollar would fall back on our own heads. In the present stage of economic development we could not preserve our own prosperity if the rest of the world were caught in the web of depression. Recognition of this interdependence gave rise to the Marshall Plan—in my judgment the greatest achievement of our postwar economic policy.

It should not have taken the Great Depression to bring these simple truths home to us. Today, as we approach the goal of the "Great Society"—to make each of our citizens a self-reliant and productive member of a healthy and progressive economic system—we can disregard these truths even less than we could a generation ago. By heeding them instead, we will have a good chance to avoid another such disaster. If monetary history were to repeat itself, it would be nobody's fault but our own.

WHAT IS THE LESSON OF 1929?

JAMES TOBIN

William McChesney Martin, Jr., chairman of the Federal Reserve System since 1951, has suffered professorial attacks longer and more patiently than most officials. On June 1, he counterattacked at Columbia.

His main message—somewhat veiled but well enough understood in Wall Street—was that the country may need, soon if not now, tighter money and higher interest rates to protect its domestic economic health and its balance of payments. Here Chairman Martin takes issue with a host of critics, mainly academics, some of whom may even have infiltrated Washington. Many think that the current expansion needs further stimulus rather than sterner discipline and that the dollar's prestige abroad already receives too high priority in U.S. policy.

Chairman Martin reads the critics lessons from the history of the twenties and the Great Depression. The irony is that before 1933 Chairman Martin's intellectual and official precursors were firmly in the saddle here and in Europe. Unlike him, they did not have to accommodate or even answer heretical financial views. The mistakes they made were all their own.

A boom is a trying period for a central banker who believes, like Chairman Martin, that recessions and depressions are inescapable retribution for the "maladjustments" of prosperity. Should he let such "excesses" develop? Or should he administer a dose of tight money? This medicine itself may turn prosperity into recession. But the doctor will always assure his perplexed and involuntary patients that they needed it to forestall much worse suffering later.

Reprinted from The New Republic, June 19, 1965, pp. 11–12.

The current expansion is especially trying. It has been proceeding for 52 months without the degree of monetary discipline the Federal Reserve became accustomed to administer in the fifties. Yet it is hard even for the hypersensitive antennae of the central bank to detect any maladjustments or excesses. Since February, 1961, a $150 billion expansion in total annual public and private spending has reduced unemployment from 7 to 4.5 per cent, without noticeably raising prices. In the spring of 1961 Chairman Martin told Congress that unemployment was structural, that it could not be reduced by more spending except at serious risk of bottlenecks and inflation. Similar warnings, similarly unfounded, have been repeated in orthodox financial circles at every step of the recovery. Had they been heeded, the country would have lost millions of jobs and billions of dollars in production and income.

Chairman Martin views economic expansion as a potentially explosive chain reaction, which only the tightest control prevents from running away. Some booms may merit this metaphor. But the current one seems in more danger of ending with a whimper than with a bang. To keep it going has required a succession of carefully timed and gauged stimuli—increases in federal spending, income tax cuts and now excise reductions. "Leaning against the wind," the favorite posture of the Federal Reserve, is not an appropriate stance when the problem is to keep the wind blowing.

What is the lesson of 1929? Chairman Martin says, "to a large extent the disaster of 1929–1933 was a consequence of maladjustments born of the boom of the 'twenties." More likely, the expansion of the twenties—non-inflationary like the present expansion—simply ran out of steam. Instead of taking action to prolong it, Chairman Martin's predecessors tightened credit and raised interest rates. Like many contemporary observers and historians, they paid too much attention to a sideshow, stock market speculation, and too little to the main ring, the real economy.

Certainly no maladjustments or overindulgences occurred in the twenties which preordained that a routine recession in 1929–1930 should become a worldwide economic and political catastrophe. That took incredible sins of omission and commission, all justified in the name of fiscal and financial orthodoxy. In the monetary area, the worst overt sins were *raising* the discount rate in September-October, 1931 (Chairman Martin agrees this was a mistake) and in February, 1933. On both occasions, the Federal Reserve's purpose was to protect the international gold value of the dollar. Chairman Martin was telling history upside down at Columbia when he blamed the severity of the depression on *insufficient* concern for the external status of the dollar. Recovery did not begin in the United States until Roosevelt gave recovery higher priority than the gold standard.

It is true that the position of the dollar as an international reserve currency today is analogous to the role of the pound sterling from 1925 to 1931. But the lesson of the analogy is the opposite of the one Chairman Martin draws. In 1925, through an excess of orthodox zeal and a Colonel Blimp conception of imperial prestige, Britain returned to the gold standard at the 1914 parity of sterling with gold and the dollar. This made British exports too expensive. The result, foreseen by J. M. Keynes, was unemployment, civil strife and depression. Nor did the sacrifices imposed on the British people and their trading partners overseas save for long the gold value of the pound or London's financial prestige. Britain was forced to devalue in 1931, and then British recovery began.

Chairman Martin deplores the ensuing destruction of the international gold standard. But this was the result of the depression, not its cause. And the depression itself owed much of its severity to the British government's previous determination to give the prestige of the pound sterling absolute priority over domestic prosperity.

It is worth noting in passing that then as now France had a "strong" currency because of previous devaluations, that then as now French threats to take gold forced deflationary policies on the United States and Britain, and that then as now France took gold anyway.

This is the history to which Chairman Martin appeals in asking us to place the international "value and status of the dollar" above all other considerations of economic policy. He excoriates "some Keynesian and neoclassical economists" for wishing the United States to follow the British 1931 example. But the issue is not really devaluation. The exchange value of the dollar in the sixties is by no means as unrealistically high as that of the pound in the late twenties. The issue is whether the maintenance of gold-dollar convertibility at the present rate has an absolute priority over all other objectives of United States domestic and foreign policy. Is "going off gold" such an ultimate catastrophe, like nuclear war, that we must avoid at all costs the slightest risk of its occurrence? And if, as Chairman Martin dubiously argues, the result would be worldwide depression, should we not expect more cooperation and forbearance from our allies than we are likely to receive so long as we define the problem, as he does, as a strictly American responsibility?

Both America and the world have more to gain from steady economic progress and sustained full employment in the United States than from timid obsession with foreign confidence in the dollar. Gratifying as it is, our long economic expansion has not yet restored full employment. The social costs of a persistent shortage of jobs can be observed daily in the streets of our cities and in the demoralization of those groups, notably Negroes and teen-agers, who get jobs only when labor markets are tight. In a real sense these people—and the mayors, social workers, police and anti-poverty warriors who must struggle with their problems—are the victims of the shortcomings of fiscal and monetary policy.

The identification of prosperity with imprudent self-indulgence may have an appealing Puritan ring. But it is wholly a vicarious Puritanism, like the austerity of the international financiers who in 1931 forced the Labour government to cut the dole of the unemployed and the salaries of teachers in a vain attempt to "save" the pound. It would be criminal folly to endanger our current economic growth either by an attack on conjectural maladjustments and imagined excesses or by subservience to gold-hungry foreign central banks. As Chairman Martin says, "If monetary history were to repeat itself, it would be nobody's fault but our own."

FEDERAL RESERVE INDEPENDENCE

Should the central bank be free to pursue a monetary
policy that is at odds with the economic policy of the President of the United States? Fear that political domination of
the central bank would lead to inflationary monetary policies led Congress to incorporate a substantial measure of
central bank independence in the original Federal Reserve
Act. The colloquy below, between a U.S. Senator and the
Chairman of the Federal Reserve Board, reveals the doctrine of independence from the Executive in an unusually
candid fashion. You should consider whether the President,
who is responsible to the people for economic results, ought
not to have a strong voice in the formulation of monetary
policy.

SENATOR LONG. Mr. Martin, I would like to talk a little bit about the
independence of the Federal Reserve Board. You made the statement
in your prepared statement that the Federal Reserve Board apparently
had an obligation to follow the administration with regard to administration policies, and that it was not independent of them, but that it
nonetheless exercised its own independent judgment with regard to
the way that those policies should be implemented. Would you elaborate upon that, as to your understanding of the degree to which the
administration fixes its policy with regard to employment, and with
regard to direction of our economic and fiscal policies, and the degree
to which the Federal Reserve Board exercises its judgment?

MR. MARTIN. Well, we feel ourselves bound by the Employment Act
and by the Federal Reserve Act. And in the field of money and credit,

Taken from *Senate Finance Committee Hearings: Investigation of The Financial Condition of the United States*, Pt. 3 (Washington: Government Printing Office, 1957),
pp. 1361–1363.

we consider ourselves to be, regardless of what the decisions of the administration may be—we consult with them but we feel that we have the authority, if we think that in our field, money and credit policies, that we should act differently than they, we feel perfectly at liberty to do so.

SENATOR LONG. In other words, you feel that you have freedom in promoting what you believe to be the full employment policy of the law?

MR. MARTIN. That is right.

SENATOR LONG. To adopt policies that may not be the policy of the administration itself?

MR. MARTIN. That is right.

SENATOR LONG. And you feel that there is the right within the Board to adopt a policy that may be completely at variance with the attitude and the direction of the policy of the administration?

MR. MARTIN. Well, I wouldn't say that—we will discuss it at considerable length.

SENATOR LONG. You have the right to disagree with them?

MR. MARTIN. Exactly.

SENATOR LONG. And you believe that the Federal Reserve Board, if it does disagree, has the right to pursue a policy that is completely contrary to the policy that the administration proceeds to follow, not meaning that you are doing this or that you have done, but that you feel that under the law you do have that right?

MR. MARTIN. Under the law we feel it is our prerogative; yes, sir.

SENATOR LONG. At the same time you believe, if I understand it correctly, that you should in a sense persuade them that the policy that you are pursuing is the correct policy, and that their policy should be consistent with yours, and that you should make your views available to the Executive for the Executive to persuade you if possible that the policy that the Executive is pursuing is the policy to which you should direct your activities?

MR. MARTIN. That is right.

SENATOR LONG. At the present time, if I understand, it, the testimony from the executive branch has been that their policy is consistent with the policy that you are pursuing?

MR. MARTIN. Well, I think in a broad sense that is correct. We have differences of opinion—differences of judgment with respect to our actions.

SENATOR LONG. Yes. Has the administration of recent date, the spokesmen for the Treasury Department or the President in any other capacity, been urging you to take a position or adopt a policy contrary to the one that you have been pursuing?

MR. MARTIN. Well, over the last year there has been no pressure, Senator, such as saying, "If you do not follow this policy, we will drop you out of office." They have tried on a number of occasions to persuade us that we should not take action which we did take, but it was a perfectly friendly discussion and honest disagreement, not about broad policies so much as about timing and judgment with respect to whether it was a wise course for us to pursue under present conditions.

SENATOR LONG. Could you give us some indication of recent decisions and recent actions that the Board has taken which you feel were not the policy that was recommended or was, perhaps, contrary to the attitude that you believed that the administration would have taken if it had been charged with the same responsibility that you have?

MR. MARTIN. Well, I think the most glaring instance of that was in April of 1956. Pursuing our method of cooperation, I began discussions with Secretary Humphrey. In February of that year Governor Balderston and I had a meeting with Secretary Humphrey and there was a disagreement as to the nature that the economy was developing. We were so convinced; we discussed it with various people, and in a series of meetings from about the middle of February until the last week in March.

By the last week in March the position in the Federal Reserve—which was not a 1-man operation; you see, the 12 bank directors were considering all aspects of this—was that it would be wise for us to go up in the discount rate.

THE OPEN MARKET

POLICY PROCESS

PETER M. KEIR

Those concerned with the study and evaluation of reserve banking policy often ask how and on what basis the Federal Reserve System makes its decisions on monetary policy.

The article that follows describes in some detail the Federal Reserve decision-making process, particularly as it applies to the formulation and execution of open market policy.

COMPLEXITIES OF POLICY-MAKING

The policy process in reserve banking involves a continuing assessment of changing economic developments and takes full account of the interaction of monetary measures and forces outside the monetary sphere. For instance, when the performance of the economy or of the balance of international payments has been falling short of longer-range objectives, Federal Reserve authorities must decide whether and to what extent changes in the financial variables more directly affected by monetary action—namely, the pace of bank credit and monetary growth, and levels of interest rates—can help to improve the situation. They must also decide whether changes in other forces—including other public policies—are working or may work to remedy the shortfall. If

Adapted from Federal Reserve Bulletin, October 1963, pp. 1359–1370.

it seems appropriate to change the pace at which bank credit and the money supply are growing or to change prevailing interest rates, then the policy-makers must decide by how much and with what timing to adjust the reserve base of member banks so that monetary action will encourage the change desired.

Judgments of this kind call for full analysis of all relevant information about the domestic economic and credit situation, the flows being generated in international payments, and the major forces affecting the world economy generally. Hence in arriving at policy decisions the Federal Reserve considers a spectrum of guides. These range from ultimate goals for output, employment, average prices, and the balance of payments to the more immediate objectives, such as bank reserve ability, which transmit System policy to money market conditions and interest rates, bank credit, and the money supply.

It would be easier for the System to make decisions on policy if there were a simple statistical norm—such as a particular rate of growth in the money supply or particular levels of interest rates—which, if it could be attained, might insure continuous realization of optimum conditions in output, employment, and the balance of payments. Neither experience nor a consensus of economic theory, however, has indicated any single norm for policy guidance. Rather, the System must consider changes in all indicators, financial and nonfinancial, that help to explain recent economic tendencies, that shed light on likely future developments, and that reflect the stance of monetary policy in relation to other influences on the economy.

Policy-makers thus place a high priority on comprehensive, dependable, and timely economic intelligence. A wide range of information, both statistical and qualitative, is available for use in making such judgments, and methods of economic analysis are much advanced over earlier periods.

Even so, opinions differ on how the available information should be interpreted. These differences arise because there are still important gaps in the data and because the information that is available currently does not fully reveal emerging economic developments in the domestic and international spheres. In addition, different participants in the decision-making process may attach different weights to the various elements in an evolving situation—not only among domestic factors but as between domestic and international.

In this complex economic world—in which data tend to run somewhat behind events and in which the effects of changes in Federal Reserve policy work themselves out over time—adaptations in policy tend to be taken step by step. In that way, they can be readily modified or reversed, if necessary, as the future unfolds. This is especially important at times when the strength of perceivable trends is not clear or when there is strong interaction between domestic and international economic developments. Nevertheless, situations may arise that clearly call for rapid and forceful policy measures. In these circumstances, too, the continuous nature of the policy process permits prompt response.

ROLE OF THE OPEN MARKET COMMITTEE

Open market operations are the instrument best suited to step-by-step adaptation of monetary policy. They can be used subtly to initiate small policy actions or aggressively to carry out large changes in reserves over relatively short periods of time. They are continuous in nature, can be undertaken quickly, and are well adapted to ready modification and reversal, if necessary. In practice, therefore, open market operations normally take the lead in general monetary policy implementation, with changes in the discount rate and in required reserve ratios being used more often to supplement and reinforce this initiative.

Most open market operations are transacted in domestic securities —mainly U.S. Government issues, and to a limited extent bankers' acceptances. But since early 1962 the Federal Reserve has also bought and sold foreign currencies in the exchange markets and in direct transactions with foreign monetary authorities. The focus of foreign currency operations is on the orderly achievement of balance in the supply of and demand for dollars in foreign exchange markets. These operations also have some effect on the supply of domestic bank reserves, but their net impact has usually been small, and any effect they may have is taken into account in the management of domestic security operations. All of the System's open market operations—in both domestic securities and foreign currencies—are carried out under policy directives of the Federal Open Market Committee.[1]

[1] The Committee consists of the seven members of the Board of Governors together with the presidents of five of the Reserve Banks. The Chairman of the Board of Governors serves as Chairman of the Committee, and the President of the Federal Reserve Bank of New York as Vice Chairman. The President of the New York Bank is a permanent member of the Committee. The presidents of the other Reserve Banks rotate as members voting in groups prescribed by law. Membership of these four is for one year.

To facilitate the execution of open market operations, all System holdings of Government securities and foreign currencies are pooled in a System Open Market Account. Each Reserve Bank participates in the holdings and earnings of this account.

Operations in Government securities and foreign currencies authorized by the

The Committee's procedures and practices have varied over the years along with the changing focus of the issues and problems faced. The practices described hereafter are those that have evolved out of past experience to meet present needs. As needs change in the future and as knowledge increases further, current practices are likely to be modified.

To keep open market policy constantly in touch with the monetary and credit needs of the economy and with the international economic position of the country, the Committee has found it essential to meet often, usually every three weeks. The primary purpose of these meetings is to develop a policy consensus that can be formulated into operating directives to the Manager of the System Open Market Account and the Special Manager for foreign currency operations. In addition, the meetings are a forum for discussion of the use of all instruments of monetary policy against the background of overall monetary objectives.

Decisions on changes in the use of policy instruments other than open market operations—discount rates and reserve requirements—are not made by the FOMC as such. But since all policy instruments are closely related, views developed in Committee deliberations are carried over into meetings of the Board of Governors and of the Reserve Bank presidents with their directors, where actions on these other instruments are decided. In this way Committee discussions have a bearing on the coordinated use of all instruments.

COMMITTEE PROCEDURES

Meetings of the FOMC are organized to facilitate wide discussions and careful assessment of available information as part of the process of coming to decisions on open market policy. To this end, all twelve of the Reserve Bank presidents attend the meetings and participate in the discussion, although only the five who are members vote on proposed Committee actions. This arrangement makes the knowledge and information of the entire Federal Reserve System available to the Committee.

Background Preparation. Between meetings, members of the Committee are kept informed about late developments in the nation's economy, in regional economies, and in the balance of payments by the research staffs at the Board of Governors and at each of the Reserve Banks. Regular briefings are provided in both oral and written form. Some of these staff reports stress only the facts of recent changes. Others assess and interpret them in relation to past trends and in terms of the key factors in economic cycles and growth suggested by various economic theories. Such analyses are helpful in the assessment of possible future trends.

In addition, Committee members receive regular reports from the Manager of the System Open Market Account and the Special Manager for foreign currency operations. These reports—provided daily, weekly, and in advance of each meeting—analyze developments in the domestic money and securities markets, in bank reserve positions, and in foreign exchange markets. They also provide a full review of System operations against the background of Committee objectives.

Before each meeting members of the Committee receive special staff reports that place developments since the preceding meeting in clear perspective. One of these is a review of the key phases of the current economic situation, domestic and international, prepared by the research staff of the Board of Governors. It sets forth recent information on the broad economic aggregates that represent the ultimate targets of domestic policy—output, employment, income, and prices—and reviews changes in such important factors as business investment, housing, consumer outlays, and Government finance that underlie movements in these broad aggregates. In addition, it reviews developments in key financial variables such as bank credit, money, and interest rates, which are the proximate targets of policy, and reports changes in the money market and bank reserve statistics that respond most immediately to monetary policy actions. Finally, it sets forth summary information on output and credit conditions abroad and the state of the U.S. balance of payments. When special problems or proposals relating to policy are under consideration, Committee members usually receive supplementary background papers.

Organization. Meetings of the FOMC are held at the Board of Governors building in Washington. The agenda for each meeting is typically divided into two parts. One focuses on foreign currency operations; the other on broader questions of general open market policy.

The discussion of foreign currency operations begins with an oral report by the Special Manager of the Account. He reviews the highlights of recent foreign exchange market experience and identifies situations likely to require Committee attention or action before the next meeting. After discussion of questions raised by his comments and recommendations, the Committee takes whatever actions may be needed to direct foreign currency operations until the next meeting.

The meeting then proceeds to a consideration of general open market policy. Discussions begin with an oral report by the Account Manager. In this he outlines recent and prospective System actions in the market and reviews money and securities market developments expected to be of special significance to the Committee in the period ahead. If Committee members have questions or reservations about the conduct of open market operations in the interval since the last meeting, they raise them at this point.

The Committee then receives oral briefings from its staff economists. These are analytical and interpretive statements that draw out the significance and implications of the more detailed written reports distributed in advance of the meeting. One statement covers key developments in domestic business; another, recent changes in domestic financial markets; and a third, recent developments in the U.S. balance of payments.

After the staff reports, each Board member and Bank president— nonvoting as well as voting—speaks in turn. Each presents his judgments on current economic and financial conditions, and the Reserve Bank presidents report any significant recent developments in the economies of their districts.

These summaries of regional conditions are useful in interpreting overall economic tendencies because they often help to spot developments not yet reflected in statistical series for the nation as a whole. Also, reports by the Bank presidents reflect a special knowledge of banking developments obtained from supervision of member banks, administration of the discount window, and other regular contacts with bankers and business leaders, including their Bank's directors.

Each speaker states his view with regard to policy, usually by indicating whether he believes that money market conditions and the volume of reserves available to member banks should be kept about the same or be changed. Recommendations to shift toward more or less ease or restraint in open market operations may include an expression of opinion as to the desirability of a near-term change in the discount rate. In addition, speakers typically relate any proposals they may have concerning money market conditions and bank reserves to broader financial variables such as interest rates, the pace of bank credit and monetary growth, or other liquid assets. They also assess these financial variables against trends in domestic economic activity and employment, the level of prices, and the balance of international payments. When all members of the Committee have spoken, the Chairman summarizes the points of view expressed and the consensus that seems to have developed on open market policy.

Following such further comments as may help to clarify differing points of view, attention turns to the current policy directive, which expresses the Committee's judgment as to the appropriate posture of monetary policy for the period until the next meeting. If the policy judgment that is reached calls for a change in the directive, alternative formulations are considered. Then a vote of the Committee members is taken on that policy formulation which seems to express most satisfactorily the majority view. On occasion the wording of the directive will be revised to acknowledge the short-run significance of some unexpected event or condition such as the Suez crisis in late 1956, the stock market break in May 1962, or the Cuban crisis in October 1962. Developments of this type may be deemed to require specific recognition in the policy directive, even though basic policy remains unchanged.

The directives of the FOMC to the System Account Managers provide the central basis for the record of Committee policy actions that is published in the *Annual Reports* of the Board of Governors. But more fundamentally they establish formal lines of policy direction from the 12-member policy-forming Committee to the System Account Managers, who execute day-to-day market operations. Thus, the directives, to be discussed in more detail in the next section, are the basis for policy execution, although the Managers' understanding of the instructions is enhanced by their presence at the Committee's discussions.

EXECUTION OF POLICY

Over its history the Committee has changed the form of its directives from time to time. At present, instructions for open market operations in domestic securities are contained in two directives. One is a "continuing authority directive," which is reviewed at least once a year. It sets the technical limits on operations—indicating such things as the types of securities that may be bought or sold, the procedures to be followed in transactions, and the conditions under which repurchase agreements may be made with dealers. The other is the current policy directive voted at each meeting. This states the present objectives of open market policy and gives guidance in light of the Committee's discussions, to the Account Manager in implementing Committee policy until the next meeting.

The current policy directive is revised rather often. Revision takes account of recent and prospective changes in the domestic economy and the balance of payments, which may require alterations in open market policy.

With regard to foreign currency operations, the policy aims of the Committee relate to the international position of the dollar as mirrored in the technical performance of foreign exchange markets and to the way in which the deficit or surplus in the U.S. balance of payments is financed. When the FOMC authorized operations in foreign currencies in 1962, it defined the goals and character of this program in a detailed statement. The statement, published by the Board in its *Annual Report* for 1962, explained the purposes of foreign currency operations, the types of currencies in which transactions could be conducted, the nature of institutional arrangements with central banks in other countries, and the administrative structure and procedures to be used for executing transactions.

At the same time the Committee adopted a set of guidelines for foreign currency operations. These define the circumstances in which the System may acquire and hold foreign currencies and specify the purposes for which it may engage in spot and forward exchange transactions. These rules guide the Special Manager in his day-to-day operations in foreign currencies. A continuing authority directive, subject to change when appropriate, lists the particular foreign currencies in which he may operate, along with the quantitative limits on various types of transactions.

At least once a year—at its annual organization meeting in early March—the FOMC reviews all of its continuing directives and operating procedures to make sure they are consistent with the present needs and objectives of effective monetary policy.

The balance of this article discusses the factors taken into account in the wording of the current policy directive and in the execution of day-to-day open market operations in domestic securities.

The Operating Problem. The main function of the current policy directive is to set forth guidelines as to the availability of member bank reserves and the degree of ease or firmness in the money market for the Account Manager to follow until the next meeting. These objectives have to be expressed in a manner that will give the Accounts Manager adequate guidance while at the same time allowing him sufficient latitude—in view of continuously evolving market conditions and expectations—to carry out basic Committee aims in relation to domestic economic activity and the balance of payments.

It might seem at first glance as if the Committee could achieve its objectives by simply stating the dollar volume of securities that the Account Manager should buy or sell in the market before the next meeting. In practice, however, this is not feasible, for the supply of reserves available to member banks is affected by changes in a number of factors that in the short run are independent of Federal Reserve monetary action. Among these are changes in the level of monetary gold, currency in circulation, and float—the last arising mainly from fluctuations in the volume of checks in process of collection. As a result the System can bring about a desired change in the general availability of reserves to banks only if reserve changes arising from these other factors have been fully allowed for.

The task of taking into account changes in these factors, together with normal seasonal movements in required reserves, is essentially an operating problem rather than a policy problem. It is a part of the Account Manager's job—with the help of the staffs at the Federal Reserve Bank of New York and the Board of Governors—to detect such variations and to make prompt adjustments to them. In other words, the execution of open market policy requires continuous and sensitive appraisal of day-to-day market conditions.

Looking ahead to the interval between meetings, the Committee itself cannot easily predict the amount of reserves that open market operations will have to supply or absorb to take account of changes in other factors affecting reserves. But as the period unfolds, the Account Manager can usually accommodate his operations to such changes. He may observe the changes through statistical measures developed by the staff, or they may become evident to him in the process of day-to-day operations in the money market. Most open market transactions are undertaken simply to respond to seasonal and other short-term reserve changes of these kinds.

For policy purposes, therefore, the FOMC is less interested in the gross volume of open market transactions likely to be needed in the period ahead than it is in the supply of reserves that will be available to support further growth of bank credit at member banks.

Several measures help to indicate the extent of reserve availability at member banks. For measuring the results of policy actions over a period of weeks or months, trends in total, required, and nonborrowed reserves are particularly useful, because they reveal changes in the reserve base that supports bank deposit and credit expansion. But these measures have only limited usefulness as very short-run operating guides for the System Account Manager—and it is in the short run that day-to-day operations must be planned and executed. To be used effectively on a day-to-day basis, these measures would have to be adjusted to allow for immediate seasonal pressures on reserves as well as for other short-run forces that may unexpectedly produce a sudden bulging or slackening of reserve needs. Such adjustments are difficult at best, and for current operations in such a complex and dynamic economy as that of the United States, where it is hard to find recurring patterns, they have to be viewed as tentative or approximate.

In the very short run various marginal measures of bank reserve positions are useful indicators of the interaction between monetary policy and market forces. These indicators include the amounts of excess reserves that member banks hold and the amounts of their borrowings from the Federal Reserve. Subtraction of total member bank borrowings from their total excess reserves provides a net measure of reserve positions for all member banks. When this difference is positive, it is popularly referred to as net free reserves; when it is negative, it is called net borrowed reserves.

When net free reserves rise, the result is an increased marginal availability of reserves, which the banking system can readily use to expand credit. But when member bank borrowings grow relative to excess reserves, credit expansion comes under restraint. In this process individual banks find extra reserves more difficult and expensive to obtain, and they come under increasing pressure to repay advances from the Federal Reserve. As this continues over time, a net borrowed reserve position emerges for the banking system as a whole.

The technical advantage of marginal reserve guides is that they help the Account Manager to accommodate seasonal and other short-run credit demands readily as they develop. For example, when net reserves are tending to fall because of a seasonal or random rise in the public's need for bank credit, the Account Manager will supply the reserves required to back the deposits created in credit expansion. Similarly, when net reserves are tending to rise because of a seasonal decline in the demand for bank credit—taking the form, for example, of seasonal repayment of bank debt by businesses—he will absorb the required reserves released by the associated decline in deposits. With smaller deposits, banks would need less required reserves and their excess reserves would rise unless absorbed by System operations.

Taken by itself, however, the net free (or net borrowed) reserve position also has its limitations as a guide. For one thing, it may not show what is happening to total bank credit over time, since a given level of net reserves at one point may be associated with a faster or slower rate of growth in total bank credit than the same level of net reserves at another point. This difference reflects differences between the two periods in the intensity of credit demands, the level and structure of interest rates, and market expectations—and hence in bank preferences for free reserves.

The danger in adhering to net reserves alone as a guide is that the System might be misled into reinforcing changing demands for bank credit generated by forces of cyclical expansion and contraction when this was undesirable. For example, in periods of vigorous credit demands and rising bank needs for reserves, free reserves tend to decline as banks use reserves that formerly had been excess or increase their borrowings from Federal Reserve Banks. If the Account Manager in such circumstances adds to the total supply of bank reserves through open market operations in order to keep free reserves from falling, this will encourage a rapid expansion of bank credit—perhaps more rapid than desired to accommodate seasonal and growth needs at the time.

Under conditions of slack credit demands and declining interest rates, on the other hand, the opposite may occur. In such periods member banks typically try to repay debt at the Federal Reserve and add to their excess reserves in an effort to build up their free reserves. If, in these circumstances, the Account Manager failed to allow free reserves within the banking system to grow enough to meet the changed preferences, open market operations would tend to encourage further contraction rather than the renewed expansion needed to help stimulate economic recovery. In short, although the net reserve measure is a useful and sensitive short-run guide to open market operations, it is not used inflexibly as a policy target. Rather, it is continuously interpreted in the light of other evidence on credit and economic developments and in the light of changes in various fundamental measures of the bank reserve base—total, required, and nonborrowed reserves.

Moreover, even in the short run the significance of any given net reserve figure must be assessed alongside a broad assortment of other information that bears on what is typically alluded to as the "tone" or "feel" of the money market. Indicators such as the intensity of demand for and the depth of supply of Federal funds, the amount of new money needed by Government securities dealers and their sources and costs of financing, and day-to-day trends in market prices and yields for Treasury securities all provide important insights into the immediate state of reserve availability and the strength of demands pressing upon that availability. In executing policy, it is essential to have these immediate indicators of money market atmosphere, because daily estimates of reserve availability may be wide of the mark and because such estimates are for the banking system as a whole and do not allow for the differing market impact of possible variations in reserve distribution.

In summary, although at first glance it might seem to be most efficient for the FOMC to express its instructions to the System Account Manager in simple and explicit terms—either as some dollar amount of net purchases or net sales to be accomplished before the next meeting, or as some given target of net reserve availability or reserve growth—this quantitative approach has not proved feasible. Experience has shown that the Committee cannot forecast the size of technical adjustments that will be needed between meetings to allow for changes in other reserve factors. Nor can it predict the precise extent to which bank credit, money, and interest rates will respond to given target levels of, or changes in, reserve availability.

Nature of Operating Instructions. In practice, therefore, the Committee finds it desirable to express its operating instructions in broader terms, which allow the Account Manager sufficient latitude to evaluate and interpret changing technical relationships among all of the relevant money market indicators. For this reason Committee instructions have typically directed the Account Manager to seek more, less, or about the same amount of reserve availability and money market ease or tightness as has been prevailing. Decisions as to the precise size, timing, and direction (purchase or sale) of any market operations needed to implement these instructions are left to the Manager's discretion, for he has day-to-day contact with the market and with the daily figures bearing on bank reserves and money market conditions, and he is therefore in a position to make the necessary and continuing day-to-day adaptations of operations to basic policy aims.

To illustrate the form of operating instructions, the current economic policy directive adopted at the meeting of September 11, 1962, follows:

It is the current policy of the Federal Open Market Committee to permit the supply of bank credit and money to increase further, but at the same time to avoid redundant bank reserves that would encourage capital outflows internationally. This policy takes into account, on the one hand, the gradualness of recent advances in economic activity and the availability of resoures to permit further advance in activity. On the other hand, it gives recognition to the bank credit expansion over the past year and to the role of capital flows in the country's adverse balance of payments.

To implement this policy, operations for the System Open Market Account during the next three weeks shall be conducted with a view to providing moderate reserve expansion in the banking system and to fostering a moderately firm tone in money markets.

In making day-to-day decisions, the Account Manager adheres to the guidelines of the current directive. As the example shows, the first paragraph contains a statement of the Committee's broad goals, and the second its operating instructions.

If changes in banking and money market conditions in the period between meetings should begin to deviate sharply from the general pattern assumed in the policy deliberations at the latest meeting, the Account Manager would call this to the Committee's attention. If the change were very rapid, he might ask for a special meeting (perhaps by telephone conference) to review alternative means of coping with the changed situation and to determine whether the Committee wished to issue new operating instructions. Any Committee member who was similarly concerned by the unexpected course of developments could, of course, also request a special meeting. In fact, Committee members could, of course, also request a special meeting. In fact, Committee members may at any time comment to the System Accounts Manager on actual System operations and market developments in relation to Committee intentions.

Basis for Day-to-Day Operations. In his day-to-day evaluation of money market developments the Account Manager considers both statistical and qualitative measures of financial activity. One key element in this continuous evaluation process is a daily projection of changes in factors affecting bank reserves. The reserve projection contains estimates for several weeks ahead of daily and weekly average changes in all of the key elements that affect the bank reserve equation—float, currency, gold and foreign accounts, and so forth—as well as in the various reserve measures—total, required nonborrowed, and free reserves. These projections show the direction and general order of magnitude of the open market operations likely to be needed in the period immediately ahead.

Every morning the daily and weekly estimates for factors affecting reserves are revised on the basis of actual reserve figures collected for the preceding business day from the System's statistical reporting network. Since the money market is especially sensitive to the current and expected reserve position of large city banks, figures on the distribution of reserves among banks are also assembled from the reported data and carefully evaluated.

Data on reserves are supplemented by other types of statistical information. For example, statistics on transactions in Federal funds are collected daily from a sample of large money market banks. These shed light on the demand for and supply of excess reserves by banks and are a sensitive indicator of changes in current bank reserve availability relative to the demand for bank credit. In addition, the Account Manager receives from the Market Statistics Department of the Federal Reserve Bank of New York aggregate data collected from Government securities dealers that show their current inventories, volume of trading, and sources of financing.

Apart from these various types of current and retrospective statistics, the Account Manager obtains through a network of telephone contacts maintained by the Trading Desk a wide assortment of information from Government securities dealers and other money market professionals on current rate and price quotations in money markets as well as estimates of customer offerings and demands in markets for Federal funds and U.S. Government securities. This information, which reflects the interaction of the volume of reserves actually available and the demand pressing upon these reserves, is needed for meaningful interpretation and evaluation of the preliminary statistical estimates on bank reserve positions. It also helps the Account Manager to come to a better understanding of market expectations and of the likely response to Federal Reserve operations.

This brief review of the guides and information that shape day-to-day activities of the Account Manager illustrates the wide range of information he takes into account in the execution of policy. The Manager, in turn, keeps members of the Committee continuously informed of the particular money market and bank reserve developments that underlie each day's actions. Insights gained from these reports of current developments, in combination with analyses of the broader but less timely indicators of general changes in the domestic economy and the balance of payments, provide the background information on which Committee members must base their new policy judgment at the succeeding meeting.

TRANSACTIONS FOR THE

SYSTEM OPEN MARKET ACCOUNT

ROBERT ROOSA

In this selection, a former official of the Federal Reserve Bank of New York explains the physical mechanics of conducting open market operations.

In recent years virtually all purchases or sales in the market for System Account on an outright basis have been made in Treasury bills.[1] Any dealer who consistently demonstrates his readiness to make markets is welcome to compete for transactions with the Account, provided the firm meets reasonable standards of credit-worthiness and provides the financial statements needed in reaching a determination to that effect.

Once the Account Management decides, for example, to purchase Treasury bills in a magnitude of 50, 75, or 100 million dollars, its approach to the market is governed by two overriding considerations. First, it must trade with all dealers on a freely competitive basis. This means, when buying, that it will take bills at the lowest offered prices (highest yields), up to the point that the intended total of purchases is reached. Second, the Account Management must give some weight, if the size and variety of dealers' offerings are great enough to permit

---

[1] This was written during the "bills only" period.

Reprinted from Federal Reserve Operations in the Money and Government Securities Markets, *Federal Reserve Bank of New York*, 1956, pp. 80–83.

any leeway, to the need for maintaining a maturity distribution of the portfolio that will best contribute to the practical administration of the Account over the months ahead. This means that when the Account holds no bills of a particular weekly issue, perhaps because it had let the preceding issue run off at maturity in order to absorb reserves at that earlier time, some preference would be given to restoring a moderate holding of that particular maturity, all other things being equal. There are other similar operating considerations that have to be taken into account.

The usual procedure, once the Vice President-Manager has reached his decision, is to brief all available members of the trading staff on the language to be used in contacting dealers, and to assign each person to two, three, or four dealers as his responsibility. On instructions from the Manager, Trading and Markets, all traders then begin simultaneously contacting dealers to ask for bids or offerings, as the case may be, specifying particular maturities where that is appropriate. Under present arrangements, it is usually possible for the traders to reach all dealers and note their bids or offers within an elapsed time of three to five minutes. It is necessary to act quickly so that no dealer can be placed in a privileged position either by obtaining knowledge of a Federal Reserve System operation in advance of other dealers or by being able to bid or offer after the initial impact on prices becomes apparent (which might be a particular advantage, in the event of Federal Reserve purchases, for example, if the purchases had an immediate upward influence on Treasury bill prices).[2] As each trader completes his contacts with dealers, all of the bids or offers he receives are promptly assembled on a single worksheet, or "blanket," which the Manager, Trading and Markets, and any other officers currently working with him, can then use in order to select those bids or offers which, in conformity with the two principles just mentioned, will fulfill the System's buying or selling objective.

The bids or offers received from the dealers are requested on a "firm" basis for twenty minutes or thereabouts, as a general rule, and by the elapse of that time the selections will have been completed and each trader can begin return calls to the dealers indicating which, if any, of their bids or offers are to be taken. Generally, this entire operation, known colloquially as a "go-around," is completed within thirty minutes. The Account Management usually conducts operations

---

[2] System action does exert an influence on prices of bills, and other Government securities as well, but fortunately the market is no longer as sensitive to this particular procedure as formerly.

in the manner described, unless unsettled conditions are so pervasive in the market that the broadside effect of a full-scale "go-around" threatens to be unduly disruptive. Under those circumstances, the Account Management may achieve its objective in terms of absorbing or releasing reserves, with less pronounced impact on market psychology, by simply taking advantage of bids or offers that are volunteered by the dealers during the course of the routine conversations continually in process between the traders or the Trading Desk and those at various dealer firms. In no event, however, would purchases or sales be made at prices out of line with those currently prevailing in the market, as checked and cross-checked by all of the traders in their continuing conversations with the market.

Outright transactions are normally executed either for "cash" (that is, same-day) or for "regular" (next-day) delivery and payment. Due to mechanical problems of physical delivery, it is ordinarily not practicable to initiate negotiations with respect to cash transactions after 12 o'clock noon, although in special circumstances, particularly when the Federal Reserve is a seller, transactions may at times be executed as late as 1:00 p.m. One advantage or disadvantage of cash transactions, depending on the circumstances, which also applies in the use of repurchase agreements to be described below, is that they provide or withdraw Federal Reserve funds to or from the market immediately. There are times when, in the nature of a developing situation, a prompt release or withdrawal of funds, is particularly desirable. Transactions for regular delivery may, of course, be executed at any time until the 3:30 p.m. closing hour. Thus, it is broadly correct to generalize, as far as outright transactions are concerned, that any action intended to influence reserves today must be decided upon, and execution must begin, before or close to noon. Any reserve effect which can suitably be exerted on the following day may be brought about through regular delivery transactions at any time during the trading day.

Because of the difficulties of assuring timely physical deliveries, particularly when dealers may have to withdraw securities already pledged on loans at other institutions in order to effect delivery, or must await deliveries of the securities from customers, the Account Management often finds on its "go-arounds" that dealers are not prepared to offer enough securities on a cash basis to meet the Federal Reserve System's objective. Conversely, when the System is on the selling side, dealers may also be somewhat reluctant to take as many securities as the Account Management may have in mind because of the difficulties of subsequently making arrangements late in the day for additional loan facilities, both in order to be able to pay for the securities when picking them up (in Federal funds) and in order to carry the securities in position after receiving them. By comparison, when the Federal Reserve policy objective indicates a need for buying, the repurchase agreement facility usually provides somewhat greater flexibility. Securities that a dealer may still be in need of financing ordinarily will be more easily accessible, right down to the last minute at which the dealer closes his own books. Repurchase agreements can physically be negotiated as late as 1:30 p.m., and timely deliveries subsequently effected. Although it is rarely practicable from the Federal Reserve System's own point of view to operate that late, there are some occasions when the Account Management is glad to take advantage of this avenue for placing funds immediately in the market at a relatively late hour in the trading day. Of course, the greater flexibility of operations in repurchase agreements is dependent upon the dealers having securities in a position that they are willing to finance through a repurchase agreement with the Reserve Bank at the rate of interest the Reserve Bank is charging on that day.

THE STRUCTURE

OF RESERVE REQUIREMENTS

ON DEMAND DEPOSITS

The Committee on Financial Institutions, appointed
by President Kennedy, was made up of the heads of government departments that deal with regulation of financial
institutions and monetary policy. The following selection is
taken from the Report of this Committee. The Committee
proposes a system of graduated reserve requirements. You
should evaluate this proposal in terms of (1) whether or not
it would improve the effectiveness of monetary policy; and
(2) whether it is more or less discriminatory than either
the present system or the one proposed in the succeeding
selection.

Member banks of the Federal Reserve System are required to hold
reserves in the form of either deposits at Federal Reserve Banks or
vault cash. The present reserve requirement against net demand deposits is 12 per cent for banks classified as "country" banks and 16½
per cent for "reserve city" banks. Under existing law, the Federal Reserve Board has discretion to set these reserve requirements between
7 and 14 per cent for country banks and between 10 and 22 per cent
for reserve city banks.

The geographical classification between "city" and "country" banks,
with differential reserve requirements, dates back to the National Bank

Reprinted from Report of the Committee on Financial Institutions to the President of
the United States (Washington: Government Printing Office, 1963), pp. 10–13.

Act (1863), under which "reserve city" banks served as reserve depositaries for country banks and in turn maintained reserves with "central reserve city" banks. Differential reserve requirements were viewed as necessary in that system as a means of protecting the liquidity of the banking system.

The ineffectiveness of required reserves as a means of ensuring bank liquidity was demonstrated forcefully by the prevalence of financial panics. Indeed it was these difficulties, resulting from the lack of a dependable source of liquidity, that led in 1913 to the establishment of the Federal Reserve System, which has come to be the ultimate provider of liquidity in our monetary system. Nevertheless the three-way geographical classification of banks was carried over from the National Banking System. It was only in 1959 that the three classifications were reduced to two by a consolidation of the two city-bank categories.

Other shortcomings of the existing structure of reserve requirements have become evident. In the past, large banks, which were located mainly in central cities, were concerned principally with serving the needs of industry and commerce and of out-of-town banks. In recent years, consumers have become increasingly important as depositors and borrowers at large city banks. Moreover sizable concentrations of population and business outside the limits of reserve cities, especially in the suburbs, have led to wider branching and substantial growth of many banks in these areas. The result has been that the distinction in size and function between "country" and "city" banks has become blurred. In these circumstances, banks of comparable size and similar activity are more likely than in the past to have different reserve requirements, depending on where they are located. Furthermore, the question whether or not a city should be classified as a reserve city, with the consequence that its banks would have a higher reserve requirement, is a difficult one and inevitably leads to arbitrary distinctions.

Recognition of these problems has stimulated numerous proposals in recent years for revision of the system of reserve requirements. One such proposal is for identical percentage requirements at all banks. The American Bankers Association is on record in favor of this proposal. Most recently, the Commission on Money and Credit recommended uniform reserve requirements.

The case for uniform requirements is usually based on two arguments: (1) that monetary policy would become a more precise instrument if all banks had the same requirements, since potential credit and monetary expansion would no longer vary with changes in the distribution of demand deposits among banks in different locations, and (2) that the present differential is arbitrary and imposes inequitable treatment on many banks.

The Committee recognizes the logic of the argument, presented by the Commission on Money and Credit and others, that completely uniform requirements would enhance the precision of monetary policy. At the same time, it is aware that, as a practical matter, the difference in reserve requirements between city and country member banks introduces only a minor imprecision into the management of bank reserves by the Federal Reserve. Greater imprecision results from the fact that small banks maintain sizable excess reserves and, in contrast to larger banks, adjust their loans and investments only with a lag when their reserves change. For this reason, required reserves would be affected when deposits shift between city and country banks even if reserve requirements were uniform.

A system of differential reserve requirements is defended on the grounds (1) that smaller banks find it necessary, in order to obtain certain services from their city correspondents, to hold a large proportion of their assets in the form of noninterest-bearing balances at other banks and (2) that smaller banks are necessarily higher cost banks, in view of their lesser ability to take advantage of economies of scale (such as avoiding excess reserves, making large individual loans and investments, and using automatic accounting equipment and other specialized facilities); a lower level of reserve requirements may serve to offset these disadvantages of smaller banks, thus helping to preserve a system of independent unit banks.

As it considered these arguments, the Committee was aware of the practical difficulty of implementing the two recommendations of the Commission on Money and Credit that all (insured) commercial banks should be required to become members of the Federal Reserve System *and* that reserve requirements should be identical for all member banks. Nonmember banks are predominantly small banks. Among the 7,000 banks that are not members of the Federal Reserve System, more than three-fourths have total deposits of less than $5 million. If these banks were required to adhere to member bank reserve requirements and if requirements were made uniform at anything like present levels (somewhere between 12 and 16½ per cent), a strain would be imposed on many of the small nonmember banks. To implement the two recommendations therefore, it would probably be necessary to lower the present average level of reserve requirements on member banks, perhaps to less than 10 per cent.

Although reserve requirements serve mainly as a vehicle for monetary policy, there is, within broad limits, little basis for judging that in the long run one level is preferable to another in terms of facilitating monetary policy. Inevitably therefore, the other effects of reserve requirements—on bank earnings, on competitive relationships with other institutions, and on net interest payments by the Government—become relevant in evaluating the advisability of a change in the average level of requirements. It is clear that a substantial reduction in requirements —to 10 per cent or less—would, at least in the short run, result in a sizable increase in net profits of banks (especially of larger banks in reserve cities now subject to a requirement by 16½ per cent) and a corresponding reduction in net receipts by the U.S. Government, taking into account payments by the Federal Reserve to the Treasury.

The Committee has examined other means of altering the structure of reserve requirements, in a way that might represent an improvement over the present arrangement for member banks, and might also accommodate small nonmember banks if they were required to maintain reserves as specified by the Federal Reserve Board, while causing a minimum of transitional disturbance.

The Committee has analyzed in specific terms a possible graduated system of reserve requirements, and a large majority was convinced that, under present circumstances, an approach along these lines was the most practical. Under such a system, every bank would maintain a low reserve against the first few million of its net demand deposits, a higher reserve against its deposits above this minimum amount and up to a substantial figure, and a still higher reserve against net demand deposits, if any, above the latter amount. By way of illustration, banks, at least initially, might be required to keep a 7-per cent reserve requirement against the first $5 million of net demand deposits; a 12-per cent requirement (the present country bank level) against the next $95 million, and a 16½-per cent requirement (the present city bank level) against net demand deposits above $100 million. As at present, ranges within which the Federal Reserve could vary the required percentages would be specified for each bracket—ranges which probably should overlap, at least for the two higher brackets.

A system of this type would represent an improvement over the present system, whether or not all commercial banks were subject to the reserve requirements of the Federal Reserve. It would bring some of the advantages of uniform reserve requirements, since banks of the same size (with respect to demand deposits) would be subject to identical requirements regardless of location. The sharp differential between classes in the present two-way classification would be replaced by a smoothly graduated system. As a bank grew and passed into another reserve bracket, the higher requirement would apply only to its marginal demand deposits. The character of the present reserve requirement structure could be preserved to the extent deemed desirable, by continuing to place higher marginal requirements on larger banks. Similarly, a graduated system would facilitate a transition to greater uniformity—or, to full uniformity—if and when desired.

MONETARY RESTRICTION THROUGH

OPEN-MARKET OPERATIONS AND

RESERVE-REQUIREMENT VARIATION

JOSEPH ASCHHEIM

The relative merits of restrictive open-market operations versus reserve-requirement increases have for several years, been in lively controversy among economists and central bankers. In the *Economic Journal* alone, a half dozen papers [1] have been evoked by this writer's essay in the December 1959 issue that had expounded the preferability of the open-market tool. This writer's subsequent reformulation of the argument in the June 1963 issue has more recently still been challenged in a 1964 article by Mr. A. D. Bain [2] of Cambridge University. Mr. Bain's is perhaps the most fundamental attack yet upon the notion of a clear-cut superiority of the open-market tool over the reserve-requirement tool. He appealingly contends that "a monetary authority endowed with both weapons will have a more flexible control of the economy which can use only one." [3]

The task of this essay is threefold. First, we examine the basis for the above quoted preference of the combination of both tools of central

---

[1] For all references see *Economic Journal*, June 1963, Vol. 73, p. 254.
[2] A. D. Bain, "Monetary Control Through Open-Market Operations and Reserve-Requirement Variations," *Economic Journal*, March 1964, Vol. 74, pp. 137–146.
[3] *Ibid.*, p. 137.

Adapted from Joseph Aschheim, "Restrictive Open-Market Operations versus Reserve-Requirement Increases: A Reformation," Economic Journal, June 1963, Vol. 73, p. 254.

banking over the open-market tool alone. We find this basis faulty. Second, we explore the general question of the choice of the number of policy instruments in light of the theory of economic policy. We find that two policy instruments are not necessarily better than one. Finally, we consider a previously unuttered implication of the entire controversy over open-market operations versus reserve-requirement variation. We find that the preferability of open-market operations remains intact even when the question of the direct control of nonbank financial intermediaries is brought into consideration.

BASIC ASSUMPTIONS IN QUESTION

Demonstration of the preferability of restrictive open-market operations to increased cash-reserve requirements rests on a set of assumptions that were chosen by this writer for their relevance to the case at issue. The case is that of commercial banks being loaned up as the monetary authority seeks to reduce the volume of commercial-bank demand deposits by a given amount. To state these assumptions symbolically, we denote with respect to commercial banks:

D = deposits
o = after restrictive open-market operations
r = after an increase of reserve requirements
C = required cash reserves
S = Government securities
L = private loans
E = earning assets
Z = total liquidity of assets
Z_c = liquidity coefficient of cash
Z_s = liquidity coefficient of securities
Z_l = liquidity coefficient of loans

Accordingly, the definitions and behavioral premises are as follows:

1. $D_o = D_r$
2. $D_o = C_o + S_o + L_o$
3. $D_r = C_r + S_r + L_r$
4. $C_r > C_o$
5. $E_o = S_o + L_o$

6. $E_r = S_r + L_r$
7. $Z_o \gtreqqless Z_r$
8. $Z_o = Z_c C_o + Z_s S_o + Z_l L_o$
9. $Z_r = Z_c C_r + Z_s S_r + Z_l L_r$
10. $Z_c > Z_s > Z_l.$

Now Mr. Bain's strictures are based upon his challenge of equation (7) above. Specifically, he states,

What I am challenging are the assumptions behind equation (7) of Professor Aschheim's formal analysis. This equation is the mathematical equivalent of the statement that the total liquidity of bank assets will be no higher after an increase in reserve requirements than after an open-market operation of equivalent magnitude. If, as in equations (8) and (9), the total liquidity of the portfolio is defined as the sum of the liquidity contributed by each of the component assets and no account is taken of the level of required reserves in determining the contribution of reserves to total liquidity I find this statement unacceptable. And if the inequality expressed in equation (7) is not accepted the subsequent analysis falls.[4]

Thus, as Mr. Bain correctly reiterates, equation (7) means that total liquidity of bank assets will be no higher after an increase of reserve requirements than after a restrictive open-market operation of equivalent size. Now, as Mr. Bain also correctly reiterates, the total liquidity of bank assets is defined as the sum of the liquidity of each of the various types of asset. Mr. Brain is, however, in error when saying, "If . . . no account is taken of the level of required reserves in determining the contribution of reserves to total liquidity. . . . " [5] In this clause, Mr. Bain misses the point,[6] that precisely because account *is* taken of the level of required reserves in determining the contribution of reserves to total liquidity, is the behavioral relationship stated as equation (7) included. In other words, it is exactly because higher reserve requirements augment the banks' capacity to meet deposit drains out of their required reserves that banks are held, as symbolized in equation (7), to be seeking to maintain no greater total liquidity of their assets after an increase of reserve requirements than after a restrictive open-market operation. Thus, rejection of the inequality expressed in equation (7) would itself mean failure to take account of the level

[4] *Ibid.*, pp. 139–140.
[5] *Ibid.*
[6] This point is referred to by this writer as the "liquidity" effect; Aschheim, *op. cit.*, p. 255.

of required reserves in determining the contribution of reserves to total liquidity. And if such failure is avoided, the basis for Mr. Bain's contention collapses.

Likewise, when Mr. Bain makes "the assumption that the maximum deposit drain against which the commercial banks maintain secondary reserves is independent of the means by which the authorities force the contraction of their deposits," [7] he fails to take into account the level of required reserves in determining the contribution of cash reserves to total liquidity. To avoid this failure, his assumption must be abandoned. And if his assumption is abandoned, his balance-sheet examination is voided. Not even his identification of a reason for the holding of securities and loans other than that of meeting deposit drains can sustain his case. For the fact, pointed out by Mr. Bain, that "reserves and securities may be held to ensure that if there is a deposit drain commercial banks may be able to maintain the legally required reserve ratios" [8] is itself taken care of in the holding of reserves and securities for the purpose of meeting deposit drains.[9] So long as commercial banks are law abiding, their capacity to meet deposit drains automatically includes the capacity to maintain the legally required reserve ratios when a deposit drain occurs.

Mr. Bain's further contention that his "objection will only be important if legal or conventional restraints on the minimum levels of cash or liquid assets are effective" [10] is equally unsustainable. Apart from the fact that this writer's analysis was explicitly directed to the case where commercial banks are already loaned up,[11] the capacity to meet deposit drains implies the capacity to maintain the legally required reserve ratios as well, not only when commercial banks have excess reserves but also when they do not. Accordingly, Mr. Bain's strictures founder regardless of whether their empirical context is the United Kingdom or the United States.[12]

---

[7] Bain, *op. cit.*, p. 139.

[8] *Ibid.*

[9] Likewise, the fact mentioned by Bain (*Ibid.*, p. 140, footnote 1) following D. C. Rowan, that "banks also hold liquid assets to avoid having to embarrass their customers" is also taken care of in the holding of reserves and securities for the purpose of meeting deposit drains.

[10] *Ibid.*, p. 140.

[11] Aschheim, *op. cit.*, pp. 254, 258.

[12] It is noteworthy that Mr. Bain's only reference to monetary policy in the United States is entirely misleading. He states (Bain, *op. cit.*, p. 144, footnote 1), "Partially compensating change in reserve-requirements and open-market operations have, of course, been carried out by the Federal Reserve System. For example, a reduction of required reserves in 1958 was timed to provide the reserves needed for subscriptions

Now, as shown by this writer,[13] the comparative advantage of restrictive open-market operations in curbing the shifting by commercial banks from securities to loans necessarily implies a smaller rise in interest rates on Government securities than would occur under the impact of an increase of reserve requirements. Mr. Bain's positive analysis, i.e., the latter part of his article subsequent to his examination of this writer's essay,[14] expounds the argument that open-market operations make for a *greater* rise in interest rates than would be brought about by an increase of reserve requirements.[15] This positive analysis, however,

---

for a new Treasury Issue." Now, in the first place, the "example" cited by Mr. Bain is quite irrelevant to his analysis. For the "example" refers to the combination of a *reduction* in reserve requirements with open-market *sales* of securities, whereas his analysis refers to "combining a *rise* in reserve requirements with open-market purchases of securities" (*Ibid.*, p. 143; the italics are Mr. Bain's). Secondly, since the restoration of American central banking to an active role as a result of the Treasury-Federal Reserve Accord of March 1951, there has not been a single instance of the Federal Reserve System combining a *rise* in reserve requirements with open-market operations. Indeed, there has been not a single increase in reserve requirements by the Federal Reserve System since the activation of American central banking with the March 1951 Accord. Thirdly, in the United States, Treasury issues are separate from, and not a component of, the open-market operations by the Federal Reserve System. Finally, the reduction of reserve requirements in 1958 was combined with substantial open-market *purchases* of securities by the Federal Reserve System, as well as with reductions of Federal Reserve discount rates. Thus, if it is an example of anything, the timing of the reduction of required reserves in 1958 is an example of "a condition of ease [being] . . . being cultivated by the active use of each of the three major instruments of Federal Reserve policy." (*Treasury-Federal Reserve Study of the Government Securities Market, Part II: Factual Review for 1958* [published in February 1960], p. 15.) In sum, contrary to Mr. Bain's reference to monetary policy in the United States, there exists not a single instance of American monetary policy since postwar activation of central banking that could serve as an illustration of his own version of a restrictive monetary control.

[13] Aschheim, *op. cit.*, p. 262.

[14] Bain, *op. cit.*, pp. 140–146.

[15] Equally as noteworthy as his reference to American monetary policy quoted in footnote 12 above is Mr. Bain's conjecture with respect to the effectiveness of the Central Bank's intention to keep the interest rate constant. He states (*Ibid.*, p. 145, footnote 1), "If the commercial banks were aware of the Authorities' intention to maintain the rate of interest they would not sell any securities, since by doing so they are exchanging a higher for a lower yielding asset. This would reduce the scale of the operation required." Mr. Bain seems to attach enormous potency to the impact upon their portfolio policy of the commercial banks' awareness that the monetary authority intends to keep the interest rate constant: he goes so far as to say that if the commercial banks had such awareness, they would sell no securities at all. Now there is certainly no great problem in imparting to the commercial banks awareness of the monetary authority's intent. One way of imparting such awareness is to *tell* the commercial banks of the monetary authority's intent, i.e., to use moral suasion. (See J.

rests on his assumption that "when forced to contract their assets the banks choose to liquidate earning assets in the proportion X of securities to $(1 - X)$ of loans under either measure." [16] By this assumption, the banks' ratio of securities to loans is fixed without regard to the level of the cash reserve requirement. Thus, this assumption—like Mr. Bain's previously quoted assumption respecting the maximum deposit drain against which commercial banks maintain secondary reserves—fails to take into account the contribution which the level of required reserves makes to the total liquidity of bank assets. The recognition of such contribution necessitates rejection of Mr. Bain's assumption of a fixed

---

Aschheim, Techniques of Monetary Control [Baltimore: The Johns Hopkins Press, 1961], pp. 99–110.) In light of recorded experience with the use of moral suasion at least in the United States, unbounded faith in the potency of substituting "open-mouth" operations for open-market operations or for reserve-requirement variation appears little short of absurd. To illustrate, consider the following comment by the Presidents of Federal Reserve Banks on their postwar experience with moral suasion:

> "A mild degree of moral suasion probably was exercised in the fall of 1950 when Board and Reserve Bank official and Reserve Bank officials on several occasions indicated that reserve requirements of member banks would be increased unless the rapid expansion of bank credit was checked. . . . Also, on different occasions during the past few years, there have been references to unorthodox or particularly restrictive reserve proposals as a possible consequence of continued monetization of government securities by banking and nonbanking investors, which might be considered as a form of moral suasion. Neither of these efforts, however, met with any appreciable degree of success." (Quoted in Aschheim, loc. cit., p. 102.)

An alternative way of imparting to the commercial banks' awareness of the central bank's intent to keep the interest rate constant is not merely to tell them of this intent but to implement Mr. Bain's suggested combination of a rise in reserve requirements with open-market purchases of securities by the central bank. This was in large part the "restrictive" policy of the Federal Reserve System during World War II and the immediate postwar period leading up to the Treasury-Federal Reserve Accord of March 1951. In other words, Central-Bank restrictiveness was exerted through increases of reserve requirements, and the simultaneous intention of the Central Bank to keep the interest rate constant was carried out by means of open-market purchases of securities in whatever volume necessary to keep the interest rate constant. Contrary to Mr. Bain's above-quoted footnote, the commercial banks' awareness of the Central Bank's intention led to substantial unloading of Government securities by the commercial banks (and others), whenever they had incentive to shift from securities to loans. It was, of course, precisely this Federal Reserve policy that led to the paralysis of central banking as a counter-inflationary weapon and that was rendering the Federal Reserve System an engine of inflation. This policy was terminated with the Treasury-Federal Reserve Accord, which has enabled the Federal Reserve to back away from the open market, indeed even to *sell* Government securities, thereby letting the interest rate rise, whenever the curbing of private lending activity is considered by the monetary authority desirable.

[16] Bain, *op. cit.*, p. 141.

ratio of securities to loans that is independent of the level of reserve requirements. With this assumption rejected, his subsequent analysis falls and with it falls his appealing conclusion that a monetary policy endowed with both weapons will be superior to a central bank which can use only one.

THE OPTIMAL NUMBER OF TOOLS

At first sight, there would seem to be an appeal that is all but self-evident in the argument that, "because their effects differ, a monetary authority endowed with both weapons will have a more flexible control of the economy than an authority which can use only one" [17] in the attempt to control the level of total expenditure. This argument is only a special case of the "note of questioning and caution" [18] that has been sounded for monetary policy generally on the grounds that "The simple fact is that precise conclusions are impossible on most matters in this area." [19] In view of this fact, "The moral is plain that central bankers require a full complement of instruments and a flexible approach to their problems. This is the only sure conclusion that can legitimately be drawn." [20] With all due respect to the authority of these pronouncements, we still venture to inquire, How sure is the foregoing conclusion? How legitimately can it be drawn? Indeed, what does the conclusion mean?

The idea that, because their effects differ, a central bank endowed with two control instruments will have a more flexible control of the economy than a central bank endowed with only one, presumably means that one instrument alone is less than a full complement of instruments. In turn, if their effects differed, three instruments would be preferable to two, and a mere two would, therefore, be less than a full complement. Indeed, if their effects still differed, four instruments would be preferable to three, and a mere three would, therefore, be

[17] Bain, *op. cit.*, p. 137.
[18] C. R. Whittlesey, "Monetary Policy and Economic Change," *Review of Economics and Statistics*, February 1957, Vol. 39, p. 39.
[19] *Ibid.*
[20] *Ibid.* A related conclusion that Professor Whittlesey finds it possible to draw is the following: "The general rule should be that 'there can be no such thing as a bad instrument of monetary policy that works.' There can be bad use of an instrument but not a bad instrument. If a particular technique is used in the wrong way or at the wrong time this is a defect of the administration, not of the technique." (C. R. Whittlesey, *Lectures on Monetary Management* [Bombay: University of Bombay, 1960], p. 82.)

less than a full complement. In general, when is the complement of instruments full?

For an attempted answer to this last question we must turn to the theory of economic policy pioneered in by Professor Tinbergen [21] and further developed by Professor Theil and associates.[22] We shall now recapitulate this theory merely in terms of its implications for the choice of the number of policy instruments.

Included in the conceptual setting within which the theory of economic policy is cast is the distinction between instruments and targets. Instruments are the predetermined variables controlled by the policy-makers. Targets are the jointly-dependent variables whose values are the object of preference of the policy-makers. The function of Tinbergen's "fixed targets" approach is to set forth the relationship between instruments and targets, i.e., to show what the numerical values are that the policy-maker would have to use in order to attain particular given values of the target variables. Essentially this is an approach to policy decision-making consisting of the solution of a system of simultaneous equations wherein the values of the instrument variables are the unknowns and the targets are specified by the policy-makers.

Now if the number of instruments is equal to the number of targets, the policy model is just-determined, making it possible to solve for all the unknowns of the model. There is, however, no *a priori* guarantee that this equality will obtain; the instruments and targets may well be different in number. If targets outnumber instruments, there will be more equations than unknowns, and the policy model is over-determined. This situation confronts the policy-maker with insoluble tasks, for the targets will, except by coincidence, be mutually incompatible. In consequence, one or more of the targets would have to be abandoned or compromised, or else the number of instruments will have to be increased.

Conversely, if the number of instruments exceeds the number of targets, there will be more unknowns than equations, and the policy model will be undetermined. In this situation there is an infinity of solutions which may, however, be easily corrected by fixing arbitrary values for the excessive instruments and solving for the remaining ones.

Tinbergen himself depicts the situation where the number of in-

[21] See especially J. Tinbergen, *On the Theory of Economic Policy*, 2nd Edition (Amsterdam: North Holland Publishing Company, 1955); and J. Tinbergen, *Economic Policy: Principles and Design* (Amsterdam: North Holland Publishing Company, 1956).
[22] See especially H. Theil, *Economic Forecasts and Policy* (Amsterdam: North Holland Publishing Company, 1961).

struments exceeds the number of targets as "the most attractive situation, from a practical standpoint, since it evidently means that there are, in principle, an infinity of solutions." [23] In other words, there is greater flexibility for the policy-makers than in the equality situation in that if the targets are inconsistent with one set of instruments, the policy-makers are free to try another set of instruments. One possible implication of this "attractiveness" of the third situation is that the greater the flexibility for the policy-makers as expressed in the magnitude of the excess of instruments over targets, the better. Alternatively stated, the ideal or optional number of instruments is the maximal number.

Yet there are considerable hazards in inferring such an implication from the "fixed-targets" approach. Tinbergen himself points to some of these. For one thing, inexperience with or ignorance of the effects of some instruments precludes their use. Specifically, "our empirical quantitative knowledge of human behavior under different structural conditions is so restricted. Statistical observation may shed some light on the reactions of consumers and producers under varying conditions of prices, incomes, or costs, but we know very little about what a man does if private property is changed into public property; or if he knows that a decline in his productivity may bring him into a concentration camp." [24] Second, there is some correlation between the number of instruments and the type of instruments. "Instruments may be overall controls or detailed controls and they may be objective or discriminatory. As a rule, policies with a small number of instruments tend to use overall instruments of an objective nature, judging each individual case on the basis of well-defined objective criteria. Policies with a large number of instruments will tend to detailed controls and to discriminatory treatment of individual cases." [25]

An alternative (and more recent) approach to the "fixed-targets" approach is that by Theil of maximizing a preference function which takes the place of the fixed targets. The policy-makers here too have in mind certain desired values but these values refer to all the variables, including the instruments. Maximization of the preference function implies choosing values for the instruments that will minimize the weighted sum of squared deviations of realized from desired values, the weights reflecting the relative priorities of the respective variables.

In the "preference-function maximizing" approach there is always a unique solution of the policy model, while in the "fixed-targets"

---

[23] Tinbergen, *On the Theory of Economic Policy, op. cit.*, p. 37.
[24] *Ibid.*, p. 72.
[25] *Ibid.*, p. 70.

approach the existence of a solution depends on the number of instruments relative to that of targets. Thus, whatever practical difficulties there may be in the specification of variables in the preference function, this approach does not connote any necessity to have equality between the number of instruments and the number of targets. Indeed, absence of the equality constraint is one of the major comparative advantages of the "preference-function maximizing" approach that has led to its supplanting of the "fixed-targets" approach in recent applied research. Moreover, while in the case of the "fixed-targets" approach, flexibility for the policy-makers is enhanced by the excess of instruments over targets, in the "preference-function maximizing" approach flexibility is a result of the freedom of this latter approach from the equality constraint.

Though lacking the charm of the rule-of-thumb simplicity of the "fixed-targets" approach, the "preference-function maximizing" approach has the greater realism and sophistication by virtue of (a) its explicit introduction of instruments as targets and (b) its avowed recognition that deviation from particular values of these instruments may have considerable disutility, especially over short time spans. Thus, the very notion of flexibility for the policy-makers that emerges from this approach is distinctive from maximization of the size of the tool kit: it is a notion incorporating the idea that certain movements of particular instruments may have negative utility. In turn, this idea implies that some conceivable or even available instruments can, in any of several respects, have a social-nuisance value that may militate against their use altogether or when certain alternative instruments are available. The modern theory of economic policy diverges, therefore, from the affirmation that a full complement of instruments is identical with a maximum complement.

Accordingly, the fact that two instruments of monetary control differ in their effects does not necessarily suggest that a monetary authority endowed with both instruments has a more *flexible* control of the economy than an authority which can use only one. If one of the two instruments carries with it drawbacks that its distinctive effects do not offset, its addition to the monetary authority's tool kit may be an outright nuisance. The comparison between open-market operations and reserve-requirement variation is a case in point. The present writer's conclusion that restrictive open-market operations are preferable to reserve-requirement increases was confined to the comparison of the effects of the two on the capital market, i.e., on the banks shifting from securities to loans and on the consequent rise in yields on government securities. On both counts, open-market operations turn out to be more moderate than reserve-requirement increases with references to a given reduction in the money supply. When, in addition, other considerations are included the preferability of open-market operations is decisive. As another writer has aptly concluded from his own comparison of the two instruments, "Since the use of two weapons of monetary control where one will serve the purpose tends to make for confusion and uncertainty, there is much to be said for doing away with redundant and ineffective controls. Accordingly, once reserve requirements have been established at what seems to be the proper level from a secular standpoint . . . it might be desirable to take away from the Board of Governors the power to change requirements in normal times. If the authority is left intact, it should be used very sparingly." [26]

RESERVE REQUIREMENTS AND FINANCIAL INTERMEDIARIES

Finally, though largely unuttered in the course of the extended controversy over the relative merits of restrictive open-market operations versus reserve-requirement increases, one particular policy implication of this controversy accounts in substantial measure for the liveliness and protraction of the controversy. This implication has been given expression in a different context, namely: in the contemporaneous discussion of nonbank financial intermediaries. The new theory of finance,[27] which has given rise to the call for extension of direct central-bank controls to financial intermediaries generally, has also led to explicit consideration of the institution of cash-reserve requirements for nonbank intermediaries. Now the conclusion that restrictive open-market operations are preferable to reserve-requirement increases tends, on its face, to militate against the extension of cash-reserve requirements to nonbank intermediaries. For while cash reserve-requirements are confined to those particular institutions that are legally or otherwise compelled to adhere to the requirements, the institutional scope of open-

[26] W. L. Smith, "Reserve Requirements in the American Monetary System" in *Monetary Management*, prepared for the Commission on Money and Credit, Research Study Two. (Englewood Cliffs, New Jersey: Prentice-Hall, 1963), pp. 215–216.
[27] J. G. Gurley and E. S. Shaw, "Financial Aspects of Economic Development," *American Economic Review*, September 1955, Vol. 45, pp. 515–538; and J. G. Gurley and E. S. Shaw, *Money in a Theory of Finance* (Washington, D.C.: The Brookings Institution, 1960).

market operations is as wide as the extent of the securities market, which encompasses financial intermediaries generally. Thus, relegation of the reserve-requirement instrument to a position of inferiority to open-market operations appears to detract from the call for extension of central-bank controls beyond commercial banks.

On further reflection, however, it becomes clear that both the feasibility and desirability of cash-reserve requirements for nonbank intermediaries do not hinge upon validity of the thesis that commercial banks and nonbank financial intermediaries are essentially similar. In other words, even rejection of the new theory of finance does not *ipso facto* imply rejection of cash-reserve requirements for nonbank intermediaries.

Thus, among scholars who recognize—indeed, emphasize—an essential difference between commercial banks and nonbank intermediaries, there are some who, nevertheless, find considerable merit in applying cash-reserve requirements to nonbank intermediaries.[28] Fundamentally, the case for such application is that it would permit the central bank to constrain the capacity of nonbank intermediaries to change the velocity of money. The question then becomes the dual one of (a) whether any regulation of the velocity of money could make a contribution to economic stability that the regulation of the quantity of money alone could not make; and, if so, (b) whether regulation of the velocity of money through application of cash-reserve requirements to nonbank intermediaries would be a more efficient, equitable and convenient regulation technique than other measures such as the direct control of spending units that are quantitatively most important in the generation of cyclical fluctuations. Thus, once outright regulation of the velocity of money is contemplated, determination of the institutional scope of direct controls should encompass the consideration not only of financial intermediaries but of spending units, too, as objects of control.

In any case, our comparison of open-market operations with reserve-requirement variation is applicable to reserve requirements for nonbank intermediaries as well as for commercial banks. Both groups of financial enterprises are participants in the Government securities market, and both would be subject to the differential "income" and "liquidity" effects of cash reserve-requirements imposed or increased at

---

[28] E. C. Ettin and W. P. Yohe, "Reserve Requirement Control of Financial Intermediaries," *National Banking Review*, June 1964, Vol. 1, pp. 551–558; see also J. M. Henderson, "Monetary Reserves and Credit Control," *American Economic Review*, June 1960, Vol. 50, pp. 362–368.

a time when these enterprises would have to liquidate earning assets to meet the requirements. Consequently, even in terms of regulating the influence of nonbank intermediaries upon the velocity of money, open-market operations are preferable to cash-reserve requirements for nonbank intermediaries in an economy with a well-developed securities market already in existence.

THE NEED FOR RESERVE

REQUIREMENTS AND RESERVE

BALANCES AT THE

FEDERAL RESERVE BANKS

DEANE CARSON

In this selection the author argues that legal reserve requirements are unnecessary to effective monetary control.

Desired cash holdings of the banking system limit the marginal expansion of bank deposits and, to the extent that they are influenced by legal reserve requirements, it can be said that the latter serve as a fulcrum for credit control. More precisely, however, the monetary control mechanism operates via changes in the level of total reserves relative to desired cash holdings of the banking system. I shall contend in this section that the necessity for legal reserve requirements and minimum cash balances at Federal Reserve banks is a function of the particular objectives of Federal Reserve policy; I shall further argue that the locus of the banking system's cash reserves is of little significance with respect to either the structure of the Federal Reserve System, or its effectiveness as a central bank.

Reprinted from Deane Carson, "Is the Federal Reserve System Really Necessary?," Journal of Finance, December 1964, pp. 658–660.

[266]

THE FUNCTIONS OF RESERVE REQUIREMENTS
AND A PROPOSAL

Reserve requirement changes are a substitute for open market operations.[1] An initial justification for the existence of legal reserve requirements is, therefore, that their levels can be changed, and with them monetary and credit expansion potentials. It is not within the scope of this discussion to weigh the merits of changes in reserve requirements *versus* changes in open market portfolio of the central bank. In a zero per cent reserve requirement banking system, however, it must be recognized that the substitute, imperfect as it now is from the standpoint of effectuating monetary control, would no longer exist.

It can be argued, therefore, that some future situation might arise that would call for the raising of reserve requirements, even though the Federal Reserve Board has not seen a need to do so since February 1951, thirteen years and several business expansions ago.[2] I recognize this possibility as a defect in the plan, but a defect which could be easily remedied through congressional action, given the compelling circumstances that would give rise to the need.

Quite apart from the above, a great deal of emphasis has been given to the *level* of legal reserve requirements as a base which limits the potential expansion of money and credit. Arithmetical exercises in standard textbooks "prove" that the height of reserve requirements determines the maximum expansion potential of any given amount of excess reserves, subject to assumptions that are usually specified.[3] It is not at all clear that this fact is relevant to the functionality of legal reserve requirements. In the first place, banks individually and in the aggregate would hold some level of desired cash reserves against deposits in the absence of legal requirements,[4] thus providing the "base" for monetary and credit expansion (or contraction).

In the second place, since the levels of reserve requirements have been progressively lowered (with few reversals) in the postwar period

[1] Cf. Joseph Aschheim, *Techniques of Monetary Control* (Baltimore: The Johns Hopkins Press, 1961), Chapter 2.

[2] On November 26, 1960, the Board raised country bank reserve requirements from 11 to 12 per cent, while simultaneously permitting the calculation of vault cash in the reserve base. This increase was a technical adjustment to the inclusion of vault cash and therefore does not count as a monetary policy action.

[3] Zero desired excess reserves, and no change in cash in circulation.

[4] For example, state chartered banks in Illinois are not subject to reserve requirements, yet they keep something in the order of 12 per cent of their deposits in cash.

without appreciably affecting the performance of monetary policy, the question can be raised as to why they are at all necessary in the present context—that is, as a limitation on the potential expansion of money and credit.

Cash reserves can be controlled by open market operations, and the tone of the market observed by the simple device of central bank hypothecation of the market's desired level of bank cash reserves. Given continuation of reporting requirements, the device of "shadow reserve requirements" suggested here would enable the central bank to observe "excess reserves," "free reserves," and "net borrowed reserves" as indicators of money market conditions without the necessity of formal requirements.

The plan would work in the following way: suppose the Federal Reserve Board were to announce that it considered X per cent of deposits (details aside) an appropriate level of cash reserves for the commercial banks (or some segment of the banking system).[5] Periodic reports to the Federal Reserve on actual cash holdings and deposits would give the monetary authorities precisely the same "feel of the market" that they now require to conduct defensive open market operations to offset very short-term disturbances in the money market.

It is of course a debatable question whether offsetting these changes is an appropriate objective of monetary control in the pursuit of longer range goals of full employment, price level stability, and economic expansion. Many would argue that day-to-day fluctuations in cash reserves need not interfere with the achievement of an appropriate level of change in the money supply which, after all, is the most important means of realizing the goals. Beyond this, it has been argued persuasively that free reserves are a misleading guide for monetary management.[6]

---

[5] It is not necessary to make such an announcement to generate the statistical indicators. However, an announced level of appropriate reserves would benefit portfolio managers and managers of reserve positions in that it would remove one source of uncertainty as to central bank policy that would exist if the announcement were not made.

[6] Cf. A. James Meigs, *Free Reserves and The Money Supply* (Chicago: The University of Chicago Press, 1962).

SLIPPAGE EFFECTS OF THE ZERO RESERVE REQUIREMENT PROPOSAL

The proposal set out in skeleton form above raises a very obvious question: Will the abolition of reserve requirements increase the slippage that now exists between policy actions and policy results? Contrary to one's first inclination to answer affirmatively, it is not at all certain that this should be the case.

We are not concerned with slippages in general, but rather with one segment of the total lag between policy actions and their ultimate effects upon income and prices. This segment is the initial one, that which spans the sequence between a change in total cash reserves of the commercial banks and the employment of these reserves in loans and investments.

While this is basically an empirical question, intuition leads to the belief that if banks individually and collectively are in equilibrium (in the sense that their cash to deposit ratios are at the desired level), changes in cash reserves occasioned by open market operations will elicit responses quickly and in the right direction. If the Federal Reserve purchases securities (presumably, but not necessarily with Federal Reserve notes), the banks will find actual cash in excess of desired cash, and will take steps (loans, investments) to return to equilibrium.

On the other hand, sales of securities by the central bank will push the banks into equilibrium in the opposite direction. If the Federal Reserve retains its discount window, the deficit banks could choose between "borrowing" from themselves and borrowing from the Federal Reserve Bank. As Sprinkel has pointed out, the discount window is itself an institutionally sanctioned source of slippage;[7] I would suggest that its usefulness would depart with the demise of legal reserve requirements.

In effect each bank would have its own discount window; but we know that banks eschew borrowing as sin, and there is no reason to believe that this attitude would change just because the lender was the bank itself. I suspect that loan and investment officers would keep an even sharper eye on the actual cash ratio than they now do on the free reserve position. Temporary departures from desired equilibrium would occasion furrowed brows in the Board room and charges

[7] Beryl Sprinkel, "Monetary Growth as an Economic Predictor," *Journal of Finance,* September 1959, p. 342.

to the operating officers to "get the cash ratio back where it is supposed to be."

Over the monetary cycle the banks might well change their levels of desired cash reserves relative to deposits in a way that would counteract monetary policy. But this is hardly a peculiar defect of the zero reserve requirement proposal, since in effect precisely the same thing occurs with existing legal reserve requirements.

THE DISCOUNT MECHANISM

AND MONETARY POLICY

After a brief statement of policy with respect to the administration of the discount window, this article discusses the role of the discount rate under conditions of credit "restraint" and credit "ease."

Discount policy at any time consists primarily of two aspects: administration of the "discount window," and setting the discount rate.

ADMINISTRATION OF THE DISCOUNT WINDOW

The twelve Reserve Banks administer the function of lending to member banks in their respective districts as well as setting the rate which is subject to approval by the Federal Reserve Board. The principles used by each Reserve Bank in judging an application for a loan are set forth in Regulation A of the Board of Governors which reads in part as follows:

Federal Reserve credit is generally extended on a short-term basis to a member bank in order to enable it to adjust its asset position when necessary because of developments such as a sudden withdrawal of deposits or seasonal requirements for credit beyond those which can reasonably be met by use of the bank's own resources. . . . Under ordinary conditions, the continuous use of Federal Reserve credit by a member bank over a considerable period of time is not regarded as appropriate.

Reprinted from Monthly Review, *Federal Reserve Bank of St. Louis, September 1960*, pp. 5–9.

In considering a request for credit accommodation, each Federal Reserve bank gives due regard to the purpose of the credit and to its probable effects upon the maintenance of sound credit conditions, both as to the individual institution and the economy generally. It keeps informed of and takes into account the general character and amount of the loans and investments of the member banks. It considers whether the bank is borrowing principally for the purpose of obtaining a tax advantage or profiting from rate differentials and whether the bank is extending an undue amount of credit for the speculative carrying of or trading in securities, real estate, or commodities, or otherwise.

Administration of the discount privilege does not change with shifts in monetary policy. The Reserve Banks are aided in their enforcement of Regulation A by the traditional reluctance of some commercial banks to remain indebted.

THE DISCOUNT RATE

The discount rate is the interest rate charged by the Reserve Banks on loans to member banks. This then becomes the cost of obtaining additional reserves through such borrowing. As brought out above a member bank has several alternatives in adjusting to short-run changes in its reserve position. The decision as to which method is adopted is determined in large part by the relative cost. The relative cost is frequently determined by: (1) the loss or gain realized on the sale of a short-term earning asset, and (2) the relation between the discount rate and other short-term money market rates.

Insofar as an individual member bank is concerned, an adjustment in its reserve position through any of the alternative methods stated above solves the bank's immediate problem. From the standpoint of monetary policy the type of reserve adjustment is important. Adjustments in reserves which are made through transactions in the Federal funds market or in Treasury bills represent merely a transfer of funds. No reserves are created or destroyed in this process. On the other hand, borrowing or the repaying of borrowing from the Reserve Banks increases or diminishes total reserves of the banking system. As we have seen, this is the variable upon which the System operates in order to affect bank credit.

Open market operations have been in recent years the primary means through which the Federal Reserve exercises control over member bank reserves. Changes in borrowing from the Reserve Banks, which are at the initiative of the individual member banks, may offset temporarily the effects of open market operations. However, since the discount rate has an influence on the decisions of member banks either to borrow from the System or make their temporary reserve adjustments in some other way, the relationship of the discount rate to other market rates may tend to cause member bank borrowing in the aggregate to supplement, rather than offset, open market policies.

The following set of examples is designed to show how discount policy combined with open market operations function first in a period when the Federal Reserve is attempting to exercise credit restraint, and then again in a period of credit ease. It will be assumed in both cases that the banking system is initially in a state of equilibrium. That is, total bank credit is at a desired level and excess reserves and borrowings from the Reserve Banks are at levels which the member banks consider satisfactory. In addition we will assume that the economy is operating at a relatively high level and experiencing growth with prices about stable.

Example 1—Credit Restraint

Assume for the moment that the demand for bank credit increases and that interest rates and prices are tending to creep up, and that the System would decide that supplying additional reserves via open market operations to meet this credit demand would be inflationary. As the demand for credit increases, member banks will seek additional reserves by selling securities or borrowing from the Federal Reserve. As short-term interest rates rise relative to the discount rate, banks will find it more desirable to adjust their reserve positions by increased borrowings from the System rather than by selling Treasury bills. As a result commercial bank credit would expand—new reserves being supplied by the System in the form of additional loans to member banks.

In order to slow up the rate of increase in member bank reserves, the System might reduce its open market purchases or allow market forces (gold outflows, cash drainage, or a rise in Treasury balances) to pinch reserves. Commercial banks would now find that in order to avoid reserve deficiencies it becomes necessary to further increase their indebtedness to the Federal Reserve. Although the intent of the System is to restrain the credit expansion, it will permit the use of the discount window to cushion the shock of reserve stringency for individual banks. In this sense the discount mechanism will act as a safety valve.

It should be recognized that the increase in member bank bor-

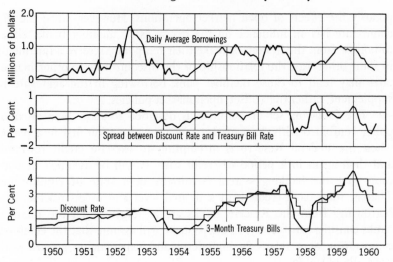

Member bank borrowings from Federal Reserve banks, discount rate and Treasury bill rate. Largest data plotted: August preliminary.

rowing will offset initially the objectives of open market policy oriented toward restraint. To make this borrowing more costly and reduce the incentive to use the discount window the System may raise the discount rate. It may be noted that the Federal Reserve policy of restraint is already underway. The rise in the discount rate is not a signal initiating a change in policy as much as it is a move to strengthen a policy already in effect.

Example 2—Credit Ease
Starting once again from our assumed initial position, let us consider what happens if the demands for credit begin to slow up or contract, market interest rates are falling, and the possibility of a weakening in economic activity appears. The banking system will probably find itself with more than the desired level of borrowing and may begin to repay borrowings from the Federal Reserve. The Federal Reserve with a view to encouraging full use of resources may supply reserves through open market purchases of securities. As interest rates continue to fall relative to the discount rate, banks would have an added incentive to repay their debt to the Reserve Banks rather than use their reserves for lending or investing. Thus, despite Federal Reserve action to increase reserves, the decline in outstanding borrowing may actually reduce reserves and total bank credit. In order to reduce the incentive

to make further adjustments in reserves through repayment to the System the discount rate might be lowered. Here, again, the change in the discount rate cannot be considered as signalling a change in Federal Reserve policy, but rather a move designed to reinforce open market operations. The marginal advantage of the new-found reserves now rests with expanding investments or loans. Thus, the reserves made available to banks as their loans decline will be used to expand investment holdings when the discount rate is lowered relative to other money market rates. If investment increases more than loans decline, total bank credit and the money supply would tend to rise.

As has been pointed out in the examples above, discount rate changes can be used to keep changes in member bank borrowing from adversely affecting open market operations. Appropriate discount rate policy may be used to supplement open market operations as well as providing a safety valve. In practice, a major difficulty in implementing discount policy is to maintain the discount rate in proper relation to other short-term rates, primarily Treasury bills.

The Federal Reserve may not find it feasible to adjust the discount rate to maintain the desired relationship between it and other rates, for reasons relating to Treasury financing, sudden changes in short-term interest rates, and public reaction to discount rate changes. Thus, it is possible that with infrequent discount rate changes, the movement of other rates can alter the effectiveness of a given discount rate. In periods of boom with rising interest rates, a constant or "lagging" discount rate would provide the same incentive to member bank borrowing as a reduction in the discount rate with other rates unchanged. Similarly, in periods when credit policy is oriented toward ease, a discount rate which lags behind the fall in market rates increases the "effective" cost of member bank borrowing, thus inducing a decline in member bank borrowings (reflected in a greater reluctance to borrow and a stronger incentive to use excess reserves to repay outstanding borrowings). In such situations the discount rate tends to reduce the effectiveness of the open market operations designed to encourage credit expansion.

In light of the above analysis, many of the discount rate changes made by the Federal Reserve System may be considered as "technical adjustments" to market rates reflecting the efforts of monetary authorities to establish a relationship between the discount rate and other market rates appropriate for the effective accomplishment of the objectives of open market operations.

LENDER OF LAST RESORT

This selection may be read with textual assignments covering monetary policy between 1929 and 1931, when, for various reasons, the Federal Reserve failed to serve as a lender of last resort. One should also note the difference in emphasis between this article and the selection beginning on p. 284.

Suppose the business community were suddenly required to pay off all debts, stop all borrowing and lending, and refrain from using credit in any form. How would this development affect the American economy?

The confusion would be enormous. Credit underlies most modern economic activity and its sudden elimination would paralyze business. But in answering this question, it is not necessary to rely on imagination. Economic history provides many vivid examples. Sudden credit stoppages imposed by defective banking systems were common in the days before central banking.

ORIGINS OF THE FEDERAL RESERVE

In this country before 1914 credit "freezes," or banking panics, occurred with discouraging regularity. Popular determination to stop these panics was an important factor in the movement to establish the Federal Reserve System. This System, framed after long study, was expected to insure that credit would always be forthcoming in the necessary amounts. In this role, the System became, in the financial

Reprinted from Monthly Review, Federal Reserve Bank of Richmond, February 1961, pp. 8–10.

language of the early twentieth century, the economy's "lender of last resort."

Credit and Liquidity Before 1914. The Federal Reserve's role as lender of last resort is best appreciated in the light of credit problems before 1914. Relatively, credit was as important then as it is today. A sudden cessation of bank loans and trade credit could seriously reduce business activity. The pyramid of credit then, as now, rested mainly on bank lending. Banks were the chief immediate lenders as well as the indirect source of much of the trade and credit extended by others.

Commercial bank operations before 1914 did not differ markedly from those of today. What did differ, however, was the system of bank organization. In particular, in the earlier period no provision was made to insure the liquidity of the banking system, as distinct from that of individual banks.

Liquidity, the ability to meet creditor claims when due, is of course a problem facing all businesses. For commercial banks it is an especially difficult one. Most creditor claims on banks are in the form of deposits payable on demand. This is technically true only of demand deposits, but in practice it is true of savings deposits as well. By contrast, the claims on most other businesses mature in the future, many in the distant future.

Before 1914 bankers sought liquidity through holding cash, deposits at other banks, and notes and securities which could be sold readily with little chance of loss. In addition, most loans were short-term, some even callable on demand. Loans were arranged so that some would be maturing, and thereby providing access to cash, at short intervals. The portfolios of most large banks also contained such assets as bankers' acceptances, call loans, and prime commercial paper. These assets were held for two reasons. First, they were regularly traded in large volume on well-developed markets which bankers could readily enter as sellers if the need arose. Second, as short maturities they involved little risk of capital depreciation.

Banking System Liquidity. These practices, which resemble those followed today, ordinarily insured the liquidity of individual banks. Faced with large deposit withdrawals, the individual banker responded first by calling demand loans and refusing to renew other loans as they came due. If this did not suffice, he then sold his more liquid securities. As long as the latter maintained their value in the market, these actions allowed the banker to meet the withdrawals and to remain in business.

If this course of action was open to all bankers, why did difficulties arise? With no central bank present, a banker selling liquid assets would be likely to sell them to other commercial banks. Under such circumstances an individual banker was able to maintain liquidity only as long as other banks would buy his offerings of liquid assets or as long as his borrowers could squeeze their own operations sufficiently to repay their loans.

But what if all banks experienced large withdrawals and were forced to sell liquid assets at the same time? Then sales at book value were possible only if nonbank buyers entered the markets on a large scale. Before 1914, however, nonbank buyers were relatively few and could take large quantities of these assets only at sharply reduced prices. Forced to sell at large discounts, bankers might not realize enough to meet their deposit obligations and remain solvent. Thus, while current practices sufficed for individual banks under normal conditions, they did not insure the liquidity of the entire banking system.

Before the Federal Reserve System was organized, deposit withdrawals from any group of banks tended to put all banks under pressure. A group of banks experiencing extraordinary withdrawals would call in their deposits at other banks, curtail loans, and sell their more liquid securities. All these actions, the first one most obviously, would lead to withdrawals from other banks. As borrowers at the first group of banks were forced to pay off their loans, they in turn would insist on payment from their customers, at least some of whom would be likely to be depositors at other banks. Similarly, sales of securities by the first group of banks would probably be paid for, in part at least, by buyers drawing down their deposits at other banks. Thus, the normal reaction of one group of banks under depositor pressure was likely to produce withdrawals from a second group of banks. In like manner, the actions of the second group would soon involve still other banks and so on, with deposit losses snowballing through the system.

Pre-Federal Reserve Liquidity Crises. The liquidity of the banking system is vitally important to the liquidity of the business community at large. Thus a liquidity crisis in the banking system quickly becomes a liquidity crisis for the entire economy.

The banking system creates most of the public's money, since bank deposits make up most of the money supply and these deposits result chiefly from bank lending and investing. The banking system generally pays new deposits to the public in return for the public's promissory notes and securities. On the other hand, therefore, deposits are reduced when banks sell their assets to the public, for the public generally pays for these purchases by drawing down deposits.

Before 1914, when the public decided to convert its deposits to cash, banks were forced to sell notes and securities, both through offers on the markets and through requiring borrowers to pay off, i.e., to "buy back," their notes. If enough banks were affected, sales to the public were sufficiently large to cause a significant reduction in the public's money holdings. At the same time, lending by banks was seriously reduced, if not stopped altogether. Business borrowers, pressed by banks, curtailed their own trade credit and insisted on cash payment. With both less money and less credit in trade channels, prices fell, interest rates rose, profit margins disappeared, and widespread business failures followed.

Major crises of this kind occurred in 1837, 1857, 1873, 1893, and 1907, with lesser ones interspersed between these dates. Each of these was marked by extraordinary deposit withdrawals, a phenomenon popularly referred to as "runs" on banks. Factors underlying these runs varied, associated sometimes with international and sometimes with purely domestic developments.

Ordinarily, business firms and many individuals held much of their money as bank deposits, for payment by check was often more convenient than payment in cash. Sometimes, however, a series of business failures or an exposé of bank mismanagement shook public confidence in banks and touched off withdrawals. At other times gold exports had the same effect, since most gold was held by banks and its purchase for export reduced deposits. Perhaps the chief factor in these runs, however, was the poor record of the banking system itself. The public was, of course, aware of this record, and many bank customers were prepared to withdraw deposits on small provocation.

The Remedy—A Lender of Last Resort. With long experience in the kinds of crises described here, Congress, in framing the Federal Reserve System, sought to establish an institution that would underwrite the banking system's liquidity. The new Federal Reserve Banks were viewed as a broad market in which commercial banks could obtain cash for some of their assets when the need arose. Confronted with extraordinary withdrawals, bankers could bring customer and other notes to the Reserve Banks and exchange them for either currency or reserve deposits, a procedure called "rediscounting." In this manner, sales of bank assets to the public, with a consequent reduction in the public's deposits, would be avoided. Banks could also maintain loan lines despite the deposit withdrawals.

In this light the term "lender of last resort" takes on an obvious meaning. It implies a central bank role as third party in credit transactions between the commercial banking system and the public. When commercial banks find the burden of meeting the public's needs to be too great, they shift part of this burden to the central bank. As a third party ready to assume this burden, the central bank becomes the ultimate support of the economy's credit structure.

CENTRAL BANK EVOLUTION

In the Federal Reserve's first years, the prevalent view was that the System's chief function should be rediscounting at the initiative of commercial banks. The basic idea was that the public's need for credit should normally be met by commercial banks. If these banks were treatened with a liquidity problem, the Reserve Banks would stand ready to provide the necessary liquidity.

Those who expected that the new system would eliminate all crises were disappointed. In 1921 and again in 1929 the country experienced credit panics not unlike those of pre-Federal Reserve days. Chiefly as a result of the 1929 crisis and the ensuing depression, the System's role as lender of last resort has been expanded and refined. Since 1935, this role has embraced not only the emergency function of preventing credit freezes but also the more positive function of maintaining the "right" amount of liquidity in the banking system and the "right" amount of credit in the economy. Here "right" must be interpreted in the light of broad policy objectives respecting employment, prices, and economic growth.

Today the Federal Reserve underwrites the liquidity of the economy not merely by responding to bank requests for loans; on its own initiative it enters the market for government securities as a buyer when it sees the need for additional liquidity, or as a seller when it feels that liquidity is excessive. The System's purchases of securities in the open market provide banks with new cash, and hence lending power, as effectively as loans to members. Similarly, System sales in the open market curtail bank lending power. The Federal Reserve now employs rediscounting, open market operations, and other controls over commercial bank lending power in an active and continuing campaign to meet the liquidity requirements of a growing, fully employed economy without generating inflationary pressures.

This change in the Federal Reserve's role, however, should not be allowed to obscure its function as lender of last resort in the old sense of the term. It is still the economy's insurance against the kinds of panics that plagued the pre-Federal Reserve era.

MEMBER BANK BORROWING:

RIGHT OR PRIVILEGE?

KARL BRUNNER AND ALLAN H. MELTZER

The authors of this selection, after an exhaustive survey of Federal Reserve monetary management, have concluded that the authorities do not really understand the monetary process. Their many suggestions for reforming the System include transforming member bank borrowing from a privilege (under present circumstances a Federal Reserve bank can, and often does, refuse credit to a member bank) to a right. This proposal would bring American practice close to that which has long prevailed at the Bank of England and other central banks.

THE DISCOUNT WINDOW SHOULD BE "OPEN" AT A PENALTY RATE

The spirit of the original Federal Reserve Act envisioned that bankers would adjust actual to desired reserves by borrowing from the Reserve banks. Since the twenties, the Federal Reserve has attempted to impose administrative restrictions on the use of the discount window, particularly in periods when banks desired to borrow. The rationale for these administrative restrictions is open to question. If banks do not borrow for profit but only for "need," and repay borrowing as

Reprinted from An Alternative Approach to the Monetary Mechanism, Part 3, Subcommittee on Domestic Finance, Committee on Banking and Currency, H.R., 88th Congress, Second Session, 1964, pp. 89–90.

[281]

promptly as possible as the Federal Reserve has maintained, why should the Federal Reserve impose administrative restrictions designed to reduce the volume of borrowing to meet these "needs"? If banks borrow for profit, the profitability of borrowing can and would be eliminated by the use of a penalty rate.

Our proposal to keep the discount window "open" would mean that borrowing at a penalty rate would be a "right" and not a "privilege" of membership in the System. A major reason for advocating this step stems from the recognition of the desirable role that member bank borrowing can play in the individual bank's reserve adjustment. Many smaller banks cannot participate in the Federal funds market regularly, if at all, because the minimum size of transactions in that market is too large relative to the size of their excess reserves. Generally, such banks hold excess reserves and do not borrow or lend. However, even the smallest member banks may at times have reserve deficiencies. The discount window permits them to adjust their position. The proposal would not change this adjustment procedure other than granting the member bank the right to expect accommodation.

A second reason for advocating the "open window policy" stems from our concern with so-called defensive operations. Many of these operations are designed to smooth the adjustment of individual banks or sectors of the banking system to the inevitable random movements that affect their reserve position for short periods. We propose to make the adjustment to such movements a matter to be resolved by the individual banker. If there is a maldistribution of reserves or some other random event, the banker may, if he wishes to pay the rate, avoid this problem by borrowing. Such borrowing would solve his temporary problem and would not involve any substitution of judgment by the Federal Reserve for judgment by the individual banker.

It may be suggested that under prevailing arrangements, bankers are rarely refused the discount privilege. This might lead many to believe that this proposal would not provide any new mechanism other than the penalty rate. Our response to that potential comment is contained in the next recommendation.

The discount window should replace open-market operations as the principal means by which the Federal Reserve handles "defensive" operations. This proposal would transfer the judgment about "defensive" operations to the individual bankers. Under present arrangements, when the Treasury withdraws balances from an individual bank, the bank may have a reserve deficiency. Why should the Federal Reserve correct this temporary deficiency by a "defensive" open-market purchase? If collection schedules are disrupted so that Federal Reserve float rises, why should open-market operations at the initiative of the Federal Reserve be used to adjust reserve positions?

We recommend that, by paying a penalty rate, the individual bank be allowed to adjust reserve deficiencies at its own discretion. Our proposal envisions that many of the deficiencies and surpluses in reserve positions would be resolved through the Federal funds market. Those that were not resolved in that way could be handled through the discount window, if the individual banker is willing to pay the price. If the individual bankers prefer to take the risk of acquiring reserves later in the settlement period, we see no reason for the Federal Reserve to substitute its collective judgment for the decisions of the bankers.

POSSIBLE REFORMS

IN DISCOUNT POLICY

WARREN L. SMITH

In the preceding selections the role of the discount rate in monetary management was discussed from the viewpoint of the Federal Reserve System. Professor Smith provides a critique of this view and discusses several alternative techniques of administering the discount window.

The discount rate as presently handled is not a very effective element in Federal Reserve policy. At times when a restrictive policy is applied, the induced increase in member bank borrowing constitutes a minor "leakage" in the controls, since it permits member banks to postpone contraction of their loans and investments and also adds to the total supply of member bank reserves. For the purpose of controlling the amount of borrowing, the Federal Reserve relies on adjustments in the discount rate, together with a tradition against borrowing that prevails among member banks and System surveillance of the borrowing practices of the banks. Due to the fact that open market interest rates fluctuate continuously, while the discount rate is changed only at somewhat unpredictable discrete intervals, the relation between the discount rate and open market rates (which largely determines the incentive to borrow) behaves in a very erratic fashion. The System relies on "free reserves" as an immediate short-run guide for monetary policy; however, the restrictive effect of a given amount of free reserves varies with

Reprinted from "The Instruments of General Monetary Control," The National Banking Review, Vol. 1, No. 1, September 1963, pp. 47–76.

(among other things) the relation between the discount rate and the yields on assets—especially Treasury bills—that banks might alternatively liquidate to adjust their reserve positions.

Discretionary changes in the discount rate may at times have rather unpredictable effects on the business and financial situation, partly because it is often uncertain whether such changes are meant to be passive adjustments to keep the discount rate in line with other interest rates or whether they represent independent moves to tighten or ease credit. To the extent that changes in the discount rate do influence business conditions directly, they do so chiefly through psychological or "announcement" effects, the nature of which depends upon the kinds of expectations held by lenders, borrowers and spenders. Although these announcement effects are quite complex and probably not of great importance in most cases, it seems likely that on occasion they may tend to increase economic instability.

A number of students of monetary affairs have expressed discontent with the present discount policy of the Federal Reserve . . . at least three fairly specific proposals for reform have been suggested. Two of these would de-emphasize discount policy—one by getting rid of the discount mechanism entirely and the other by tying the discount rates and thereby eliminating discretionary changes in it. The third would move in the opposite direction by trying to reform the discount mechanism in such a way as to make the discount rate a much more powerful weapon of credit control. We shall discuss each of these proposals in turn.

ABOLITION OF THE DISCOUNT MECHANISM

The proposal has been advanced quite forcefully by Professor Milton Friedman that the discount mechanism should be abolished altogether. Friedman argues that the legitimate function of the central bank is to control the stock of money and that the discount rate is an effective instrument for this purpose.

One difficulty with the complete elimination of discounting is that the discount mechanism serves a useful function as a "safety valve" by which banks are able to make adjustments in their reserve positions and the Federal Reserve is able to come to the aid of the banking system—or individual banks—in case of a liquidity crisis. In order to provide a means for individual banks to make short-run adjustments in their reserve positions, Friedman proposes the establishment of a fixed "fine" to be assessed on reserve deficiencies; the fine to be set high enough to be above likely levels of market interest rates, in order to prevent the device from becoming an indirect form of borrowing from the Federal Reserve.[1] As far as liquidity crises are concerned, he contends that, due to the success of deposit insurance in practically eliminating bank failures, such crises are now scarcely conceivable and that the "lender of last resort" function of the Federal Reserve is now obsolete, so that we need not worry about its elimination. It may be noted that if the discount mechanism were eliminated, it would be possible to use the repurchase agreement technique as a means of providing emergency assistance to the banking system in times of crisis.

TYING THE DISCOUNT RATE TO THE TREASURY BILL RATE

An alternative to the complete abolition of borrowing would be to change the discount rate at frequent intervals in such a way as to maintain an approximately constant relation between it and some open market interest rate, such as the Treasury bill rate. For example, each week as soon as the average rate of interest on Treasury bills at the Monday auction became known, the discount rate could be adjusted so as to preserve a constant differential between the two rates.

Under this arrangement, the discount rate would no longer be a discretionary credit control weapon, and the unpredictable and often perverse announcement effects on the expectations of businessmen and financial institutions would be done away with. To the extent that the Federal Reserve wanted to influence expectations and felt that it could manage such effects so as to contribute to economic stability, it could implement these effects through the issuance of statements concerning its intentions, the economic outlook, and so on. While the present writer is rather dubious about the value of such activities, it is surely true that to the extent that they can contribute anything useful they can be handled better by verbal means than through reliance on such a crude signal as the discount rate.

The major question involved in the adoption of an arrangement for tying the discount rate to the bill rate would be the choice of the proper differential between the two. Obviously, the discount rate should be above the bill rate; beyond this the establishment of the differential is a matter of judgment. The larger the differential, the smaller would be (a) the average amount of borrowing and (b) the swings in bor-

---

[1] Milton Friedman, *A Program for Monetary Stability* (New York: Fordham University Press, 1959), pp. 44–45.

rowing that would occur as credit conditions changed. In view of the wide variations among individual banks with respect to both portfolio composition and expectations, the present writer feels that a fairly large differential of perhaps 1 per cent would be desirable, in order to keep down the amount of borrowing, which, for reasons discussed earlier, represents a minor leakage in monetary controls. But there does not seem to be any analytical principle that provides a basis for selecting the proper differential. Doubtless the best procedure would be to experiment with various differentials, retaining each one long enough to observe its effectiveness.

Under this arrangement, in contrast to the complete elimination of discounting, the discount mechanism would continue to be available to serve as a means of making temporary adjustments in bank reserve positions and as a "safety valve" that could be used in times of crises. If this approach were adopted, it would probably be desirable to give up the efforts to rely on such an intangible and unreliable means of controlling discounting as the traditional "reluctance" of member banks and the so-called "surveillance" of the Federal Reserve, recognizing borrowing as a "right" rather than a "privilege" of member banks, and relying entirely on the discount rate (in relation to the bill rate) as a means of controlling it.

A procedure of the kind discussed above was employed in Canada from November 1956, to June 1962. During this period, the Bank of Canada adjusted its lending rate each week so as to keep its ¼ of 1 per cent above the average rate on auction. The reasons given for adopting such an arrangement in 1956 were similar to those set forth above. The policy was abandoned at the time of the Canadian balance of payment crisis in June 1962, when, as part of a program for dealing with the crisis, the discount rate was raised to 6 per cent as a signal to the rest of the world of Canada's determination to defend the external value of the Canadian dollar. The traditional discretionary discount rate policy has been employed in Canada since that time.

INCREASING THE EFFECTIVENESS OF THE
DISCOUNT RATE

A proposal for reform of the discount mechanism very different from the two discussed above has recently been advanced by Professor James Tobin.[2] Instead of dismantling the discount mechanism entirely

[2] James Tobin, "Towards Improving the Efficiency of the Monetary Mechanism," *Review of Economics and Statistics,* XLII, August 1960, pp. 276–279.

or abolishing discretionary changes in the discount rate, Tobin would greatly increase the importance of the rate and turn it into a major weapon of credit control.

The Tobin proposal calls for two changes in present procedures:

(1) The Federal Reserve would pay interest at the discount rate on member bank reserve balances in excess of requirements.

(2) The prohibition against payments of interest on demand deposits and the ceilings on the payments of interest on time and savings deposits would be repealed.

These changes would greatly increase the leverage of the discount rate by making it an important consideration for banks that are not in debt to the Federal Reserve as well as for those that are. The opportunity cost to a bank of increasing its loans and investments would be the return it could earn by holding excess reserves, and this cost would be firmly under the control of the Federal Reserve. Moreover, the interest rate offered by the banks to holders of idle deposits would presumably be linked rather closely to the rate paid on excess reserves, since the bank could always earn a return on its deposits at least equal to one minus its reserve requirement times the discount rate. Thus, if the Federal Reserve wished to tighten credit, it could raise the discount rate, and this would increase the opportunity cost of lending for all of the member banks (whether they were in debt or not) and would, therefore, make them willing to lend only at higher interest rates than previously, while at the same time causing the banks to raise interest rates on deposits, thereby increasing the attractiveness of bank deposits relative to other assets on the part of the public.[3] The discount rate

---

[3] Allowing the banks to pay interest on deposits would have two related advantages. One is that it would probably reduce the propensity for the velocity of deposits to increase when a restrictive policy was applied, since the banks would be able to raise interest rates on deposits making them more attractive and weakening the tendency for rising interest rates on other claims to induce shifts of deposits into the hands of persons having a high propensity to spend. The other advantage is that it should reduce the amount of real resources devoted to the task of economizing the use of cash balances. Since the revival of flexible monetary policy, many large corporations, as well as state and local governments, have developed extensive facilities for handling short-term investments in order to minimize their holdings of sterile cash balances, and the amount of skilled personnel devoting its time to this kind of activity at present is certainly not trivial (see C. E. Silberman, "The Big Corporate Lenders," *Fortune*, August 1956, pp. 111–114, 162–70). Resources devoted to this purpose represent a form of economic waste, since the real cost of creating deposits is virtually zero so that there is no economic gain from exercising economy in their use. This is pointed out by Tobin and is emphasized even more strongly by Friedman (*A Program for Monetary Stability, op. cit.,* pp. 71–75). The two advantages (reducing destabiliz-

could be used independently to control credit, or it could be combined with open market operations. It is not clear, however, what principle should govern the division of responsibility between the two weapons.

The proposal is ingenious and would certainly be practical and capable of being put in operation without causing disruption. And it might have the incidental advantage that the payment of interest on excess reserves might encourage more banks to become members of the Federal Reserve System. What is not clear, however, is why a flexible monetary policy could be implemented more effectively by means of the discount rate under this proposal than is now possible by means of open market operations. It is true that the proposal would presumably permit the Federal Reserve to control the cost of bank credit very effectively, but this can already be done—in principle at least—by open market operations. In part, the problems of monetary policy seem to stem from the fact that the demand for bank credit is not very sensitive to changes in interest rates and other monetary variables, so that it has proved to be difficult to operate forcefully enough to produce prompt changes of the degree necessary for effective stabilization. Perhaps it would be possible to bring the forces of monetary policy to bear more rapidly by means of the Tobin proposal, but this is by no means obvious. If the proposal merely provides another way of doing what is already possible, it hardly seems worthwhile.

The repeal of the existing restrictions relating to payment of interest on deposits is in no way dependent upon provision for the payment of interest on excess reserves, and there is much to be said for the repeal of these restrictions, even if the remainder of the Tobin proposal is not adopted.

CONCLUSIONS

Of the three proposals for reforming the discount mechanism, the present writer feels that the strongest case can be made for the procedure of changing the discount rate each week in such a way as to maintain a constant spread between the discount rate and the Treasury bill rate. This would be a less drastic reform than the complete elimination of discounting, would eliminate the unpredictable effects of dis-

---

ing velocity changes and discouraging efforts to economize in the use of costless deposits) are related in the sense that the propensity to waste resources in economizing cash balances tends to increase during periods of credit restriction and rising interest rates, and this increased application of resources helps to permit a destabilizing rise in velocity.

cretionary changes in the discount rate, would preserve the discount mechanism as a safety valve, and would eliminate the effects on credit conditions that now result from erratic variations in the relation between the discount rate and open market rates. The Tobin proposal for increasing the potency of the discount rate as a credit-control weapon is worthy of careful study, but it is not yet clear that the proposal would greatly strengthen the hand of the Federal Reserve.

If the present system of making discretionary adjustments in the discount rate at irregular intervals is retained, it would be desirable to reform the administration of the discount mechanism, perhaps by shifting the authority for making changes in the rate from the individual Reserve banks to the Federal Open Market Committee. The purpose of such a change would be to reduce the number of persons involved in decisions regarding the discount rate so that it would be easier to agree on the reasons for making changes. This would facilitate the issuance of explanatory statements at the time changes are made, in order to eliminate the confusion that often results due to the varying interpretations that are frequently placed on rate changes in the absence of explanations. It should then be feasible to make more frequent technical adjustments in the rate with less need to worry about the danger of disruptive effects on the credit situation, thereby permitting closer coordination of the discount rate with open market operations.

OPEN MARKET OPERATIONS
IN LONG-TERM SECURITIES

WINFIELD W. RIEFLER

In the conduct of open market operations, the Federal Reserve Open Market Committee generally confines itself to purchases and sales of short-term securities, preferably Treasury bills. The existing policy was adopted five years ago on the basis of recommendations presented by an Ad Hoc Subcommittee of the Federal Open Market Committee. It was believed that such a policy would be conducive to a resilient market for United States Government securities and would also facilitate open market operations directed primarily toward influencing the general credit situation. The present article re-examines some implications of the policy in the light of operating experience since that time.

At the time the policy was adopted, it was criticized on the grounds that it prevented the System from directly stimulating or restricting the volume of funds available to the long-term money markets. The analysis underlying this criticism was that System transactions in short-term securities influenced primarily the short-term money markets and short-term interest rates. A comparable direct influence on the availability of funds in the long-term money markets, and on long-term interest rates, it was contended, required similar direct operations in the long-term market.

The fact that interest rates on both short-term and long-term securities have tended in the past to move generally in the same direction, whatever the terms of the securities purchased or sold by the Open

Reprinted from Federal Reserve Bulletin, November 1958, pp. 1260–1274.

Market Committee, was attributed primarily to arbitrage. There were expressions of fear that, if the Federal Reserve continued its operations to short-term securities, arbitrage might not work efficiently or might work so slowly in a recession market that unduly high long-term interest rates would impede the borrowing of long-term funds in the capital markets.

The course of market developments over the past five years has shown that this view of the way System purchases or sales of Government securities affect the money and capital markets is oversimplified and inadequate. Even though System open market operations have been confined almost wholly to Treasury bills, the response to those operations in the long-term capital markets and in movements of long-term interest rates has been in general anything but lethargic. There is currently less doubt concerning the System's ability to exert an influence on long-term interest rates without direct intervention in the long-term market. This influence is not necessarily confined to the effects of open market operations. It may reflect changes in discount rates or anticipation of future Federal Reserve action.

In the latter part of 1957, for example, System operations were a decisive influence in one of the most rapid breaks in market interest rates, both long and short, on record. In this instance, the main drop in rates followed a lowering of Federal Reserve Bank discount rates in mid-November without any marked immediate change in System holdings of either short-term or long-term United States Government securities. The basic factor in this dramatic break was an abrupt turnabout in market expectations as to the direction of monetary policy rather than an immediate increase in the supply of reserves available to the banking system or a decline in the demand for funds.

Subsequent experience has shown, on the other hand, that System actions are not in all cases the decisive influence on interest rates. In the early summer of 1958, for example, a change in market expectations with respect to prospective credit and business conditions uncovered a condition of widespread, and to some extent thinly margined, speculation in the market for United States Government securities. There followed a dramatic rise in the level of interest rates that persisted despite supporting purchases of United States Government securities of more than $600 million by the Treasury and $1,300 million by the Federal Reserve System. Treasury support purchases consisted almost entirely of intermediate-term maturities. Federal Reserve purchases included a small amount of intermediate- and long-term maturities, but for the most part consisted of short-term issues involved in the July refunding.

Interest rates rose even further during late July and August 1958 as Federal Reserve operations were directed first to absorbing redundant reserves injected into the market in the course of these supporting operations, and later, to establishing a technical money position more consistent with the strong recovery in business activity then in process. By mid-September, a 2 per cent discount rate prevailed at the Federal Reserve Banks in contrast with the earlier 1¾ per cent rate. Free reserves were still positive but at a level just under $100 million as compared with nearly $550 million in May. The rapid rise of long-term interest rates came to a halt in October, but their general level remained exceptionally high relative to the technical money position, as expressed in the level of Federal Reserve discount rates and of free reserves.

This episode demonstrated that a variety of forces, in addition to those flowing from Federal Reserve actions, affect the level of interest rates. One of the most important in this instance was a diversion of investment funds from bonds and similar long-term fixed interest obligations to common stocks, reflecting partly the recovery but partly also a hedge against a resumption of inflation. The episode also demonstrated some of the difficulties the System faces when it operates to support the market. The July purchases, made to correct a disorderly condition in the market that arose on the eve of a Treasury financing, at the same time helped to create redundant bank reserves that gave additional strength to the expectation of renewed inflation.

Finally, the episode highlighted the problem the Federal Reserve faces at all times when it diagnoses an emerging credit situation, in differentiating between market developments that reflect forces originating in the economy and those that reflect the response of credit markets to the technical money position established by the Federal Reserve System. The former, clearly dominant during the summer of 1958, are in most circumstances the more difficult to identify. Such differentiation is facilitated when System operations are confined to bills.

In view of developments such as these, it seems appropriate to re-examine (1) the ways in which Federal Reserve policy actions affect the availability of funds and market rates of interest, (2) the manner in which these actions permeate the various sectors of the money and capital markets, and (3) certain features of the organization of the open capital markets that engender instability when expectations of lower or higher interest rates are not firmly based on actual changes in the supply of loanable funds relative to the demand. The re-examination in this article is supplemented by a review of the empirical experience of recent years to assess the relative influence of different System operations on the availability and cost of funds.

The purpose of the analysis is to provide background against which to evaluate the suggestion that direct System intervention in the long-term market for United States Government securities might be helpful in situations other than those calling for correction of disorderly conditions in the market. The analysis suggests that the lasting contribution of such additional use of direct intervention would be small, and that under certain conditions there would be considerable risk that such action might not only obstruct the functioning of the market but also make it more difficult for the Federal Reserve to judge the adequacy of its own actions.

AVAILABILITY AND COST OF CREDIT AND CAPITAL

Federal Reserve operations in the Government securities market can be said to influence prices and yields of outstanding securities in three fundamentally different ways. (1) They affect the volume of securities available for trading and investment, (2) they change the volume of reserves available to member banks for making loans and investments or paying off debts, and (3) they influence the expectations of market professionals and other investors regarding market trends.

Change in Outstanding Securities. Open market operations bring about a direct change in the volume of securities available in the market for trading and investment. Thus, Federal Reserve purchases withdraw securities from the market and tend to raise the prices of those that remain. Conversely, Federal Reserve sales add to the total volume of securities in the market and tend to depress prices.

This relationship of System transactions to the volume of market-held securities is one to one, that is, each dollar of securities bought or sold withdraws or adds a dollar of securities to those available in the market. The effect is the same as that produced by any other buyer or seller of an equivalent amount. The price or interest rate response to the change in market supply is registered most strongly on the particular issues that are bought or sold, but, as will be noted later, it will also be reflected in some degree throughout all maturity sectors of the market by reason of actual or anticipated substitution and arbitrage in the market.

Change in Member Bank Reserves. Federal Reserve open market operations also affect the prices and yields of Government securities because they change the volume of free reserves available to the member banks. System purchases of securities add to the volume of free reserves. Because the banking system operates on a percentage reserve basis, System purchases add roughly seven times the amount of the purchase to the total potential demand of the member banks for earning assets, including both loans and investments. Conversely, System sales of securities withdraw reserves from the banks, frequently causing member banks to borrow reserves through the System's discount window; such borrowing must generally be temporary and by definition does not avert the contraction of free reserves. Again, because of the percentage reserve requirements, the System's sales decrease the potential demand of the member banks for earning assets by a multiple of the amounts sold.

The relationship here of System open market transactions to market demand and supply is not one to one. The effect is a multiple of the dollars added to or subtracted from the reserve base. Furthermore, when impulses toward expansion or contraction of bank earning assets arise from a change in the availability of reserves, effects of System transactions are not confined to the securities that happen to be bought or sold. They are dispersed over all types of assets commonly found in bank portfolios.

The same effects take place whenever the volume of free reserves changes, irrespective of the factor responsible for the change. To be specific, the effects are the same whether the factor responsible is a change in reserve requirements, a change in the demand for currency, a purchase or sale of gold, or an open market operation. It follows that the effects are the same irrespective of whether open market operations are conducted in the short- or the long-term sector of the market for Government securities.

Change in Expectations. Finally, Federal Reserve open market operations also affect prices and yields in the United States Government securities market, particularly over the short run, by influencing market expectations, especially among dealers and market professionals. The System is a larger holder of United States Government securities than any private investment institution, and is not restricted in its operations by considerations of profit. When it enters the market, it always operates for a public interest purpose, and can bring to bear far greater means than are at the disposal of any individual operator in the market. Finally, the System operates from the very center of the market with far more knowledge than any other transactor of the total of investment and financial transactions currently taking place.

Under these circumstances, market transactors, particularly the market professionals, including the dealers, go to great lengths to probe the significance of all System policy actions, particularly operations in the securities market. As professional participants in the market, they are, of course, quickly aware of practically all such transactions. It is vital to their business for them to assess correctly the potential impact of System operations and to govern their own actions accordingly. They are not likely to operate against any trend in rates they think the System is trying to establish. Rather, they will try to anticipate such trends, both by closing out positions they expect to become less profitable and by establishing or strengthening positions consistent with the trend. As a consequence, when System actions give rise to firm expectations among market professionals with respect to interest rate trends, relatively small System operations may have important short-run effects on market quotations.

These effects, it should be reiterated, are only short run. Market professionals, including dealers, do not originate the savings that supply investable funds; nor do they originate the demand for investment funds. They are essentially middlemen located at the heart of the market, seeking to anticipate by their trading the prices (or yields) that will clear the market. Not infrequently, the professionals overshoot the mark in trying to estimate either supply or demand even apart from the effects of System policy or the direction of that policy. There is always the possibility that they may assume that a given purchase or sale by the System foreshadows larger changes in bank reserve positions than in fact develop. In such cases, they may take positions and establish, for a period, an unsustainable level of prices or yields that is inconsistent with the actual supply-demand situation.

The possibility that an unsustainable level of prices or yields will prevail temporarily because market expectations are not borne out is a major reason for the System's policy of nonintervention in the intermediate- and long-term sectors of the market. Its operations in longer term securities would be much more subject to comment and possible misinterpretation by market professionals than are its operations in Treasury bills. This would probably be the case even if the market were accustomed to frequent System operations in these sectors. The very fact that the System took the initiative in buying or selling long-term securities, where the market is almost always thin as compared with the bill sector, would indicate a feeling on the part of Federal Reserve authorities that existing prices and yields on long-term securities were out of line. Market professionals perforce would have to try to assess this implication in their subsequent trades. Bill operations can also give rise to false or misleading expectations, but they are much less likely to do so.

In other words, operations by the System in long-term securities can give rise to expectations not only regarding the direction of general monetary policy but also regarding specific prices and yields of long-term securities—a double set of possible misinterpretations. Bill operations lead mainly to expectations about general monetary policy.

FLUIDITY—SUBSTITUTION AND ARBITRAGE

The major open money markets, particularly the markets for United States Government securities, are usually characterized by a high degree of fluidity as between the various maturity sectors, in the sense that fluctuations of any magnitude in one sector are likely to be paralleled by fluctuations in other sectors. This phenomenon is often attributed to arbitrage. It is often said, for example, that movements of prices and yields originating in the most sensitive and liquid sector of the market, that for Treasury bills, are transmitted to other sectors by reason of arbitrage with or without a certain amount of delay.

The term arbitrage, as used in this context, refers to closely timed purchases and sales of securities in different maturity sectors by professional operators, which have the effect of generalizing movements in rates and yields. For example, a withdrawal by outside investors of funds from the Treasury bill sector would be reflected in a rise in bill rates, both absolutely and in relation to rates on Treasury certificates. This might induce professional operators simultaneously to sell certificates and buy bills, a transaction which would tend to restore the previous relationship between yields on bills and certificates. At the same time, it would tend to leave both yields higher than they were before the initial action took place.

In accounting for fluidity among the various sectors of the market, too much importance should not be attributed to the transactions of the market professionals who engage in arbitrage. Much more important and basic to their operations as professionals, is the high degree of substitutability of security instruments that exists for many lenders and many borrowers in the credit and capital markets. Large commercial banks in particular, when their liquidity positions permit, operate actively and have positions for their own account in all major areas and in all major maturity sectors of the money markets. Large commercial banks are also important sources of financing for other transactors in those various areas and sectors. Since commercial banks, with their ability to expand or contract the means of payment, are always a major, and at times the dominant factor in the availability of funds, their operations in all major areas of the market and in all maturity sectors have the effect of integrating the different sectors.

In addition, managers of investment portfolios such as those of insurance companies and pension and trust funds, in seeking to maximize income, operate with great flexibility as between categories of investments and, when they think it will pay, between different maturity sectors.

Among borrowers, also, many can adopt a variety of financial plans to meet their financing needs. If they think the terms necessary to obtain more or less permanent funds will improve, they may postpone coming to the capital market. Instead, they may meet immediate needs by drawing down their liquid assets or by borrowing at short term from banks or other lenders.

For example, finance companies are more or less continuously borrowing large amounts in the short-, intermediate-, and long-term markets. Within limits, they are free at any time to shift a large part of their borrowing to the sectors where financial costs are most reasonable. Governments and other public bodies are typically heavy borrowers in all maturity sectors, both of new money and of funds for refinancing. Because they enter the markets for large amounts, they are alert for signs of congestion in the different maturity sectors and are careful to offer their issues in sectors that appear capable of readily absorbing the offering.

These factors of broad substitutability on both sides of the money and capital markets are more fundamental than arbitrage in accounting for the fluidity, homogeneity, and responsiveness of the securities markets. This flexibility links the various sectors of the money and capital markets into a somewhat loosely integrated whole in which yield changes tend to move together in the various sectors. Furthermore, broad substitutability in the market accounts for the fact that arbitrage operations by professional specialists can be undertaken at a profit. At any point in time, of course, the operations of professionals, though they do not determine its shape, are primary in accounting for the smoothness of the yield curve.

In the light of these considerations, two broad observations may be made: (1) a considerable amount of interchangeability or substitutability on both the demand and the supply side of the organized money and capital markets tends to communicate stringency or ease in any one sector to all sectors; and (2) commercial banks are a particularly important element in this responsiveness inasmuch as they can operate on their own account, as well as finance the operations of others, in all major sectors of the markets. In doing so, they can expand or contract the means of payment.

These two observations about the functional characteristics of securities markets help to explain the fact that changes in the tone or direction of the money markets that appear first in the bill sector of the Government securities market soon spread to the other sectors. Moreover, any change in availability of funds is likely to be reflected first in the bill sector.

The speed with which changes in the availability of reserves are reflected in parallel changes in any individual sector of the market, such as the long-term sector, will depend basically (1) on the strength of demand in that sector relative to demand in other sectors, (2) on the attractiveness of the yield offered in the light of the risks involved, and (3) on the liquidity position of the banking system, that is, the size of its highly liquid asset holdings and the position of its loan-deposit ratio.

Ease in reserve positions will not be quickly reflected in an increase of commercial bank investments in the long-term capital markets if banks generally are concerned about an insufficiency of short-term liquid assets or a high loan-deposit ratio. Under either condition, time is needed before bank activity in long-term investments is likely to be affected.

It takes time for banks to improve their liquidity by investing fresh accretions of reserves in liquid assets. As they do, rates in the short-term open money markets will tend to fall. It also takes time for borrowers, such as finance companies with access to short-term open markets, to refinance through these markets to repay bank loans, an operation that would bring about an improvement, that is, a reduction, in bank loan-deposit ratios.

The time taken for these two processes to operate sometimes accounts for what may seem to be a sluggish response in the long-term markets to changes in the availability of funds in the short-term markets. Time for these adjustments to take place is indispensable when net free reserves have increased but liquidity in bank earning assets is low. Long-term markets will not respond until bank portfolios have become more liquid and banks are again in a position to extend direct support to long-term issues. The banks would need this time interval before extending such support even if the Federal Reserve System itself operated in the long end of the market.

OPERATION OF LONG-TERM MARKETS

A third broad observation applying to the money and capital markets is that any decision to borrow or lend a given dollar amount has much greater significance when it is taken in a long-term market than when it concerns short-term investments. This increased significance results from the fact that a commitment undertaken in a long-term market fixes the borrower's costs and the lender's income for a longer time. This is one reason why long-term rates fluctuate so much less widely than shorter term rates. It is also a reason why relatively small changes in long-term interest rates have greater implications and consequences than much larger fluctuations in short-term rates.

For example, it is generally realized that a fluctuation of, say, 1 per cent in interest rates on short-term securities would normally be associated with a much smaller fluctuation in interest yields on long-term bonds. It is also generally realized that the relative change in capital values of the securities in the two maturity areas would be the opposite, that is, that the market price of a long bond would swing over a wider range than the market price of a short-term issue. It is less generally recognized, however, just how wide this swing would be. For example, the cyclical swing in average prices of long-term United States Government securities from 1953 to 1958 was in a range roughly 10 times greater than the corresponding fluctuation in prices of 9–12 month securities.

These differences are reflected in the manner in which borrowers approach the two areas. In general, approaches to the long-term markets are carefully timed, with an eye among other things to avoiding congestion of competing offerings. Investment bankers bringing out new long-term bond issues try to offer them, if at all feasible, at a time when the calendar is not clogged with competing issues. To the extent that long-term borrowing is postponable, this planning in a sense tends in the short run to ration the supply of new long-term securities to the volume of funds currently available in the market for investment. It acts to minimize short-run variations in prices and yields in the capital markets by limiting the amount of long-term securities offered to the amount of funds available at prevailing yields.

Under these circumstances, if for any reason the level of long-term yields quoted in the market is lower than is justified by the basic supply-demand position, the lower yields will tend to persist for a period until the volume of prospective issues, previously withheld but currently seeking a place on the calendar, grows to the point where nervous congestion develops and the true nature of the basic supply-demand position is disclosed. Unjustified market expectations with respect to prospective conditions in the long-term markets are thus likely to be dangerous to the effective functioning of money and capital markets—much more so than are unjustified expectations regarding conditions in the short-term markets.

GENERAL EMPIRICAL EVIDENCE

Market behavior is compounded of almost innumerable strands, and so it is difficult to substantiate or illustrate specific aspects of these observations by direct empirical evidence. Nevertheless, many of the features of behavior described above can be subjected to a considerable degree of indirect factual testing and confirmation.

Broad Movements of Interest Rates. If there is sufficient option for substitution of credit instruments as between different maturity sectors of the capital markets on both the demand and the supply side, one would expect the markets in general to move as a whole, that is, one would expect that broad movements in interest rates would usually be in the same direction in the long, intermediate, and short sectors. One would expect that divergent movements as between maturity sectors would be less frequent and of shorter duration than parallel movements.

Yield Curve Patterns. If the effect of arbitrage and dealer portfolio activity is primarily to establish prices and yields that will clear bids and offers in the different maturity sectors of the market, it would be expected that curves showing the distribution of yields on United States Government securities by maturities would be continuous rather than discontinuous as between the various sectors. Typical yield patterns in the United States Government securities market on particular days [show] how professional activity, including arbitrage, results generally in a relatively smooth and consistent yield curve. In addition . . . the yield curve, according to maturity for a given category of security, changes its shape from time to time, reflecting the presence of differential supply-demand pressures in various maturity sectors of the market. In other words, substitution and professional activity have the effect of linking the various maturity sectors into an organic whole. They do not, however, completely obliterate differential pressures as between the sectors.

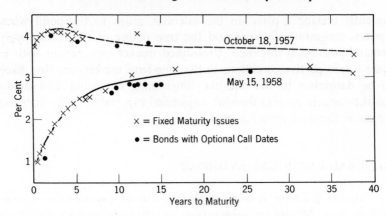

Yield curves—U.S. Government securities.

Bank Reserve Positions and Interest Rates. If commercial banks with their ability to create money are fundamentally important factors in the supply of funds for investment, interest rates would be expected to be highly responsive to changes in the reserve position of the commercial banks. This expectation with respect to the importance of the reserve position is confirmed by statistical evidence for member banks. . . . This response would not always be overriding, of course. This was indicated by developments at the end of 1956, when bank liquidity was low and many rates remained firm despite an easing in the reserve position. It was also indicated by the developments in the summer of 1958 referred to earlier. Interest rates on occasion would also reflect changes in such factors as market demand for credit and capital, the supply of funds from others than banks, loan-deposit ratios of banks, and Federal Reserve discount rates.

BANK RESERVES VERSUS SUPPLY OF SECURITIES

Current market reporting is largely concerned with changes in the demand for and supply of investments in the various individual markets for Treasury bills, Treasury certificates, United States Government bonds, municipal bonds, etc. Day-to-day developments, in fact, are almost entirely described in terms of changes in demand for and supply of specific categories of issues.

If the general analysis set forth here is valid, a change in the aggregate volume of reserves available to the banking system would be expected to have much more effect on the availability of funds, and therefore on interest rates, in all the various maturity sectors of the market than would an equal dollar change in the volume of securities held or available for trading in the market. This would be expected because the impact of a change in reserves is a multiple one whereas the impact of a change in the volume of securities held or available in the market reflects a one-to-one relationship. In a rough general sense, the relative impact on interest rates or security yields of these two factors should be proportional to the required reserve ratio of the commercial banking system.

For example, if the Federal Reserve System buys or sells a given dollar amount of Treasury bills at a time when effective required reserves average one-seventh of demand deposits, something like seven-eighths of any resulting effect on market yields should reflect the changes

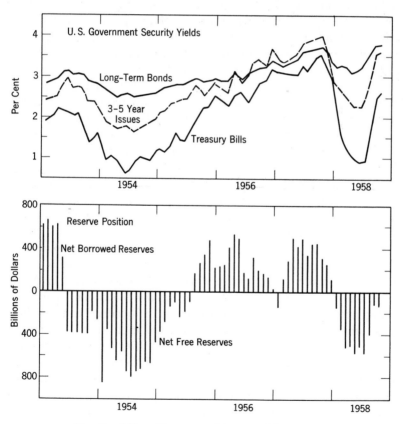

Security yields and reserve position, monthly averages.

in the volume of reserves available to the banks and only one-eighth the fact that the operation was executed in bills and therefore changed the volume of bills available for investment in the market. These same general principles would be applicable if the open market operations were executed in the long end of the market.

It is impossible to test these principles by a study of the response of the market to given open market operations, since such operations exert various types of influence simultaneously. On the one hand, they add to or subtract from the volume of free reserves available to the commercial banks, while at the same time they add to or subtract from the volume of securities to be carried in some sector of the market.

There are other ways, however, of testing whether open market operations exert greater effect through their impact on reserves than through their impact on the market supply of instruments of particular maturities. For example, if, as general analysis suggests, something like seven-eighths of the effect of an open market operation on the availability of funds in the market represents the effect of that operation on bank reserve positions, and the multiple expansion of credit therein, while only one-eighth reflects the fact that bills were simultaneously put into or withdrawn from the market, it follows that a comparable change in the level of net free reserves from whatever cause ultimately should affect the general credit situation and interest rates to roughly the same extent as the open market operation or within seven-eighths of the same extent. This should work out whether the change in bank reserve positions is brought by movements of gold or currency or by changes in reserve requirements, neither of which in itself affects the volume of securities outstanding, or whether it is induced by open market operations that simultaneously change the volume of securities to be carried in the market.

Observation of the response to changes in reserve requirements reinforces this point. The System reduced reserve requirements on five occasions [between] the Treasury-Federal Reserve accord in March 1951 [and November 1958]. On some of these occasions, partly off-setting open market sales by the System actually added to the volume of securities outstanding in the market. On each occasion, however, a greater availability of funds reflected the resulting free reserve position, and interest rates declined. That reaction, furthermore, was very close to what would have been expected if the same reserve position had been achieved solely through open market purchases, which, it may be noted, would also have removed securities from the market. In short, reductions in reserve requirements that remove no securities from the market have been as effective in easing the money and capital markets as open market purchases in which securities are removed.

Still another source of empirical data, one that is completely free from any complications arising from changes in market expectations such as are frequently induced by Federal Reserve policy actions, may throw light on this problem. The data pertain to recurrent Treasury operations undertaken to refinance maturing issues of its huge outstanding debt.

Each year more than $20 billion of market-held certificates, notes, and bonds are refinanced by exchange for new issues. Frequently intermediate securities, and sometimes long securities, have been included in the offers for exchange. Such occasions, consequently, furnish a prime opportunity to develop empirical data with respect to the effects of the availability of funds and on interest rates of changes in the maturity composition of market-held debt.

In the big refinancing of early 1958, for example, nearly $10 billion of market-held debt was refinanced, more than one-third into the 3s of 1964 and more than one-sixth into the 3½s of 1990. This refinancing, in the course of a very few days, effected a huge redistribution in the market supply of investments as between the short-, the intermediate-, and the long-maturity sectors. More that $3.5 billion of securities were shifted out of the very short to the intermediate sector, and more than $1.5 billion additional issues were shifted from the very short to the very long maturity sector.

On this occasion there was a shift in the distribution of securities to be carried in the various maturity sectors of the market that was analogous to what would have been induced had the Federal Reserve System undertaken a huge swapping operation in which it purchased some $5 billion of certificates in the market, and simultaneously sold some $3.5 billion of issues maturing in 1964 and some $1.5 billion of issues maturing in 1990. However, had a Federal Reserve open market operation rather than a Treasury refunding caused this great shift in maturities, the action would have given rise to market expectations about prospective changes in yields of long-term securities that would have affected quotations independently of any effects arising from the shifts of the operation itself.

The reaction of the market to such refinancing operations of the Treasury, however, is free from this influence. It provides, consequently, empirical evidence on three interrelated questions. (1) What is the nature of the market response to additions to or subtractions from market-held debt when the response is not complicated by expectations arising out of the fact that the Federal Reserve had decided to enter the market? (2) How much of the impact of the response is modified or absorbed by the high degree of fluidity that exists among the various maturity sectors on both sides of the market? (3) How large would direct operations by the Federal Reserve System in long-term United States Government securities have to be to exert a significant influence on the availability of long-term funds for investment if the expectations of market professionals and others had no impact on the market?

The reaction of market interest rates to this huge operation is shown in the chart at the foot of the page, where the yield curve on January 13, 1958, before the nature of the refunding was known, is compared with the yield curve on February 5, 1958, after the refunding had been completed. This comparison, of course, does to some extent reflect other market influences. For example, the decline of short-term interest rates from January 13 to February 5 was also affected by the general shift to easier money conditions then under way. Similarly, had it not been for the change in money conditions, long-term rates would probably have advanced more than they did. On the whole, however, the answers to the first two of these three questions, as provided by the response to the recent Treasury refinancing, are (1) that the effect on yields of the redistribution of maturities among the various sectors of the market was noticeable but still limited considering the magnitudes involved, and consequently, (2) that substitutability is a very important market phenomenon in limiting these responses in specific maturity groups—sufficiently important to mitigate appreciably the effects of very large shifts in the volume of securities outstanding in the various maturity sectors of the market.

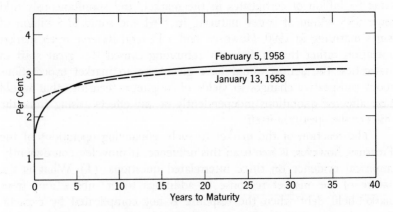

Impact of refunding on yield curves, U.S. Government securities.

In this recent case, for example, bill rates, which had been dropping for some time previous to the refinancing, dropped appreciably further as the volume of short instruments available for investment diminished more than $5 billion. That the reaction was limited in view of the amounts involved is indicated by the fact that bill rates did not drop even to 1½ per cent, and remained much above levels that usually prevail when member banks have $500 million of free reserves. Long-term bond yields, which had also been dropping rapidly, concurrently leveled off and then rose somewhat as these large volumes of additional securities were absorbed in the intermediate and long sectors of the market. There was, however, no sharp upward reaction. Nevertheless, the long-term capital markets continued to absorb new issues in record volume.

These responses were certainly tangible and definite, as would be expected on general grounds. At the same time, considering the huge amounts of securities involved, the effects both on interest rates and on the ability of the capital markets to absorb new securities suggest, in answer to the third question, that the Federal Reserve System would have to undertake very large swapping operations indeed if it wished to use this device to affect appreciably the availability of funds as among the short-, the intermediate-, and the long-maturity sectors of the market.

RECAPITULATION OF ANALYSIS

The kinds of problem that would be encountered should the System intervene directly in the market for long-term Government securities are suggested in the foregoing analysis. The steps in the analysis may be briefly recapitulated.

System actions in the open market affect quoted interest rates in two major ways: (1) by altering basic demand-supply relationships in the credit and capital markets; and (2) by inducing a shift in expectations among market professionals and other investors.

With respect to the first of these responses, System actions influence demand-supply relationships in two ways: (1) by changing the volume of reserves available to the commercial banks for lending or investing; and (2) by changing the volume of securities in the market available for investment. Since the first effect is of overriding importance compared with the second, enduring effects either on short-term or on long-term interest rates differ very little as between operations in bills and operations in bonds, either of which changes the volume of reserves available to the banks.

Under present reserve requirements, one would expect that something like seven-eighths of the interest rate response to any given open market operation would reflect the effect of that operation on the free reserve positions of banks and only one-eighth would reflect the fact that the open market operation also changed the volume of market-held debt. These general expectations accord with experience. Logically and empirically it makes no difference, in this respect, whether operations are in bonds or in bills. Thus the major effect of direct operations in *long*-term securities on *basic* supply-demand relationships would come from the fact that reserves were supplied or withdrawn, not the fact that *long*-term securities were purchased or sold.

But Federal Reserve operations, especially operations in long-term securities, also affect market *expectations*. Federal Reserve actions may induce shifts in expectations among market professionals, even when the effects of those actions on market quotations are ephemeral and supply-demand relationships remain unchanged. Such shifts in expectations may have adverse effects in the sense that they may distort or obscure the basic supply-demand position.

The consequences of mistaken expectations are most serious when they concern the long-term markets. The organization of the money and capital markets is such that long-term yields may persist for a time at lower levels than are justified by the volume of funds available for investment. In this interval, the volume of capital offerings tends to be rationed to the level of market demand, though eventually the pressure of offerings leads to obvious market congestion. Any shift in expectations induced by Federal Reserve policy actions creates the possibility of this type of problem.

In judging the technical effectiveness of its own actions and therefore in determining its own future operations, the Federal Reserve must continually guard against blind acceptances of movement in prices and yields as evidence of basic supply and demand conditions in the market. The quality of this evidence deteriorates the more the long-term sector is affected by shifting expectations. Shifts in expectations affecting the long-term sector would almost surely be more disturbing should the System intervene in it directly.

THE BILLS ONLY DOCTRINE

IN RETROSPECT

DEANE CARSON

INTRODUCTION

As an early and constant critic of the Federal Reserve System's bills only doctrine, the writer might be condemned for flaying a dead horse in proposing to survey the controversy once again—a controversy that has seemingly been laid to rest by the central bank's operations in longer-term securities since 1961. My defense is severalfold: first, it is far from certain that the Federal Reserve's view has fundamentally changed; second, the official policy of the 1950's, which was defended initially on basically institutional considerations, was later vested with theoretical trappings that deserve more complete critical consideration than they have received; and finally, a useful purpose can be served by pointing out the sources of conflict between the academic community and the Federal Reserve Board concerning the proper role of the latter in economic stabilization.

In reviewing and evaluating the rationale of the Federal's decision to confine its open-market operations to short-term securities,[1] one must first note that things were not what they seemed, at least to the outsiders, at the time the new ground rules were promulgated. Indeed,

[1] See Board of Governors of the Federal Reserve System, *Annual Report*, 1953, p. 88, for a complete statement of the new "ground rules" governing open-market operations.

Reprinted from M. J. Brennan, ed., Patterns of Market Behavior: Essays in Honor of Philip Taft (*Providence: Brown University Press, 1965*), pp. 155–172.

while the board emphasized its desire to improve the "depth, breadth, and resiliency" of the government securities market by avoiding operations outside the short-term sector, the basic motivation certainly lay elsewhere. Briefly, the bills only doctrine appears in retrospect to have been an outgrowth of the long struggle for authority between the Federal Reserve Bank of New York, where open-market operations are executed, and the Federal Open Market Committee in Washington, where market policy is formulated. The board, along with some of the reserve bank presidents who sit on the Open Market Committee, wished to exercise greater control over the discretion exercised by the manager of the Open Market account in New York. Prior to bills only, the latter had considerable leeway with respect to the sector in which the general prescription of the Open Market Committee was executed.

In this connection, it is significant that the committee's objective of "maintaining orderly conditions in the government securities market" was changed to read "to prevent disorderly conditions in the market" at the time the bills only policy was adopted. This subtle distinction in mandate to the manager was of utmost significance, since it essentially abrogated Federal Reserve responsibility for the term structure of interest rates except at times of extreme market crisis.

In addition to the difference in views held by the New York Federal Reserve Bank and the board concerning the execution of open-market operations, the bills only doctrine was based upon the experience of postwar monetary management. This experience, which involved a continuation of wartime pegs on government yield structure as a whole until 1947, and pegging of the long-term bond rate until the Treasury-Federal Reserve Accord in 1951, was interpreted by almost all observers, especially the board itself, as directly responsible for the postwar inflation. In its report to the full Open Market Committee, an *ad hoc* subcommittee continually referred to the period of market pegging and strongly suggested that long-term purchases or sales were equivalent to pegging the market.[2] This, of course, was nonsense; but one should not underestimate the trauma that gave rise to such statements and, given the subcommittee's own bias toward protecting the dealer market from exceptional hazards, its desire to avoid the very appearance of evil.

The principal recommendations of this subcommittee were adopted

---

[2] The full text of this report is published in *U.S. Monetary Policy: Recent Thinking and Experience*, Hearings before the Subcommittee on Economic Stabilization of the Joint Committee on the Economic Report, 83rd Congress, Second Session. Hereafter referred to as *Hearings*.

on March 5, 1953, following the submission of its report to the Open Market Committee in November. The proposals adopted were three in number: first, that open-market operations henceforth be confined to the short end of the market; second, that support of the market during periods of Treasury refinancing be discontinued; and third, that operations be conducted solely for the purpose of effectuating credit policy, and not for the purpose of supporting any pattern of prices and yields in the market.[3] The long-standing directive to the manager of the Open Market Account to "maintain orderly conditions in the Government securities market" was changed to one of "correcting disorderly conditions." While the latter phrase was not defined, it was interpreted to mean a qualification, in extreme circumstances, of the "bills only" doctrine contained in the first recommendation.

In commenting on the import of the new directives, Chairman Martin declared they "gave notice that the . . . Committee would not intervene to prevent fluctuations of prices and yields such as normally . . . occur as markets seek to establish equilibrium between supply and demand factors and to allocate savings. . . ."[4] It was his conviction, furthermore, "that we do the most service . . . consonant with the concept of private competitive enterprise by giving the play of the market the maximum influence that it can have without disruptive effects."[5]

The free market thesis was not unqualified; the System stood ready to correct disorderly conditions should they develop. This possibility was considered "remote."[6] Furthermore, "the System would be called upon rarely, if ever, to intervene in securities with longer than one-year maturity and . . . the only justification for System intervention would be to correct disorderly conditions resulting from some emergency, such as an unexpected development in international relations."[7]

Further evidence of the commitment to a free market is inferred from the subcommittee's repeated assertion that the committee should

[3] Board of Governors of the Federal Reserve System, *Annual Report*, 1953, p. 88. These "ground rules" were rescinded by the Open Market Committee on June 11, 1953, on motion of Mr. Sproul, only to be reinstated at the next meeting held September 24, 1953. Members Sproul and Powell were alone in opposing the latter action.
[4] *Hearings*, p. 23.
[5] *Ibid.*, p. 229.
[6] *Ibid.*, p. 304.
[7] *Ibid.*, p. 298. The fact that long-term federal bonds "broke 90" without System intervention shortly after the new directives were adopted indicates the strength of its conviction in this respect.

restrict its intervention in the market. In general, this meant that operations should be conducted for the single purpose of regulating the reserve position of the banking system. In formulating its report, the subcommittee declared that "the present wording of the directive of the . . . Committee on 'maintenance or orderly conditions' carries with it an unduly, *and even dangerously strong*, implication of continuing intervention in all sectors of the market. This prospect . . . seriously impairs the ability of the market to stand on its own feet or to evaluate correctly the real forces of demand and supply in the economy." [8] Testifying in December 1954, Chairman Martin stated that open market operations "have come to be limited to providing and withdrawing reserve funds. . . ." [9]

The emphasis of the *ad hoc* subcommittee report was placed upon the need for improving the technical performance of the government securities market. Rather less attention was given to the question of the impact of a bills only policy on the effectiveness of monetary control, although we are repeatedly assured that changes in short-term yields will be accompanied, after a (presumably short) lag, by same-directional changes throughout the yield curve via the mechanism of arbitrage. As Professor Samuelson has remarked, however the relevant premise raised by the bills only policy is that "by confining operations to short terms, the monetary authorities can realize all the desired effects on credit and spending and can do this in the manner that is philosophically most compatible with the ethical goals of a free society." [10]

It is possible, and indeed rather probable, of course, that neither the *ad hoc* subcommittee nor members of the Open Market Committee actually wished their remarks on the subject of the free money market to be taken literally. In a sense, at least, they were addressed to themselves and to the layman, including market participants and legislators, rather than to the academic economist. The latter's view has nearly always been that the Federal Reserve should exercise a powerful influence on market rates of interest and their structure. On the other hand, central bank officials have nearly always attempted to minimize the public's image of their power, if not the power itself.

A prime example of the attempt to "play down" the impact of central bank action in recent years is contained in the phrase "leaning against the wind" used by Federal Reserve officials to describe their operations. Essentially, "leaning against the wind" implies that the

[8] *Ibid.*, p. 268, italics mine.
[9] *Ibid.*, p. 21.
[10] *The Three Banks Review*, No. 29, March 1956.

central bank simply *modifies* the basic private forces making for expansion and contraction of credit and changes in the level of interest rates. Many economists, on the other hand, tend to assume that the central bank's role is either to *establish* the supply of funds available for bank credit or to *establish* rates of interest and their structure.

These different views of central bank power are not simply the products of difficulties in communication. The monetary economist is inclined to believe that there is a rate of interest, or a structure of rates, that is uniquely appropriate to the attainment of full employment without inflation. As a corollary, many contend that it is the task of the central bank to make this rate level and structure effective. The Federal Reserve's view has increasingly been that its task lies not in establishing interest rates but in modifying the availability of bank reserves on which credit expansion is based. In the quaint vernacular of a recently received undergraduate paper, the Federal Reserve seems to have "flushed the interest rate."

Two reasons may be given the Federal Reserve position *vis à vis* its own market powers. On the theoretical level, the monetary authorities are inclined to doubt the utility of the academic economist's models as guides for policy. This in turn has led to one or the other of two attitudes: first, that the model (for example, the Hicks-Hansen-Lerner formulation) is so abstract that it does not adequately explain the forces that determine interest rates and the level of income, or, second, that to follow its prescription would involve the exercise of "arbitrary" power by the Federal Reserve. We will return to these attitudes when we discuss the Riefler-Young-Yager defense of the bills only doctrine which itself involves a model of monetary behavior.

The second reason for the present view of the Federal Reserve *vis à vis* its responsibilities is largely political in nature. The position of the American central bank in the governmental structure is, if not unique, at least unusual. Its basic responsibility is to Congress, modified by legal, extralegal, and informal relationships to the Executive. Congress itself is made up of hundreds of individuals representing various economic and regional interests, and with varying degrees of responsibility and power. Federal Reserve officials tend to be highly sensitive to the views of this heterogeneous body in general and to those of certain more powerfully placed members in particular. Criticism of its policy is pervasive, unrelenting, and at least occasionally unjustified and uninformed. There is not a little sentiment in Congress that the System is part of a monstrous conspiracy of the banking community to destroy the small farmer and businessman; at the same time, it has been accused of being an engine of inflation. Tight money policies invariably generate anguished complaints from constituents whose congressmen duly reflect them in the multitude of committee hearings at which Reserve officials are asked to testify.

Given this responsibility to Congress, and the need to serve the national interest, the Federal Reserve is forced to explain its sometimes politically distasteful policies in ways that will minimize political hostility. This is done, if our interpretation is correct, by de-emphasizing the role that the Federal Reserve plays in determining the level and structure of interest rates, and by adopting operating techniques which, while somewhat arbitrary, give the appearance of impersonality and, in fact, are less arbitrary than some available alternatives. This involves reliance principally on the purchase and sale of short-term securities (in which market sector the *price* effect will be least) to modify the aggregate supply of excess reserves available to the member banks. The resulting increase (or diminution) in commercial-bank reserves is then allocated to loans and investments or to idle cash as the banking system desires; interest rates in the various markets for funds, furthermore, respond to the changes that have taken place in asset portfolios according to privately determined choices. Finally, the structure of rates is allowed to reflect free market allocation of funds and private demand, with no attempt being made by the monetary authority to establish a particular pattern. This image of the board's powers is certainly more acceptable to the general public than that of a monolithic monetary authority; unfortunately, the desire to project it may lead the central bank to adopt attitudes and techniques that interfere with its own—as well as the public's—ultimate goals. And, ironically, it does not appear that criticism is blunted by the projection of a "weak" central bank.[11]

THE RIEFLER DEFENSE OF BILLS ONLY

In response to criticism of the bills only doctrine which the System adopted in 1953, economists connected with the Federal Reserve Board in Washington developed a further rationale for the policy. This work was largely the responsibility of W.W. Riefler, a long-time economist of the board and assistant to Chairman Martin.[12] Thus it represents official board thinking at the time of its publication in late 1958.

[11] See, for example, Allan Meltzer's testimony before the House Banking and Currency Committee's subcommittee on Domestic Finance on February 11, 1964.
[12] W. W. Riefler, "Open Market Operations in Long-Term Securities," *Federal Reserve Bulletin* (November 1958), pp. 1260–1274.

Riefler's analysis, while avoiding the explicit reference to a free money market that had so confused monetary theorists who had read the *ad hoc* subcommittee report in early 1955, rests, to a great extent, on an implicit preference for minimizing the impact on interest rates of any given operation by the central bank. His major points are listed and discussed below.

(1) Bill operations are preferable to long-term security transactions because "operations by the System in long-term securities can give rise to expectations not only regarding the direction of general monetary policy but also regarding specific prices and yields of long-term securities—a double set of possible misinterpretations. Bill operations lead mainly to expectations about general monetary policy." [13]

(2) Market arbitrage by government securities dealers, and the high degree of substitutability of securities and credit instruments that exists for many lenders and borrowers, results in the transmission of sustained changes in yields in one market sector to other sectors, with or without a time lag.

(3) The effect of open-market operations on interest rates is predominantly the result of change in bank free reserves and only slightly due to the addition or withdrawal of securities in a certain sector of the government securities market.

(4) Since (2) and (3) above lead to the conclusion that it really doesn't matter whether the System's open-market operations are conducted in short- or long-term securities as far as the interest rate effect is concerned, (1) above is the basic justification for operating in the short-term sector.

(5) Interest rate changes are a means to an end, not an end in themselves. The effectiveness of monetary policy rests upon its ability to modify the supply of bank reserves and the flow of bank credit. Changes in interest rates are thus conceived of as the by-product of the reserve effect.

Riefler's central point, (1) above, requires elaboration. Centrally located in the money market are some twenty dealers in government securities whose function is not only to serve as brokers, matching buy and sell orders, but also to make markets in various maturity sectors. The latter requires them to take positions (accumulate inventories) in various issues on their own account, using relatively small amounts of their own capital and relatively large amounts of borrowed money. Their willingness to undertake the latter function depends upon profit expectations. These are determined by a set of conditions

[13] *Ibid.*, p. 1264.

involving the availability and cost of borrowed money, anticipated changes in prices of potential inventory, and the yield of such securities during the inventory-carry period.

Dealers will be encouraged to assume positions in longer-term securities, and thereby to stabilize the market, whenever (1) financing is readily available, (2) the cost of financing is favorable relative to the yield on carried securities, and (3) there is an expectation of an increase in the price of the security over the inventory-carry period. In brief, the dealer must expect to realize a carry-profit after all explicit and opportunity costs have been deducted. Future expectations as to (1) and (2), as well as (3), are important in the decision process.

Since dealers operate on extremely thin margins, small changes in the price of a long-term security held in inventory cause large changes in the rate of profit on capital invested. At the same time, *ceteris paribus*, the more costly are borrowed funds relative to the yield of long-term bonds (as in periods of extremely tight money), the less the attraction of speculative carries in the long-term sector of the market.

To continue with Riefler's argument, dealers constantly seek to discover and correctly interpret Federal Reserve policy. Since they handle all System purchases and sales, they can easily discover the volume of System operations. But this is not enough, for they must also correctly assess the *meaning* of the transactions if their speculative activity is to yield a profit. A somewhat lengthy quotation from Riefler points out the consequences of a misinterpretation of Federal Reserve intentions by market professionals:

> There is always the possibility that they may assume that a given purchase or sale [in any market sector] by the System foreshadows larger changes in bank reserve positions than in fact develop. In such cases, they may take positions and establish, for a period, an unsustainable level of prices or yields that is inconsistent with the actual supply-demand situation.
>
> [The above possibility] is a major reason for the System's policy of nonintervention in the intermediate- and long-term sectors of the market. Its operations in the longer-term securities would be much more subject to comment and possible misinterpretation by market professionals than are its operations in Treasury bills. . . . The very fact that the System took the initiative in buying or selling long-term securities, where the market is almost always thin as compared with the bill sector, would indicate a feeling on the part of Reserve authorities that existing prices and yields on long-term securities were out of line. Market professionals perforce would have to try to assess this implication in their subsequent trades.[14]

[14] *Ibid.*

While Riefler's analysis is essentially correct, it hardly constitutes a compelling reason for avoiding long-term operations. In essence, the argument is that long-term operations increase the uncertainties to which dealers and other professionals are subject when monetary control is exercised through the bill market. Furthermore, however, the fact is that dealers, misinterpreting the objective of a given volume of long-term operations, will tend to operate in the same direction as the Open Market Committee, thus bringing about a change in yields that is inconsistent with basic conditions of demand and supply in the capital markets. That is to say, dealers will seldom go against a trend which they believe the Federal Reserve is trying to establish.

A yield inconsistent with basic supply-demand forces will, according to Riefler, cause later congestion in the capital market if the market has initially been brought to an abnormally low level by dealer expectations generated by System long-term purchases. Indeed, "the lower yields will tend to persist for a period until the volume of prospective [capital] issues, previously withheld but currently seeking a place on the calendar, grows to the point where nervous congestion develops and the true nature of the basic supply-demand position is disclosed." [15]

Although Riefler is not entirely clear on this point, the basic supply-demand position to which he refers is apparently determined in part by the supply of bank reserves. In this context, if the System wishes to augment reserves by, say, $100 million through long-term bond purchases, the following effects obtain. First, yields fall as prices are bid up by the System. Second, dealers and others, riding with the expected trend of monetary ease, also purchase long-term securities, thus further reducing long-term yields. But while the initial fall in yield was consistent with the new supply of bank reserves, the secondary decline is not. One can also infer that the desired increase in investment was consistent with the initial change in yield and additional bank reserves, while the secondary change in yield brings into the new capital issue market an increase in demand that is greater than the supply of loanable funds. This is the basic cause of "congestion" in the capital market.

Riefler does not carry this part of the analysis to its conclusion. In the first place, the excess of capital demand over the supply of loanable funds at the new lower yield induced by both System operations and dealer expectations will not be stable. The long-term yield

15 *Ibid.*, p. 1267.

will tend to rise until the market is cleared, quite possibly at the level originally reached as a result of the initial System purchases. The congestion cannot possibly last for very long. Some prospective investors will be disappointed, of course, but unless investment demand is very elastic with respect to interest rates, the magnitude of congestion will be of little consequence. On the other hand, dealers who have taken positions in long-term issues will be "burned" as prices of long-term bonds rise to reflect the basic supply-demand position. We will return to this particular effect after further considering the conclusions that follow from Riefler's analysis.

A second conclusion to be drawn is that induced dealer expectations which bring long-term yields to an abnormally low point (given the initial assumptions) imply that a relatively small System operation in this market can generate relatively large changes in long-term yields.[16] In recession, when the latter tend to be sticky and in some cases have tended to *rise*, this effect constitutes a powerful argument for System purchases in the longer maturities! In such cases, when lenders are shifting to more liquid assets, dealer expectations of the sort Riefler contemplates, so far from being a disruptive market force, actually serve monetary policy objectives rather well.

At this point we must distinguish between normal day-to-day defensive operations of the System, and operations undertaken to effect changes in basic monetary conditions.[17] The former involve both purchases and sales to counteract factors bringing about changes in bank excess reserves that are not desired from the standpoint of existing monetary policy. These include such things as gold flows, changes in Federal Reserve float, and currency shifts. In this type of open-market operation, there is no particular reason for preferring long-term purchases and sales to short-term. Indeed, the latter should be preferred on the basis that Riefler suggests: In this sector, while "false" expectations can be generated by System operations, the impact on the security prices is much smaller and, therefore, somewhat less disruptive to the performance of dealer functions. Riefler, however makes no distinction of this sort.

Riefler further defends bills only on the grounds that the effect of operations in the short-term sector are transmitted to the long-term sector through dealer arbitrage and the high degree of lender asset

---

[16] Riefler, in fact, states this explicitly on page 1263.

[17] An excellent discussion of defensive and dynamic System operations is found in R. V. Roosa, *Federal Reserve Operations in the Money and Government Securities Markets* (Federal Reserve Bank of New York, 1956).

substitution that exists between market sectors. The discussion of the latter is particularly perceptive. His general position is that the existence of these links between market sectors accounts for the smoothness of the yield curve and provides the transmission lines through which changes in short-term yields and bank reserve positions are carried to the longer-term sectors. He concludes that the existence of these links makes the choice of sector in which the System should conduct its operations a matter of indifference, if there were no other considerations.

The common observation that long- and short-term interest rates tend to move in the same direction has tended to obscure the really important policy considerations involved. Reserve officials contend that short-term operations which increase or decrease short-term yields will bring about similar directional effects, perhaps with a lag, in the intermediate- and long-term sectors. As a corollary, they believe that direct purchases and sales in the latter maturities are unnecessary. This position is untenable as a defense of bills only *dynamic* operations on two grounds.

First, the time lag between an easy money condition in the short-term market and its subsequent impact on long-term yields and investment expenditures has been extensive at certain times in the past. The classic example of this is the depression of 1929–1932, when short-term yields were brought to an extremely low level without noticeable impact on long-term yields. Only after the financial system had been flooded with liquidity in subsequent years did the long-term yield decline. Timing of this sort is certainly incompatible with accepted goals of countercyclical monetary policy.

But even if the time lag does not present a problem, changes in the direction of monetary policy initiated in the bill market may exert a weak impact on the long-term rate. The latter typically moves sluggishly upward or downward relative to similar changes in bill yields. On the other hand, the *price* of long-term bonds drops sharply with a relatively small increase in yield, and vice versa. As far as inhibiting or encouraging long-term investment expenditures is concerned, it is the yield effect which is of paramount importance in monetary control.

In recession, for example, short-term open-market purchases by the System usually bring down long-term rates very little in terms of what a countercyclical expansion of long-term spending on investment would require where demand is inelastic. On the other hand, during an investment boom (conceptually, the investment demand schedule shifting to the right), long-term yields may not move up sufficiently to have much dampening effect.

The bills only approach to monetary control is ill-suited to the problems presented by large changes in investment expenditures and income. Since sustained booms and depressions present many other control problems to the authorities, it seems unwise to limit the arsenal of defense so severely.[18]

Riefler's final point in defense of bills only may be passed over rather quickly. He contends in point (3) that most of the interest rate effect of open-market operations derives from the resulting change in bank reserves, and only a small fraction of the effect can be attributed to the withdrawal or addition of securities in a particular market sector.

To test this hypothesis, he examines a period of Treasury refunding in early 1958 in which a substantial volume of maturing securities was exchanged for long-term bonds. Since the refunding did not in itself cause a change in bank reserves, he observed the security-supply effect on long-term yields more or less in isolation. Making the assumption that the swap of very short-term debt for long-term bonds was equivalent to a system open-market sale of an equivalent amount in the long-term sector, he was led to conclude that the resulting small increase in yield was significant.

Like many other similar experiments, this one is not immune to criticism of its design. In the first place, a Treasury refunding of the kind observed is *not* equivalent to System sales in the long-term market in one important respect. When the Open Market Committee sold $1.5 billion in this market (the amount actually involved in the refunding), dealers would very quickly appraise the operation as intended to raise long-term rates. The exceptional effect that Riefler discusses would lead dealers to ride the trend, mark down prices, and liquidate their own positions, thus raising interest rates by more than the amount generated by the open-market operation. Dealers had no reason to expect that the Treasury's move was anything more than its usual attempt to lengthen the debt during recession periods.[19]

In the second place, interest rates did not rise as much as might be expected under other circumstances. The testing period was one that immediately followed a shift in monetary policy from extreme stringency to active ease. Member bank free reserves averaged $(-)$ $476 millions in September 1957. By January 1958, the date of announcement of the Treasury's refunding terms, free reserves averaged $(+)$ $122 millions. The Federal Reserve Bank of New York discount rate

---

[18] Since early 1961 more flexibility has been adopted in response to peculiar domestic and international balance of payments conditions.
[19] Unfortunately, the use of debt management as a countercyclical device has been inhibited by lack of demand in booms and emerging demand in recession. Dealers have come to expect the Treasury to lengthen debt whenever conditions are favorable.

was reduced both in November 1957, and *during* the period between the announcement of terms and the completion of the refunding on February 5, 1958. These are hardly conditions in which one might expect a System sale of $1.5 billion in the long-term market. Riefler's test is at best inconclusive regarding the interest rate effect of long-term operations by the System, and more statistical testing of this matter is clearly needed.

SUPPLEMENTAL VIEWS ON "BILLS PREFERABLY"

As a backstop to Riefler's defense of bills only, two other members of the Federal Reserve Board staff subsequently published additional views on the problem.[20] Quite aside from the rechristening of the doctrine "bills preferably," which did not change the official position in the least although it provided a more accurate descriptive title,[21] Young and Yager offer largely the same defense as did Riefler, with some additional analysis. To this we now turn.

Major attention is devoted in this analysis to the suggestion that the System should endeavor to reshape, at certain times, the yield curve in the government securities market. Much of what we have argued in the preceding section would lead to this conclusion. Young and Yager deny that this is either desirable or feasible.

Pointing out that although long-term yields may indeed fail to decline during recessions after an initial fall, or fail to rise after an initial increase during booms, the authors argue that this is no evidence of monetary policy failure, let alone failure of the links between market sectors. Taking the recession of 1957–1958 as a case in point—a case in which the differential between long- and short-term rates reached a record high level—they contend that this disparity "suggests that, by the Spring of 1958, monetary policy had come to make its maximum contribution to economic recovery." [22] That long-term yields did not fall further, after the initial decline, "reflected strong private and governmental demands for funds, current and prospective, at the reduced levels of long-term rates." [23]

Examination of flow of funds and saving data for this period in-

[20] R. A. Young and C. A. Yager, "The Economics of 'Bills Preferably,'" *Quarterly Journal of Economics*, LXXIV (August 1960).

[21] The System, in fact, did not confine its operations to Treasury bills during the period. Other short-term debt was involved, ranging up to eighteen months in maturity.

[22] Young and Yager, *op. cit.*, p. 366.

[23] *Ibid.*, p. 367.

dicates that credit and equity funds fell from an increase of $11.8 billion in the fourth quarter of 1957 to an increase of only $3.0 billion in the first quarter of 1958. The third quarter of 1957 increase had been about $900 million higher than the fourth quarter. Long-term government bond yields fell from 3.73 to 3.30 in the fourth quarter of 1957, when investment demand was still high, and only to 3.25 by the end of the first quarter of 1958, when demand had fallen to a very low quarterly level. In the second quarter (spring) of 1958, funds raised increased by $13.7 billion over the previous quarter and then fell again to an increase of 5.9 in the third quarter of 1958. Beginning in the spring quarter, long-term bond yields began to increase. Most of the increase came in the slack third quarter when the average yield went from 3.19 to 3.75. This was prior to the very large fourth-quarter 1958 increase of $22.7 billion in equity and credit funds raised.

These data tend to indicate a substantial lag between changes in long-term rates and changes in spending and are not inconsistent with the Young-Yager hypothesis stated above. However, for every fortuitous example of the benefits that flow from a hands-off policy in the long-term market, the economist can offer a different period to illustrate the need for intervention. From the beginning of the recession in the early summer of 1953 to the end of November, for example—a period of seven months—long-term bonds fell by just more than ⅛ of 1 per cent. One could hardly describe this stability as the result of heavy prospective and present demand for funds.

As a second major defense of bills only, Young and Yager assert that "little empirical evidence is available to illuminate the problem of the relative elasticities of financing demand and total demand to changes in long- and short-term interest rates. It can hardly be contended, accordingly, that a firm basis exists for specifying what shape of yield curve is most appropriate to the given stage of the economic cycle." [24] This contention leads to the conclusion that the central bank should confine itself to the control of bank reserves on which credit is based, leaving to private market forces the tasks of allocating available funds between market sectors and establishing interest rates.

This argument is really not against long-term operations, but rather against an attempt by the Federal Reserve to establish a particular yield curve during a particular phase of the economic cycle. That the two kinds of arguments differ can be seen from the fact that the System could conduct its dynamic open-market operations in the long end of the maturity range, leaving short-term rates to adjust to their

[24] *Ibid.*, p. 365.

own level. While it is true, furthermore, that the appropriate yield curve is not always known, much can be inferred from particular existing yield curves. Failure of monetary policy to stem inflationary investment booms in the period following the Accord suggests that, at least possibly, the yield curves that developed were *not* appropriate. These were marked by rapidly rising short-term yields, slowly rising long-term yields, and, often, a pre-recession yield curve in which short-term securities were yielding nearly as much as, or more than, long terms. This suggests that booms are rather insensitive to short-term yield changes and that higher long-term rates would have been appropriate. This is also suggested by economic theory.[25]

Young and Yager would prefer the use of market techniques that yield the least possible market disruption and undesirable "feedback" effects consistent with the achievement of policy goals. This would be agreed to by all students of the problem. A difficulty exists, however, in that long-term operations, which we have contended will be desirable at certain times, are more disruptive to dealer functions than short-term purchases and sales. As we have seen, dealer functions include taking risk positions in all sectors of the market. Such positions in the long-term sector are more hazardous, and therefore less likely to be assumed, when the System is operating in the long maturities.

The writer believes that the disturbances in the long-term market occasioned by System purchases and sales have been considerably exaggerated by the proponents of bills only. In the first place, there is little evidence that System withdrawal from intervention in this sector materially improved its depth, breadth, and resiliency. One empirical study of the matter offers the conclusion that the market behaved less well in the period after the adoption of bills only than before. Price spreads became wider on a day-to-day basis (lack of depth); the ownership of debt had not widened when important investor groups were considered (lack of breadth); and nonself-correcting price movements have occurred in at least two periods (lack of resiliency).[26]

In the second place, the proper functioning of the long-term market depends at least as much on adequate dealer financing of inventory as on the possible impact of System intervention. Indeed, deal-

---

[25] Young and Yager apparently feel that one "received theory" is as good as another, or perhaps equally bad, as a guide to monetary policy. Their reference to the theory that short-term rates are of primary causal importance to the business cycle was last seriously entertained by R. G. Hawtrey in the 1920's, and had reference to an economic organization that probably antedated World War I.

[26] D. G. Luckett, " 'Bills Only': A Critical Appraisal," *Review of Economics and Statistics*, XLII (August 1960), pp. 301–303.

ers complain of the forced withdrawal from long-term positions occasioned by tight-money policies. When dealer financing is short and expensive, a clear-cut tendency to avoid taking positions in long-term securities is often observed. In this view, a poorly functioning long-term market is the natural concomitant of tight money. If long-term operations are at times required, and dealers cannot live with them, it would seem that, so far from seeking to accommodate the present market institutions, the feasibility of other arrangements should be explored.

BILLS ONLY AND THE TERM STRUCTURE OF INTEREST RATES

In one very important sense, the bills only controversy involves the question of whether the central bank can affect the term structure of interest rates, apart from its acknowledged power to influence the *level* of the yield curve of government securities. This question is of considerable practical importance at certain times; for example, when the economy is in severe recession and the spread between short- and long-term rates is unusually large, or when international payment considerations appear to dictate high short-term yields at a time when domestic economic conditions dictate lower rates and monetary expansion. At such times the ability of the central bank to generate a yield curve different from that which would obtain in the absence of its direct intervention in various maturities is of crucial importance and involves the validity of hypotheses concerning the term structure of interest rates.

One such hypothesis which has dominated monetary thought is that long-term rates are averages of current and expected short-term rates. This expectational hypothesis has been challenged by the institutional hypothesis, according to which the term structure of interest rates is influenced by the existence of suppliers of funds to certain segments of the market for whom securities of other maturities are not perfect substitutes. According to the latter view, yields in any maturity sector may be permanently affected by the *supply* of securities in that sector, a result that cannot be explained by the expectational hypothesis.[27]

In his recent work on the term structure, Meiselman has reconciled

[27] See F. A. Lutz, "The Structure of Interest Rates," *Quarterly Journal of Economics*, LX (1940–1941), 54–55 n.

the two theories by pointing out that the expectational hypothesis only requires that

> Market excess demand schedules of securities of given maturities tend to be infinitely elastic at rates consistent with current and expected short-term rates. Of course, it is not necessary that all transactors have infinitely elastic schedules. . . . It is only necessary that one class of adequately financed transactors have [such a schedule]. . . . Speculators with given expectations adjust quantities of securities taken from or supplied to the market in order to maintain the structure of rates consistent with expectations.[28]

It is apparent that the institutional hypothesis is consistent with the probable success of central bank attempts to impose a given yield structure in the market. As long as excess demand schedules are highly inelastic at current and expected short-term rates, so long can the monetary authority (or the Treasury, for that matter) permanently impose a given yield structure by controlling the relative supplies of securities in particular maturity sectors.

The interposition of "adequately financed transactors" with infinitely elastic excess demand schedules complicates the central bank's task. For example, if the bank wishes to bring down long-term yields *relative* to short-term yields, the impact of its operations in the long-term market (purchases) may be largely offset by sales by speculators, the purpose of which is to maintain the structure of rates consistent with their expectations. Since the proceeds of such sales are unlikely to be kept idle, the speculators will undoubtedly purchase short-term securities, a fact which, given our initial assumptions, should lead to concurrent sales by the central bank. In effect this situation leads to a two-way swapping operation between speculators and the central bank.

The outcome of the game would seem to depend upon the resources of the players. Here Meiselman's qualification that transactors be "adequately financed" is not important; what is required is that speculators have enough long-term bonds in inventory (or power to issue them) to offset the purchases of bonds by the central bank. Since the bank is at worst constrained by its supply of short-term securities, it seems unreasonable to suppose, given the supplies of securities in the Federal Reserves portfolio, either that (1) speculators' supplies will be adequate or that (2) ultimately expectations will not

---

[28] David Meiselman, *The Term Structure of Interest Rates* (Englewood Cliffs: Prentice-Hall, 1962), p. 57. Italics mine.

be modified by the central bank's action.[29] In effect, speculators can ignore the central bank in their calculations only if the bank is in fact committed to a neutral policy with respect to "the rate of interest."

CONCLUSIONS

The bills only controversy has engaged the attention of academic economists and Federal Reserve officials for more than a decade. Until recently, the latter tended to a rather adamant position against the use of direct operations in long-term government securities. This position has been based upon both broadly philosophical grounds, stressing the values of a "free money market," and upon pragmatic considerations involving the possible impact of such intervention on the functioning of the securities markets and the effectiveness of monetary policy.

Most academic economists have argued that circumstances and the objectives of monetary control can best be served at times by direct purchase and sales of long-term bonds. They contend that private market allocation of funds does not always result in a structure of interest rates that is most appropriate to monetary control. We have concluded that this view is essentially correct.

The contention that long-term operations are justified at certain times is made in spite of full agreement with Federal Reserve officials that day-to-day defense operations can best be effected in the short-term maturities. This, however, should not obscure the fundamental differences between monetary theorists and practitioners that have come to light as a result of the bills only controversy. Needless to say, many of these remain to be resolved.

---

[29] If one accepts the expectations theory, or better, Meiselman's variant of expectations theory, the conclusion is inescapable that long-run changes in the yield curve consequent upon Treasury or central bank alterations in the supply of securities of various maturities must be accompanied by a change in expectations as to "the interest rate."

Some have cited the "failure" of "operation twist" or "nudge" in the period after 1961 as evidence that the monetary authorities cannot permanently change the shape of the structure of rates. See J. R. Schlesinger, "The Sequel to Bills Only," *Review of Economics and Statistics*, XLIV (1962), 184–189. On the contrary, this episode is not conclusive, since the Federal Reserve's operations in the long-term market were neither vigorous nor sustained.

SIX

INTERNATIONAL
MONETARY RELATIONS

CONCERN about the United States' adverse balance of international payments, beginning in 1958, has prompted many studies of the system of payments and international monetary arrangements. The role of gold, the dollar as a key currency, the merits of fixed versus flexible exchange rates, the need for more international liquidity to finance expanded world trade—all have been subjected to close scrutiny both here and abroad.

The readings in this final section provide considerable insight into the complex nature of our international monetary problems. In addition, they examine a few of the many proposals for reform that have been suggested.

INTERNATIONAL

MONETARY ORGANIZATION

HARRY G. JOHNSON

The International Monetary Fund was constructed with four specific problems of the 1930's very much in mind. In the first place, the collapse of the gold exchange standard had revealed the weakness of a system in which a shortage of monetary gold was made good by substituting holdings of national currencies convertible into gold, or reliance on negotiation of borrowings of reserves from other countries. The IMF was therefore designed to provide a stock of international credit facilities that could be drawn on by members in balance-of-payments deficit. The specific plan adopted involves members contributing a quota to the Fund, of which 25 per cent is in gold and 75 per cent in the member's own currency; in return they can borrow other members' currencies by purchasing them from the Fund, up to the limit of a Fund holding of their currency equal to 200 per cent of their quota, these purchases being subject to increasingly restrictive terms and conditions as the percentage of currency quota held by the Fund rises. It should be noted that the "currency fund" device has two built-in features that can be (and have been) sources of difficulty in its operation. One is that the fund may not contain a sufficient stock of the currency or currencies that a member wishes to borrow. The other is that an increase in the size of the fund, designed to provide more liquidity, requires additional subscriptions of gold; and to obtain the requisite gold, members may resort to converting their holdings of other

Reprinted from The World Economy at the Crossroads (Montreal: Canadian Trade Committee, 1965), Chapter 3.

members' currencies into gold, thus aggravating the balance-of-payments problems of the latter.

Secondly, the experience of the collapse of the gold exchange standard and its aftermath had shown that, while exchange rate changes were necessary to remedy fundamental disequilibrium, such changes could not be left to the free decisions of national authorities, both because countries might resort to "offensive" devaluation as a substitute for appropriate domestic expansionary policies, and because countries could cancel out each other's exchange rate changes. The International Monetary Fund was therefore designed to be an institution through which internationally agreed changes in particular exchange rates could be implemented, when such changes were necessitated by "fundamental disequilibrium." Thirdly, since movements of "hot money" from country to country had been a major initiating factor in the 1930's collapse and subsequent disturbances, the rules of the IMF allowed countries to exercise control over short-term capital movements. Finally, since it was generally agreed that a major defect of the gold standard system was its "deflationary bias"—due to the fact that while the efflux of reserves put pressure on the deficit country to remedy its deficit, the influx of reserves put no such pressure on the surplus country to remedy its surplus—the Articles of Agreement of the IMF included a "scarce currency clause" permitting members to discriminate in their commercial policies against any member whose currency became scarce in the Fund. This clause was more or less explicitly designed for use against the United States, whose propensity to accumulate gold in the interwar period, and especially in the latter 1930's, was widely held to have been responsible for the interwar difficulties and was expected to continue to present a problem in the future.

The IMF was therefore designed to start the postwar world off with an international monetary system free of the defects of the previous system. But both defects in its design—particularly the small size of the initial Fund and the erroneous basic assumption that all currencies can be treated as equal in international trade and payments—and the nature and magnitude of the immediate postwar monetary disequilibrium problem conspired to set the Fund outside the mainstream of developments. The immediate postwar problem was the reconstruction and economic recovery of the European countries, which required large-scale assistance from the only area capable of supplying the necessary real resources, North America; on the monetary side, this problem appeared as the problem of "dollar shortage." The real resources needed were beyond the capacity of Europe's own financial resources and those of the Fund to supply; instead, the dollars were supplied directly by the United States under the Marshall Plan; and, as a logical corollary, use of the Fund by the European countries was suspended during the period of the Marshall Plan. The isolation of the Fund from European developments during those years had important implications for the future: in the first place, various incidents in 1947–1949 fostered the feeling in Europe that the Fund was an American policy instrument, at a time when Europe was peculiarly sensitive about American domination. Secondly, largely as a consequence of the form in which Marshall Aid was given—in dollars to finance dollar balance-of-payments deficits, with the corresponding real resources having to be reallocated among countries according to their recovery requirements —the European countries had to develop their own institutions of international monetary cooperation on a regional basis—the successive Intra-European Payments Schemes and the European Payments Union, which after the end of the Marshall Plan became the European Monetary Agreement. Thus there became established a tradition of European monetary cooperation, outside of and apart from the IMF.

Meanwhile, the dominating position in world trade, payments, and capital movements that the United States had perforce assumed was rapidly fostering another development that bypassed the IMF system— the growth of use of the U.S. dollar as an international reserve currency, in substitution for the use of gold. The growing use of the dollar as an international reserve currency, together with the gradual transfer of gold reserves from the United States to other, mainly the European, countries that accompanied it, played an important part in permitting the rapid postwar expansion in international trade and payments, which otherwise would have been constricted by a growing shortage of monetary gold, since current new supplies of monetary gold (the excess of new production over hoarding, which has been substantial) have not added to monetary gold stocks as rapidly as the demand for international reserves has grown. On the other hand, the emergence of the dollar as an international reserve currency has re-created the gold exchange standard of the 1920's, which broke down so disastrously in the 1930's, and all of its inherent problems. These problems began to appear very rapidly after 1957, when as a result of European economic recovery, the delayed effects of the 1949 European devaluations, and to some extent of domestic inflation and its own foreign military and economic assistance programmes, the United States balance of payments moved into chronic and substantial deficit. They have been aggravated by the return of the European currencies to convertibility at the end of 1958, which has provided an international environment conducive to the international mobility of capital, and by strong resistance on the part of the monetary authorities and governments of the major countries to exchange rate changes as a means of correcting international disequilibria. On the United States side, that resistance is associated with the obligation not to devalue that a reserve currency country is assumed to have towards its creditors. On the European side, it is associated with the experience of the 1949 devaluations, which by hindsight appear to have been unnecessarily harsh and disturbing, and especially with the notion emphasized by the Americans at that time, that deficits are a consequence of inflationary sins that must be atoned for by devaluation by the deficit country, not condoned by appreciation by the surplus country. The result has been that the present international monetary system has become a system of rigid exchange rates like the old gold standard, contrary to the intentions of the planners of the IMF; further, contrary to the assumption of the planners, it has proved impossible (or at least inexpedient) to devise effective controls over short-term capital movements, which have returned to plague the stability of the system.

What are the major defects of a system of fixed exchange rates based on gold but entailing large-scale holdings of national currencies as international reserves in substitution for gold? International monetary experts have come to distinguish three major problems that characterize such a system—the confidence problem, the long-run liquidity problem, and the adjustment problem.[1]

The confidence problem is concerned with the danger that a loss of confidence in one of the reserve currencies—or a gain in confidence in another—will lead to massive conversions of funds out of or into a particular currency, precipitating demands for gold that cannot be met (since the gold backing of the reserve currencies is inadequate) and so bringing about a collapse of the system in a scramble for nonexistent gold through the liquidation of reserve currency holdings. It is important to note that since only central banks are entitled to convert currencies into gold, such a collapse could only occur as a result of central bank actions, so that the confidence problem is a matter of central banks' confidence in each other's country's economic policies; this feature, besides putting possible conflicts of national interest at the center of operation of the system, gives altogether undue power to central bankers in the operation of the international economic system.

The long-run liquidity problem is as follows: if total international

---

[1] See Fritz Machlup and Burton G. Malkiel (eds.), *International Monetary Arrangements: The Problem of Choice*, report on the deliberations of an international study group of 32 economists (Princeton, N.J.: Princeton University Press, 1964).

reserves are to grow faster than basic reserves in the form of gold, holdings of reserve currencies must grow faster than the gold reserves backing them; so that the liquidity position—ratio of gold reserves to short-term liabilities to foreign countries—of the reserve currency country or countries must deteriorate over time; further, the reserve currency country can only supply additional reserves to other countries by running a continuous deficit on its balance of payments. Both the deficit and the deterioration of the liquidity position sap the confidence in the reserve currency on which its use as a substitute reserve depends; thus the system contains an internal contradiction which can only be corrected by voluntary agreement by other countries to tolerate the deficit and steadily reduce their holdings of gold relative to reserve currencies, or by provision of an alternative supplement to gold other than national currencies. In addition, the system makes the long-run growth of reserves depend on the vagaries of new gold production and hoarding, the balance-of-payments experience of the reserve currency countries, and whatever *ad hoc* arrangements are made from time to time to supplement the gold and national currency reserves with international credit facilities.

The adjustment problem derives from the consideration that the function of international liquidity is to finance deficits that are in process of being corrected, not to remove the need for correction, and is concerned with what mechanisms the system provides for bringing about adjustment. Adjustment is fundamentally a problem of the international realignment of prices and costs. A fixed exchange rate system rules out one mechanism for accomplishing such realignment—changes in exchange rates. The objectives of price stability, high employment, and economic growth adopted by modern economic policy rule out the major mechanism relied on under the old gold standard—deflation in deficit countries and inflation in surplus countries. Adjustment in the present system has therefore come to depend on two other mechanisms: the use of interventions in trade and payments on an *ad hoc* temporary basis to secure improvement in the balance of payments in the short run—which is not "adjustment" in the fundamental sense but a means of averting the consequences of nonadjustment—and reliance on the inability of governments to succeed in achieving the objectives of price stability and full employment in the face of sustained balance-of-payments pressures to the contrary, a reliance reinforced by resort to intergovernmental lecturing on the subject of the responsibilities of deficit and surplus countries to the system.

These problems have, as already mentioned, become acute since the emergence of the United States as a chronic deficit country after

1957. So far as the confidence and long-run liquidity problems are concerned, there have been two alternative practical lines of development to follow—to strengthen the reserve currency system built on the U.S. dollar, and to strengthen and increase the role of the International Monetary Fund in the international monetary system.

To describe these as the practical alternatives is, of course, to exclude two proposals that have been strongly advocated by some academic experts in recent years—to return to the gold standard by means of a sufficient increase in the price of gold and subsequent adherence to the gold standard rules of the game, and to replace the present system by a system of freely floating exchange rates. Both proposals seek to replace the discretionary management of the present arrangements by an automatic self-regulatory system, the difference between them being that gold standard proponents seek to subject national monetary authorities to international discipline, whereas floating rate proponents seek to free national monetary authorities from such discipline—if one distrusts one's own government, one favours the gold standard; if one distrusts other countries' governments, one favours floating exchange rates.

Up until the middle of 1963, the main line of evolution of the international monetary system lay along the route of strengthening the reserve currency system rather than the Fund. The potential role of the Fund was indeed strengthened by an increase in quotas agreed in 1958, by its own development of the technique of "stand-by" credit facilities for countries in balance-of-payments difficulties, and by the General Arrangements to Borrow agreed on in 1961–1962. These Arrangements ensured the Fund an adequate supply of the major European currencies, thereby overcoming the defect of the quota system mentioned earlier, that the Fund may lack a sufficient stock of currencies a member in deficit desires to purchase; but the terms on which the Arrangements to Borrow can be invoked vest discretionary power over the availability of the currencies in the countries supplying them, reflecting the interest of the European countries in keeping control in their own hands and out of the IMF. The main line of evolution, however, lay outside the Fund, a consequence on the one hand of the stance taken by U.S. policy towards the deficit—which was largely shaped by Mr. Robert V. Roosa during his period as Under Secretary for Monetary Affairs in the United States Treasury—and on the other of the attitudes towards and suspicions of the United States and the IMF on the part of the European countries. Until 1963, the United States consistently took the view that its deficit was temporary and due soon to disappear, that the dollar was fundamentally sound, and that it was the obligation of other countries to assist in supporting it through a period of difficulty always expected to be short. Accordingly, the United States, at the instigation and with the active participation of Mr. Roosa, became involved in a succession of *ad hoc* arrangements with various European countries—currency swaps, prepayments of past loans, the issuance of medium-term securities denominated in foreign currencies—designed to improve the appearance of the U.S. balance of payments and finance it without serious loss of gold. The European partners to these arrangements joined in them partly out of growing recognition that they were in fact obliged to do so to keep the international monetary system functioning, partly out of appreciation of the political leverage they acquired thereby over the United States.

In the late summer of 1963, however, the United States changed its position, presumably because the opportunities for further *ad hoc* arrangements had reached the point of exhaustion and because new evidence indicated that the U.S. deficit was likely to continue for some years. The European countries had also been becoming restive about the amounts of credit they had supplied to the United States, and about some of the implications of recent *ad hoc* arrangements. A Study Group of representatives of the ten participants in the General Arrangements to Borrow was set up to review the functioning of the international monetary system and its probable future needs for liquidity. A parallel study was conducted by the IMF; the findings of both were published in time for discussion at the September 1964 annual meeting of the IMF.

The important document here is the *Ministerial Statement* of the Group of Ten, and its *Annex* prepared by Deputies.[2] Its importance lies as much in the issues it leaves open as in those it settles. Not unexpectedly, the Statement affirms the adequacy of the present system of fixed exchange rates based on the present price of gold; where it makes a new departure is in admitting the possibility of a future need for new international reserve assets and setting up a further study group to examine this question. In this connection the Statement supports a "moderate" increase in Fund quotas combined with some adjustment of individual country quotas to align them with the relevant countries'

---

[2] *Ministerial Statement* of the Group of Ten and *Annex* prepared by Deputies, reprinted in *Federal Reserve Bulletin*, 50, no. 11 (August 1964), 975–999; see also *International Monetary Fund, 1964 Annual Report*, Part II (Washington, D.C., 1964).

importance in world trade—such an increase, on the order of 25 per cent, has been set in train by the IMF, though it may pose some problems for the United States by inducing conversions of dollars into gold for subscription of the gold portion of the quota increase. The strains that have arisen in the operation of the international monetary system in recent years are reflected in the Statement on the one hand in the emphasis given to problems of adjustment, which are to be subjected to further study, and on the other to new arrangements for something called "multilateral surveillance" of ways and means of financing payments disequilibria—a term obviously chosen to paper over disagreement about the extent to which third parties should have a voice in bilateral credit arrangements of the type that have become common in recent years.

In terms of the three problems of the present international monetary system outlined earlier, the strengthening of international monetary cooperation evident on and under the surface of the developments of 1963–1964 clearly implies that the confidence problem has been resolved, though some residual areas have been left for bickering among central banks. This fact was indeed dramatically demonstrated by the promptness and adequacy with which international financial support was provided for the pound sterling in the balance-of-payments crisis of late 1964. There remain, however, the long-run liquidity problem and the adjustment problem. These problems, and especially the adjustment problem, have become more urgent in consequence of the sharp deterioration of the United States deficit in the last quarter of 1964, and the increasing impatience of the European surplus countries with the balance-of-payments performance of the United States, expressed most dramatically in General de Gaulle's attack on the present international monetary system and demand for a return to the gold standard in his speech of early February 1965.

As regards the long-run liquidity problem, the recognition by the Group of Ten of the existence of such a problem is at least encouraging; but the real question is how much will be done about it and in what way. The Ministerial Statement leaves open the question whether the new reserve asset envisaged should be provided through the IMF or outside it; and the Group's support for the enlargement of Fund quotas agreed on in September 1964 was clearly intended not to pre-judge that question, nor will the increase in quotas do more than preserve the *status quo ante* recent developments. According to all indications, the Europeans would much prefer future increases in liquidity to be provided outside the IMF, through implementation of the Bernstein multiple-reserve-currency plan.[3] Under this plan, new reserve assets would be provided in the form of bundles of national currencies combined in fixed ratios, which countries would be obliged to hold within a margin of ratios to their gold holdings. The plan has the attraction of building on and stabilizing the reserve currency system by spreading the reserve currency role among the major national currencies; but one suspects that its chief attraction to the European countries is that it will give them control over the amount of the new reserve asset to be created, control which will enable them to resist what they regard as the inflationary influence of the United States. (This question of the alleged inflationary impact of the United States deficit has been a source of much confusion and misunderstanding between Europe and the United States; the Americans argue that American prices have been relatively stable, and that the United States current account has shown a large surplus, so that, if anything, the United States has exercised a deflationary influence; what the Europeans mean is that financing the overall deficit of the United States has faced them with problems of unwanted monetary expansion.) This motivation gives reason for fear that the adoption of the multiple-currency-reserve plan would exercise a deflationary drag on the growth of world trade and payments. From the point of view of ensuring growth of international liquidity at a rate sufficient to support stable growth of world trade and payments, a preferable solution would be for holdings of currency reserves to be centralized and internationalized through transformation of the IMF into a world central bank, with powers to govern the aggregate growth of international reserves through appropriate open market operations, on the plan propounded on various occasions by Professor Robert Triffin of Yale University.[4]

Finally, as regards the adjustment problem, it has already been mentioned that adjustment under the present system is a matter of

---

[3] The Bernstein plan, originated by Dr. Edward F. Bernstein, former Research Director of the IMF, has been circulated privately but not published in an easily accessible source.

For details of other plans advanced in recent years, see Herbert G. Grubel, *World Monetary Reform: Plans and Issues* (Stanford: Stanford University Press, 1963).

[4] The main outlines of the Triffin plan are presented in Robert Triffin, *Gold and the Dollar Crisis* (New Haven: Yale University Press, 1960), though the details have been modified in Professor Triffin's numerous subsequent writings on the subject.

For discussion of the proposal for a world central bank, see Harry G. Johnson, "International Liquidity—Problems and Plans," *Malayan Economic Review*, VIII, no. 1 (April 1962), 1–19, reprinted in Grubel, *op. cit.*, 369–391, and Harry G. Johnson, *The Canadian Quandary* (Toronto: McGraw-Hill of Canada, 1963), 297–322.

ad hoc interventions in trade and payments designed to disguise disequilibrium, coupled with dependence on the passage of time in disequilibrium conditions to bring about genuine adjustment contrary to the other policy objectives of the countries concerned. There is, indeed, a strong prevailing tendency to gloss over the difference between spurious and genuine adjustment, and in so doing to sanction the use of interventions in trade and payments to preserve the appearance of balance-of-payments equilibrium. To do so is to lose sight of the ultimate purposes of international monetary organization in the pursuit of a functioning international monetary system. The ultimate purpose of the international monetary system is to facilitate freedom of competition in trade and payments, and to free international transactions from arbitrary interventions prompted by monetary developments themselves. When freedom of international competition becomes subservient to the maintenance of a particular set of exchange rates, as it has increasingly done in recent years, means have exchanged places with ends. It may be suggested that the trend towards the use of interventions for balance-of-payments purposes calls for re-thinking of the monetary system itself. Under the present system, adjustment occurs by natural competitive realignment of prices and costs so slowly that the resultant deficits are too large to be manageable under existing international monetary arrangements, and have to be handled by what Roosa has termed "systematic *ad-hoc*-ery." One alternative would be to recognize that payments imbalances are of this magnitude, and to seek to finance them not by banking credits but by long-term intergovernmental loans (and possibly grants) following the precedents of war finance, the Marshall Plan, and development assistance. Another would be to revive and make use of the machinery for changing exchange rates in cases of fundamental disequilibrium, which the International Monetary Fund was intended to provide but which has been allowed to fall into disuse.

THE INTERNATIONAL

MONETARY SYSTEM

IRVING S. FRIEDMAN

In this selection the author discusses the structure of the international payments mechanism and the foreign exchange markets through which it operates.

EXTERNAL CONVERTIBILITY

Most of the world trade in goods and services is paid for in currencies [1] which can be freely exchanged for other currencies, including that of the original supplier of the goods or services. With few exceptions, the governments of countries outside the Soviet bloc allow their currencies, when acquired by nonresidents, to be converted into other currencies. Some limitation may be placed, however, on the conversion of such currencies acquired through capital transactions, such as direct or portfolio investments. In this sense, the currencies earned may be said to be "externally convertible" (i.e., convertible by persons outside of the country concerned) for "current transactions" (i.e., not of a capital nature). In practice, an importer of goods or services in a country whose currency is externally convertible is free to pay the exporter of the goods or services in (1) the currency of the importing

---

[1] The word "currencies" is used here to cover all the many forms of means of payment actually employed.

Reprinted from an article in International Monetary Fund Staff Papers, July 1963, pp. 219–245.

country (which the exporter can then sell for other currencies or can hold in a bank deposit—i.e., a nonresident convertible account—which can later be used for any purpose, including conversion into other currencies), or (2) other convertible currencies (including that of the exporting country) obtained by the importer in the foreign exchange market. The latter kind of payment merges into internal convertibility, discussed below.

External convertibility makes it unnecessary for countries whose exchange receipts are very largely in convertible currencies (as are those of the industrial countries) to discriminate, by means of licensing systems, in regard to the currency used for payments for imports and invisibles. As a consequence, discrimination has become much less important in international trade, although some remains as a result of continued bilateralism; however, bilateral agreements (as well as other forms of discrimination for balance of payments reasons) are used primarily by the developing countries. While bilateral trading agreements are still used to some extent by the industrial countries, they are not of major significance in determining the pattern of international trade and payments because, as a general rule, these countries do not try to discriminate in favor of particular bilateral partners. These statements must be qualified with respect to recipients of tied aid. Although this aid is usually extended by countries whose currencies are convertible, the recipient countries, in order to use it, may have to resort to some form of discrimination in their exchange and trade policies; thus such aid, taken beyond certain limits, recreates the economic effects of inconvertibility.

INTERNAL CONVERTIBILITY

Internal convertibility confers on residents the same right to convert their national currency into other currencies which external convertibility confers on nonresidents. After World War II, countries whose currencies were inconvertible restored external convertibility first. Therefore, under present conditions, if a currency is internally convertible, it is necessarily externally convertible as well. Residents of most industrial countries do not yet have complete freedom to exchange their own currency into foreign currencies at official rates of exchange. However, the list of purposes for which foreign exchange is freely made available to residents has by now been greatly extended. Whereas, formerly, payments for many imports of goods and services were severely restricted, existing restrictions are confined mainly to capital payments.

The freedom to purchase foreign currencies for certain purposes does not mean, in practice, that all externally convertible currencies are used to an important extent to make international payments. Payments are generally made in U.S. dollars or sterling even when no residents of the United States or the United Kingdom are parties to the transaction; prices, shipping documents and other contracts, freight charges, etc., are frequently expressed in one of these currencies. Occasionally, other currencies are used, particularly in transactions between two nondollar, nonsterling countries. Payments may also be made by crediting the convertible currency account of the payee (or his bank), but if this is done conversion when requested is usually into U.S. dollars or sterling. Gold itself is used from time to time to make international settlements, particularly those of a governmental character or between central banks; however, the use of gold for these purposes is relatively infrequent. Part of the explanation for the use of the U.S. dollar as a reserve currency is its convertibility into gold at a fixed price, but its widespread use for international payments is another important recommendation, and this applies even more forcibly to sterling. It is noteworthy that during recent years, when the U.S. balance of payments has been in deficit and there has been talk of dollar "weakness," the international use of the dollar seems actually to have increased. The pound sterling also, despite the United Kingdom's balance of payments difficulties, remains a widely used international medium of payment.

Countries exercising controls over capital transactions find it difficult to refrain from screening payments for all purposes, including payments for imports and invisibles, in order to prevent disguised capital flight. The screening process may not be onerous and, through the use of such devices as open general licenses for broad categories of transactions and the delegation of authority to commercial banks to deal even with doubtful and borderline requests for permission to purchase foreign exchange, it may result in having little, or virtually no, effect on current transactions. Nevertheless, so long as there are limitations on the amount of foreign exchange which residents can purchase, whatever the reasons and however valid they may be, a full convertibility system does not exist. All that can be said is that the significance of the inconvertibility still remaining is much less than in the 1950's both because it now affects only slightly the international exchange of goods and services and because it does not interfere with the convertibility of earnings or other foreign exchange receipts by nonresidents.

It is true that many industrial countries retain quantitative restrictions on some imports, and that these restrictions on international trade affect the volume and pattern of payments. Generally, however, these trade restrictions in the industrial countries are not, technically, restrictions on international payments as such. Thus, countries with convertible currencies may employ quantitative restrictions and quotas without technically impairing the convertibility of their currencies, even though the economic effects of these restrictions are very similar to limitations on internal convertibility. This similarity is reflected in the provisions of the General Agreement on Tariffs and Trade (GATT) dealing with such quantitative restrictions—especially in the role given to the Fund in judging the extent to which such restrictions are needed for balance of payments purposes and in the closeness with which the definition of discrimination in the exchange field, authorized under the Fund Agreement, is paralleled by that of discrimination authorized under the GATT. Where trade restrictions are maintained to protect the balance of payments, there is close cooperation between the Fund and the GATT on the question of whether the restrictions are more intense than the balance of payments position requires.[2] However, the trade restrictions maintained today by the industrial countries are not usually maintained for balance of payments purposes; this means either that the country does not claim that its balance of payments necessitates the maintenance of such restrictions, or that it considers that they could be eliminated without intolerable effects on its balance of payments. The General Agreement also contains provisions requiring countries to account for import restrictions not maintained for balance of payments reasons. Thus, trade restrictions which significantly affect the volume and direction of payments are subject to international discussion, whether or not they are maintained to protect the balance of payments.

PAR VALUES AND MARGINS

In countries where par values have been agreed with the International Monetary Fund, the purchase and sale of currencies are supposed to take place at exchange rates based upon these parities and within limited margins. Par values are expressed in gold, or in terms of

[2] The only important industrial countries not members of the International Monetary Fund are Switzerland and those in the Soviet bloc.

the U.S. dollar of the weight and fineness in effect on July 1, 1944. The par values of the principal industrial countries are given in Table 1.

Par values are thus unitary rates, although, as discussed below, they can be part of multiple currency systems. In the industrial countries the exchange rates are essentially unitary; where multiple currency features exist, they do not alter the fundamental character of the system.

The Articles of Agreement of the Fund provide that the maximum and minimum rates for spot exchange transactions between the currencies of its members taking place within their territories shall not differ from these par values by more than 1 per cent. This 1 per cent is called the margin; the combination of margins on either side of par can result in a spread of 2 per cent between the lowest and highest limits between any two members' currencies. In practice, the industrial countries have fixed their currencies in terms of the U.S. dollar. If the exchange rate of each currency vis-à-vis the U.S. dollar varies within a margin of one-half of 1 per cent, giving a spread of 1 per cent, the exchange rate between two such currencies can vary within a margin of 1 per cent or a spread of 2 per cent. Therefore, margins of more than one-half of 1 per cent vis-à-vis the U.S. dollar could give rise to margins of more than 1 per cent between other currencies and therefore margins greater than specified in the Articles of Agreement. A decision taken by the Fund in July 1959, however, permits the spread between the maximum and minimum rates to be as much as 4 per cent whenever such rates result from the maintenance of margins of no more than 1 per cent from parity for a convertible currency. Thus, even currencies that are based on par values agreed with the Fund can fluctuate considerably in terms of other currencies without changes in par values or any other official action. The importance of the width of this spread can be seen by calculating the possible cost to a speculator of taking an uncovered position within the spread, keeping in mind that his costs are calculated on a per annum basis. An error in forecasting a movement of the exchange rate during the period of the transaction (from one day to many months), even if the movement of the rate is within the permitted spread, may well involve a considerable loss. Thus, from a business point of view, the existing spreads are by no means "narrow." In this connection, attention is drawn to the steps taken by Japan in April 1963 to widen the margins of exchange rates for the yen to magnitudes similar to those prevailing in connection with European currencies (see Table 1).

For a business engaged in international transactions, the possibili-

TABLE 1 PRINCIPAL INDUSTRIAL COUNTRIES: PAR VALUES AGREED WITH THE INTERNATIONAL MONETARY FUND

(In units of national currencies per U.S. dollar)

Member Country	Currency	Initial Par Values		Changes in Par Values		Central Bank's Buying and Selling Rates for U.S. Dollar		Margins of Selling (+) and Buying (−) Rates for U.S. Dollar (as per cent of par value)
		Rate	In effect for period	Rate	In effect for period	Buying	Selling	
Austria	Schilling	26.000	May 4, 1953 to present	—	—	25.80	26.20	±0.769
Belgium	Franc	43.8275	Dec. 18, 1946 to Sept. 21, 1949	50.000	Sept. 22, 1949 to present	49.625	50.375	±0.750
Canada	Dollar	1.000	Dec. 18, 1946 to Sept. 18, 1949	1.100	Sept. 19, 1949 to Sept. 29, 1950	—	—	—
				No par value	Sept. 30, 1950 to May 1, 1962	—	—	—
				1.08108	May 2, 1962 to present	1	1	±1.000

Country	Currency	Par value	Period	Par value	Period	Buying	Selling	Margins
France	Franc	119.107[2]	Dec. 18, 1946 to Jan. 25, 1948	No par value	Jan. 26, 1948 to Dec. 28, 1958	—	—	—
				493.706[2]	Dec. 29, 1958 to Dec. 31, 1959	—	—	—
				4.93706[3]	Jan. 1, 1960 to present	4.90[3]	4.974[3]	+0.748 / −0.751
Germany, Fed. Rep.	Deutsche Mark	4.200	Jan. 30, 1953 to Mar. 5, 1961	4.000	Mar. 6, 1961 to present	3.97	4.03	±0.750
Italy	Lira	625.000	Mar. 30, 1960 to present	—	—	620.50	629.50	±0.720
Japan	Yen	360.000	May 11, 1953 to present	—	—	357.30	362.70	±0.750
Netherlands	Guilder	2.65285	Dec. 18, 1946 to Sept. 20, 1949	3.800	Sept. 21, 1949 to Mar. 6, 1961	—	—	—
				3.620	Mar. 7, 1961 to present	3.5925	3.6475	±0.760
Sweden	Krona	5.17321	Nov. 5, 1951 to present	—	—	5.135	5.2125	±0.759 / −0.739
United Kingdom	Pound Sterling	.248139	Dec. 18, 1946 to Sept. 17, 1949	.357143	Sept. 18, 1949 to present	2.82[4]	2.78[4]	±0.714

[1] No official buying or selling exchange rate has been announced. It is understood that the authorities maintain the exchange rate within the margins of 1 per cent on either side of parity with the U.S. dollar.
[2] Old francs.
[3] New francs.
[4] U.S. dollars per pound sterling.

ties of variations within the spread create conditions not too unlike a free market with a fluctuating rate—the difference being, of course, that the monetary authorities will intervene to prevent the emergence of rates beyond the limits of the spread. In practice, this means that if a currency is under pressure—in that demand for that currency to consummate international transactions is less than supply (whatever the source of demand and supply) and the exchange rate falls in terms of foreign currencies—the monetary authorities will provide additional foreign exchange to keep the rate from falling below the agreed margin. In these circumstances, the country is using its monetary reserves to defend its exchange rate. On the other hand, if a currency is strong, so that the demand for it is outrunning the supply, the exchange rate will be bid up to the upper limit and the monetary authorities will buy foreign exchange to prevent further appreciation of the currency.

In recent years, the central banks of a number of the industrial countries have adopted a rather passive attitude toward intervention, in the sense that the spot exchange rates have been allowed to reach or come very close to either the upper or the lower limit before foreign exchange is bought or sold. Such passivity may well lead to an expectation of a change in the par value, and there are indications that central banks are now intervening more actively to influence trends in the exchange markets and particularly to narrow the range of fluctuation. Although institutional differences are marked from country to country, the intervention of the central banks normally takes place through the commercial banking system; this practice is usual in the United Kingdom. The Bank of England, as manager of the Exchange Equalization Account, has for many years operated to prevent unwanted fluctuations of the rate, and so far as possible to prevent it from bumping against the margins. It does not stand committed to protect the spot rate at any one point within the margins, but it endeavors to keep the rate at a level which reflects the underlying state of the market. Its operations are usually conducted secretly, so that the public does not always receive information about its intervention. Speculators know, however, that attempts to exploit temporary weaknesses in the position of the pound may prove very costly.

In so intervening, the central banks may be motivated by a desire to influence not only the rate of exchange, the reserve position, or the flow of capital, but also domestic liquidity. Of course, in practice its operations affect all these, and perhaps other, factors simultaneously, and they may merely afford different routes by which to achieve the same end—the defense of the external value of the currency at a desired level and without impairment of its convertibility.

ROLE OF FOREIGN EXCHANGE MARKETS

The basic structure of the international payments system comprises the "external" and "internal" convertibility of currencies, the system of par values and margins, and central bank intervention on the exchange markets. The system operates through foreign exchange markets made up principally of commercial banks. Thus, most international financial transactions are handled on a commercial basis through the operation of foreign exchange markets linked through exchange rate and interest rate arbitrage. Commercial banks in the industrial countries are, by and large, free to deal in all of the currencies of these countries (as well as some others), so that they are free to take advantage of interest rate differentials in different money markets. The excellence of modern communications obviates disparities in exchange rates through the ability of commercial banks to consummate quickly foreign exchange purchases and sales. This re-creation of the function of the foreign exchange markets has been one of the most important and yet neglected developments in postwar international finance. It began on a regional basis shortly after the establishment of the European Payments Union (EPU) in 1951. For some years, separate exchange markets for EPU currencies and the dollar existed simultaneously. The establishment of external convertibility of the main currencies in 1958 meant the elimination of the wall between these separate markets and their merger into one exchange market for convertible currencies.

However, experience soon indicated that, despite the many similarities to prewar exchange markets, the new conditions in the world economy created novel situations in the exchange markets, calling for a constant reappraisal of central bank policies. These new conditions included, for example, large accumulations of dollar balances, commitments to full employment policies, limitations on capital movements, and eagerness to maintain the foreign currency value of direct investments. A major policy instrument for coping with these situations has been direct intervention by the central bank in the exchange market.

Such direct intervention works instantaneously, whereas other influences exerted by the monetary authorities through open market operations, other public debt measures, or changes in relevant rates or reserve requirements, are usually taken after a time lag and are subject to a further time lag before they take effect. Aside from central bank intervention, the position of currencies in the exchange markets is largely the result of transactions made by private individuals, reflecting all the factors that affect any commerical market. In particular, apart from such intervention, the differences between rates for forward transactions and those for spot transactions are determined by market conditions. Given the possibility of exchange rate variations, as described above, as well as interest differentials, the forward market becomes an important indicator of expectations with respect to exchange rates. It is simple arithmetic to calculate whether, at any given moment, commercial traders, whatever their motives, are expecting a fall or a rise in the exchange rate, and whether that fall or rise reflects an expectation of a change in the par value. For this reason, forward exchange rates have become increasingly important as indicators of the external financial position of a country and its prospects. Indeed, it may be said that such quotations are becoming more important than changes in gold or foreign exchange reserves as indicators of the strength or weakness of a currency. The exchange market has become the battlefield for defending the external value of a currency.

ALTERNATIVE INTERNATIONAL

MONETARY SYSTEMS

J. M. CULBERTSON

In this selection Professor Culbertson examines the virtues and shortcomings of the orthodox gold standard and the gold exchange standard. He then proposes a new international monetary standard that would retain the virtues and avoid at least some of the defects of present international monetary arrangements.

Principal holders of international money are national governments, which are pledged to maintain their national currencies in a fixed relation to those of other countries and to gold. They hold reserves to protect their ability to do this, just as individuals and business hold reserves of money and liquid assets to assure their ability to meet their obligations. A national government that is short of international money and liquidity may adjust in various ways (discussed below), according to whatever agreed rules of international economic behavior are in operation. However, principal means are by applying a restrictive domestic monetary policy or other measures to limit its domestic income and employment, by imposing impediments to its imports, by restrictions on its capital outflows, and by a reduction in the external value of its currency. Thus, a shortage of international money leads to

Reprinted from Recent Changes in Monetary Policy and Balance of Payments Problems, Hearings before the Committee on Banking and Currency, 88th Congress, First Session (Washington: Government Printing Office, 1963), pp. 331–344.

a predominance of international deflation or unemployment,[1] increased restrictionism, or competitive devaluation of currencies. An excess of international money would lead to predominance of inflationary pressures, to easing of restrictionism, or increases in the value of national commodities in relation to gold (or another international money).

What is needed is a behavior of the amount of international money that avoids both of these extremes. The other requirement is that the international monetary system should be stable, that the amount of international money should not be potentially subject to an abrupt decline, such as that following the breakdown of the gold-exchange standard in 1931. Such a drop in the amount of international money can occur either because of a reduction in the amount of that thing that serves as money, or because of a change in usage that deprives of its monetary function, demonetizes, a part of what had been the stock of money.

The construction of a satisfactory international monetary system, thus, is one of the foundations of a workable and stable economic system embracing the free nations. The choice among directions in which to build the international monetary system is one of the crucial ones presently affecting U.S. policy. The considerations involved are best illustrated by outlining the principal alternative courses that are available.

GOLD AS THE INTERNATIONAL MONEY

The traditional international money is gold. One direction for policy would be toward an exclusive reliance upon gold as the vehicle for the holding of international reserves and the making of international payments. This course has one strong point in its favor. Gold is quite firmly monetized. Its acceptability in international payments rests firmly on tradition and past experience.

The difficulties with an exclusive reliance upon gold as interna-

---

[1] Presently there are powerful resistances in most countries to reductions in wages and prices. Therefore, a deficiency of total demand in a nation arising from a payments deficit (either through deliberately restrictive government policies or the automatic result of the monetary and income drain of the deficit) is likely to show up in the short run mainly in increased unemployment, rather than falling prices. Thus, in the event of a deficiency of international money, what is to be feared is a predominance of large unemployment and economic slack in the free world, more largely than dangerously rapid price reductions.

tional money are: (1) Its amount is grievously deficient at the existing value of gold (in terms of national currencies), (2) it would be extremely difficult to change the general price of gold, and (3) the future rate of increase in the gold stock is, in any case, somewhat unpredictable and therefore possibly inappropriate, and gold is an expensive international money because of the costs of mining, storing, and shipping it.

The world's monetary gold stock long has failed to increase proportionately with world income and trade. This meant that the amount of gold used as international money did not grow fast enough to prevent pressures for deflation and restrictionism. As a result, presently gold is supplemented by the use of a large amount of national currencies as international money, in the gold-exchange system discussed below. In order to go back to an exclusively gold international money and demonetize (as international money) these national currencies, it would be necessary to do one of two things: (1) Reduce world prices sufficiently to bring down the international reserves desired by the nations into line with the existing stock of gold, or (2) increase the price of gold (devalue national currencies in terms of gold) so that the value of the existing gold stock suffices to meet needs for international money at existing incomes and prices. The first course obviously is uninteresting. The second might be followed, and is one of the candidates for consideration.

A general increase in the price of gold would have two effects: (1) It would increase the value of existing gold reserves. If done to just the right extent, thus, it would provide enough international money to meet the world's present needs and to permit the demonetization as international money of national currencies, yielding a more stable system, and (2) it would increase the profitability of mining gold and might attract gold from speculative hoards into international reserves. Thus, it might raise the future rate of growth in the monetary gold stock more nearly into line with future growth in world monetary needs.

It has been argued, thus, that a single, once-for-all increase in the price of gold could solve both problems, of present reform and future adequacy of international money. However, this is an optimistic view of the matter: It would be a happy coincidence if the increase in gold value that just sufficed to meet the present problem also sufficed to meet the future one. In any case, future output of gold cannot be predicted with confidence. Neither is there any reason for assurance that the rate of increase will be stable. There is no reason to believe that the production function of the gold-mining industry is one of the great constants of nature. It has not been so in the past.

Thus, thoroughly to tame gold, to make the amount of gold as international money behave in a controlled and acceptable way, presumably would require a continuing series of revisions of the price of gold. The increase in the price of gold, upon each successive reconsideration of the matter, would be whatever amount was required to bridge the gap between the rate of increase in the world's stock of monetary gold, at the existing price, and the rate of increase in the gold stock required to satisfy the nations, on balance, and prevent a predominance of restrictionist or inflationary pressures.

This necessarily involves the translation of gold from a traditional, or natural, international money into a managed money. It breaks the fixed link between national currencies and gold that in the minds of some observers is the crucial element in the international monetary arrangements.

This is not an altogether unpromising system, but it is subject to some substantial defects:

(1) It would be very difficult to get from here to there, since a large devaluation of all the world's currencies would be very difficult if not impossible to manage in an orderly way. It would involve breaking commitments and obligations on the part of the dollar (which might be met a least in part by reimbursement of some holders of dollars for all or a part of their missed benefits from gold appreciation), reward those who have speculated against the dollar and other national currencies and hurt those who have played generously and showed trust, and generate present and future speculation in gold. The adjustment could not be made without warning, and the problem of preserving order in the international financial system while it was being negotiated would be extraordinarily difficult. Given the sort of behavior to be expected of the various nations, it very likely is impossible. The passage would hold considerable hazard for the free world. This is the more true in that opinions on the matter are divided, and a large segment of the financial community (as well as others) does not favor this course.

(2) The benefits of the gold appreciation would be unevenly distributed, accruing mainly to the United States and other large gold holders (if reimbursement to dollar holders were not given) and to the producing areas, mainly South Africa and the Soviet Union.

(3) A continuing encouragement would be given to the private hoarding of gold by its probable appreciation in price (in terms of national currencies). This would complicate the management problem.

(4) The appreciation in gold price would encourage its production, and would continue to involve the world in considerable costs

of producing, storing, and transporting gold, which could be avoided by alternative systems.

(5) To make gold, the international money of tradition, into a managed money, may involve an awkward and unstable compromise. Those who take the traditional approach to international money will oppose the continued revaluation of gold, as being the opposite of orthodoxy. On the other hand, those who favor a managed money will not desire to give the expensive and tradition-based gold the central place within the system. Thus, it can be argued, if we are to go to a managed system, we should assign a lesser role to gold and create a new international money, as discussed below.

These are substantial defects, but none of the candidates is without defects, so their relative defectiveness is appraised when they have all been considered. An important virtue of gold is its defenses against demonetization, and the protection thus afforded by a gold-only international money against an abrupt deflationary shock to the free world.

THE GOLD-EXCHANGE SYSTEM

The inadequate growth in the world's stock of monetary gold has resulted in major use of national currencies as international money, presently the dollar and the pound sterling. This system is termed the gold-exchange or gold-plus-key-currency system. It involves the making available to other countries of balances in the key currency through deficits in the international payments of the key-currency country, and the use of these balances as reserves and as an instrument for the making of international payments.

This system has a quite different characteristic behavior, and quite different difficulties, than the straight gold system. In the straight gold system, the amount of international money is likely to misbehave because it depends upon the fortuitous factor of techniques of mining gold. In the gold-exchange system, the amount of international money is likely to misbehave because it depends upon this plus another equally fortuitous factor, the (international) payments deficit of the key-currency country. If there existed a mechanism to assure that the key-currency country ran just that payments deficit that would provide to other countries just that amount of its currency that, together with the increase in the gold stock, would meet the world's need for international money, then the management problem would be under control. No such effective control over the state of international payments has ever yet been achieved. In the absence of it, the gold-exchange system operates somewhat haphazardly, as is illustrated by recent gyrations in the payments position of the United States and their effect upon the state of international liquidity.

In order to transform the gold-exchange system from a haphazard to a managed one, it would be necessary to develop an apparatus for the precise control of the payments deficit of the key-currency country. This would have to use the potential adjustment mechanisms discussed below. However, the problem—difficult enough at best—is complicated by the fact that the key-currency country cannot change the external value of its currency, and perhaps must suffer special limitations in its access to other adjustment devices. Thus, the payments position of the key-currency country is even less subject to effective control than those of other countries. This argues that the adjustments ought to be made on the other end. Other countries, on balance, ought to so adjust their payment positions that the key-currency country's payments position comes out to be what it ought to be. But to achieve this in any very complete way would require a complex sharing of responsibilities by other nations, and would run into the political difficulties mentioned below.

If the management problem of the gold-exchange system could somehow be solved, there would be a second problem. Characteristically in the past, those national currencies used as international money have had the status of a second-class international money. The first-class international money was gold. The acceptability of the key currency was not firmly established but depended upon its presumed convertibility into gold on demand. In a situation in which the rate of growth in the monetary gold stock is less than that in demand for international money, this system suffers from a basic flaw. The amount of key currency used as international money must increase more rapidly than the gold stock, which means that the gold-reserve ratio of the key-currency country must decline, which means that the status of the key currency will weaken. When the key currency falls into the unstable position of being subject to demonetization under pressure, then the free world is in a precarious position. The abrupt demonetization of the key currency as its former holders forsake it and flee to gold can cause violent pressures for deflation, restrictions, competitive devaluation, international animosity, and can bring the collapse of the international economic system.

The gold-exchange system could be saved from its potential instability if the key currency could be converted into a first-class money, one acceptable on its own right and not merely because of its convertibility into gold. However, an effort to achieve this runs into a third problem, the weak political foundations of the key-currency system. In the absence of a more basic change in the nation's views on international money or in international political relations, the key currency could be made into a first-class international money only by a commitment of other nations to hold their reserves to some minimum extent in this form, rather than gold. Yet a status as a key currency, a strong or hard currency, commonly is taken to confer political and economic advantage upon a nation and, indeed, may be used by it as an instrument for its own advantage. This, plus the profit that the financial community in the key-currency country derives from its status, is likely to generate jealousy abroad, and to prevent the granting of the required commitments.

Even if such jealousies were avoided, it is not clear that a satisfactory political basis for the required commitments could be found. Why should other nations thus tie themselves irretrievably, say, to the dollar, and to the economic policies of the United States? What commitments on the part of the key-currency country would be required to justify this? Is such an arrangement conceivable, in the present political state of the world?

On this basis, it appears that what is required to make the gold-exchange system into a controlled and stable international monetary system is very difficult to do. There is a good deal of question whether it could be done, in the present state of things. In any case, no serious effort to take these steps is presently being made.

Attention has been focused on the immediate problem of strengthening the dollar as a key currency by reducing or eliminating the U.S. payments deficit. Such action will strengthen the dollar, but it also will cut off a major source of growth in the stock of international money. Thus, some other international monetary mechanism must be provided to fill the gap, if restrictive pressure on an international scale is to be avoided.

If the decision is made not to attempt to take the steps required to make the gold-exchange system manageable and stable, but rather to cut off the supply of additional key currency, this essentially involves rejection of this system as the basis for further expansion in international money. The question, then, is what is to take its place.

One line of attack is to further develop or refine the key-currency system. This is seemingly the intention of recent U.S. policy, and, under its leadership, the direction of development of the international financial system. This is a new and untested system. Indeed, it has as yet received but little understanding and approval, considering what is being staked upon its workability.

There are several possible elements in this program, which are considered further in the appendix, the relative importance of which is perhaps yet not entirely clear. One of these is to achieve the strengthening of the key currency (which for brevity here is associated with the dollar) by reducing the U.S. payments deficit, and then to provide other nations with the additional dollars needed for adequate growth in their reserves not through a U.S. payments deficit, but rather through currency swaps. Other countries get dollars, which they use as international money. The United States gets other currencies, which it uses as backing for the international dollar (the dollar used as international, rather than domestic, money) along with gold. The additional international dollars coming into existence, then, could be fully backed by gold plus holdings of other currencies. It might be argued that this should suffice to assure that the dollar would continue indefinitely to be acceptable as international money, no matter how large the amount of international dollars rose over time.[2]

The question must be raised whether this device effectively escapes the basic flaw of the gold-exchange standard. This flaw is that international dollars, for example, are treated by their holders as a second-class international money, one deriving its acceptability from its convertibility into gold, the first-class international money. Under one swap system, the dollar is backed by a falling ratio of gold plus a rising ratio of other currencies, the other currencies, in turn, being backed by a falling ratio of gold. If the problem is to stretch the limited supply of gold, it is not clear that this stratagem suffices to do it.

To put the matter in another way, the United States when it exchanges dollars for other currencies either could give a pledge not to use the other currencies in international payments—not to present them for payment—or else could avoid giving such a pledge. If it gave the pledge, then its holdings of other currencies would be an illiquid asset, and it is difficult to see that they would be regarded as conferring strength on the international dollar. After all, it is only liquidity and the convertibility of the dollar into gold that is in question. There is no doubt but that the United States is a solvent enterprise, and a net creditor on international account.

On the other hand, if the United States gave no such pledge, its

---

[2] As the ideas and objectives lying behind U.S. policy are characterized in the available statements by Under Secretary of the Treasury Robert V. Roosa, this device seems to play the central role. See the statements by Under Secretary Roosa in "Factors Affecting the U.S. Balance of Payments, Compilation of Studies Prepared for the Subcommittee on International Exchange and Payments of the Joint Economic Committee, 1962," pp. 325–351.

holdings of other currencies would be a more meaningful backing for the international dollar—setting aside the ultimate question of what they add to its convertibility into gold. At least, the dollar would be fully backed up by liquid assets of some sort. In this event, however, it is not clear that the countries engaging in the swaps with the United States would have gained any international liquidity. They would have gained a ready asset in their dollars, and a demand liability in the U.S. holdings of their currency. It is not clear that they should feel any better off. Such a country that actually used its newly gained dollars to meet a payments deficit would seem to find itself in a weak position, having lost the demand asset but retained the demand liability. Would it not be under pressure to apply deflation or restriction?

Moreover, this arrangement would seem, like the gold-exchange standard itself, to be potentially unstable. The key currency is not transformed into a first-class international money nor supported more strongly by the first-class international money, gold. Rather, any additional liquidity that was created would be based upon frame of mind, a set of attitudes, that might change under pressure. The system confers liquidity only if other countries somehow regard the dollar as being firmly supported by U.S. holdings of currencies such as theirs, but at the same time regard the claims against them represented by U.S. holdings of their currency as certain not to be exercised. In a situation of stress, it seems altogether probable that one or the other of these beliefs would break down, pulling the other down with it. The structure built on a fragile foundation of optimism would give way to its inherent inconsistency, resulting in generally restrictive policies and threatened demonetization of the dollar.

In this instability, there is a close parallel to that of unstable financial arrangements within the domestic economy. During a period of optimism people are willing to place themselves in an illiquid position because of their certainty that things will go well. They are willing psychologically to concentrate attention on their illiquid assets and discount their short-term liabilities. But when this system of arrangements is tested, it does not merely weaken, but collapses. For people abruptly are forced to give full weight to their short-term liabilities, and the general scramble to liquidate ruins all.

If U.S. holdings of foreign currencies would suffice to monetize the international dollar so firmly that these awkward questions would never be raised, then the system would be stable. However, the approach proposed does not seem to be based upon such a conception of firm monetization, but rather upon a conception of mutual trust, sound financial policies, and strong balance sheets. Approached with this frame of mind, the proposed system seems to display the usual characteristics of an unstable financial arrangement. With a growing superstructure of mutual financial claims rising up from a limited base of solid liquidity in the form of gold, the balance sheets would not be strong, and they would grow progressively weaker.

An associated, but distinguishable, proposal is for an increase in the number of key currencies. This need not involve currency swaps or mutual holdings of national currencies. It could reflect only the fact that some nations other than the present key-currency countries hold substantial gold reserves that could be the basis for creation of additional amounts of international money in the form of key currencies. The validity of the key currencies, then, would continue to be only their convertibility into gold based upon the gold reserves of the key-currency countries.

In the simplest, and perhaps most workable, version of the key-currency system, there is only one key currency. Other nations regard this as so firmly monetized that they have no desire to hold gold (or established rules prohibit them from holding it). Therefore, the world's monetary gold stock is entirely held by the key-currency country. The maximum amount of the key currency that can come into existence, then, is determined only by how low the gold reserve ratio of the key-currency country can fall before the arrangement becomes suspect. (With the right set of institutions and understandings, perhaps this need never happen, the key currency could become first-class international money.)

In our world, the gold-exchange system has not been played under such well-defined or tight rules. Other countries have used the U.S. payments deficits not as a means of increasing the amount of international dollars, but rather to pull gold from the United States and hold it themselves. If the full mileage that is possible in stretching the limited available supply of gold is to be derived from the system under these looser rules of the game, evidently every country that insists upon holding some gold must also become a key-currency country. If this were practicable, it would seem to permit the aggregate amount of key currencies to rise as large in relation to the given gold stock as the tighter system.[3]

[3] Lutz sees it as an advantage of the "multiple-currency standard," as he terms it, that for a given use of key currencies it permits a higher gold reserve ratio (Friedrich A. Lutz, "The Problem of International Liquidity and the Multiple-Currency Standard," *Essays in International Finance*, No. 41, Princeton University, March 1963). He does not seem to take account of the fact that the greater uncertainty as to the monetization of each key currency will require a higher gold reserve ratio, which could more than offset the enlargement of the potential gold reserve base.

It would seem that this arrangement magnifies the defects of the gold-exchange system, rather than curing them. In the multiple-key-currency system, what must be governed in order to produce a proper behavior of international money is not the payments deficit of a single nation, but the aggregate deficit with the rest of the world of a group of key-currency nations.[4] The difficulty of building any system that would achieve this is apparent.

The suspectibility of the system to instability evidently would be greater, for there would exist not a single key currency whose position as international money might be rather firmly established, but a number of currencies competing for this status. Evidently, no one of them could be so firmly monetized in this fluid situation. Thus, the minimum gold reserve ratio that would be sustainable might well be a higher one. Because of the weak monetization of the key currencies, the total amount of key currency that could be created under this system might be much less than with concentrated gold reserves and a single key currency. The system also might tend to run to continual turmoil, as some key currencies inevitably would be weakening and others strengthening at any given time, and efforts would have to be made to keep nations from moving their funds from the former to the latter and thus aggravating the discrepancy in their positions. In view of the active competition among the key currencies for "strength," the stage would be set for a competition in domestic restrictiveness and economic slack, with each nation fearful of following another course in view of the international threat to its currency.

What seemingly is contemplated is some sort of combination of these ingredients, a multiple-key-currency system in which the key-currency countries hold one another's currencies (and perhaps others also) as reserves, and an increase in the amount of key currency in existence is partially managed through currency swaps. The only definite thing that can be said about the operation of this system is that it is enormously uncertain. If there were a developed rationale and a set of rules of national monetary behavior that it was proposed to try to enforce, an effort on this basis might be made to predict the consequences of its installation. In the absence of this, there is a good deal of mystery.

However, such a system would seem to retain the faults of its ingredients. Its management would suffer from involvement with the

---

[4] If every nation that was a substantial holder of international reserves insisted upon holding some gold and becoming a "key currency," then obviously they would have to hold one another's currencies, and we should then come to the combination arrangement.

payments deficits of a number of countries (and the specific patterns into which these fell), as well as from variations in the confidence reposed in the various key currencies and in the whole arrangement. Since the net effect of the system in creating psychological liquidity would be rather uncertain, since it would depend upon the viewpoint from which the offsetting claims were considered by the various participants, the additional step of controlling the amount of such liquidity would seem to offer insuperable obstacles. Moreover, the system would seem to be subject to abrupt failure, because of the pyramiding and the tenuous psychological foundations on which it rests.

The political implications of such a system also merit attention. Proponents assume that management of the system will be left to the central bankers of the various nations, governed by their rules of gentlemanly behavior, of financial soundness, and their group "esprit de corps." However, critics object that the powers involved are so great that it is undemocratic to confer them upon a group of men who are not directly responsible to governments and whose actions are not subject to public scrutiny. If the central bankers did, indeed, behave as independent agents, free of the ideas and political desires of their governments, then the free world should have turned over very important powers concerning its future to a group of men who are beyond political control. If, as is more likely, the central bankers cannot divorce themselves from the political positions of their governments, then political rivalries and animosities represent another potential basis for instability of the system. Each key-currency country would be under the threat of pressure exerted upon it by shifts out of its currency by other nations. There is no suggestion that any explicit set of rules would be developed to govern these relations. They are to be left to mutual confidence. It is relevant to ask how national rivalries and political pressures would affect the system.

Another difficulty is that the key-currency countries would make themselves subject to the ideas on economic policy of the central bankers of other countries. The central bankers characteristically have been given to conservative economic and political beliefs. If they hold over each key-currency country a major threat in the event of withdrawal of their "confidence" in its economic policy, this could impose an important constraint upon the national economic policies of the major nations. Whether such an arrangement is acceptable is an important political question.

In the absence of more complete specification of the program than has yet been given and of demonstrations that the difficulties pointed out can be overcome, it seems reasonable to fear that the proposed extension of the gold exchange system would be quantitatively unmanageable, politically objectionable, and potentially unstable.

A NEW INTERNATIONAL MONEY

Since there are difficulties in creating a sufficient growth in international money by revaluing the world's monetary gold stock, or by stretching the gold stock by using national currencies for international money, it is necessary to consider the possibility of creating a new international money. This may seem a radical approach, in the sense that it involves something that has not been done before. However, it must be observed that to operate any of the other approaches successfully would be something that has not been done before for very long. There is no tried and true method to which we may turn back.

In another sense, the development of a new international money would not be radical, but quite the expected thing, for it would apply to the international sphere what is universally done within the domestic economies of the various nations. Moreover, we have learned from bitter experience in the United States the hazard of a dual-money system, including a second-class money whose acceptability may come into question, and thus cause the collapse of the system. We instituted Government guarantee of bank deposits so that there would no longer be a second-class money from which people would be prone to flee into currency with consequences that were illustrated in 1933. In domestic economic affairs, also, we would think it a precarious arrangement if people ran down their cash balances and relied to finance growing expenditures upon a network of mutual loans, with each person ignoring his liabilities and his net liquidity position. The fragility of such arrangements also was illustrated in the 1930's. Thus, to demand in the international sphere a system using only first-class money in an amount sufficient to preclude fragile structures of mutual credits would only be to apply lessons that have been learned at great cost in the past.

The essential elements in a new system are the creation of a new international money, provision for the control over its rate of growth, specification of the means of introduction of the new money into circulation, and providing arrangements to assure that the new money will be a first-class international money secure from demonetization or depreciation in terms of gold.

The new money would be in the form of deposits or certificates that serve as a generally acceptable means of international payment, and therefore a first-class vehicle for the holding of national monetary reserves. What is required to establish the new money in this status is an understanding or firm usage of the nations in accepting it in payment and holding their reserves partially in this form.

To protect the new money from demonetization or depreciation, several things could be done: (1) A guarantee of its value in terms of gold, but with limited conversion right. (2) An agreement among the participating nations to hold no less than a stipulated proportion of their reserves in new money (as against gold). (3) Provision of efficient services for the making of payments in the new money. (4) Payment of interest on balances and/or rights to "dividends" in the form of free annual increments in holdings of the new money to the participating nations. (5) Restriction of the use of national currencies as international money.

The determination of the rate of expansion in the amount of the new money would presumably be determined by a specific rule agreed upon at the time of the setting up of the system. The matter could be left to the decision of a discretionary management, but this would involve nations in a grant of power that they might be reluctant to make. In view of the past performance of national central banks, this reluctance would seem justified.

If the requirement for a rule governing the bahavior of the new international money is that it would be the optimal one, then we are in a hopeless situation. If the requirement is that it should perform better than the alternative systems, then there is but little doubt of our ability to succeed. The formula need not be a simple one, and could provide for meeting unusual conditions, even granting limited discretionary powers to a management body under specific conditions.

The new money probably would be injected into the system through loans to participating nations and open market purchases of securities denominated in their currencies. In this case, the interest earnings would cover administrative costs of the system and permit interest to be paid on balances in the new international money. The new arrangement then would operate very much as an international central bank conducting its operations under a defined rule of behavior. Alternatively, prescribed additions to the stock of new money, beyond any needed for loans to participating nations, could simply be allocated free to these nations in accordance with some formula. In this case there would be no open market operatings to make and less interest to distribute.

In either case, there would be problems of some political content in determining the conditions of lending of new money, the formula for purchases of particular kinds of securities of the various countries, or the formula for free distribution of increments to the stock of new money. These problems, however, are perhaps less formidable than the ones involved in putting the alternative systems on a solid basis.

This approach has at least the educational merit, through its close parallelism to national monetary systems, of making clear the monetary nature of the problem and the requirements of a successful system. The firm monetization of the new money would rest—as is the case with the dollar within the United States—upon an assurance of its continued acceptability as money, more largely than upon its relation to gold or the character of the assets that would be available to back it if—as would not be conceivable—the whole system were to be liquidated.

This system must face the same problem as the gold-exchange standard in that it must guard the new money against depreciation against gold, especially against abrupt demonetization. This approach seems to have more adequate resources in this connection. A thoroughly internationalized new money could better be established in a position of firm and permanent monetization than could a national currency for several reasons: (1) Its behavior is based upon a defined rule agreed to by the members of the system, while the amount of any key currency created is somewhat haphazard and insofar as controlled (in present institutions), it is mainly responsive to the policies of the key-currency country. This country assumes no definite obligations in this connection, and what is done depends upon domestic political developments in the key-currency country. Considerable uncertainty is inescapable. (2) The new money would be genuinely international and symmetrical in its operation, while the political asymmetry of the key-currency system is a force for instability. (3) The new system would provide for only one international money to supplement gold. There would be no competition among moneys that would raise uncertainties as to the future of each—and therefore all—of them. At a fixed price of gold, the role of gold in the system presumably would decline over the years. The expectation would be that, as this happened, experience would monetize the new money so firmly that it would be considered a first-class international money, superior to gold because of its greater stability of value in relation to goods and services, its interest privileges, its greater convenience and lower cost. Then the declining ratio of gold backing behind the new money would no longer matter.

There are formidable obstacles to the adoption of this approach. It is foreign to the thought and practice of the financial community, and therefore is taken in that quarter to be radical. It is taken to affect adversely the interests of the financial community in key-currency countries. More basically, there is a fear, based largely upon misunderstanding, of loss of sovereignty from creation of such an international money. This matter requires some attention.

One danger is that the amount of the new international money will be inappropriate. The fear usually expressed is that it will be excessive, and thus tend to cause world inflation. This is, of course, possible if the formula agreed upon were misconceived. However, if the formula must be a compromise agreed to by all participating nations, we perhaps should assume that it will be a safe-and-sane one and not an inflationary one. It would be desirable that the formula provide some self-correcting provisions such that a preponderance of world inflation would cause corrective adjustment. Perhaps it is at least as likely that an excess of conservatism will prevail and the formula would encourage continued restrictionism. The probable performance of this system, however, must be judged against the alternatives, none of which seems to earn so high a grade.

The other fear is that a country that runs its affairs soundly, especially a rich country such as the United States, will find that other countries are using their accessions of the new international money to make inroads upon its output and wealth, forcing upon it an unwanted hoard of the new international money. That is to say, the United States (the opposite of its present problem) might find itself running a large payments surplus and piling up an undesired amount of the new international money. However, if the total amount of international money is not excessive, it is not clear that there is any more threat of such a development under this than under any other system.

The crux of the matter, obviously, is the assumption of an excessive payments surplus. The protection against the situation is access to instruments for correcting payments imbalance sufficient to eliminate such an excessive surplus. As is pointed out below, this is a requirement of any reasonable system. There is no special problem in this connection associated with the new international money.

So far as its basic political footings are concerned, the new international money might be judged sounder than its competitors. The key-currency systems are politically shaky because they place the key-currency countries in a position that at once confers on them some advantages and prestige and at the same time makes them vulnerable to noncooperation by other countries. The multiple-key-currency system would involve temptations to political use of economic warfare in an unstable setting. Gold revaluation or the new international money would avoid this situation by divorcing international money from national currencies. Because of this either of them would be on a solider political footing than the gold exchange system. However, the gold-revaluation approach, from the political viewpoint, suffers from its differential impact upon gold-producing nations and others, and between those that do and do not hold large reserves in the form of gold. Moreover, if any effort were made to impose some sort of uniform limitation upon private hoarding of gold, because of its added profitability, this would be a ticklish political matter. Thus, the system with the solidest political foundation, if the necessary understanding could be achieved to attain it, perhaps is the new international money.

EXCHANGE RATES—

HOW FLEXIBLE SHOULD THEY BE?

MILTON FRIEDMAN

Professor Friedman is the outstanding proponent among American economists of flexible exchange rates. In this selection he presents the case against fixed exchange rates.

Discussions of U.S. policy with respect to international payments tend to be dominated by our immediate balance-of-payments difficulties. I should like today to approach the question from a different, and I hope more constructive, direction. Let us begin by asking ourselves not merely how we can get out of our present difficulties but instead how we can fashion our international payments system so that it will best serve our needs for the long pull; how we can solve not merely this balance-of-payments problem but the entire balance-of-payments problem.

A shocking, and indeed, disgraceful feature of the present situation is the extent to which our frantic search for expedients to stave off balance-of-payments pressures has led us, on the one hand, to sacrifice major national objectives; and, on the other, to give enormous power to officials of foreign governments to affect what should be purely domestic matters.

Statement before The Joint Economic Committee, 88th Congress, First Session, Hearings: The United States Balance of Payments (Washington: Government Printing Office, 1963), pp. 451–459.

Foreign payments amount to only some 5 per cent of our total national income. Yet they have become a major factor in nearly every national policy.

I believe that a system of floating exchange rates would solve the balance-of-payments problem for the United States far more effectively than our present arrangements. Such a system would use the flexibility and efficiency of the free market to harmonize our small foreign trade sector with both the rest of our massive economy and the rest of the world; it would reduce problems of foreign payments to their proper dimensions and remove them as a major consideration in governmental policy about domestic matters and as a major preoccupation in international political negotiations; it would foster our national objectives rather than be an obstacle to their attainment.

To indicate the basis for this conclusion, let us consider the national objective with which our payments system is most directly connected: the promotion of a healthy and balanced growth of world trade, carried on, so far as possible, by private individuals and private enterprises with minimum intervention by governments. This has been a major objective of our whole postwar international economic policy, most recently expressed in the Trade Expansion Act of 1962. Success would knit the free world more closely together, and, by fostering the international division of labor, raise standards of living throughout the world, including the United States.

Suppose that we succeed in negotiating far-reaching reciprocal reductions in tariffs and other trade barriers with the Common Market and other countries. To simplify exposition I shall hereafter refer only to tariffs, letting these stand for the whole range of barriers to trade, including even the so-called voluntary limitation of exports. Such reductions will expand trade in general but clearly will have different effects on different industries. The demand for the products of some will expand, for others contract. This is a phenomenon we are familiar with from our internal development. The capacity of our free enterprise system to adapt quickly and efficiently to such shifts, whether produced by changes in technology or tastes, has been a major source of our economic growth. The only additional element introduced by international trade is the fact that different currencies are involved, and this is where the payment mechanism comes in; its function is to keep this fact from being an additional source of disturbance.

An all-around lowering of tariffs would tend to increase both our expenditures and our receipts in foreign currencies. There is no way of knowing in advance which increase would tend to be the greater and hence no way of knowing whether the initial effect would be toward a surplus or deficit in our balance of payments. What is clear is that we cannot hope to succeed in the objective of expanding world trade unless we can readily adjust to either outcome.

Many people concerned with our payments deficits hope that since we are operating further from full capacity than Europe, we could supply a substantial increase in exports whereas they could not. Implicitly, this assumes that European countries are prepared to see their surplus turned into a deficit, thereby contributing to the reduction of the deficits we have recently been experiencing in our balance of payments. Perhaps this would be the initial effect of tariff changes. But if the achievement of such a result is to be *sine qua non* of tariff agreement, we cannot hope for any significant reduction in barriers. We could be confident that exports would expand more than imports only if the tariff changes were one sided indeed, with our trading partners making much greater reductions in tariffs than we make. Our major means of inducing other countries to reduce tariffs is to offer corresponding reductions in our tariff. More generally, there is little hope of continued and sizable liberalization of trade if liberalization is to be viewed simply as a device for correcting balance-of-payments difficulties. That way lies only backing and filling.

Suppose then that the initial effect is to increase our expenditures on imports more than our receipts from exports. How could we adjust to this outcome?

One method of adjustment is to draw on reserves or borrow from abroad to finance the excess increase in imports. The obvious objection to this method is that it is only a temporary device, and hence can be relied on only when the disturbance is temporary. But that is not the major objection. Even if we had very large reserves or could borrow large amounts from abroad, so that we could continue this expedient for many years, it is a most undesirable one. We can see why if we look at physical rather than financial magnitudes.

The physical counterpart to the financial deficit is a reduction of employment in industries competing with imports that are larger than the concurrent expansion of employment in export industries. So long as the financial deficit continues, the assumed tariff reductions create employment problems. But it is no part of the aim of tariff reductions to create unemployment at home or to promote employment abroad. The aim is a balanced expansion of trade, with exports rising along with imports and thereby providing employment opportunities to offset any reduction in employment resulting from increased imports.

Hence, simply drawing on reserves or borrowing abroad is a most unsatisfactory method of adjustment.

Another method of adjustment is to lower U.S. prices relative to foreign prices, since this would stimulate exports and discourage imports. If foreign countries are accommodating enough to engage in inflation, such a change in relative prices might require merely that the United States keep prices stable or even, that it simply keep them from rising as fast as foreign prices. But there is no necessity for foreign countries to be so accommodating, and we could hardly count on their being so accommodating. The use of this technique therefore involves a willingness to produce a decline in U.S. prices by tight monetary policy or tight fiscal policy or both. Given time, this method of adjustment would work. But in the interim, it would exact a heavy toll. It would be difficult or impossible to force down prices appreciably without producing a recession and considerable unemployment. To eliminate in the long run the unemployment resulting from the tariff changes, we should in the short run be creating cyclical unemployment. The cure might for a time be far worse than the disease.

This second method is therefore most unsatisfactory. Yet these two methods—drawing on reserves and forcing down prices—are the only two methods available to us under our present international payment arrangements, which involve fixed exchange rates between the U.S. dollar and other currencies. Little wonder that we have so far made such disappointing progress toward the reduction of trade barriers, that our practice has differed so much from our preaching.

There is one other way and only one other way to adjust and that is by allowing (or forcing) the price of the U.S. dollar to fall in terms of other currencies. To a foreigner, U.S. goods can become cheaper in either of two ways—either because their prices in the United States fall in terms of dollars or because the foreigner has to give up fewer units of his own currency to acquire a dollar, which is to say, the price of the dollar falls. For example, suppose a particular U.S. car sells for $2,800 when a dollar costs 7 shillings, tuppence in British money (i.e., roughly £1 = $2.80). The price of the car is then £1,000 in British money. It is all the same to an Englishman—or even a Scotsman—whether the price of the car falls to $2,500 while the price of a dollar remains 7 shillings, tuppence, or, alternatively, the price of the car remains $2,800, while the price of a dollar falls to 6 shillings, 5 pence (i.e., roughly £1 = $3.11). In either case, the car costs the Englishman £900 rather than £1,000, which is what matters to him. Similarly, foreign goods can become more expensive to an American in either of two ways—either because the price in terms of foreign currency rises or because he has to give up more dollars to acquire a given amount of foreign currency.

Changes in exchange rates can therefore alter the relative price of U.S. and foreign goods in precisely the same way as can changes in internal prices in the United States and in foreign countries. And they can do so without requiring anything like the same internal adjustments. If the initial effect of the tariff reductions would be to create a deficit at the former exchange rate (or enlarge an existing deficit or reduce an existing surplus) and thereby increase unemployment, this effect can be entirely avoided by a change in exchange rates which will produce a balanced expansion in imports and exports without interfering with domestic employment, domestic prices, or domestic monetary and fiscal policy. The pig can be roasted without burning down the house.

The situation is, of course, entirely symmetrical if the tariff changes should initially happen to expand our exports more than our imports. Under present circumstances, we would welcome such a result, and conceivably, if the matching deficit were experienced by countries currently running a surplus, they might permit it to occur without seeking to offset it. In that case, they and we would be using the first method of adjustment—changes in reserves or borrowing. But again, if we had started off from an even keel, this would be an undesirable method of adjustment. On our side, we should be sending out useful goods and receiving only foreign currencies in return. On the side of our partners, they would be using up reserves and tolerating the creation of unemployment.

The second method of adjusting to a surplus is to permit or force domestic prices to rise—which is of course what we did in part in the early postwar years when we were running large surpluses. Again, we should be forcing maladjustments on the whole economy to solve a problem arising from a small part of it—the 5 per cent accounted for by foreign trade.

Again, these two methods are the only ones available under our present international payment arrangements, and neither is satisfactory.

The final method is to permit or force exchange rates to change— in this case, a rise in the price of the dollar in terms of foreign currencies. This solution is again specifically adapted to the specific problem of the balance of payments.

Changes in exchange rates can be produced in either of two general ways. One way is by a change in an official exchange rate; an official devaluation or appreciation from one fixed level which the Government is committed to support to another fixed level. This is the method used by Britain in its postwar devaluation and by Germany in 1961 when the mark was appreciated. This is also the main method contemplated by the IMF which permits member nations to change their exchange rates by 10 per cent without approval by the Fund and by a larger amount after approval by the Fund. But this method has serious disadvantages. It makes a change in rates a matter of major moment, and hence there is a tendency to postpone any change as long as possible. Difficulties accumulate and a larger change is finally needed than would have been required if it could have been made promptly. By the time the change is made, everyone is aware that a change is pending and is certain about the direction of change. The result is to encourage flight from a currency if it is going to be devalued, or to a currency if it is going to be appreciated.

There is in any event, little basis for determining precisely what the new rate should be. Speculative movements increase the difficulty of judging what the new rate should be, and introduce a systematic bias, making the change needed appear larger than it actually is. The result, particularly when devaluation occurs, is generally to lead officials to "play safe" by making an even larger change than the large change needed. The country is then left after the devaluation with a maladjustment precisely the opposite of that with which it started and is thereby encouraged to follow policies it cannot sustain in the long run.

Even if all these difficulties could be avoided, this method of changing from one fixed rate to another has the disadvantage that it is necessarily discontinuous. Even if the new exchange rates are precisely correct when first established, they will not long remain correct.

A second and much better way in which changes in exchange rates can be produced is by permitting exchange rates to float, by allowing them to be determined from day to day in the market. This is the method which the United States used from 1862 to 1879, and again, in effect, from 1917 or so to about 1925, and again from 1933 to 1934. It is the method which Britain used from 1918 to 1925 and again from 1931 to 1939, and which Canada used for most of the interwar period and again from 1950 to May 1962. Under this method, exchange rates adjust themselves continuously, and market forces determine the magnitude of each change. There is no need for any official to decide by how much the rate should rise or fall. This is the method of the free market, the method that we adopt unquestioningly in a private enterprise economy for the bulk of goods and services. It is no less available for the price of one money in terms of another.

With a floating exchange rate, it is possible for Governments to intervene and try to affect the rate by buying or selling, as the British exchange equalization fund did rather successfully in the 1930's, or by combining buying and selling with public announcements of intentions, as Canada did so disastrously in early 1962. On the whole, it seems to me undesirable to have governments intervene, because there is a strong tendency for government agencies to try to peg the rate rather than to stabilize it, because they have no special advantage over private speculators in stabilizing it, because they can make far bigger mistakes than private speculators risking their own money, and because there is a tendency for them to cover up their mistakes by changing the rules—as the Canadian case so strikingly illustrates—rather than by reversing course. But this is an issue on which there is much difference of opinion among economists who agree in favoring floating rates. Clearly, it is possible to have a successful floating rate along with governmental speculation.

The great objective of tearing down trade barriers, of promoting a worldwide expansion of trade, of giving citizens of all countries and especially the underdeveloped countries, every opportunity to sell their products in open markets under equal terms and thereby every incentive to use their resources efficiently, of giving countries an alternative through free world trade to autarchy and central planning—this great objective can, I believe, be achieved best under a regime of floating rates. All countries, and not just the United States, can proceed to liberalize boldly and confidently only if they can have reasonable assurance that the resulting trade expansion will be balanced and will not interfere with major domestic objectives. Floating exchange rates, and so far as I can see, only floating exchange rates, provide this assurance.